THREE ALLITERATIVE SAINTS' HYMNS:
LATE MIDDLE ENGLISH STANZAIC POEMS

EARLY ENGLISH TEXT SOCIETY

No. OS 321

2003

Oxford, Bodleian Library, MS Bodley Rolls 22, head

THREE ALLITERATIVE SAINTS' HYMNS: LATE MIDDLE ENGLISH STANZAIC POEMS

The Alliterative Katherine Hymn
by Richard Spalding
(Bodleian Library MS Bodley Rolls 22)

The Alliterative John Evangelist Hymn
(Lincoln Cathedral Library MS 91)

The Alliterative John Baptist Hymn
(British Library Additional MS 39574)

EDITED BY

RUTH KENNEDY

Published for
THE EARLY ENGLISH TEXT SOCIETY
by the
OXFORD UNIVERSITY PRESS
2003

OXFORD
UNIVERSITY PRESS

Great Clarendon Street, Oxford OX2 6DP

Oxford University Press is a department of the University of Oxford.
It furthers the University's objective of excellence in research, scholarship,
and education by publishing worldwide in

Oxford New York

Auckland Bangkok Buenos Aires Cape Town Chennai
Dar es Salaam Delhi Hong Kong Istanbul Karachi Kolkata
Kuala Lumpur Madrid Melbourne Mexico City Mumbai Nairobi
São Paulo Shanghai Singapore Taipei Tokyo Toronto

Oxford is a registered trade mark of Oxford University Press
in the UK and in certain other countries

Published in the United States
by Oxford University Press Inc., New York

British Library Cataloguing in Publication Data

Data available

Library of Congress Cataloging in Publication Data

Data applied for

ISBN 0-19-722324-9

1 3 5 7 9 10 8 6 4 2

Typeset by Joshua Associates Ltd., Oxford
Printed in Great Britain
on acid-free paper by
Print Wright Ltd., Ipswich

PREFACE

The 'Wheatley Manuscript' belongs to the Early English Text Society and publication depends upon permission from the society; grateful acknowledgement is made here for that permission, granted by the Director, John Burrow. The plates are reproduced by kind permission of the Bodleian Library, Oxford, the Dean and Chapter of Lincoln Cathedral, and the British Library. I acknowledge here the invariably helpful assistance of the staff of the Bodleian Library, the British Library MS Room, and staff and archivists of the Public Record Offices at London, Lichfield, Norwich, the University libraries of Cambridge, Durham, Leeds, Manchester and Nottingham, and college libraries at Trinity and Gonville and Caius, Cambridge. I wish to thank my friend, Philip Jebb OSB and his colleagues for the privilege of using Downside Abbey Library.

This edition had its origins in a dissertation for the degree of Ph.D. in the University of Bristol under the direction of Dr Myra Stokes to whom I owe an enormous debt of gratitude for her meticulous supervision of every aspect of that work, her constant good advice and kindness, and the outstanding example of her own attitudes and critical acumen. The Library and Computer staff of the University of Bristol, particularly Madeleine Chinnick and Cyd Roberts, deserve my special gratitude for their unfailing, prompt, intelligent and friendly assistance in the most arduous initial stages of production. I also wish to acknowledge how much I owe to the fine minds and attentive scholarship of my past teachers, John Burrow and the late Ian Bishop. My examiners, Thorlac Turville-Petre and H. L. Spencer, made innumerable helpful suggestions for improvement; Malcolm Godden and Ronald Waldron read the manuscript for the Early English Text Society and made astute suggestions about turning it into a suitable edition. I am deeply indebted to Bella Millett for her painstaking reading, and to H. L. Spencer, Editorial Secretary, for her constant and patient guidance. I should like to thank Joshua Associates for their care and patience in devising a professional layout for a complicated typescript.

I would like to thank all of my family and friends for support, forbearance and encouragement. Christopher Bright must be singled out for especial thanks for untold assistance, advice and deliverance from error. For many years I have been lucky to have had the enlivening goodwill and support of my past and present colleagues in the Department of English, Royal Holloway University of London, and of our skilled and endlessly-obliging secretaries and librarians; I would also like to thank the college for granting sabbatical leave.

Finally I wish to honour the life and work of the late Basil Cottle, for his inimitable teaching, for his suggestion that I undertake the project, and for his interest and joy throughout its progresses. This volume is dedicated to his memory.

CONTENTS

INTRODUCTION ix
  The Manuscripts and Textual Histories ix
  Construction, Metre and Alliteration xxviii
  Language xliii
  Provenance and Dates lxiv
  Sources and Affiliations lxxv
  Treatment of the Texts xciv

BIBLIOGRAPHY AND ABBREVIATIONS xcix

THE TEXTS
  The Alliterative Katherine Hymn by Richard Spalding 1
  The Alliterative John Evangelist Hymn 10
  The Alliterative John Baptist Hymn 19

NOTES
  Notes to Katherine 25
  Notes to Evangelist 68
  Notes to Baptist 86

GLOSSARY AND PROPER NAMES 97

PLATES
  I Oxford Bodleian Library MS Bodley Rolls 22, head
                          frontispiece
  II Oxford Bodleian Library MS Bodley Rolls 22, foot
                         Facing p. xi
  III Lincoln Cathedral Library MS 91, f. 231^r Facing p. xix
  IV British Library Additional MS 39574, f. 15^r Facing p. xxvii

INTRODUCTION

This edition presents the three extant texts of a narrow sub-genre in Middle English verse: 14-line-stanza, alliterative and rhyming poems addressed to saints, only 686 lines in all. All three appear to be naïve, provincial works of the North and East Midlands *c.*1400. Each survives in a unique manuscript, and, as far as can be ascertained, is by a different author; each is an ode to a very popular saint, the details of whose life and passion were common knowledge. These fragments of the late medieval alliterative tradition invoke the popular saints, Katherine of Alexandria (Bodleian Library Bodley Rolls 22), John the Evangelist (Lincoln Cathedral Library MS 91), and John the Baptist (British Library Add. MS 39574), hereafter abbreviated to *Katherine*, *Evangelist* and *Baptist*, respectively. During their edited history and critical mention the poems have been entitled 'hymns'.

The present edition provides the first English publication of a thorny, crux-ridden, but unique and significant alliterative work, one of the many Middle English life writings of St Katherine of Alexandria. The distinctive cognate poems venerating St John the Evangelist and St John the Baptist were last edited in 1889 and 1921 respectively.[1] It is now possible to make more sense of the manuscripts, and to contextualize the works in other ways, so that a new edition of these three texts should contribute to the scholarship of various fields: hagiographical, linguistic, historical, and stylistic.

THE MANUSCRIPTS AND TEXTUAL HISTORIES

The three poems occur in unique witnesses, *Katherine* on a formal roll, *Evangelist* and *Baptist* in private devotional anthologies. There are no evident links between these three witnesses.

---

[1] For editorial histories of *Katherine*, *Evangelist* and *Baptist*, respectively, see pp. xii, xx–xxi and xxv–xxvii.

Katherine: **Bodleian Library Bodley Rolls 22** (*Summ.Cat.* **30445**)

The Bodley Rolls are part of the Bodleian Library Bodley Collection—a small collection, 'formed in about 1761 for Western MSS not included in other definite collections, so that it became the ultimate depository of miscellaneous MSS received singly or in small groups since the foundation of the library'.[2] The deputy librarian, Falconer Madan, then responsible for the relevant volume of the *Summary Catalogue of Western Manuscripts*, describes this collection of miscellaneous and multinational books and papers as 'waifs and strays of which the date of acquisition is not certainly known, but which presumably came in after 1695'.[3] It comprises 27 miscellaneous rolls, mostly unrelated, mostly donated in the seventeenth century, and largely *chronica* and genealogies.

It can be deduced from the cataloguing that Bodley Rolls 22 was acquired at some point between 1680 and 1890, but the name of a donor or details of a sale are not recorded. It is a medieval parchment roll, 1230 mm in length and 280 mm wide, in very good condition. Some of the ink has, at some time, flaked, and subsequently the parchment has been badly stained by five large patches of chemical reagent at the ends of the first five stanzas of the first text (see 'Frontispiece'); but apart from this, there is no damage to the manuscript.[4] At the time of cataloguing (*c.*1880) a mitred linen headpiece was stitched to the roll for protection, and this headpiece, together with its attached tape-ties, now forms the outside of the cylinder. Various other nineteenth-century identifications are now on or attached to the roll in the same hand that has catalogued the entire Bodley Rolls collection. Below this clean linen top, the top of the

---

[2] Falconer Madan *et al.*, *A Summary Catalogue of Western Manuscripts in the Bodleian Library at Oxford which have not hitherto been catalogued in the Quarto series*, 7 vols in 8 [II in 2 parts] (Oxford, 1895–1953; reprinted with corrections in I and VII, Munich, 1980). See V: *Collections received during the second half of the nineteenth century and miscellaneous MSS. acquired between 1695 and 1890*, 801–08, Accession No. 30445 (Bodley Rolls 22) at V, 808.

[3] Ibid, at p. 801.

[4] Such reagents were in use at the Bodleian Library at the time of the cataloguing of the roll (see Bodleian Library Records, 1878). It cannot now be deduced whether these here are from the standard hydrosulphate of ammonia or from the innovative but more lethal Leyden reviver which involved a two-part process using first oxalic acid and then tannin; both left the same brown stain. As recipes for reviving faded writing are found from as early as the seventeenth century, no date can be ascribed to the application, which could have been made before the Bodleian's acquisition. I am grateful to Dr Bruce Barker-Benfield, Assistant Librarian in the Department of Western Manuscripts, for information on this matter.

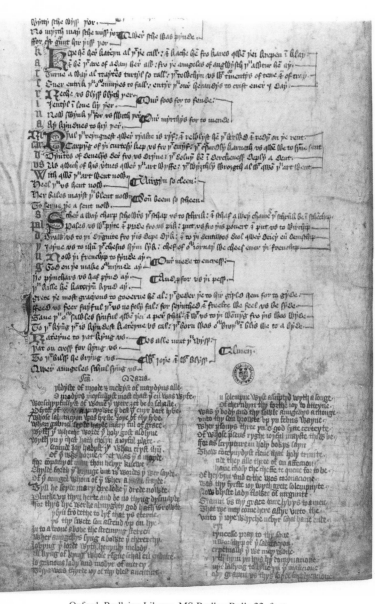

Oxford, Bodleian Library, MS Bodley Rolls 22, foot

dorse of the original parchment roll is darkened with dirt, age, and (apparently) handling, and about 20 mm from the join of the linen is a seventeenth- or eighteenth-century pen sign which appears to read *M S*, perhaps indicating that the roll belonged to an earlier collection. It could be read as *M 8*, perhaps indicating previous classification; there is no other identification on the roll.

The parchment section is formed of two membranes of sheepskin, the upper one carefully glued with a small overlap on to the top of the lower. There are no signs of earlier stitching, and, from the handwriting over the join, it can be seen that this gluing preceded the scribal writing. The mitred linen headpiece is approximately 400 mm in length, the top membrane 505 mm, and the lower one 725 mm. The entire roll, with headpiece, is thus 1630 mm in length. The manuscript is ruled vertically and horizontally with an extremely fine pen, in some places barely discernible. A left-hand margin of approximately 35 mm is ruled and maintained throughout the two texts which appear on the manuscript (see below), but this does not necessarily say anything about the relationship of these texts, as it is likely that the entire roll was previously prepared for writing. The right-hand margin is vertically ruled by a fine pen to be approximately 40 mm, but naturally varies; it is never less than 5 mm. The ruled horizontal line is approximately 205 mm in length. There are no pricking or holding marks on any part of the roll, and it must be assumed that it was held to the desk under strings or by weights.

There are two texts in Bodley Rolls 22. The first, in a neat bookhand, *Anglicana formata*, begins *Katereyn þe curteys . . .*, with an illuminated initial, and is an arrangement of 200 lines of English verse in twenty stanzas, with mostly two verses to a line, extending down to the penultimate 143 mm of the roll. It reveals two acrostics, the first *katerina*, and the second *Ricardus spaldyng*. The text is indented at these points and the acrostics are paralleled in the margin by equivalent red letters. The second text on the roll, in a less controlled later hand, *Anglicana formata*, is discussed here because of its value in ascertaining provenance; see also Plate II, facing, and pp. lxvi–lxvii below. It starts with the heading *Sancta Maria*, and comprises forty-seven lines of English verse, written in two columns, which have been fitted into a small space (280 × 143 mm). It embodies two acrostics: the first *maria*, and the second *pipwel*, with these eleven letters merely sketched in for rubrication. The last line of this text ends up so close to the extreme edge of the parchment roll that it might seem that the roll has since been shortened, but there are some pen tries, in the dark ink of the first text, on the dorse of the document at this level, with a short bottom margin beneath them; this position is where pen tries would appear if the foot of the roll had been turned up for this purpose, and suggests that this was the original lower edge of the roll. There are no other markings on the document.

As far as can be ascertained, the manuscript had no printed notice until the German edition of both of its texts by William Heuser.[5] It can be assumed that Heuser had learnt of the roll's existence from the publication of the *Summary Catalogue* in 1905. Heuser's first edition of *Katherine* was short but comprehensive. He was mistaken on some minor details of the manuscript, but, as might be expected, his phonology and dialectology were astute, as was his knowledge of the legend of Katherine of Alexandria and its species. Heuser's work was subsequently 'improved on' by Ferdinand Holthausen in a second German edition.[6] Holthausen emended on grounds of metre, spelling and sense, and his edition bears scant resemblance to a transcription of the manuscript, but several of his emendations are intelligent, and can be retained. Both editors appear to have worked from photographs, the negatives of which are no longer registered in the Bodleian Library. The poem has received no editorial or critical treatment and virtually no mention since 1937. The MED incipit is 'Katereyn þe curteys', which defines the text, and a case could be made for the retention of this title. But there is more to the poem than Katherine's courtesy. I have entitled the poem *The Alliterative Katherine Hymn* (sometimes shortened to *The Katherine Hymn*). The word 'alliterative' differentiates this rendition from the dozens of others on the Katherine legend; and I follow the two previous editors in using the word 'hymn' to mark the invocatory and supplicatory nature of this distinctive version.

Katherine is illuminated with one initial capital *K*, some surrounding two-sided decoration and much rubrication. The reproduction of the manuscript (see 'Frontispiece') does not do justice to the quality

[5] 'Die Katherinenhymne des Ricardus Spaldyng und eine Marienhymne derselben Pergamentrolle', *Anglia*, 30 (1907), 523–48. The short poem, which I have entitled 'Pipwel's St Mary', was subsequently edited by Ferdinand Holthausen in *Anglia*, 59 (1935), 319–21, and by Carleton Brown in *Religious Lyrics of the Fifteenth Century* (Oxford, 1939), No. 31, pp. 55–6; see also Kennedy, 'Alliterative Katherine Hymn', pp. 39–64.

[6] See 'Ein Mittelenglischer Katharinenhymnus von Richard Spalding', *Anglia*, 60 (1937), 150–64.

of the illumination with its unusual combination of clear blue, brown and gold on the off-white sheepskin background, very much highlighted with some white paint in the initial. This illumination is professional in its proportions and execution, but somewhat primitive in form: basically curvilinear, with S-curves, curls and curvifoliate acanthus leaves that approach reversed S-chains, the surrounding leaves lanceolate, but developing to trifoliate and trifid shape. On the sparse outer filigrees are kite-shaped leaves, underscored by inverted engrailing; these also form a simple cusped corner to the initial. It is not easy to draw a comparison between the character of this illumination and that of any other manuscript in British libraries or in print. It appears older in style than the script of the manuscript, perhaps indicating that the roll was produced in a provincial centre—a notion suggested by Ian Doyle and endorsed by Malcolm Parkes (for whose personal communications I am most grateful). I have sought advice about this illumination from Janet Backhouse, Lucy Sandler Freeman, Christopher de Hamel and Kathleen Scott, all of whom have been generous in their detailed replies, and all agree that its style and execution would fit in well with the provenance and dating suggested in this edition. No comparable manuscripts have come to light, and few characteristics that are directly comparable can be found in printed notices or catalogues of late fourteenth- or early fifteenth-century illumination.[7] However, the illuminated letters in the sizeable and luxurious Carmelite Missal (BL Add. MSS 29704–5, 44892, produced in London $c.$1390) have some rather impressive similarities, not only in the many trefoils with roundels (not always shown in the facsimile edition), but in the acanthus pattern that accompanies these in several initials, such as those on ff. 161^v, 163^v, 171^r and 176^r. Our illuminator concludes his initial at top and bottom with a gold roundel of leaves that encloses a trilobate leaf, and this small feature is writ large and beautiful in many of the gold leaf capitals of the missal. These observations could be prejudiced by the case for Carmelite influence that is being put forward in this edition (see pp. lxiv–lxviii).[8] The main body of the text is demarked by eighteen small red and blue initial capitals (see 'Frontispiece'). The indentation

---

[7] See *The Reconstructed Carmelite Missal*, ed. Margaret Rickert (London, 1952), e.g. plates xxxiia and xxxvi.

[8] About this similarity Professor Scott writes: 'As the *Missal* borders are of a much higher quality of production, it would be rash to make much of this. It may simply be a conventional design' (private communication). I especially wish to record my thanks here to Dr Scott for searching her 300–400 slides of manuscripts $c.$1400.

for the rubricated acrostics, the use in the acrostic at K259 of the scribe's normal *p* graph, used for both *þ* and *y*, and the use of the same graph for the rubricated *þ* initials all suggest that the rubricator was the scribe, and the execution of this rubrication suggests a professional production. A concluding decorated capital *I* on the 20th stanza is different again, as it is in the margin, and forms a small tailpiece, with its surrounding fine work echoing the first large illuminated initial. The second text is undecorated, because its drafted capitals were never rubricated; see Plate II, facing p. xi.

The general execution of the text is neat and professional, as might be expected in what appears to be commissioned work. The hand is a compact, rounded but upright, book hand of the first half of the fifteenth century, *Anglicana formata* with some secretary features, but with no readily discernible tapering and splay. The deft carefulness of the handwriting is maintained throughout, emphasized by the short, but mostly hooked, ascenders and descenders. *i* is normally diacritized, and certain graphs, such as the dotted *p* which is used for *þ/y* and the 2-shaped *r*, are embellished with minute hairlines.[9] Secretary forms are as follows: *e*, *o* and *q*, which are consistent throughout; *r*, which is always short and is occasionally 2-shaped after *o* (7 times), after *p* (4 times) and after *þ* and *d* (once each); *a*, employed 97 per cent of the time; the *B*-shaped secretary *s*, almost invariably at the ends of words; sporadic distinctive horns on *f* and long *s*; *g*, found occasionally; and *y*, found twice. *Anglicana* forms of *d* and *p* = *þ/y* (invariable), *g* and *w* (usual), *a* in 15 instances and *8*-shaped *s* at the ends of words (employed once or twice), together with the predominant long *s* at the beginnings of words, help to date the manuscript as probably belonging to the first half of the fifteenth century. The graph *t* rises above the line of writing, and so is almost always distinguishable from *c*; the letters *n* and *u* are indistinguishable; discernible capitals are employed at the beginnings of the verse lines, often embellished with points and hairlines; there are no apparent majuscule letters within the lines except for an indeterminate *I/J* which is employed both for the personal pronoun and for the past participle prefix; double *ff* is employed as a capital, but only once medially, and as if accidentally, in *ffro* K2. There are no deletions, and alterations are not perceptible except for one or two current superimpositions and a very fine vertical line that divides two words, *be|rwd*, written as one in

---

[9] In this edition the graph *p* will sometimes be used to indicate this MS graph that looks like *wynn* and is used for both *þ* and *y*, except in two instances: *fpfty* (K36), *longly* (K88).

K240. Flourishes consist in (i) a bar over the Tyronian *et* for *and* (⁊) which is unvarying; (ii) an embellishing dot over $p = þ/y$ about 90 per cent of the time (omitted when the graph is followed by superscript letters, as in p^u, and periodically apparently omitted by accident, as, for example, in *hpr* ('Frontispiece', K20) and *fesawnt'ps* ('Frontispiece', K36)). In almost every instance an oblique hairline can be discerned following this dot; (iii) final *n* is embellished 10 times, medial *n* once and final *m* once with a superior bar that can almost certainly be read as otiose (see, for example *Qweñ* ('Frontispiece', K7)). The instances are discussed in 'Treatment of the Texts', below. There are no other flourishes in the manuscript apart from those embellishing the punctuation.

Abbreviations are unexceptional, and consist in: the *nomen sacrum*, *íhū*; barred vowels indicating a nasal—where every possible medial vowel is barred at some point to indicate an ensuing *m* (8 times), and every possible medial vowel is barred at some point to indicate an ensuing *n* (42 times). There is also an *o* graph in *wōwndpd*, K102 that appears to have been barred in error. Only the vowels *e, i/p = y* and *o* are so marked to indicate a terminal *m* (26 times), and only the vowels *a, e* and *i* are barred to indicate a terminal *n* (45 times). The apostrophe is employed to indicate the missing letters *er*, and found over *t, p = þ/y*, or *u/v = [v]*. This apostrophe is almost invariably decorated with an oblique hairline, as, confusingly, is the ubiquitous dot over $p = þ$ or *y*. It is most usual for this apostrophe to be used over *t* (it is found in *Katerepn* in 12 of the 14 occurrences of that name), which is why there is a compound confusion in the interpretation of MS *fesawnt'ps* K36; see 'Frontispiece' and Notes to K36. The apostrophe is sometimes imperceptibly elongated into a lozenge-shaped stroke that evidently equals the standard abbreviation ꝰ = *er* or *re*. Its total occurrences representing *er* are as follows: over *t* in *port* (K74) and *katepn(e)* (K15, 29, 433, 71, 74, 75, 127, 169, 200, 225, 273, 275); over *p* (K46, 58, 66 and 77); over *nep* (K18); *epp* (K106); over *u = [v]* in *neu* (K47) and *reues* (K204); over *v* in *vtuuswerk* (K143); and *vtues* (K245). The same apostrophe, but evidently signifying *re*, as is usual, is employed over *p* in *preued* (K211). The same apostrophe is used over the secretary *r* and signifies a terminal *e* only. This suspension (a precise equivalent to the *Anglicana* ẏ which is *not* employed) is used very heavily throughout the copy. Further suspensions, or curtailments, are not problematic and consist in the unvarying crossed double *l* for graphs *lle* (6 times), as in *aₜℋℓ* (K1; see

'Frontispiece'), and crossed double long *s* for *-sse* (13 times). The established brevigraphs (e.g., ꝯ = *us*, ꝰ = *ur*) are used logically and uniformly. Superscript *i* is also employed to indicate *ri* (an uncommon contraction in English, especially with letters other than *p*); it is used in *sacrifice* K130, and *crist* K199 and 223. Some superscript letters appear for no apparent reason; among them a raised *s* is found 8 times.

The punctuation is influenced by the visual indication of verse form, shown by diverse highlighted capitals, the bracketing in red, and the regularly emphasized blue capitula. Only three other punctuation marks are found, the punctus, colon and punctus elevatus, but it is debatable whether these last two were intended to be differentiated, or are not merely stroke variants of the same mark, a mark which, for convenience, is here called the double punctus. It is also debatable whether the scribe was aware that he was using two forms of the punctus: the light point that in many MSS is raised above the line of writing, and a strong one that corresponds to a modern full stop. In the octets there is a remarkably regular arrangement of markings, in that the mid-couplet pauses between the first and second, the third and fourth, the fifth and sixth, and the seventh and eighth lines are always marked by a double punctus. The stronger pauses at the end of the second, fourth, sixth and eighth lines are invariably marked by a single (strong) punctus. In the octets, it could be said that the punctuation conforms more closely to modern usage, with the single mark being more potent than the double. The 120 short lines of the sestets are very distinctly set out, with uniform format, definite bracketing and an unexpectedly consistent scheme of punctuation marks which can be examined in the 'Frontispiece'. Among these 20 sestets there is only one inconsistency in the punctuation: the substitution of a punctus elevatus for the expected punctus in K26, a twelfth line. Apart from this, the entire copy reveals that the scribe has been able to repeat a fairly elaborate blueprint of punctuation no less than 19 out of 20 times. Because the pattern of punctuation in the octets is also, to all intents and purposes, completely regular, the aberration of K26 is, indeed, the only real inconsistency in punctuation throughout the 280 lines of the copy. This makes for an unusually regular achievement in medieval punctuation and furthers the presupposition that the manuscript was painstakingly executed, even though its content makes such nonsense in places. The punctuation also conveys some sense of syntax and rhetorical pause, particularly in the sestets, and in general shows a highly systematic methodology.[10]

Evangelist: Lincoln Cathedral MS 91: the 'Thornton Manuscript'

Evangelist is one of the many works of the Alliterative Revival preserved solely because of Thornton's two anthologies, Lincoln Cathedral MS 91 and British Library Add. MS 31042. This edition of one of its texts will not substantially rehearse descriptions or studies of Lincoln Cathedral MS 91; considerable scrutiny has been made of this remarkable book, and of Robert Thornton as a scribe, most conspicuously in the introductions in the facsimile edition by D. S. Brewer and A. E. B. Owen,[11] the important study of Thornton's London manuscript by John J. Thompson,[12] and the work of George Keiser.[13] However, it is surprising that so much work remains to be done, in particular detailed, more literary investigations of each composition in its context.[14] The book contains at least 64 texts, copied by Robert Thornton on what originally must have been 340 paper leaves stitched in 17 folio gatherings, and it has been well established (in the face of some early doubts) that all the texts were copied by Thornton himself. Scholars of the make-up of the compilation have come to various conclusions about the possibility and status of original 'booklets', self-contained quire units that may have had an independent existence before compilation.[15]

[10] The decisive punctuation of this text is dealt with in more detail and with reference to a diplomatic transcription in Ruth Kennedy, 'The Alliterative Katherine Hymn: A Stanzaic Poem of the Late Fourteenth Century' (Unpublished Ph.D. thesis, University of Bristol, 1991).

[11] D. S. Brewer and A. E. B. Owen, *The Thornton Manuscript: Lincoln Cathedral MS. 91* (London, 1978); *Introduction* by Brewer and *Collation and Handwriting* by Owen.

[12] John J. Thompson, *Robert Thornton and the London Thornton Manuscript* (London, 1987); see also his 'The Compiler in Action: Robert Thornton and the "Thornton Romances", in Lincoln Cathedral MS 91', in *Manuscripts and Readers in Fifteenth-Century England*, ed. Derek Pearsall (Cambridge, 1983).

[13] Particularly his '"To Knawe God Almyghten": Robert Thornton's Devotional Book', in *Spätmittelalterliche Geistliche Literatur in der Nationalsprache*, ed. James Hogg (Analecta Cartusiana 106, Salzburg, 1984), pp. 2103–29; this paper made significant advances in its close examination of the religious section of the codex.

[14] For instance, there is no fuller representation of the contents than the basic, and what now seems inexact, list in Brewer and Owen, *Thornton Manuscript*, pp. xvii–xx, or that in R. M. Thompson, *Catalogue of the Manuscripts of Lincoln Cathedral Chapter Library* (Cambridge, 1989); this latter replaces Lincoln Cathedral Library, *Catalogue of the Manuscripts in Lincoln Cathedral Chapter Library*, ed. Reginald Maxwell Woolley (London, 1927).

[15] See, e.g., Pamela R. Robinson, 'The "Booklet": A Self-Contained Unit in Composite

It has often been remarked that the Lincoln manuscript divides generally into three sections: romance (roughly the first half of the book), devotional (approximately the next third (100 folios)) and medicinal (the last 60 folios). *Evangelist* comes in the last quarter of the compilation, as the 33rd of the 47 short devotional items as classified by Brewer and Owen. However, as the third text in the middle quire of the five main quires devoted to religious material, it could be described as being in a very central physical place among the pious pieces. It is the third text in the 13th gathering (Brewer and Owen's gathering N). This quire (ff. 223^r–236^v), made from a single stock of paper, contains three religious prose treatises in English and the text of *Evangelist*. Within the two Thornton manuscripts the watermark of quire N is unique to this gathering. It is a simple vertically-divided circle, which, because of foliation, appears on ff. 230 and 232; it corresponds to Briquet 2921, dated 1401. In the two Thornton manuscripts the only other watermark with so early a *terminus a quo* is the letter 'A' and cross, which is found only in the *Liber de Diversis Medicinis* at the end of the Lincoln book (Briquet 7900, dated 1385–1442). More commonly the Lincoln MS watermarks are of the 1420s, 30s and 40s; on this see further, below. Some leaves have been lost at each end of the quire, probably three each at the beginning and the end, so that a large part of the first text and the end of the last are missing,[16] but, from the aggregate of evidence, it seems likely that Thornton started to copy *Evangelist* on the right-hand side in the centre of the quire, and that it is not a 'make weight'. Each leaf, as in the volume as a whole, is approximately 291 × 210 mm and there has been some attrition at the edges. The order of the four texts of the quire is as follows:

Manuscripts', *Codicologia*, 3 (1980), 46–69, and Ralph Hanna III, 'Booklets in Medieval Manuscripts: Further Considerations', Chapter I in *Pursuing History: Middle English Manuscripts and Their Texts* (Stanford, 1996), pp. 21–34.

[16] Owen suggests that a minimum of one leaf is missing from the beginning of quire N (*Thornton Manuscript*, pp. xiv–xv), and states, 'The textual evidence here offers no guidance as to the amount lost', but Horstmann's edition of the opening, supplied from the Vernon Manuscript (C. Horstman, *Yorkshire Writers*, I: *Richard Rolle of Hampole, an English Father of the Church, and his Followers* (London, 1895), pp. 264–70), shows clearly that about three pages must have been missing. The initial letter of quire signatures noticed by John Thompson on the bottom right-hand corners of ff. 226^r, 228^r and 230^r (kindly supplied through personal communication) show only that these folios definitely belong to the first half of the quire. The corner of f. 231 is badly worn and no trace of a signature remains.

In hete and in wildynesse was þi wonyng
Neythir purpil ne palle ne pelle of price
But of camel skyn þou toke þi clothyng
Halfes þou toke and iotes of þe Iyse
With bonon and beis in the blomyng
Hony comes and wylde mete wanted þo þo
folk Lonely þou lerned Un to þi lykyng
Unto þi lykyng he toke it t in thoght
Baty þynkyng
Syþen ne syne þ negheþ it noght
Seye it neu so fyne
Blissed be þou baptist bothe fer and neye
Dwellyng in deserte with ful goddes wille
þou baptist Ihu withouten any weye
In þe flume iordan þe faith to fulfille
for þe incarnación of the thyes zeye
As fel on þe twelfth day he payde
Unto þe holy gost of heuene become to þe yeye
And as a dowfe on þe he satt þanne ful stille
He sat on þe sulstille A voyce sayde in haast
As it was his wille

Lincoln Cathedral Library, MS 91, f. 231ʳ

ff. 223^r–229^v: end portion of a prose text beginning: 'men*e* pat
 ware in p*r*elacpe'[17]

ff. 229^v–231^r: prose text beginning: 'Wit thou well dere ffrende'

ff. 231^r–233^v: alliterative verse text in 14-line stanzas beginning:
 'Of all mankpnde pat he made'

ff. 233^v–237^r: prose text beginning: '[P]raping is a'.[18]

On these texts see further details and discussion under 'Provenance
and Dates' below. One or more of the missing leaves of the gathering
could have been of a different paper, but this seems unlikely. It is
possible that Quire N may have been a self-contained booklet, though
the fact that the texts in Quires L, M, O and P are also devotional,
instructional texts by Northern writers such as Rolle, Hilton and their
imitators makes it more likely that, if any booklets were compiled,
they would be larger ones.[19]

The scribe has chosen to start the poem on a new leaf because only
about 55 mm remain at the foot of the previous leaf, and he formally
inscribes the heading: 'Of Sapne John p^e the eu*au*ngelist' (see Plate
III facing). The execution is one of Thornton's standard neat formats
for stanzaic alliterative verse, with the eleventh and fourteenth lines
to the right of the bracketed ninth, tenth, twelfth and thirteenth lines.
The text fits the frame except in the very long E260. John Thompson
has noticed the remains of forty-nine quire and leaf signatures in the
Lincoln manuscript, not all wholly legible, but none are now visible in
this gathering.[20] Near the base of the outer margin of f. 231^r there are
some small faint graphs drawn sideways, apparently in the scribe's

[17] There is a large marginal catchword (*?frenes*) from the previous text at the beginning
of this decapitated text, but this could have been added later by someone puzzled about the
sequence.

[18] [P]: MS S (sketched letter *P* in margin). This can provide fuel for each side of the
discussion about whether Thornton did his own initials. For a useful graphic reproduction
of the collation with titles, see Keiser, '"To Knawe God"', pp. 2125–9.

[19] On this and 'Sections', see further Brewer and Owen, *Thornton Manuscript*, p. ix; and
see especially Keiser's argument ('"To Knawe God"', *passim*) that the 100 folios of the
religious pieces were planned to form a distinct 'book'. That the religious pieces begin at
the end of the quire containing *Sir Percival* might seem contraindicative, but the *Charm for
the Toothache* on f. 176^r towards the end of Quire I, followed by the first of the short
religious pieces, rather suggests that they were copied as folio fillers before the large
religious section proper. I have necessarily drawn a strict boundary within the textual
compilation of the entire Lincoln Thornton MS, and indeed the devotional section in it,
both of which still require book-length studies. For the organization of the gathering in
which *Evangelist* appears see Ruth Kennedy, 'The Evangelist in Thornton's Devotional
Book', forthcoming in *Journal of the Early Book Society for the Study of Manuscripts and
Printing History*, 8 (2005).

[20] See Thompson, *Robert Thornton*, p. 270.

hand; these look like a long cursive *s*, a gap and three minims, but do not appear to bear any relation to the matter in the text, and are not like Thornton's current marginal lacunae, which he always indicates with caret marks. It is not like this scribe to write sideways in his margins (in a similar manner, say, to the later scribbling on f. 188^r), but nothing can be made of these faint marks except a conjecture that they are Thornton's own inadvertent pen tries. They are very like those on f. 255^r.

The textual history of the Lincoln Cathedral MS 91, from its life with the Thornton family in North Yorkshire for three centuries, to its place in the archive of Lincoln Cathedral Library by 1735, is delineated in two important articles by G. R. Keiser, following Halliwell and Ogden.[21] *Evangelist*, together with other devotional material from Lincoln Cathedral Library MS 91, was first edited for the Early English Text Society by G. G. Perry, then Dean of Lincoln Cathedral.[22] His anthology is a miscellany from the Lincoln manuscript, prose first and verse last, though arranged in a rather haphazard order. It was designed to 'serve somewhat towards illustrating the religious teaching of the fourteenth and fifteenth centuries, as well as towards exhibiting the peculiarities of the Northern English, in which all the pieces are written' (Introduction, p. v). Perry furnished the text with two sentences of introduction, one page of notes and a glossary, for which he acknowledges Skeat's assistance with difficult words. The poem subsequently found a place in C. Horstmann's *Altenglische Legenden: Neue Folge* (Heilbronn, 1881) where it was given some further brief introductory mention. For the second edition of the EETS volume in 1914, some of Perry's work was amended by C. W. Foster of Timberland, and it was given a new glossary by O. T. Williams,[23] but there were no noticeable

---

[21] Keiser examines the possible sources from which Thornton derived his copy texts; see G. R. Keiser, 'Lincoln Cathedral Library MS. 91: Life and Milieu of the Scribe', *Studies in Bibliography*, 32 (1979), 158–78, and 'More Light on the Life and Milieu of Robert Thornton', *Studies in Bibliography*, 36 (1983), 111–18. See also *The Thornton Romances*, ed. J. O. Halliwell (Camden Society 30, London, 1844), pp. xxv–xxvi, and *The Liber de Diversis Medicinis in the Thornton MS*, ed. Margaret S. Ogden (EETS, 207, 1938 (for 1936)), pp. vii–xv.

[22] See *Religious Pieces in Prose and Verse* (EETS, os 26 1867), pp. 88–95 (2nd revised edition 1914 (for 1913), pp. 97–105).

[23] See Furnivall's notes (in his reformed spelling) in the contemporary EETS circular, often bound at the end of early editions: 'Though called "Reprints", these books are new editions, generally with valuable additions, a fact not notist by a few careless receivers of them, who have complaind that they already had the volumes'. Page references in the present edition are to the 1914 volume.

modifications to *Evangelist*, and the poem had virtually no critical mention during the twentieth century, though Mabel Day, in her 1921 edition of *Baptist*, cites both texts with a list of common collocations (pp. xi–xii), in order to point out that they share certain phrases.[24] J. A. Oakden briefly describes the rhyme schemes, vocalic alliteration and alliterative collocations in his first volume, but was apparently unaware of the existence of either *Katherine* or *Baptist* to enable him to compare or contextualize; four years later, the companion volume accorded a detailed paragraph (opening with '*St. John the Evangelist* is not a noteworthy poem') to the 'unfortunate style' and 'lack of originality [and of] 'poetic style'.[25]

The entire manuscript has ruled frames within generous margins. These frames have been made with the help of pricks, and have sometimes been made before folding and then drawn in ink. In this quire and the preceding one only, Thornton seems to have experimented with red ink frames, but, as in the London manuscript, ff. 125^r–143^v (a section with a single watermark (crossed keys) and the first part of the text of *Richard Coeur de Lion*), they have occasioned some smudging from a ruler in a way that brown ones did not. The handwriting is certainly the same in both quires: neat and upright, the letter forms about the same size. This suggests that Thornton may have been creating these booklets at the same time.[26] No lines are drawn for writing, but straight lines are maintained and *Evangelist* is a tidy item. The ink of the text is dark brown. Thornton's familiar hand is a working current early fifteenth-century book-hand, cursive but upright, *Anglicana* with a few secretary features such as secretary *v*, *g* and *p* graph = *y/þ*. Lower case *t* is crossed and distinguishable from *c*; long and 2-shaped *r* are employed, as are sigma as well as long and secretary *s*. Thornton's *d* graph is characteristic, its body descending below the line in a sharp diamond. As with all of Thornton's copyings, the writing is always legible but in the editing of other texts there has sometimes been difficulty in distinguishing between his *Anglicana e* and *o*. This is not the case with the manuscript of *Evangelist*.

[24] For edition see p. xxii and n. 27.
[25] J. P. Oakden, *Alliterative Poetry in Middle English*, 2 vols (Manchester, 1930, 1935), I. 215, 217–32, *passim* and II. 2, 79. For the sum of critical notice since 1934 see Thorlac Turville-Petre, *The Alliterative Revival* (Cambridge, 1977), pp. 44 and 66, and A. I. Doyle, 'The Manuscripts', in *Middle English Alliterative Poetry and its Literary Background: Seven Essays*, ed. David Lawton (Cambridge, 1982), pp. 88–100, at p. 97.
[26] See p. xvii and n. 15.

There is little mechanical error in the witness. In E62, E86, E89, E115, E118, E128 and E156 there are several current deletions (see apparatus and 'Notes'), some perhaps occasioned by less familiar forms in the exemplar, as in E89 *supere* (*sop* deleted), and E115 *thede* (*tude* deleted); others are common types as in, e.g. E128 *dide* (*dede* deleted) and E156 *delſpnge* (*def* deleted). One is a correction of an exemplar—or far more likely a self-correction—on grounds of sense and alliterative form: in E118 an ampersand is deleted before *ledden*. None are of dialectal interest or can say much about the exemplar except that it was evidently not difficult to read. The text is finished off with the word *Explicit* placed centrally beneath it.

One large decorated initial *O* is drawn at the start of E1 in the brown ink of the text. It has an insert of two acanthus leaves and is set in a simple square frame with some unrefined engrailing. The body of the initial *O* is strongly filled in with the same red as the margins, showing, as elsewhere in the compilation, that Thornton was almost certainly his own limner. Capitals are fairly formal and calligraphic throughout, especially at the opening of the colophon and the stanzas. As is normal for Thornton, there is no punctuation in this witness apart from capitalization at the start of more than half of the lines (notably at the start of each stanza) and bracketing of the ninth and tenth and the thirteenth and fourteenth stanzas in the brown ink of the current hand (sometimes, elsewhere in the book, Thornton brackets in red). A punctus appears twice in the entire text: at the caesurae in E15 and E203. A mark like a modern colon, but with three rather than two dots, punctuates the rhetoric in E70 precisely as a colon might today. Current capitulum marks are made at the caption line, and before stanzas 1, 2, 3 and 4 on f. 231^{r}.

Baptist: British Library Additional MS 39574: the 'Wheatley Manuscript'

BL Add. MS 39574 is a small fifteenth-century book of religious writings in prose and verse, copied on 10 octaves of vellum and later much cut down. Unlike Thornton's large 'family' books, it gives the appearance of having been commissioned for the purposes of private devotion, and then executed by professional scribes. The pages now measure 158 × 100 mm. A description of the book's organization, scribes and fourteen items of religious verse and prose can be found in its first edition by Mabel Day.[27]

[27] Mabel Day, *The Wheatley Manuscript: Middle English Verse and Prose in British*

Because the book was taken apart for rebinding in 1929, some years after first being edited, Day was not aware of some fragments that are probably of significance for the provenance of the anthology. The volume now has 24 flyleaves, 11 at the front, formed: 1 new laid paper, 6 old paper and 4 old parchment; 13 at the end, formed: 7 old parchment, 5 old paper and 1 new laid endpaper. The BL Catalogue is best cited for f. v^r:

In the rebinding of the MS there were found in the old binding fragments of a document apparently connected with wardrobe accompts, mentioning Thomas Bek (Keeper of the Wardrobe 1274, d. 1293) and Philip de Wilueby (for whose connection with the Wardrobe see P. R. O. Lists and Indexes, xxxv, pp. 220, 221). These have now been bound in the back of the volume on the 7th flyleaf as f. v^r.

On these see further, under 'Provenance and Dates', pp. lxxi–lxxii below.

There are 14 texts written on the 10 gatherings of the book. The present edition deals only with the text of *Baptist* and does not attempt a re-examination of the whole volume, its foliation and contents, but, as with the treatment of *Evangelist*, the nature of the neighbouring items should be conveyed. The arrangement of the first five of the fourteen texts is as follows (titles as Day):

ff. 1^r–4^v: Rhyming poem on Christ's passion, beginning 'Ihesu þ^t haste me dere bought' ('An Orison on the Passion')[28]

ff. 4^v–12^v: Prayer, beginning 'Hayle bote of bale blissed qwene' ('A Prayer to the Blessed Virgin')[29]

ff. 12^v–15^v: Stanzaic alliterative poem beginning 'Blissed be thow Baptist' (*Baptist*)

ff. 15^v–45^r: Seven psalms, beginning 'lord in þi angir vptake me noght' ('The Seven Penitential Psalms')[30]

Museum Additional MS. 39574 (EETS, 155 (1921 (for 1917)). Day's description of the manuscript is at pp. vii–xxxii.

[28] Ed. Day, *Wheatley MS*, pp. 1–6; 152 lines in thirty-seven 4-line stanzas (stanza 35 is 6 lines) of alternating duple rhythm; anonymous; found in at least 8 other manuscripts.

[29] Ed. Day, *Wheatley MS*, pp. 6–15; 320 lines of octosyllabic rhyming couplets with refrain and acrostic *Maria*; unique witness.

[30] Ed. Day, *Wheatley MS*, pp. 19–59. Attributed to Richard Maidstone, Carmelite Friar of Kent (d. 1396); found in multiple witnesses and in various forms. See Day, *Wheatley MS*, pp. xii–xviii, and *Richard Maidstone's Penitential Psalms*, ed. Valerie Edden (Middle English Texts 22, Heidelberg, 1990).

ff. 45ʳ–50ᵛ: Nine penitential prose *lectiones*, beginning 'Spare me lord forsope my dayes ben nouȝt' ('Lessons from the *Dirige*').[31]

Baptist is thus the third text of fourteen, the only alliterative poem in the book. It begins two thirds of the way down the verso page. Its striking format of long lines and wheels appears between the octosyllabic couplets of the anonymous and imaginative *Prayer to the Blessed Virgin* and Maidstone's more-or-less-octosyllabic, stanzaic *Penitential Psalms*. Folio 12ᵛ, at the centre of a gathering, is a very rough page, from which half of the ink has disappeared; hence Stanza 1 of *Baptist* is unclear.

Day does not mention the loose scribbles on the first two flyleaves in brown ink in a hand of the first half of the sixteenth century. They consist of two very large initials: *CS* on the first leaf, and then, on the next leaf, in what appears to be the same hand, the same or similar initials and several apparently disconnected words. Most can be deciphered under ultraviolet light, and they start with the words 'Sancta Maria', seemingly as a title. What follows, examined for signs of ownership, is a curious melding of two texts, as if two sets of scribbles ran over the edges of one or more, now missing, loose sheets. The apparent title is followed on the left side of the page by words which are actually some of the penultimate and rhyme words of the nailing to the cross in 'An Orison on the Passion', the first item of the book (ll. 42–60). The spellings of the scribbles exactly match those on f. 2ʳ, including one obvious scribal error, signifying that whoever was scribbling was copying from the text.[32] Each of the rhyme words is succeeded on its right by at least one (mostly decipherable) word which appears to be part of a prose work or prayer, almost certainly to the Virgin. Therefore, proceeding down the right-hand side of the page, words such as the following from 'An Orison' can be deciphered: *Saluations / mindfull / augth / so do so please / to God / Lord mercy that yt*. By line 60 of the 'Orison' text (at the point where f. 2ʳ ends) the 'Orison scribbles' on the left break off,

---

[31] Translation of the Latin from the Matins of the Office of the Dead, otherwise known as the *Dirige*, found in primers and books of hours, and often versified. For their use by the devout laity see W. A. Pantin, 'Instructions for a Devout and Literate Layman', in *Medieval Learning and Literature: Essays Presented to Richard William Hunt*, ed. J. J. G. Alexander and M. T. Gibson (Oxford, 1976), pp. 398–422, especially pp. 405, 413–14. See also editions in Day, *Wheatley MS*, pp. 59–64, and *The Prymer or Lay Folks' Prayer Book*, ed. H. Littlehales (EETS, os 105, 109, 1895, 1897), I, 56–70.

[32] 'An Orison', line 43; MS: ~*þy baak to þe rode was lent*. Day emends to *[b]ent*.

and in the next five lines some individual letters and words can be deciphered under ultraviolet light:

	lorne	was A i	son	Mary
anothir		suram	of	loue Jhu it ?is
mynot acouour[33]			Amen tha	
Amen		tho hit		
s				

These scribbles, like all of the texts in the anthology, are clearly words of meditative devotional matter.

The codex has only a brief known history, for it was acquired by the Early English Text Society for the British Library from Maggs in 1917, and searches through Maggs's archive have not uncovered any earlier documented record. The manuscript was named at the time of the sale in memory of the EETS treasurer and secretary, H. B. Wheatley, and was edited by Mabel Day, then a lecturer at King's College, London, and assistant director of the society in 1921.[34] It was rebound in 1929.[35] Some pertinent correspondence is affixed to the clean parchment flyleaves that appear to have been added to the front of the book on rebinding. On one of these is attached an extract from a letter of Israel Gollancz, dated 11 October 1917, finely copied, with catchwords. Naturally this was not published by Day, but it is of interest today, some eighty-six years later, and helps illustrate the unusually fugitive textual history of all three hymns:

Dear Mr Gilson,
. . . the Director has decided to recommend to the Trustees of the British Museum the grant of (a sum equal to 50% of the purchase money)[36] towards the purchase of the Early English MS. which I handed to you recently, so that it may be secured for the Museum.

I beg leave to add a few particulars:- Some months ago Messrs Maggs showed me the MS., and I at once recognised that it was valuable from several points of view, and especially for some of the poems it contained. With the permission of the firm I transcribed one remarkable poem, found no where else, and of greatest interest for Early English literary history, viz.

[33] Omission of a vowel is a common scribal trait, and a reading 'may not' is possible, as in a phrase such as 'may not recouour'.

[34] See n. 27.

[35] Black morocco, embossed on the spine with 'The Wheatley Manuscript', on the front cover with the inscription 'Acquired with the help of contributions in memory of Dr. Benjamin Wheatley F. S. A.', and inside the back cover with the date.

[36] Despite this decorous parenthesis, the booksellers' price '£210—' is visible in a pencilled note on the verso of the first old paper flyleaf.

a poem on S^t. John the Baptist—a companion poem evidently to S^t. John the Evangelist, found in the Thornton MS., hitherto regarded as the only example of a Stanzaic Alliterative Poem of the 14 line stanza type.[37] The MS. so far as its contents are concerned is of value as containing a text of 'God's Complaint', which next to the Perle is the best example of the stanzaic twelve-line alliterative rhyming poem: of this there are several MSS., but I think none in the Museum. . . .

I trust it may be possible to mention what we desire in respect of associating D^r. Wheatley's name with the volume, and also to reserve for the Society the right to copy and edit the text[38]—It is a long time since so interesting a volume has come into the market . . .

Yours very sincerely
(sd.) I. Gollancz.

Day's edition of *Baptist* is a near-perfect transcription of the text,[39] though the Notes and Glossary are minimal.

As far as can be ascertained, this religious compilation had no printed notice until its mention in Carleton Brown's *Register of Middle English Religious and Didactic Verse* in 1920,[40] and then the edition of 1921 for the Early English Text Society; thus the short textual history of the manuscript consists solely in Mabel Day's volume, as described above. There are no apparent clues as to ownership or history of the manuscript. Day noted the apparent derangement of the stanza order of *Baptist*, but did not attempt to reconstruct it.

That Gollancz had not noticed the edition of *Katherine* which appeared in the 1907 volume of the German philological serial *Anglia* is understandable, though relations with Germany were good until the outbreak of war. But that Oakden, publishing in 1930 and 1934, had not been apprised of the existence of either *Katherine* (described in the Bodleian *Summary Catalogue* in 1905 and edited in 1907) or of *Baptist* (both in Carleton Brown's *Register* of 1916 and 1920, and published by the EETS only nine years before him) is mildly astonishing.[41] It suggests that, though he may have been a member

---

[37] Heuser's edition of *Katherine* had appeared in *Anglia* in 1907.

[38] The present editor was formally granted permission by the Honorary Director of the Early English Text Society, J. A. Burrow.

[39] Gollancz made a transcription of the poem in 1917 before acquiring the MS for the British Museum (see also Day, *Wheatley MS*, 'Prefatory Note', p. v). He would probably have made his transcription available to Mabel Day, if only for verification and comparison.

[40] Carleton Brown, *Register of Middle English Religious and Didactic Verse*, 2 vols (Oxford, 1916, 1920), II, v, vii, 39, etc.

[41] Oakden, *Alliterative Poetry*, *passim*. There is notice and analysis of *Evangelist*, but of

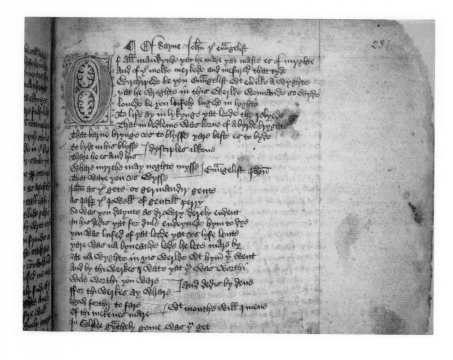

of the EETS and have bought the books, he did not find the time to read them.[42] Critical notice consists in similar brief allusions as for *Katherine* and *Evangelist*.[43]

The writing in the 'Wheatley Manuscript' is professional and conventional, as might be expected in what looks like a commissioned work, and the work of the two scribes is competent and clear in execution. The whole manuscript is ruled vertically and horizontally (averaging about 23 lines) with a fine pen, and the top and bottom margins are now only about 20 mm and those at the side about 10 mm. Two scribes copied the texts, the second scribe starting in the middle of the psalms at f. 33^r. The hand of the first scribe, who copied all of *Baptist*, is a capable, not unusual early fifteenth-century book-hand that employs an upright script with many *Anglicana* and charter features, decorated on the top lines of the folios by stylish elongated ascenders (see facsimile, facing). The *þ* and *y* graphs are very clearly distinguished in the hand of Scribe A, and there is only one word in the text in which these graphs appear to be confused: in *hpm*, B6, though here the *p* graph is dotted (for the possible significance of this and for the fairly systematic spelling, see 'Language', p. lxiv below). There are only three mechanical errors in the text: at B22 where the word *and* is clearly deleted having been written in error before *at*; at B95 where a *t* is erased but left visible before the word *in*; and at B127 where the *p* in *Baptist* has been inserted by means of a caret.

Red and blue decorated capitals are used throughout the volume, and one fairly large decorated initial capital *B* starts the poem, though it is not followed by the smaller plain red or blue capitals at, for example, stanza beginnings, that are found in other parts of the book. The body of the initial is solid blue ink, and it is filled with open red acanthus leaves and surrounded by some fine engrailing.

Punctuation consists of a punctus at the end of about half of the lines, notably absent in twelve lines of one stanza. It is twice used for

neither *Katherine* nor *Baptist*. In II, 'Preface', Oakden thanks Mabel Day 'for granting access to the text of *Mum & Sothsegger* without which this work would have been most incomplete'. Day could not have read his significant first volume or she would have pointed out that he had missed the discovery and edition of *Baptist*. It is interesting, too, that E. V. Gordon, thanked for reading the typescript for Oakden's second volume, evidently had not become aware of the 1907 and 1921 editions of *Baptist* and *Katherine*.

[42] The evidence suggests that he was not a member, and that the state of the texts, as with the status of witnesses, was not a priority with him.

[43] See above, pp. xx–xxi and n. 25. Turville-Petre, *Alliterative Revival*, has two observations, at pp. 26 and 66.

rhetorical pause mid-line (at B7 and B35), and in two instances the mid-line pause is indicated by a colon (at B45 and B87). Neither the punctus elevatus nor the virgule are employed. The rhymes of the sestets are bracketed except in three instances: in Stanzas 1 and 2 (at B12–13; B23–24; and B26–27). Catchwords appear at the foot and head of every page, missing only on f. 24ᵛ, where the rhyme is still maintained. Scribe B does not punctuate his English material at all, but the degree of punctuation that appears in the whole of Scribe A's section is about the same as that found in the text of *Baptist*: just when it seems that some coherent method is being followed, it breaks off, only to resume methodically a line or two later. The *Penitential Psalms* of BL MS Royal 17 C. xvii, a similar but earlier compilation, are completely unpunctuated (except for red bracketing), possibly indicating that the punctuation of *Baptist* is this scribe's own. Marginal capitulum marks denote what seem to be a random three of the stanzas, all on right-hand pages. The margins are too cut down on the verso leaves for any relics of these to be noted.

CONSTRUCTION, METRE AND ALLITERATION

The three hymns are intricately constructed of various numbers of stanzas (*Katherine* 20, *Evangelist* 19 and *Baptist* 10), the 14 lines of which are divided into octet and sestet. The stanzas are not only composed in strong-stress alliterative metre with the addition of rhyme-schemes, but are also linked sporadically by concatenation, and knit at the conjunction of octet and sestet by varying degrees of iteration of word or phrase. Although each stanza, terminated by its metrical 'wheel', forms a definite narrative episode, much of the expression is apostrophe, and all three poems are constructed to form earnest and measured hymns, two of which end with the word 'Amen'.

The term 'Alliterative Revival' (henceforth without inverted commas) designates the flowering of Middle English alliterative verse around the late fourteenth century. Arguments about the continuity of the OE alliterative line are not strictly pertinent to this edition, but it can be noted that the tendency to what has commonly been known as 'alliterative metre' (though the term 'strong-stress metre' with its emphasis on the metrical skeleton is more definitive)[44] never died out in the vernacular, and that in the reign of Edward III, and for a variety of reasons, some stylistic initiative was well received, and led in and shortly after the Ricardian period to an expansion of verse in strong-stress metre with an optimum aa/ax alliterative pattern, producing a 'classic' unrhymed corpus, generally consisting of histories and romance.[45] The heterogeneous lesser, or 'informal', corpus of the minor works of the Revival comprises more ornate, stanzaic, rhymed compositions embodying diverse subjects and didactic intent, in various forms, and with somewhat disparate alliterative patterning. They embody the late fourteenth-century devotional mode of thought, and a taste for short, episodic, homiletic stories in which closures can be effected at short regular stages, as is manifest also in stained glass and pictorial series. The wide distribution of authorial and manuscript provenance of the earliest long-line stanzaic texts—ranging from *The Three Dead Kings* copied in Staffordshire,[46] to *The Awntyrs of Arthure* in Essex, and *Susannah* in Lincolnshire, Essex and Worcestershire—shows that abundant models of stanzaic structures that had not originated in the North West Midlands would have been available to the authors of our three hymns in the late fourteenth or early fifteenth centuries.

14-line Stanza Form

Much of the informal corpus is composed in the distinctive 13-line stanza form.[47] Similar eight- or nine-line stanza forms in strong-stress

[44] See the comment of C. S. Lewis, 'Alliteration is no more the secret of this verse than rhyme is the whole secret of syllabic verse', 'The Alliterative Metre', *Lysistrata*, 2 (1935), reprinted in *Rehabilitations and Other Essays* (London, 1939), pp. 119–13, at p. 119, and *Selected Literary Essays by C. S. Lewis*, ed. Walter Hooper (Cambridge, 1969), pp. 15–26, at p. 15.

[45] Arguments for some continuity of the alliterative tradition through Early Middle English have been made elsewhere. See especially Derek Pearsall, 'The Origins of the Alliterative Revival', in *The Alliterative Tradition in the Fourteenth Century*, ed. Bernard S. Levy and Paul E. Szarmach (Kent, Ohio, 1981); Turville-Petre, *Alliterative Revival*, pp. 1–22; David Lawton, 'Middle English Alliterative Poetry: An Introduction', and Angus McIntosh, 'Early Middle English Alliterative Verse', in Lawton, *ME Alliterative Poetry*, pp. 1–19, and 20–33; Ralph Hanna III, 'Defining Middle English Alliterative Poetry', in *The Endless Knot: Essays in Honor of Marie Borroff*, ed. M. Teresa Tavormina and R. F. Yeager (Cambridge, 1995), pp. 43–64.

[46] Title given by Thorlac Turville-Petre in his edition in *Alliterative Poetry of the Later Middle Ages: An Anthology* (London, 1989), pp. 148–57; previously edited by E. K. Whiting as 'De Tribus Regibus Mortuis', in *The Poems of John Audley* (EETS, 184, 1931), no. 54.

[47] See, e.g., *The Awntyrs off Arthure at the Terne Wathelyn*, ed. R. Hanna III (Manchester, 1974), and *The Four Leaves of the Truelove*, more commonly known as

metre, as well as more complex thirteen- or fourteen-line forms, are employed in the York and Wakefield mystery cycles. Our poems belong to this informal corpus of minor alliterative works, and are in the unusual 14-line stanza form.[48] This small family comprises three saints' hymns, two plays of the York cycle, and one political poem of the fifteenth century which, in three of its nine stanzas, alternates stanzas of strong-stress metre with stanzas of iambic tetrameter.[49] The fourteen-line compositions in rhyming verse share one defining feature, the clear split into an octet of alliterating long lines and a sestet of short lines based on two new rhymes. The saints' hymns alone have sestets which are composed throughout in strong-stress hemistichs; thus these do form one tiny clan, and the remainder (the above-mentioned two plays and satire) another. All of it is, like much verse of the period, religious and didactic.

As yet it cannot be deduced from where these poets took their alliterative fourteen-line stanza form—a form which they handled with comparative assurance—but there is perceptible correspondence with other alliterative stanzaic forms, especially as seen in the later redactions of the drama; and, taking into account the probable guild affiliations of *Katherine* and the plays (see under 'Provenance and Dates', below), we might conjecture that the same local authors were commissioned for both occasional verse and dramatic productions. The thirteen-line stanza form (octet and five-line wheel) of, e.g., *Susannah*, is distinctive and was used early within the alliterative tradition. That there is little difference between the octets of the

The Quatrefoil of Love, ed. I. Gollancz and M. M. Wheale (EETS, 195, 1935 (for 1934)); *The.iiii.leues of the trueloue* is the name of the Wynkyn de Worde edition of *c.*1520, BL Huth 102, and is re-adopted by Susanna Greer Fein (ed.), in *Moral Love Songs and Laments* (Kalamazoo, 1998), pp. 161–254. See also the later Scottish works, e.g., Richard Holland's *The Buke of the Howlat*, *c.*1450, the anonymous *Rauf Coilȝear*, and *Golagros and Gawaine*, *c.*1470, all best edited in *Longer Scottish Poems I, 1375–1650*, ed. Priscilla Bawcutt and Felicity Riddy (Edinburgh, 1987).

[48] Although Turville-Petre gives brief consideration to all three poems in his *Alliterative Revival*, they are missing from the otherwise useful checklist that completes Lawton, *ME Alliterative Poetry*, pp. 155–8. The 14-line stanza corpus is surveyed in Ruth Kennedy, 'Strong-Stress Metre in Fourteen-Line Stanza Forms', in *Medieval English Measures*, ed. Ruth Kennedy, *Parergon*, n.s. 18.1 (Special issue, July 2000), pp. 127–55, at 129–30.

[49] See Plays XXVI, The Cutlers' 'The Conspiracy' and XXXI, the Litsters' 'Christ Before Herod', in *The York Plays*, ed. Richard Beadle (London, 1982), pp. 220–7 and 270–82; and Bodleian Library MS Digby 102, f. 115^r; for editions see *Twenty-Six Political and other Poems*, ed. J. Kail (EETS, OS 124, 1904), pp. 69–72; *Political Poems of the XIVth and XVth Centuries*, ed. R. H. Robbins (Oxford, 1959), pp. 50–3; 'Strong-Stress Metre', appendix, ed. Ruth Kennedy, pp. 152–5.

thirteen-line or fourteen-line stanza forms may suggest that the six-line ending was an independent and in some ways more satisfactory development of the five-line *cauda* found in most of the thirteen-line stanza poems. The lack of bob and the stanza resolutions certainly render more appropriately sober endings to the religious hymns.[50]

The framework of the fourteen-line stanza is made by the rhyme scheme operating in conjunction with metre and alliteration. It falls into two sections: a first group of eight, four-stressed, long lines in *rimes croisées*, abababab—a *frons*, octave, or 'octet'; and a second group of six two-stressed short lines—a *cauda*, sestet or 'wheel' which rhymes variously (e.g., *ccdccd* in *Katherine* and *Evangelist*, and *bbcddc* in *Baptist*).[51] A further feature of this corpus is that more often than not alliteration is carried through two long lines at a time, so that the normative pattern, aa/aa, can result in alliteration of a letter in sequences of eight. Although the short lines are more emphatic because of their close rhymes, they are fully employed to carry the narrative and deliver the forceful stanza closures; they are invariably made up of patterns of a- and b-verses, the latter always ending the stanza.[52] In all three hymns the ninth, tenth, twelfth, and thirteenth lines are metrically a-verses, and the eleventh and fourteenth lines are b-verses; this means that the a-verse patterns of the ninth and tenth lines are always resolved by the shorter, stronger b-verse patterns of the eleventh line, as in, e.g.:

> Thay go agayne in degre,
> As þaire kynde was to bee,
> Stones as þay ware.   (E205–7)

The same happens again with the last three lines of the stanza, as so:

> For he wolde þe aungel noght leue
> Ful sore it gan hym greue:
> He stode doumbe as stone.   (B40–42)

This is also made plain by the manuscript layout of all three witnesses, where the eleventh and fourteenth lines are always bracketed to the right (see Plates I–III).

---

[50] This aesthetic is explored in Kennedy, 'Strong-Stress Metre', *passim*.

[51] *Baptist* exhibits a rhyme scheme unique to the 14-line stanza corpus: though still operating on 4 rhymes to a stanza, the rhyme scheme of the sestets, tied into the octet (*abababab bbcddc*), makes a more intricate structure than found elsewhere.

[52] The currently conventional terms 'a-verse' and 'b-verse' are used to designate these half lines or hemistichs.

Concatenation, as found in *Somer Soneday* and *Awntyrs*, links some stanzas through repetition of a phrase, word or syllable from one stanza to the following. It is realized by the *Evangelist*-poet, possibly by chance, only between Stanzas 10–11 and 13–14; the *Baptist*-poet does not attempt stanzaic concatenation at all, and the *Katherine*-poet manages to sustain it in only eight of his twenty stanzas, for, although diverse concatenation links virtually all of the first eight stanzas of *Katherine*, where much of the *passio* is being recounted, after K99 the poet seems unable to maintain it, and it only reappears between Stanzas 10 and 11: *Turnyng of qweles. / Wyth wrenchis and wylys.* . and Stanzas 14 and 15: *In Syna þei sett. / To Syna ful scherply.* . It is noticeably (and effectively) absent when there is a dramatic leap in the narrative, as at K113: *þan sprong þat cursed kayesere . . .*, or when the narrative moves into an address to the saint, as when the final prayer begins: *Kepe hem here Katereyn . . .* (K225).

Mid-stanza iteration is a more pronounced integrative device. Here the eighth and ninth lines (thus the octet and sestet) are linked, more often than not, by means of a phrase which is repeated, usually with some inversion of its content. This mid-stanza iteration is rare in the thirteen-line stanza form. It is consistent in *Three Dead Kings* and occurs in *Awntyrs*, where it wanes as the composition progresses. However, in the three hymns such verbal echoing is maintained in forty-six of their total of forty-nine stanzas. A deterioration of the ninth-line iteration has been cited as evidence that *Awntyrs* was once two separate poems.[53] The evidence from *Katherine*, where iteration is maintained in only seventeen of the twenty stanzas, indicates that it is more likely that a poet's technical powers can flag. However, the mid-stanza iteration in the two 'John' hymns is sustained throughout.[54] This constraint, when conjoined with alliteration, rhyme and concatenation, serves to create an extremely tight and challenging stanzaic structure.

The varying number of stanzas (*Katherine* 20, *Evangelist* 19 and *Baptist* 10) suggests some focus around the numbers 10 and 20. The acrostics that are such a striking feature of *Katherine* are of some consequence for the structural plan. Heuser posited an original

---

[53] See Hanna, *Awntyrs*, pp. 19–21.

[54] This depends on reversal of MS ll. 37 and 38 in *Baptist* on grounds of sense (see Notes to B61–6 and apparatus to text). Stanza 14 of *Katherine* has been editorially emended so that the iteration of *flayn* and *flik* links the eighth and ninth lines (the MS witnesses it between the sixth and ninth lines).

nineteen stanzas, bringing the poem into line with *Evangelist*, and suggesting that the twentieth stanza of *Katherine* was a later addition.[55] Indeed the acrostic ends at Stanza 19, Stanza 20 is especially nonsensical in syntax, and the allusion to a *giyld* in only the last stanza (see p. lxiv, below) may indicate an addition to an existing nineteen-stanza hymn to make it suit a guild occasion. However, *Baptist*, its existence unknown to Heuser, has a ten-stanza shape, exactly half that of *Katherine*, making two of the three hymns shaped with what one might think of as more equilibrium than nineteen stanzas. Further, the final line of *Katherine*'s Stanza 19, *And profor vs þi pesse* (K266), does not, in fact, effect closure so well as that of Stanza 20, *With joye and with blisse* (K280). Moreover, it would be easier to embody the acrostics at a penultimate position where there is some interesting invocatory vocabulary; the poet may have recognized the difficulty of fitting the name 'Ricardus Spaldyng' into the lexis of the usual closing platitudes where 'joy' and 'bliss' normally abound. Thus it seems more likely that the poem was written in twenty stanzas, and that conjecture about the nineteen of *Evangelist* is more in order; see p. lxxxiv and Notes to E168–9.

Metre

Recent metrical theories differentiate the metrical and alliterative habits of the poets from those of the scribes.[56] In the first edition of *Katherine*, the editor, Heuser, rehearsed a laborious theory of a seven-stress long line, and argued, e.g., that a short thirteenth line conforming to a-verse metre, such as *As fyre doth of flynt þere~* (K13), carried three stresses.[57] The neglected older theories of two stresses in hemistichs, except for some of the a-verses, now appear obvious.[58] More recently metrists such as Hoyt N. Duggan, Thorlac Turville-Petre and Thomas Cable have shown that metrical constraints operated in the 'classic' unrhymed alliterative corpus, and that homomorphic rhythms (particularly noticeable in the second half-lines, or b-verses) that would seem to be quite natural to our ears

---

[55] Heuser, 'Die Katherinenhymne', p. 529.

[56] For a useful recent summary, see *The Wars of Alexander*, ed. Hoyt N. Duggan and Thorlac Turville-Petre (EETS, ss 10, 1989), pp. xvii–xxiv.

[57] Heuser, 'Die Katherinenhymne', §3. Heuser did not, in fact, emend according to his metrical theories, and, considering the contemporary limitations of Middle English dictionaries and of reprographic methods, made a creditable edition of *Katherine*.

[58] See, e.g., Jacob Schipper, *A History of English Versification* (Oxford, 1910), pp. 64–124.

were avoided by the poets, if not by the scribes, over 99.9 per cent of the time.[59] Through careful comparisons with scribal variants, they have developed distributional metrical theories for the unrhymed corpus, mainly showing that the rhythmic moulds, such as ~xx/xx/ and ~x/x/ (i.e., homomorphic, or 'even-beat', phrases that we can hear as anapaestic or iambic), were distasteful to the poets' own 'aural templates', but were installed by copyists who did not have an ear for the subtle unevennesses of strong-stress metre.[60] The constraints that operate in the b-verses of this metre result in heteromorphic rhythms like (x)/xx/ or xx//(x);[61] that is, having one, but only one, poly-syllabic (or 'long') dip between the two stresses.

As yet, much less consideration has been given to the complexity of a-verse metrical patterning than to that of the b-verses, which are so often formulaic in origin, and, with their function of effecting closure, generally shorter and tighter in metrical expression. On the basis of studies so far (and this includes such standard works as those of Oakden and Borroff),[62] very few a-verses in the entire alliterative corpus can be shown to be unmetrical; the impression has always been that anything goes, as long as it has two lifts and a minimum of four syllables.[63] They are certainly more variable and allow for two long

[59] The poets avoided symmetrical, 'even-beat', alternating metrical patterns by juggling with such alternatives as aphetic forms, by using *to* or *for to* with the inf. (as in K30 'to lede' where the poet's more usual *for to* would give an unmetrical line), or by the use of fillers such as an adverbial *ful* to give a required extra syllable. Accounts of such techniques are given in, e.g., H. N. Duggan, 'The Shape of the B-Verse in Middle English Alliterative Poetry', *Speculum*, 61 (1986), 564–92, at 584–7.

[60] See Duggan, 'Shape of the B-Verse'; Duggan and Turville-Petre, *Wars Alex.*; Thomas Cable, *The English Alliterative Tradition* (Philadelphia, 1991), pp. 85–103.

[61] (x) indicates the indeterminate phonology of final -*e* and vowels in unstressed syllables.

[62] J. P. Oakden, *Alliterative Poetry in Middle English*, 2 vols (Manchester 1930, 1935); Marie Borroff, *Sir Gawain and the Green Knight: A Stylistic and Metrical Study* (Yale Studies in English 152, New Haven, 1962).

[63] The a-verse criteria are examined by Duggan in two articles, 'Alliterative Patterning as a Basis for Emendation in Middle English Alliterative Poetry', *Studies in the Age of Chaucer*, 8 (1986), 73–105, and 'Extended A-Verses in Middle English Alliterative Poetry', in Kennedy, *Measures*, pp. 53–76. They can be epitomized as 'A-verse rhythms are far more flexible [than b-verse rhythms]. There are rarely more than eight unstressed syllables, and the most common rhythmical patterns involve three or fewer syllables in each dip. None to five unstressed syllables may occur before the first lift and from none to seven immediately follow it. Though any two dips may have three syllables, the third dip in such lines tends to be light, and when any one dip contains four or more syllables, the other two dips tend to have two, one, or no syllables' ('Patterning', p. 78) and, on the problematic of three possible stresses in an a-verse: 'The evidence suggests that none of the studies thus far offered, including my own, constitutes anything beyond a crude approximation of this aspect of metrical patterning' ('Extended A-Verses', p. 66).

dips (and less work has been done on them), but they come out most often as something like xx/x(x)x/; and a-verses sounding /x/x appear, though are not proven to be unmetrical. So, although a-verse patterns (x)/x(x)x/(x) are usual, they are utilized for only 55.83 per cent of the whole.[64]

Through study of the multiple manuscript witnesses of a control corpus it can be shown that even though alliterative practice was different, the same metrical rules of the b-verse were operating with even greater stringency for the rhymed verse than for the unrhymed, the evidence of compared witnesses showing that writers who composed in rhymed stanzas never violated the peculiar metrical constraints of the b-verse paradigms. Scribes can be shown to have brought this astonishing 100 per cent metricality down by a significant degree, generally to about 98 per cent.[65] In our three hymns the metricality of the b-verses ranges from the characteristic 98.5 per cent of *Evangelist* and *Baptist* to the unprecedented 93.5 per cent of *Katherine*, showing a normal degree of scribal disruption in the 'John' hymns and a problematic degree in *Katherine*. Thus, the two 'John' hymns are metrically unexceptional. The percentages of unmetrical b-verses in them (an average of 1.5 per cent) are consistent with an average from any witness to any alliterative work that we might care to examine.[66]

The disordered metricality in the witness of *Katherine* with its 6.5 per cent of unmetrical b-verses demonstrates a degree of metrical corruption that goes along with its lexical confusion—with subsequent consequences for editing.[67] The customary patterns of (x)/xx(x)/, xx// (lines with clashing stresses), and the rare, but authorial xx/x/ make up most of the text, but fewer than thirteen of the 200 b-verses appear in homomorphic metre (7 in a driving, triple, anapaest rhythm (K87, K115, K123, K126, K187, K189, K226), and 6 in an

[64] This would appear to conflict with Cable's argument that the ~xx/xx/(x) pattern is the metrical *norm* for a-verses (Cable, *Alliterative Tradition, passim*), but his arguments are premised on a sounding of final -*e* that the evidence of rhyme makes hard to accept.

[65] See Ruth Kennedy, 'New Theories of Constraint in the Metricality of the Strong-Stress Long Line, Applied to the English Rhymed Alliterative Corpus, *c.*1400', in *Métriques du Moyen Âge et de la Renaissance*, ed. Dominique Billy (Paris, 1999), pp. 131–44. The control corpus embodies eleven witnesses: *Awntyrs* (4), *Susannah* (5) and *Truelove* (2, plus one early printed book from a separate tradition).

[66] That is a scribal substitution rate of anything from as low as 0.04 per cent to as high as the 5.9 per cent of the *Parlement* Ware manuscript. In the control corpus it is only 0.63 per cent—largely because of the sound Vernon and Simeon *Susannah* manuscripts. See Kennedy, 'Constraint in Metricality', *passim*.

[67] This is noticeable among the pronouns, e.g. K88 (MS him/*hir?*); K100 (MS sche/ *he?*); K145 (MS his/*hir?*). See also 'Treatment of the Texts', below.

iambic duple rhythm (K17, K36, K56, K142, K201, K203)). This is an unprecedented percentage in the rhymed corpus and raises the question whether they are authorial, and thus whether the poet had a penchant for alternating rhythms. But the overwhelming evidence is that poets writing in strong-stress metre did not employ such syllable arrangements, and a likely metrical equivalent can be substituted for each of them. Each fits into the types of scribal patterns that can be highlighted in comparisons of variant witnesses—addition or omission of particles being the general factor.[68] Further details of their unmetricality and suggested solutions are described in the Notes to each of these thirteen lines.

As regards a-verses, the *Katherine*-poet appears to be establishing a homomorphic triple measure so thoroughly that it is difficult to tell whether he intends it to be broken in the same ways and for the same effect as in the unrhymed corpus (as done particularly well by Langland and the *Gawain*-poet[69]). The problem is compounded in that either will depend on the position adopted on the stress status of three alliterating words in the first hemistich. These nine problematic a-verses in *Katherine* are K58, K74, K102, K128, K130, K162, K253, K269, K271. Each can be scanned at least two ways: the first as in traditional scansion which slows the line down while three stresses are honoured; or, secondly, scanned with the options that ensue from the subordination of one stressed word in an open class. As we are far from knowing how strong stress metre was scanned with regard to word classes, none of the possible ways of scansion should be seen as especially problematic, though it seems particularly difficult to suppress a stress or elevate an adjective over a noun in the interests of a 'metrical' triple rhythm in K128.[70] It is possible to pinpoint only one possibly defective a-verse (one without a long dip) in the entire poem: K6: *Bot tholyd thykly* (x/(x)/x~). Duggan's observations have not discounted this metrical pattern in an a-verse, but it is unusual, and breaks the expected rhythm in an awkward way. Again, an emendation suggests itself (see Note to K6), but, as with every aspect of this troublesome poem, the metre is problematic.

Evangelist presents extremely regular metrical patterning (and extremely regular alliteration, for which see below).[71] There is only

---

[68] See n. 59.

[69] As in *SGGK*, l. 2346: 'And roue þe wyth no rof-sore~', etc.

[70] See further Duggan, 'Extended A-Verses', *passim*.

[71] Thornton's accuracy in that regard is clear, and it should be noted that he is so often

one defective b-verse in the entire poem, and that is an eleventh line: *Noghte assentand to synne* (E67)—a line that has moved into 'forbidden' double pairs of unstressed syllables.[72] From the evidence of other witnesses to alliterative texts copied by Thornton (as, for instance, by comparing the four dissimilar manuscripts of *Awntyrs* or the two each of *Truelove* and *The Parlement of the Thre Ages*[73]) it can be seen that, although Thornton is a careful scribe and almost never mismetres a line into duple, alternating rhythms, he shows an eagerness to smooth out and add explanatory pleonasms by inserting fillers such as *ful*, frequently supplying full forms where an aphetic one was metrical, and altering the metrical pattern of the b-verses to make triple-beat 'anapaestic' lines. Thus a Thornton alliterative text generally makes good sense and retains alliterative regularity, but is not necessarily as metrically legitimate as might be expected.[74] It is probable that Thornton did this when he had a *bad* exemplar, as in *Parlement*, and the evidence is here that he had a good one. In contrast to the above other witnesses, Thornton does not transcribe one hypermetric b-verse in *Evangelist*. Possibly he was copying from an exemplar so clear and rhythmic that he did not feel the need to help the line along in his typical manner. The a-verses are entirely unproblematic but ring the changes agreeably on a variety of metrical frames.

The metrical structure of *Baptist* is regular, the pattern $(x)/xx/$ of about 96 per cent of the b-verses showing a customary awareness of strong-stress composition. But inelegant moments do occur more than is typical in works of the Revival. For example the hobbling rhythm of the unusual (but in other texts authorial) pattern $x(x)x/x/$, as in B3, B6, B34, B65, and B83 (and possibly B33 and B35 with sounded inflections) together with frequent breakdown of alliteration, suggests a bad writer or a problem in the copying tradition.[75] The a-

copying Northern exemplars that he does not encounter difficulties in dialect that Southern scribes smooth out, altering alliteration and metre in the process.

[72] But it is possible that the original half-line read: 'Noghte sentand to synne', as in K242, '~when we to synne sent'; or, alternatively, the *Evangelist*-poet may have judged an elision between *Noghte* and *assentand* to be within the parameters of his metricality (I am indebted to my colleague, Professor John Creaser, for this latter suggestion). Either emendation would establish 100 per cent metricality in the b-verses of the poem.

[73] See *The Parlement of the Thre Ages*, ed. M. Y. Offord (EETS, 264, 1959).

[74] See Kennedy, 'Constraint in Metricality', p. 139.

[75] B19 and B132 are b-verse lines without a polysyllabic dip: *~on ground myght gone*; *~þat hath no pere*. In the former, a missing auxiliary verb such as *han* is suspected, or, more likely, an inflection on the acc./dat. *grounde*. In the latter, an original *withouten any pere*

verses of *Baptist* are idiosyncratically short, matching, as they do, the
initial apostrophic blessing that opens each stanza. The homomorphic
B34 is the only unmetrical a-verse : *Watir drynkyng~*. The sense of
drinking nothing but water, as John did in the desert, is missing, but
it is not easy to suggest a metrical version. However, this line appears
in the 'wheel' where the *Baptist*-poet's latitude regularly disregards
alliteration. Here there also appears to have been a disregard for
metre.

An analysis of multiple manuscripts in the informal corpus
demonstrates that rhymed, stanzaic verse permits a greater variety
of alliterative patterning than is found in the unrhymed.[76] This was,
of course, observed by Oakden, and is, indeed, evident to the eye,
but it is useful to confirm that four alliterating sounds (aa/aa) is
evidently the attempted norm, but conversely that only one
alliterating sound in each half-line (for example, ax/xa, or ax/ax)
is equally permissible, as, of course, is aa/bb—a pattern particularly
useful for the exigencies of rhyme. So, where the optimum
alliterative pattern of the classic corpus is aa/ax, that of the
rhymed corpus is more likely to be aa/aa, aa/xa or aa/bb.[77] The
alliterative patterning of the 390 long lines of the three poems can
be systematized as follows:

would restore both alliteration and metre. We have few rules for knowing how to scan a b-
verse such as that in B115: *~his dere derlyng*; but it does not produce a happy line. Three
similar instances in the b-verses, at B38, B40 and B135, result in a notably average rate of
2.14 per cent, but there are no easy explanations for each of them, and authorial
incapability is suspected (see 'Notes').

[76] The evidence from the aggregate witnesses of the control corpus of rhymed
alliterative verse showed authorial (or restored) alliteration at about 98 per cent of such
normative patterning (cf. the 100 per cent b-verse metricality), with varying degrees of
scribal loss of the alliteration. The average degree of alliteration in the manuscript
witnesses was about 93 per cent.

[77] This is premised upon stress and scansion. *qw/v/w/wh* groups in *Katherine* generally
do not alliterate together (but see Note to K245). The alliteration of the [s] and [ʃ] groups
is discrete except in one possible instance: K197: 'to Syna ful scherply || sothly þei flye'
[sʃ//sf]. There are no lines where [s] or [ʃ] or OE *cw* or *hw* makes a necessary *second*
alliterating sound to its opposite number; they always create a third sound. Thus there is
no clear-cut evidence that [s] and [ʃ] or [hw] and [kw] were meant to alliterate. However,
scansion of alliteration on alliteration across these groups is made on the grounds that if a
desired combination of four sounds is found 50 per cent of the time, then obviously it
seems better to scan an [s]/[ʃ] line (e.g., K72) as aa/aa rather than aa/bb; and that if aa/ax
is the second most common pattern, then common sense dictates that aa/ax is a more
obvious patterning of K197 than the much rarer ax/ax.

RECURRENT PATTERNS

	Katherine (160 lines)		Evangelist (150 lines)		Baptist (80 lines)		Total (390 lines)	
aa/aa	78	49%	95	63%	24	30%	197	51%
aa/ax	21	13%	20	13%	2	3%	43	11%
aa/xa	21	13%	15	10%	4	5%	40	10%
aa/bb	11	7%	3	2%	14	18%	28	7%
xa/aa	12	6%	7	5%	3	4%	22	6%
ax/aa	6	4%	2	1%	4	5%	12	3%
Total	149	93%	142	93.5%	51	64%	342	88%

NON-RECURRENT PATTERNS

	Katherine (160 lines)		Evangelist (150 lines)		Baptist (80 lines)		Total (390 lines)	
e.g., aa/xx	5	3%	4	3%	9	11%	18	5%
xx/aa	2	1%	0	0%	4	1%	6	2%
xx/xx	0	0%	0	0%	5	6%	5	1%

Added to these are ax/ax, xa/xa, etc.

	Katherine		Evangelist		Baptist		Total	
Total	11	7%	6	5%	29	36%	46	12%

The differences in the way the poets use the non-recurrent patterns (see bottom line, above) are one of the many contra-indications of common authorship. The *Evangelist*-poet is the highest user of normative patterning (note also his regular metrical patterns, above), and, as regards conformity to regular patterning, the *Baptist*-poet is off the scale. Furthermore, only two or three of the 75 pairs of lines in the long lines of *Evangelist* do not alliterate on the same letter. So, 96 per cent (or even 98 per cent—see Note to E179–80) do alliterate through the pairs of lines, as compared with the 80 per cent of *Katherine*, and mere 20 per cent in *Baptist*.

In *Katherine*, there is a notable preponderance of xa/aa lines over ax/aa lines, occurring four times because of the use of the name *Katereyn* (and once the name *Porphyri*) at the opening of a line, though this does not explain the poet's preference for its use elsewhere. Both provide an unusual variation in the rhetorical cadences, with their initial strong stresses, as in, for example:

K161: liȝthly with a swerd || hire lyf schuld be leyd   ax/aa
K106: eyþer to beryen || hir bones or hyr blode.   xa/aa

Subsidiary alliteration is found sixteen times in the 160 long lines of *Katherine*, and in each case it pushes the alliteration in the direction of an obviously optimum aa/aa pattern. Furthermore, in three of the ten instances of 'defective' alliteration, subsidiary alliteration provides a necessary or third alliterating sound.[78] Three of the most unorthodox lines provide secondary alliteration as when a compensatory third sound in the a-verse makes up for none in the b-verse, as in K90 and K162; and, in the case of K21, the secondary alliteration is provided to furnish something approaching an aa/bb line:

K21: fyfti fyne retorikes || in hast þei hem hent

Of the 120 short lines of *Katherine*, 70 (58.33 per cent) alliterate on both stresses. Sometimes whole stanzas do, including virtually all of the 1st and 2nd, and the 16th and 17th. These latter two are the opening stanzas of the final prayer, where the poet might be restarting, as it were, in his intended vein, and so the position of all four of these stanzas suggests that the poet actually wished to alliterate the short lines as aa throughout, just as the aa/aa pattern seems to be that most evidently aspired to for the long lines. However, it also appears that the 41.67 per cent of short lines that do not alliterate was acceptable.[79]

Taking into account the self-evident and unavoidable emendations to letters, the alliterative patterning of *Katherine* presents few problems.[80]

The metrical and alliterative evidence shows that Thornton's copy of *Evanglist* is a clear one. Evidence of the clarity of the exemplar (and its probable closeness to the archetype) is also seen in the striking regularity of alliterative patterning. There is not one line of the 150

---

[78] See K 21, K114 and K232. It could be argued that initial alliterating letters must form the alliterative patterns, irrespective of stress. This would, on the last example, give *ff/hh*, ignoring the stress in *retorikes*, and providing a statistically more 'normal' alliterative pattern: aa/bb.

[79] There is no apparent scheme to these or to their occurrence, and little about scribal activity can be deduced from this evidence except the fact that 65 per cent of the a-verses (the ninth, tenth, twelfth and thirteenth lines) alliterate, whereas only 45 per cent of the b-verses (the eleventh and fourteenth lines) do. But the rhyme is so insistent in the eleventh and fourteenth lines (the two d-rhymes) that they are able to compensate in principally masculine endings and strong rhymes for a lack of alliteration. In the less punchy 'a-verses' of the sestets (the ninth, tenth, twelfth and thirteenth lines), the rhyme arguably always falls on the *penultimate* syllable, and the alliteration is rather more necessary for the momentum.

[80] See Notes to K107, K118, K270. K227 is emended on grounds of metre and alliteration.

long lines that is seriously impaired in alliteration, and a remarkable figure of 63 per cent of the long lines alliterate aa/aa as compared with the equally notable figure of almost exactly 50 per cent for many other poems of the stanzaic corpus except *Baptist*.[81] Furthermore, virtually all of the remainder of the long lines conform to ax/aa, aa/xa or aa/ax patterns. It would be impossible to induce from either *Katherine* or *Baptist* an archetype of such alliterative regularity as this—a regularity which is outstanding in the entire corpus of rhymed, stanzaic alliterative verse. As might be expected, the *Evangelist*-poet maintains alliteration in the sestets (63 per cent) more often than his fellow poets do.

Baptist is as unpolished in alliteration as in metre. The expected 50 per cent aa/aa is there, and the aa/bb pattern occurs at an unprecedented 18 per cent, giving this poem its characteristic bumpy antiphonal rhythm, but it is in aa/xx, xx/aa and the non-alliterating lines that differences show up. Together with the intricate rhyme scheme and the steady mid-stanza iteration, the *Baptist*-poet does attempt, where possible, to keep to the same alliterative letter (whether an aa or a bb alliteration) for two lines at a time (e.g. B1–2 or B85–86), but manages it in only 20 per cent of the long lines, as compared with the 80 per cent of *Katherine* or the 96 per cent of the *Evangelist*-poet. Yet, in complete contrast to the alliterative proficiency of the *Evangelist*-poet, there are many lines in *Baptist*, almost certainly authorial, where the alliteration breaks down altogether. Occasionally (as mentioned above, and in the Notes to, e.g., B61) the substitution of a synonym, particularly one of Northern dialect, could restore a recognized pattern, but it is clear that this poet does not have the verbal dexterity to produce alliterative fireworks in a structure that must also maintain a stanzaic form, consistent mid-stanza iteration, and an even tighter rhyme scheme than that of the other two poems. As with the *Katherine*-poet, the *Baptist*-poet alliterates less than half the time in the sestets, but there is so much going on in the emphatic syntax and complex rhyme scheme that it is hardly missed.

Emendation on Metrical and Alliterative Grounds

Duggan regards the avoidance of specific patterns as a *condition* of metricality,[82] whereas Cable believes them to be merely a *norm* of

---

[81] The seriously defective *Baptist* has a mere 30 per cent (see table above).
[82] Duggan, 'Shape of the B-Verse', p. 564, n.

metricality.[83] Like many recent editors, I attempt to take up a position between the two. Although I am convinced by Duggan's theories, for the purposes of this first edition of this group of single-manuscript poems, it has seemed most helpful to see the avoidance of certain patterns as a *principle* of metricality. However, the manuscript evidence of the metre of *Katherine* does not help us to be sure that this principle was consistently adhered to by the poets, for this begs two questions: 'Who were these poets?' and 'Were there such things as bad poets?' If these three poems were written for events connected with saints' guilds or similar parochial activity, were their authors unpractised guild members with literary leanings, whose knowledge of strong-stress metrical theory was imperfect? Or were they all practised poets who had the good fortune to learn their metrics from perfect manuscripts now lost to us?

Single-witness manuscripts bring their own troublesome problems, and only one conjectural emendation has been made on metrical grounds (the addition of a syllable to MS *herborgh* (*herb[or]ogh*) in K203). However the few that have been made on grounds of sense, or alliteration, or both, have often restored or improved metre (see, e.g., K227 and B45).

However, evidence of more severe metrical constraints than hitherto perceived can be of consequence for the sense of a line, and some readings have been confirmed through collected evidence that the caesura does always fall at the end of a syntactic unit.[84] The most lucid readings of several ambiguous lines in the problematic *Katherine* have been premised on this, so, e.g.:

Cumlyest *kepyng* kaytefs fro kare (K2)
Verbal n. = 'defence' qualified by *cumlyest*, not pres. participle dependant on *cumlyest* used substantively.

To þo buntiful beerdes *abooue* sche hem bilde (K156)
Adv. = 'openly', not adv. = 'above' governing *beerdes* (which sense is supported by neither phonology nor caesura).

Qwen þei hadd fet þat feiþful *farly* to feel (OE *feolan* = to bury) (K198)
Adv. = 'fairly, honourably' with *feel*, not adj. with *þat feiþful*. See Note to K198.

To Crist for þat curteys *comly* þei crye (K199)
Adv. with *crye*, not adj. with *þat curteys*, or adj. as n. qualified by *curteys*.

[83] Cable, *Alliterative Tradition*, Ch. 3, pp. 66–84.
[84] Kennedy, 'Constraint in Metricality', p. 142.

Dyntes of deuelys *dere* fro vs dryue (K243)
Adv. with *dryue*, not adjective with *deuelys*.

With the exception of the total of a dozen self-evident and unavoidable emendations that restore alliteration (eight in *Baptist*, three in *Katherine* and one in *Evangelist*) the alliterative patterning in the three texts presents few problems. It can be posited that there is an 'ideal' underlying norm in this patterning for both long and short lines, just as there seems to be a metrical norm, achieved wherever possible. Suggestions could sometimes be made for 'improving' the alliteration, and pushing it towards the more desired norm, but, because in *Evangelist* and *Katherine* there are no 'defective' lines (according to the norms of the rhymed control group), there are no grounds for such editorial implementation. However, as with metre, there seems little reason why more heavily emended texts might not be presented in future editions.

LANGUAGE

Note: the sign '↔' is used to denote 'rhymes with'. The scribe's use of þ = *þ/y and his use of abbreviations are discussed on pp. xiv–xvi above.*

Katherine

The most conspicuous features of the orthography are the *-th* endings for spirant *-(ȝ)ht*, the doubling of vowels and diverse recruitments of the letter *w*. Final *-e* is frequently shown by rhyme to be scribal or redundant, e.g., *mane* ↔ *ranne*; *wyffe* ↔ *cnyf*; *encresse* ↔ *pesse*. See also the rhymes of K261–266, the last 2 of the 14 spellings of the name *Katereyn(e)* in K273 and K275, and, most telling, unetymological *-e* added to, e.g., nom. *rithe* (K16) and *trewþe* (K58). By the presence of some of these same nouns which historically had no vocalic ending, it can be seen, through rhyme, that final *-e* was not sounded in the preterite verbs *wanne*, *ranne* ↔ *mane* or adv. *þane* ↔ *mane* (K49). Note also K261–6, where the nom. sing. adj. *kynd* alternates with spellings of the n. *mynde*, the pp. *pynd* and the inf. *fynde* ↔ *-nd(e) ay*. There is virtually no evidence in either rhyme or metre that final *-e* was intended to be sounded. Many infinitives in *-e* which rhyme on words that lack historical final *-e* show that the sound was already lost, e.g., *lowte* ↔ *stowte*; *wynne* ↔ *gynne*; *fynde* ↔ *mynde*; but see Note to K56–7.[85]

A distinct feature of this witness is the use of *w* in diphthongs and as a spelling variant, both for vowels and consonants, e.g., *aw* in *lawth* and *sawes* represents OE *ag*; *ew* in *rewly* represents OE *ēo*; and *ow* in *rowth* represents OE *ōh*; but *w* in *rwd* or *dewre* represents an OF vowel sound, variously written, but most likely the sound usually represented by OF *ü*. Unless the spelling is in error, the letter appears to indicate a diphthong after the initial *w*- in *wowndyd* (though cf. also *woundid*). The reflex of OE/ON *ū* is generally written *ow*, as in *dowf*, *lowte*, *schowres*. Related to this is the occasional coupling of short vowels—for obscure reasons. Examples are *fyendys*, *foundyed* (possibly because it is being treated as a weak v.; see below), *flyit* (because the stem apparently ends in an [i] sound and may represent a diphthongization of ON *y*), and perhaps *vnknyit*, if it means 'unknitted' (for no apparent reason; see 'Notes'). The spelling in *giyld* must indicate the reflex of OE *ie* rather than that of ON *i*; that in *selcouyth* plainly shows the diphthongization of OE *ū* (see *ū*, below). Conspicuous doubled *ee* and *oo* vowels appear to indicate length, but this is not invariable; e.g. *reel*, patterned in its rhyming vowels to match *feel*, *keel*, *meel*, is followed by *releþ* in the next line. Orthography here and elsewhere (e.g., the rhymes in Stanzas 10 and 11) shows that the scribe of this witness had his own ideas, one being that, as with punctuation, the rhymes in octet and sestet should be patterned visually. Thus the spelling is not a true guide to the author's pronunciation. The following forms are used:

A. In reflexes of OE stressed vowels:

(1) OE *ў̆* appears as *i* or *þ* = *y* before *n* or *t*, as in *mynt*, *kitte*, *dyntes*; it is found as *e* before *r* in *sterne* (↔ *lerne*, *derne*, *berene*) and *herde*, *merde* (↔ *lerede*, *aferde*), although these should rather be related to the lowering of earlier *i*, shown by spellings such as *beryen*. When long it is written *i* or *þ* = *y*, as in *fyre*, *fylde*, *pride* (see *kiþ* ↔ *blyth*, *liþ*, *swith*; *fylde* ↔ *þilde*, *milde*; *kynd* ↔ *fynde*, *bynde*, *mynde*). The form *fyendys* suggests an earlier *fÿnd* (but cf. *fendys*, OE *fēondas*, and the remark on doubling of vowels above).

(2) OE *i* appears commonly as *i*/*y*, as in *qwith*, *thik* (cf. *thyk*),

wychcraft. When long it appears as *i/y*, as in *fyfty, qwyles, stiffenes*. It appears once as *e* in *blely*.

(3) OE *e* generally appears as *e*, as in *breyd, tretest, wrenchis*. It appears as *a* in *away* (cf. *awey*). OE *ē* appears as *e*, as in *fere(s)* (cf. *feer*), *frede, wende*. It appears as *ee*, as in *keel, queen, scheen*.

(4) OE *æ* appears as *a*, as in *after, fast, craft*; *wrake* and *schake* rhyme on *take* and *make*. It also appears as *ee*, as in *cleen*. When long it is usually *e*, as in *herandys, reche, wed(e)*; but it also appears as *ee* in *deel, leede*, and, by analogy, probably, *meel*. It rhymes on the reflex of OE *ē* and *ēo*, e.g.: *clene ↔ qween, beene; drede ↔ lede, dede; schede ↔ mede, frede*; but also on the reflex of OE *y*, as in *lerede ↔ herde, merde*.

(5) OE *a* before a nasal not in a lengthening group is regularly written *a*, as in *mane, thank(e)*. In a lengthening group it is *o*, as in *longly, sprong, throng* (n. and v.). Lengthened in an open syllable it rhymes on the reflex of OF or ON *a*, as in *aschamyd ↔ blamyd, famyed*; and *name ↔ tame*. When long it normally appears as *o*, as in *know ↔ below, ouerthrow, trow*, and *lore ↔ ibore, icore, before*. See also *qwo, quoso*. There are three spellings as *oo*: *dool, foos, woo*.

(6) OE *o* appears as *o*, as in *doluyn, tholyd, throng*, but as *u* in *schuld*. OE *ō* appears as *o*, as in *broþur, grof, throwe*, as *oo* in *bloode, good(e)*, and as *u* in *mut*.

(7) OE *u* appears as *o*, as in *sonbeem, sondur, wonnyng*, as *ou* in *loue, þour, woundid*, as *u* in *schrunk, tunge, turtyl*, and as *ow* in *wowndyd* (cf. *woundid*). OE *ū* appears as *o in bot*, as *ou* in *þou, oure(e)*, as *ouy* in *selcouyth*, as *ow*, as in *lowte, thowsand, bowed* (although here the *w* might be a relict of OE *ġ*), and as *u/v* in *but, vs*.

(8) OE *eo/ēo* almost invariably appears as *e*, as in *to-ches, derlyng, krepen*, but appears as *ou* in *four*, as *ow* in *rewly*, and as *w* in *trw*.

(9) In unstressed inflexional syllables the vowel is primarily written *-e*, as in *vnwrapped, retorikes, karueth*. But *-y* is found in nine of the forty-one pl. nouns, e.g.: *wylys, fyendys, balys* (cf. *bales*). It is also found in four third-person cases: *tholyd, tredyd, stranglyd, sendys*, and in eight past participles, e.g.: *blamyd, chosyn, wowndyd*. There is one odd spelling in *-ye-*, *foundyed* (surely from OF *fondrer*, though this may indicate OE *fundian* (see Note to K190)). The vowel is written *-i* in four instances: *labowrid, wrenchis, woundid* (cf. *wowndyd*) and *karis* (cf. *kares*). It is found as *-u* in three clear instances: *cursud, cursurdly* (cf. *cursed*), *chesus; bemus* and *briddus* are found with the *ꝰ = us*

abbreviation, but cf. *briddes*. The vowel before final *r* is predominantly written as *e*, as in *schofferes, koueres, commyneres*, but in several instances (from OE *-or* and OF *-our*) it is *ur*, as in *wondur, broþur, traytures*. Two OE class I weak verbs ending in *-rian* become *-ur* in the inf.: *sondur, tempure*. In four cases (all from OF) the vowel is *-ou*, as in *honoure, traytour*; once it is *o* in *profor*, and once *a* in *pynchars* (almost certainly a casual Northern suffix analogous to, e.g., *syngar*, rather than a Latinate suffix on analogy with Modern English *scholar* which is virtually always *-er* in ME (see OED *-ar*$^{1-3}$ *suffixes*)).

B. In reflexes of certain OE consonants:

(1) OE medial *f* is most often found as *f*. Apparent unvoicing of the consonant [v] is common, as shown by words rhyming with *chef* (i.e. *lef, gref, mef*); see also *kerf, lif, schaf*. No *f-* spellings appear in inflected v. forms. However, the forms spelt with *-ue* are found in about equal quantity, often in the same stanza, e.g., Stanza 10, where *mef* (inf.) ↔ OF *chef* is iterated as *meue* (inf.), ↔ *greue, leue, preue*; and conclusive evidence of the sound must be demonstrated by *dryue* ↔ *ryf, cnyf, wyffe* in K239–45. OE medial *f* is found as *u* in *preuyd*, and written with *v* only once in *sterved*. For the voicing of the labial spirant see the use of *w* above. There is a tendency to employ *w* as consonant to represent not only OE *w* as is usual (e.g., *wardeþ*), but also OF *v*, as in *wow* (OF *vou*), *dentiwos, dentywos* (OF *daintif-*) and perhaps also ON *v* in *wylys* (ON *vēl*). These features suggest a Northern bilabial sounding of the OF/ON spirant somewhere in the tradition (cf., e.g., *Wars Alex*. 1236 and 1854), but, with no alliterative stress on such words in this text, we cannot tell. However, *v* and *u* are also employed for OF consonant *v*, as in *vertuus, uirgin*.

(2) Initial OE * g̵(e)* is written as *ȝ* in *aȝens* and *i* in *icore, ibore*, but is otherwise *g*. Medially and finally it is *y* after OE *æ/e/i*, as in *breyd, fayn, tarying*.

(3) Reflexes of OE *-ht* indicate a fricative, and are never rendered by *-t* alone. They are usually written with *-ȝt, -ȝth* or (most commonly) *-th*, as in *bryth(e), liȝthly, rowth*; but sometimes the *g* is also included, as in *laȝgth* (cf. *lawth*), *brogth, wro(ȝ)gth*. The *-ht* spelling is retained only once, in *myht* (K10) (cf. *myth*, K24).

(4) Historical *h* is retained in *hit* but dropped in *it* and in *mawment*. Initial *h* is written superfluously in *herandys*. Superfluous *n* is found in *mawment, reyngnest, dyngnite*, and possibly in MS *faunchon/*

fauuchon. Parasitic *t* is not found in prep. *aӡens,* and there is a probable superlative with loss of final *-t* in *curteys.*

(5) OE *lc* becomes *ch* in *soche* but *lk* in *ilka, milk.* OE *-ig* is *-i/y*, as in *fyſti, fyfty, sory.* OE *-lice* is always *-ly*, as in *blely, farly.* Uninflected adverbs are frequent, e.g., *oriӡth, soft, wondur.*

(6) The initial spelling of words earlier beginning with *hw-* is invariably *qw-*, e.g.: *qwen, qwerefore, qwat, qweles, qwom.* The phonology of this reflex is problematic, as such words rarely take alliterative stress (in fact, *qweles* (K140) is the only metrical Class I word from OE *hw-* in the poem). The reflexes of OE *hw-* and *cw-* do not appear to alliterate together, as they do only in Northern alliterative verse (e.g., *Destr. Troy* 3055 and 13681). The thin evidence is rather that the *qw-* spelling was still sounded as [hw] and alliterates on *w*. See, e.g., K141, where the n. *wylys* (ON *vél*) is meant to provide phonic concatenation with *qweles* (OE *hweol*) from the previous line. This provides evidence that the OE *hw- < qw-* spellings in the poem are probably not to be sounded as stopped. See also K246, where a [hw] sound on *qwom* would give the optimum alliterative pattern, aa/aa.

(7) OE *cw-* becomes *qu-* in *queen* (cf. next), and *qw-* in *qween, qwith.*

(8) OE *sc* is represented mostly by *sch*, as in *sche, schope,* but sometimes by *ch*, as in *chames* (cf. *schame, schenchip*), and once by *s* in *scort.* It was probably sounded [sk] in *schoffers.* There is no apparent reason for the inconsistency; words ending in what was the earlier suffix *-scip* are written *-chip* in four of the five cases, the exception being *demschip.*

(9) Initial *p = þ* is used invariably for short monosyllabic words such as *þis, þan, þou, þour,* but medial and final *p = þ* is employed in about equal proportions with *th* in substantive words, e.g.: *feythful/broþur; myrthys/myrþe; commeth/deieþ.*

C. Features of Accidence:

(1) In nouns, the pl. and poss. n. endings are nearly always *-es* (thirty-six times), as in *kares, bales, feres,* and *-ys* (nine times), as in *balys, herandys, turmentys; -is* is found twice in *karis, wrenchis, -us* twice in *bemus, briddus; -s* is found in *foos, kaytefs, maydens, pynchars, resons.* Weak or uninflected plurals do not occur, except perhaps in the gen. pl. *goddesse* (K131). The only other gen. pl. in the text is *deueles* (K103).

(2) The pronouns are fairly fixed, but in 3 acc., dat. are spelt in many ways. 1 sg. nom. is always *I*. 2 sg. nom. always appears as *þou*; the acc., dat. is always *þe*, and the poss. *þi*, except before a vowel when it is *þin*. 3 sg. nom. is always *he* and *sche* (once fem. *he*). Neut. is always *it* (gen. *his*). Acc., dat. is *him*, *hym*, *her(e)*, *hir(e)*, *hyr(e)*, and gen. always *his*, *hys*, *her(e)*, *hir(e)*, *hyr(e)* (pl. *þei*, *hem*, *her(e)*, *hir*).

(3) Fully inflected inf. mostly ends in *-e*, as in *dewre*, *grame*, *tempure*, and many are uninflected, as in *deel*, *kerf*, *schrik*. Inf. *-en(e)*, *in* occasionally occurs, as in *berene*, *fecchen*, *wirkin*. The verbal n. ending is always *-yng*, as in *bawmyng*, *carpyng*, *punchyng*. The only pr. p. ending is *-ing* in *tarying*.

(4) Pr. 2 indicative is *-st*, *-est*, *yst*, as in *mayst*, *tretest*, *reyngnest*. 16 of the 28 imperatives (all sg.) are uninflected, as in *pik*, *schaf* and MS *awtur*; 12 end in *-e*, as in *joyne*, *kache*, *schere*. Pr. 3 sg. ending is *-eth*, *-eþ*, as in *karueth*, *releþ*, *wardeþ*, but also *-es*, *-ys*, *-us*, as in *koueres*, *sendys*, *chesus*. There are seven uninflected pr. subjunctives, e.g., *keþ*, *pondur*, *put*; three end in *-e*: *make*, *sprunge*, *wysse*. Pr. pl. is uninflected in *chees*, *feel* (v.²), *reel*, *reygn*, *schaþ*; it ends in *-e* in *apere*, *crye*, *departe*, *dowte*, *flye*, *love*, in *-en*, *-yn* in *krepen*, *redyn*, *towchyn*, and in *-es* in *worchipes*.

(5) Pa. 2 sg. in strong verbs ends in *-e* in *wanne* and in *-te* in *stynte*; and in weak verbs the *-est* ending has gone in *tholyd* (cf. *woldest*). Pa. 3 sg. is mostly uninflected in strong verbs, as in *drof*, *hyng*, *sprong*; the ending is *-e* in *gane*, *sawe*, and *-de* in *abode*, *stode*, *wonde*. Weak pa. 3 sg. ends in *-d(e)*, as in *bilde*, *schewd*, *seyde*, as *-(n)t(e)*, as in *brast*, *hent(e)*, *pytte*, as *-t(h)(e)*, as in *dyth*, *lawth*, *wro(3)gth*), as *-ed*, as in *dispised*, *spared*, *thyrsted*, as *-id* in *labowrid*, as *-yd* in *preuyd*, *stranglyd*, *tredyd*; and *-yed* in *foundyed*. Five forms are uninflected: *commaund*, *flyit*, *graunt*, *hythe*, *throng*. The first four of these are OF or ON derivations, and the last a ME weak v. modelled on possible OE **þrongian*.

(6) There are two strong past participles with relicts of the OE prefix *ge-*, *ibore*, *icore*, but these are almost certainly added to provide an extra syllable for the metrical requirements. Otherwise strong pp. endings are usually *-e*, as in *ronne*, *schake*, *wrunge*, but uninflected in *schrunk* and *throw*. The *-n/-yn* ending appears in *born*, *chosyn*, *doluyn*, *flayn*, *slayn*. The pp. forms of weak verbs are mixed. Two are uninflected: *lyft*, *thyrst*. The endings are *-e* in *schake*, *kitte*; *-t(e)*, *-th*, as in *adent*, *fet*, *schente*, as *-ed(e)*, *-ud*, *urd*, *-id*, *-yd*, as in *aschamyd*,

cursud, disjoyned, woundid, woundyd, and as *-d(e)*, as in *fylde, merde, pynde*. The weak verbs of Class II are generally not distinguished from Class I, as in the infinitives *grame, lef, prik*, but note the endings of *sondur* and *tempure*; cf. also *foundyed* K190 (OF *fondrer*, which appears to have been formed on OE *fundian*), and *flyit* (ON *flytja*) where a disyllabic sound was possibly felt necessary (though cf. also *giyld* (K268) and *vnknyit* (K187), discussed on p. xliv above).

Vocabulary and Syntax

The fundamental vernacular of the text is a literate but unrefined Midland English of the late fourteenth century, but Spalding's copious vocabulary is a striking feature of the poem; there are 2060 words in the text, with a total vocabulary of 685 words. Of these, about 450 (66 per cent) are from Old English, 170 (25 per cent) are of French or Romance derivation, and about 35 (5 per cent) are from Old Norse. About 4 per cent of the vocabulary is of other, mixed or indeterminate origin. Few of the words are of the special poetic, alliterative stock that produces, e.g., *frekes, athels, gomes* and *schalkes* in other texts, but singular words of Germanic or Norse origin have been used for alliterative purposes, e.g., *cantly in rees, carpyng, cast, flyit, momyl, schrik, thref*. The OF technical vocabulary is drawn on for the refinements of prison and torture, e.g., *gynne, punchyng, turnement*, as well as for the celestial elements, as in *bawmyng, dentiwos, melodye, orisoun*. Monosyllables dominate; the most complex words are adverbs like *cursurdly* and *myꝫtthily*, the longest substantives forms such as *herandys* and *derckeness*. That about 25 per cent of the vocabulary is of French derivation, much of it Anglo-Norman, suggests an author with at least some degree of learning. Although the French element is not as evident as in the works of the *Gawain*-poet (on average, nearly one third of the vocabulary in those works being of French derivation), it can be compared with the proportion of only about 19 per cent of the vocabulary of *Susannah*. A somewhat exotic vocabulary of Romance origin (e.g., *faunchon, mawment, senatour*) is occasionally employed in this 'Egyptian' story, contrasting with a lexis that may have come from an Anglo-Norman administrative background, as, e.g., *apere, encresse, entryk, herandys, surauns*. Virtually all of the Romance words have descended into Modern Standard English, and are not distinctly poetic or elevated. The Scandinavian element in the vocabulary, though greater than in many other texts of a non-Northern or non-alliterative nature, accounts for

only about 5 per cent of the total; compare, e.g., the 7 per cent in
Evangelist, or 9 per cent in *Cleanness* and *Patience*. There are about
twenty-seven etymons of definite Norse derivation, e.g., *lyft*, *oloft*,
thref, and a dozen or more words whose forms suggest the possible
influence of Scandinavian cognate forms, e.g., *flik*, *tynt*, *wylys*.
Although some of these words were to enter Modern English,
many of them are not found in, e.g., Chaucer's vocabulary. For the
most interesting of them, e.g., *flyit*, *thref*, see 'Notes'. Their presence
must help define the provenance of the poem, but the text contains no
unequivocal dialect words distinctive to any one neighbourhood.

The lexis is robust, and the compacted syntax contributes to this,
yet also provides some tortuous expression. The poet appears to have
been in command of reasonably literary late fourteenth-century
English constructions. Some of the apparent incoherencies seem
due to scribal blunderings; others are from idiomatic but rather
oblique usages, mostly of alliterative convention. Inversion of normal
prose word-order is employed in 25 per cent of the 280 lines; this is
typical of alliterative verse, especially in the iteration of the sestet, but
is particularly intricate here, and is one of the features that makes the
poem so laborious in places, as in, e.g., *To hym þe to low þus* (K54),
and *Heel þou vs hent now* (K248). Complex sentences with many
relative and consecutive clauses, and sometimes an idiomatic omission
of the rel. pron., make for elided syntax, as in, e.g., *for þei schal lif at þi*
lust on þi loue haf lerede (K172), and, as in much alliterative verse,
expression is shaped by the omission of the pron. subject in a
subjunctive clause, as in *And send our syre þi sacrifice, no schame*
schal þe gref (K130). Idiomatic usages of the inf. occasionally occur, as
in K 251, and further intricacy results from idiomatic separation of a
relative from its antecedent, as in K243–4, K245–6 and K272–4. In
the parts of the narrative where there is a well-founded story line,
much of the narrative style can be direct and rudimentary (ten lines
begin with *þan* and eight with *Qwen*), and there is little or no
enjambement, each line forming a syntactic unit. Spalding frequently
employs negatives, and his use of adverbs is prolific. Particles such as
so, *þan*, *þus*, *þere* are used repeatedly for metrical fillers, especially in
an unabashed use of them for rhymed metrical fillers in all but six of
the twenty sestets (the twentieth stanza verging on the deranged in
this matter). There are fewer of the superlatives favoured by other
alliterative poets. Where some would employ phrases such as *wlonkest*
in wede or *stiffest in stowre*, the most pronounced feature of Spalding's

syntax is his preference for the use of disyllabic adverbs in a regular
'grammetrical frame':[86] *cantly in rees, freschely had fylde, prestly sche
prayed, farly to feel, comly þei crye, deply adent.*

Dialects of Scribe and Author

The dialectal evidence presented above is not at variance with the
grid position that the *Linguistic Atlas of Late Middle English*
(LALME) has assigned to the manuscript. Bodley Rolls 22, Hand
a was one of the documents chosen for analysis by LALME as a
scribal witness that can be localized on its dialectal and orthographic
features, and was examined, as part of this research, by Dr Margaret
Laing.[87] In Dr Laing's thesis the hand of *Katherine* is assigned to the
town of Spalding in Lincolnshire. Regarding the acrostic *ri car dvs s
pal dyng*, she notes: 'There is no evidence that the extant copy of this
text is autograph, or that Richard Spalding (or his amanuensis) wrote
in Spalding dialect, but the language does indeed fit there' (I, 143).
The MS reading *he* for 'sche' in K26 was not selected by Dr Laing,
but if it had been, it would not necessarily have altered the Atlas's
grid mark to a significant extent (see Note to K26).

In order to outline the location of manuscript and author in as
many ways as possible, some of the dialectal evidence from the
foregoing sections highlights the main south-east Lincs features,
both in scribal habits and in authorial usage. Conventional dialectal
analysis would designate *Katherine* as a text of the central Midland
regional standard with a homogenous mix of regional features, due
perhaps to its central location in the kingdom, rather than to the work
of scribes from different areas; for this distinction see LALME, I,
§3.5, 19–20. There is much scribal carelessness and corruption in the
copy, but no apparent spoiling by substitution, e.g., of synonyms in
rhymes or alliteration. Because Spalding (and Stamford—see
pp. lxiv–lxviii below) are on the eastern edge of that central Midland
zone where a fairly standardized English was spoken and written, and
not in an area with notable graphemic and dialectal characteristics
(such as, e.g., Scotland or Kent), we might expect to see some
linguistic features from all the regions that abutted the area: the
Northern, the East Midland, East Anglian and perhaps some West

---

[86] For this useful term, see R. F. Lawrence, 'Formula and Rhythm in *The Wars of
Alexander*', *English Studies*, 51 (1970), 97–112, and Duggan, 'Alliterative Patterning', 84–6.
[87] Margaret Laing, 'Studies in the Dialect Material of Medieval Lincolnshire' (Unpublished Ph.D. thesis, University of Edinburgh, 1978).

Midland and ON influence. This is exactly what we do have, in both scribal habit and authorial usage, with no anomalies or striking dialectal features.

A comprehensive understanding of the habits of a South Lincs scribe can be gleaned from the extensive documentary evidence of LALME. Clear testimony that places the witness consists in the employment of *y* for *þ*; the lack of extreme regional, such as Scottish, Western or Kentish, distinguishing features; the noticeable East Anglian *qw-* and *-th*; *v* becoming *w*; the use of the pronouns *sche* and *þei* with the South East Midland acc./dat. *hem*; the contrast of East Midland vowels (as in certain salient words such as 'sword' and 'work') with the Northern use of forms such as *euere ilka*; the mix of pr. 3 sg. *-es*, *-ys*, *-us* and *-eth*, *-eþ* inflexions. All of these fit with this witness.

The phonology is characteristic of South East Midland texts, and is especially apparent in the normal rising of OE *ā* to long open *o*, the *-e* spellings and sounds, e.g., *be* 'by', *keel* 'cool', *chees* 'choose', *derlyng*, *swerde*, and so on; but that parameter is modified by features that are characteristic of Danelaw texts. First is the tangible Scandinavian element in the vocabulary that is *not* an alliterative vocabulary, e.g., *ay*, *bothe*, *fro*, *sche*, *þei*, and, second, the sporadic preference for Norse forms of a word when there is a Saxon equivalent: *flik* is perhaps derived from ON *flikka*, not OE *flicche*; *wirkin* is perhaps influenced by ON *yrkja*; *brest* and *brast* (OE *berstan* and *barst*) appear to have been influenced by the ON *bresta* and *brast*. Such localization is modified by the following Northern characteristics: the *-ch-* spelling for [ʃ], as in *charp*, *chames*, *worchip*, *frenchip*, etc., but cf. also *demschip*; Northern *-f* endings such as *drof*, *salf*, *sterf*, *strof*, although these are counterbalanced by *save*, *-selue*, *sterved*, often in the very next line; the occasional *-i* spelling in unstressed syllables, as in *labowrid*, *karis*; spellings such as *walde*, and vocabulary such as *euere ilka* and *farly*. The most striking characteristic of East Anglian texts, spelling *x* for initial [ʃ], does not occur, but *qw-* for the initial aspirant (OE *hw-*), found in both East Anglian and Northern texts, does. Although distinctly Western forms do not occur, one or two Western traits do show up: fully written inflexional ending *-ur* occurs in MS *awtur* (see Note to K228); *-u(r)d* occurs in the adjectives *cursud-* and *cursurd*; *-us* occurs in *chesus*. Scribal ꝋ and ꝗ contractions occur in the nouns *briddus* (followed immediately by *briddes*), *broþur*, *thondur*, *wondur*, the verbs *pondur*, *sondur*, and the adv. *wondur*. Such scribal spellings would be fairly characteristic of a locality west of Spalding and

Stamford (for the latter, see pp. lxiv–lxviii) such as, say, Leics, and would not be out of the ordinary in a few contractions in a South Lincs witness. Distinctly Western forms do not occur at all.

Such graphemic features establish the provenance of the one scribe (established by LALME through more detailed scientific criteria), but some evidence of the author's own dialect comes through. As in the copy, there is no suggestion of extreme regional (such as Scottish, Western or Kentish) elements in the author's own dialect; e.g., earlier *ȳ* is shown by rhyme to be unrounded; see *kynd* ↔ *fynde*, *bynde*, *mynde* (K163–7). There are, unfortunately, no dialectically significant inflexions in rhyme, but details such as the absence of cross-alliteration of the scribal *qw*- sound (OE *hw*-) with the reflex of OE *cw*- indicate that the author was probably not a northerner, and from rhyme it can be deduced that the reflex of OE/ON *ā* was sounded [u]; see, e.g., *none* ↔ *alone* in K39 and K42, and the rhymes of K1–3 and K29–35. This means that the poet almost certainly came from south of the Humber; see also *hyng* (K276) ↔ *kyng*, *bryng*, *syng*. This is a decidedly East Anglian or East Midland feature; cf. similar *ȝynge* 'young' ↔ *bidding*, *þing* in the Northampton *Abraham* play. Elements that indicate a Northern influence on the author's dialect are, first, the apparent [f] sound of OE *f*, as shown by the rhyme of *dryue* (K243) ↔ *ryf*, *cnyf*, *wyffe*, and, second, the striking loss of sounded inflexions as shown by rhyme, e.g., inf. *wynne* ↔ *gynne* (OF *(en)gin*), K142–4; although this could indicate a late date of composition, we have other evidence of a date of composition around or even before 1400, and such a loss of inflexion would probably suggest some Northern influence in the author's own dialect. Indeed, it can implicitly be proved that his provenance was an area of Danish occupation; Scandinavian words or forms are found both in rhyme and in alliteration; e.g., *hythe* (ON *heita*, rather than OE *hāten*) ↔ *rithe*, *bythe*, *sythe*; *oloft* ↔ *soft*, *croft*, *oft* (K127–33—the same rhymes repeated in K205–9); the ON form *flik* rhymes with *wik* (OE *wicca*), as *fliche* could not have done; the Scandinavian *ay* and *tray* rhyme with the Saxon *klay* and *day*. The unusual word *thref* is shown by alliteration to be authorial. The large proportion of romance vocabulary would be expected in a literary saint's life of this date, and can not help to localize the place of origin of such a short text, but the dialectal parameters outlined above tell us that the poet almost certainly came from the area shown in his own acrostic.

Evangelist

The spelling is Robert Thornton's recurrent mix of his own habits with only a few possible relics from a MS tradition, giving a straightforward and lucid witness with mixed forms such as *connande*, *cunande*; *many*, *mony*; *hally*, *holly*. The main points of interest are in variant reflexes of OE/ON ā/á (e.g., *fra*, *fro*, *froo*); OE ĭ < *e* (e.g., *beschope*, *bese*, *es*); variable use of non-etymological final -*e*, a letter that Thornton uses generously (see, e.g., nom. *buke*, *childe* on nom. adjectives and suffixes, e.g., *ilke a*, *vpe-ryghte*, -*ande*, -*ynge*); an interchange of *e*, *i* and *y* in unstressed syllables; and a rich variety of usage in the spellings of particles, e.g., *þare* (7 times) + *þartill*; *þaire* (8 times) + *thare* (3 times) + *thair* + *thaire* (4 times) + *thayre* + *þere*; *þam* (3 times) + *thaym* (9 times) + *thayme*. Otherwise OE -*ht* is always -*ght(e)*; *þ*- is employed only in initial and medial position in particles (e.g., in *alþer*, *toþer*). Apart from the word *with*, the dental fricative at the ends of words is always -*the*, as in, e.g., *mirthe*, *mouthe*, *forsothe*, *welthe*. A doubled consonant is sometimes employed to indicate a short vowel, thus: *didd*, *fedd*, *godd*, *sett*, *tonn*, *wonn*. The following forms are used:

A. In reflexes of OE stressed vowels:

(1) OE ẏ́ appears as *i*, as in *birdyn*, *dill*, *firste*, and as *y* in *by(e)*, *(man)kynde*, *wyrkynges*. OE ȳ appears as *i/y* in *filede*, *filthe*, *fylthe*, as *ou* in *defoulede*, *foulely*, *foullede*, and as *u* in *cumly*.

(2) OE *i* appears commonly as *i/y*, as in *childe*, *prikkynge*. It appears as *e* in *bees*, *beschope*, *es*. OE ī appears as *i* only in *hir*, *thi*, *þi*, *whils*. It appears commonly as *y*, as in *habyde*, *lykynge*, *pyne*, *yren*, and appears once as *e* in *blethely*.

(3) OE *e* appears as *e*, as in *ʒelde*, *segge*, *wrechid*. It appears as *y* in *thynk* and as *a* in *way(e)*. OE ē appears as *e*, as in *bekende*, *heledide*, *slepede*. It appears once as *oo* in *ʒoo*.

(4) OE *æ* appears as *a*, as in *fadir*, *laghte*, *warely*, and as the first component of the digraph *ai/ay* in *agayne*, *faire*, *mayden*. Its appearance as *e* in *redy* probably shows a reflex of the OE *ʒeredig*. OE ǣ appears as *a*, as in *lare*, *thayre*, *wrate*, and appears as *e*, as in *dredles*, *flesche*, *techyng(e)*. It is found once as *ee* in *see* (E41, OE *sǣ*) among a set of unstable rhymes.

(5) OE *a* followed by a nasal appears as *a*, as in *fanding*, *lande*,

mankynde and as *o* in *fondyng*. It appears as *u* in *gun*. OE *ā* appears fairly equally as *a*, *o* and sometimes as *oo*, as in *ane*, *one*; *fra*, *fro(o)*; *go*, *goo*; *hally*, *holly*; *hame*, *home*; *famen*, *foo*; *many*, *mony*; *mare*, *more*; *na*, *no(ne)*; *sta(n)nes*, *stone(s)*; *hally*, *hame*, *wo(o)*, these variants are not always in rhyming positions. See also *gaste*, *hande*, *knawen*, *laythely*, *laytheste*, *many*, *sare*, *wate* and *so*, *two*. It is *e* in *cledde* and in *clethyng*.

(6) OE *o* appears as *o*, as in *besoghte*, *folowe(d)(e)*, *quod*, and once as *ou* in *boustoure*. OE *ō* appears as *o*, as in *alsone*, *brothire*, *thoghte*, and as *u*, as in *buke*, *gudnes*, *rude*. It appears once as *oo* in *doo*.

(7) OE *u* appears as *o*, as in *connande*, *sones*, *wondir*, and as *u*, as in *cunande*, *lufely*, *murnande*; it appears as *ou* in *couthe*, *thou*, *þou*, as *ow* in *thow*, and as *y* in *lyste*. OE *ū* appears as *u* in *burghe*, *full*, as *o* in *bot*, *down(e)*, *how*, as *ou*, as in *bouxsom*, *mouthe*, *selcouthe*, and as *ow* in *bowand*, *down(e)*, *owte*.

(8) OE *eo/ēo* appear as *e*, as in *derlyng(e)*, *deuyls*, *fende*, *werlde*, as *i/y* in *wirchip(e)(d)(e)* and possibly in *bryght*, as *o* in *ʒow*, *ʒonge*, and as *ee* in *free(ly)*, *theefe*.

B. In reflexes of certain OE consonants:

(1) The OE medial *f* is found as *f*, as in *delfynge*, *lyffede*, *lufende*, and as *u*, as in *knaues*, *lyuande*, *saluede*.

(2) Initial OE *ġ* appears as *ʒ*, as in *ʒelde*, *ʒit*, *ʒow*, but as *g* in *gates*, *gerne*. It is unsounded in *if*. Medially and finally it is *y* after OE *æ/e/i*, as in *mayden*, *redy*, *witty*; it is *i* in *worthi* and *e* in *sare*. OE final *g* appears as *g* in *segge*, and as *w* in *lawe(s)*.

(3) OE *-ht,-hð* is almost invariably *-ght(e)*, as in *(be)soghte*, *ryghte*, *wroghte*, but not in *mote*.

(4) OE *lc* becomes *lk*, as in *folke*, *swylke*, *walke*. OE/ON adverbial endings appear as *-ly*, as in *frely*, *thraly*, *worthyly*, and as *-ely*, as in *blethely*, *graythely*, *vnwysely* – possibly when Thornton appends an adj. which he thinks of as ending in *-e*, and so not necessarily sounded. But note *semly*, *semely*.

(5) OE *sc* is represented mostly by *sch*, as in *schipe*, *publischede*, *puneschede*, but by *ch* in *wirchip(e)*, *wirchiped(e)*.

(6) The initial spelling of words earlier beginning with *hw-* is almost invariably *wh-*, e.g., *whas*, *what(e)*, *when*, *whils*; but cf. *ware* (E79) and *werkes* alliterating on *whare* (OE *w-*, *hw-*). The reflex of OE initial *cw*

is *qu* in *quod*. The graph *w* is employed to make a diphthong in some reflexes of OF, as in *drowry, jowell, mawmetis*.

Historically expected final *-e* is almost never absent, and generally appears on acc., gen. and dat. nouns (but cf., e.g., *kepyng(e), techyng(e)*). Of the infinitives, not one has an *-n* ending; nearly all end in *-e*, as in *byde, ȝelde, suffire*, and about a quarter are uninflected, as in *affy, doo, thynk*. A marked feature of the text is that many infinitives are used with the prep. *to*.

Superfluous final *-e* appears on several nominatives (e.g., *golde, beschope, sybbe*) and can be seen to be redundant to the rhyme (e.g., *brothire ↔ oþer*). It also appears in many instances where, if sounded, it would spoil the metre, e.g., *whate* (E78), *þaire* (E197), *downe* (E227), where in each instance, and whichever way the line is scanned, a sounding of the final *-e* would make an unmetrical b-verse, and also in E89, where sounding the *-e* on *thorghe* would give two long dips in the b-verse.

The sound in unstressed syllables is generally written as *e* in pl. nouns, e.g., *dedes, gyftes, wandes*, and in pa. 3 pl., as in *wepede, weryede*, but as *i*, as in *mawmetis, prechide, wandis*. The *þ = y* graph is found in the *-yng(e)* ending, but not otherwise in pl. or verbal unstressed syllables. OE *o* before final *r* is found as *i*, as in *fadir, modire, brothire*.

C. Features of Accidence:

(1) Pl. and gen. endings are nearly always *-es*, as in *dayes, Goddes*, and once as *-eȝ* in *tyraunteȝ*; a simpler gen. inflexion occurs once in *deuyls*, but the uninflected gen. that occurs in *hir syster sone* (E71) is unmetrical, and the prevalent *-es* inflexion would restore the metre.

(2) Pronouns are variable in spelling but apparently consistent in sound. In the second person, sg. nom. appears as *thou, þou/thow*; the acc., dat. is far more often *the* than *þe* (which mostly appears towards the end of a line), and the poss. *thi* occurs 34 times, *þi* only three times. Third person sg. nom. is always *he* and *scho*. The neuter is always *it*. The acc., dat. is always *hym/hir* and the gen. always *his/hir*. Plurals are *þay/thay, þam/thaym(e)*.

(3) There are no fully inflected infinitives. The ending is generally *-e*, as in *grete, lere, mene*, and occasionally uninflected, as in *affy, doo, frayst*. The pr. p. ends in *-ande* eight times and *-and* twice. The verbal

n. ending is normally *-yng(e)*, as in *clethyng, doynge, forthynkyng*, but
is found once as *-ing* in *fanding*.

(4) Pr. 2 indic. does not occur; pr. 3 sg. ending is twice *-es* (*comes,
gyfes*) and once *-e* (*witnese*). The imp. always ends in *-e*, as in *graunte,
luke, mone*. The pa. 2, 3 sg. predominantly ends in *-(e)de*, as in
endeynede, noyede, profirde, but occasionally in *-ed*, as in *dedeyned*. In
strong verbs it is *-e* as in *bare, broghte, laghte*; but see also *fet, lete, sett,
tuk*. The strong pp. with prefix does not occur, and the endings are
similar to pa. 3 sg. (e.g., *mesured, puneschede, wirchiped(e)*) except in,
e.g., *chosen, halden, gyffen*, and the *-dde / -t(e)* ending, as in *cledde,
defast, endent*. Uninflected pp. endings occur in *fun, ledd, sett*.

Vocabulary and Syntax

A vocabulary of approximately 600 words of determinate origin is
used in the 2,392 words of the poem, revealing a more impoverished
resource than those of the other two poets. 73 per cent is of Old
English derivation, 20 per cent of French, and 7 per cent of Norse.
The Norse component is stronger than in either of the other two
hymns, and although it is only 2 per cent more than in *Katherine* and
Baptist, it is prominent in the syntax and alliteration, so that, apart
from the Northern *ay, gayne, get, scho, thay(m), tuk*, stressed function
words such as *graythely, kirkes, lythes, menskede, thraly, traysted,
wandis* are conspicuous. Yet this Norse element does not approach
the 9 per cent that is such a striking feature of, e.g., *Cleanness* and
Patience. In its general disposal in the rambling syntax, the French
constituent does not impose, and it is noticeably less than that of
Katherine. In fact there are more French and Latinate elements than
in the 15 per cent Romance component of the vocabulary of *Baptist*,
but there nouns in prominent positions (e.g., *poyntil, roser*) in a
tighter syntax give a more exotic flavour. Words such as *barett, menȝe,
pousté, suggeourned, toylede* disclose an everyday Romance vocabulary,
rather than the more genteel wordings of *Katherine* and, e.g., *SGGK*;
but typical collocations are abundant, e.g., *mendynge of mysse,
prikkynge of penance*, though more resourceful are, e.g., *daynte as
drowry derely endent*, and *swylk menesyng men mase*.

Evangelist is more instructive than either of the other hymns; this
obtains not so much from the lexis as from the actual content, which
is 'explained' in a prolix way, and from its plethora of particles,
present participles, infinitives with prepositions, past participles with

auxiliaries, and some ingenuous expressions. In the use of prepositions, this poet does not use one syllable when two will do. This is
often for metrical purposes, but versification is inefficient, and can
depend upon manifold instances of complex particles, as in, e.g.,
alsone, alþer, forthi, ilke-a, in-with, vpe-ryghte, partyll. When this is
compounded with the emphatic prefixes of, e.g., *defoulede, forthynkyng*, and the laborious syntax of, e.g., . . *þat I ʒow declare* and
. . . *þan þay euer hadde*, it can be seen that the language of *Evangelist*
contrasts very much with that of the other two hymns, yet its cogency
consists in its very simplicity of diction: '*Luke þat ʒe lufande be /
Ilkone to oþer.*'

Dialect of Scribe and Author

As a matter of course, scribal provenance would be seen in the verbal
endings and some other features of orthography that are generally
associated with a Northern provenance, such as the spellings *fra,
famen, gaste, many, mare, stanes, hally, hame*; pronouns *scho, þay, thay,
þam, thaym(e)*; present participle ending *-ande*; and *-ir, -es* and *-is* in
unstressed syllables. The unvoiced fricative in *delfynge* and *lyffede* is
Northern, and there is more which need not be expanded on here, as
it has been well established that the scribal dialect fits the area where
Robert Thornton was operating as a tax collector in an approximate
twenty-mile radius of York from his base in the parish of Stonegrave
in Rydale.[88]

Authorial language is obviously Northern, too, though not Scots.
The language has none of the East Midland characteristics of the
dialect of *Katherine*, and, from the evidence of rhyme, is decidedly
more Northern in origin than Spalding's; see, e.g., *mare ↔ fare,
w(h)are; sare ↔ bare, spare, thare; hate ↔ plate; hame ↔ name*. The
author's infinitive has lost the final *-n*, as in *to wende ↔* n. *fende*.
Another main pointer to a Northern authorial origin is in rhyming
of words of Norse origin (e.g., in the use of *-till, -tyll* for '-to'
rhyming with, e.g., *still, will, dill, ille*). Words such as *dill* in
rhyming position and the false division in *toþer*, necessarily pl. for
the sense, are particularly associated with Yorkshire. Much of the
vocabulary that appears authorial because of its well-functioning
alliterative or rhyming capacity is also entirely Northern in

---

[88] For this in the work of Keiser, see notes 13, 21, 111. See also Halliwell, *Thornton
Romances*, and Ogden, *Diversis Medicinis*. Authorship of the texts is not investigated in any
of these studies.

character, e.g., *wanes* (E45), *by-dene* (E50), *derfe* (E127), *weled* (E254), *graythely* (E146).[89]

Several North Midland features can be noted in, e.g., the alliteration of OE *w-/ hw-*, as found in Notts and in the Lincs *Katherine*, and may suggest authorship south rather than north of York, but this is not crucial. As with *Katherine*, there is little perceptible Western element in the dialect, but a decided Norse element is present, together with some striking parallels in vocabulary with the *Cursor Mundi* and the York plays (see 'Notes', *passim*). Margaret Laing and Frances McSparran have each kindly made a detailed study of the scribal and authorial features of the text.[90] Both find forms that (according to similar profiles in LALME) would suggest a layer of transmission of a dialect somewhat to the west rather than east of York; these include *mony* 'many', *warre* 'were', *thurghe* 'through', *gun* 'began to', *bathe* 'both', *keste* 'cast', *the* 'thee', *thi* 'thy' and *appon* 'upon', but, as none of these is in rhyming or alliterative position, little more can be deduced from them about the poet's own dialect.

Baptist

The fifteenth-century scribe evidently intended to spell consistently, and did so, except in the inflexions of the past participle, which suggests one or more layers of copying from inflexions of a different dialect. Main variations are in a variable use of non-etymological final *-e*; an infrequent exchange of *i* for *y* and *vice versa* (mostly in inflexions); the occasional interchangeability of $þ^u$, *þow* (see 'Treatment of the Texts', p. xcv); and some minor details of the particles. Otherwise OE *-ht* is always *-ght*; 'than' is nearly always *þanne* (though cf. *whan* × 2 and *when* 4 times); 'through' is always *thorgh*. There are only two other variations in a root syllable: first in the metrically stressed vowel of *Jon*, *Joon*, and second, the variation of [ʃ] in *schinest*, *scyneth*. Omission of the more usual *h* in the latter may be a slip of the current hand. For the scribe's use of *p* = *þ/y*, see 'The Manuscripts', p. xxvii above; *þ-* is used more often than *th-* in initial position of the prevalent particles (mostly abbreviated) and in an occasional adverb or preposition such as *þanne* or *þider*. It is never employed medially or terminally (so, e.g., *myrth(e)*, *brothir*, *faythful*, *hath*).

[89] For a bibliography of study of the dialect features in the texts that Thornton copied, see also Thompson, *Robert Thornton*, pp. 4–5.

[90] Personal communications for which I am most grateful.

The most interesting feature of the spelling is in occasional doubling of stressed vowels, apparently to indicate a degree of length. These appear in *haast* ↔ *moost* (B109–12); *pees* ↔ *ryse*, *sese*, *chese*, *deyse* (B114–22); *foos* and *moo* in unrhyming positions (B73 and 129); *good* ↔ *rood*, *mode*, *stode* (B29–35); and *Joon* ↔ MS *o none* (B67–70; cf. *Jon*, B7 and 138). The first and last of these may indicate a degree of metrical quantity, coming as they do at the ends of lines, but, as both scribes of the codex employ many doubled vowels when copying from Northern, Southern and East Midland sources, this might be better ascribed to their local habit. The following forms are used:

A. In reflexes of OE stressed vowels:

(1) OE *ў* appears as *i* in *first*, *-fille*, *kist*, *listen*, but before *n* as *y* in *kyn*, *synful*, *synne*.

(2) OE *i* appears commonly as *i/y*, as in *a-plight*, *myght* (n + v.), *wildirnesse*. It appears as *e* in *sekir*. OE *ī* appears as *i/y*, as in *ryse*, *schinest*, *scyneth*, *tyme*.

(3) OE *e* generally appears as *e*, as in *awey*, *rekynde*, *twelft*. OE *ē* appears as *e*, as in *bemes*, *grett*, *nede(ful)*.

(4) OE *æ* appears as *a* in *gadrid*, *ware*, *-fast*, and as the first component of the digraph *ai/ay* in *day*, *said*, *saith*, *saiyng*, though as *ei* in *seid* (B4). It appears as *e* in *lere*, *togedir*. OE *ǣ* appears as *a*, as in *maste*, *stalworth*, *þare*, and as *e*, as in *speche*, *sprede*, *wede*. The reflexes *o*, *oo* are found in *most*, *foos*, *moo*, and in *moost* (where it spoils the rhymes of B109–12). The spelling *or* (OE *ǣr*, B52) could be noted.

(5) OE *a* followed by a nasal appears as *a* in *man*, *many*, *name*, *þanne*, *whan*. Note also *whennes*, B76. For *hende*, B77, see 'Notes'. OE *ā* appears as *o*, as in *blowe*, *gost*, *holy*, but as *e* in *neythir*.

(6) OE *o* appears as *o*, as in *doghter*, *folk*, *lorne*, and once as *ou* in *bourn* (B34). OE *ō* appears as *o*, as in *brothir*, *molde*, *rotes*, and once as *oo* in *rood*.

(7) OE *u* appears as *o*, as in *honey-*, *wode*, *wonyng*, as *ou* in *ground*, *louely*, and as *u/v*, as in *ful-*, *-ful*, *lufly*, *schul*. OE *ū* appears as *ou*, as in *aboute*, *doumbe*, *loutid*, and as *u/v* in *but*, *buxum*, *vs*.

(8) OE *eo/ēo* appear as *e*, as in *be*, *chese*, *trewly*, *heuen*.

B. In reflexes of certain OE consonants:

(1) The OE medial *f* is most often found as *u*, as in *craue, heued, louely* (cf. *twelfi*). The spellings *greue, craue, leue*, rhyming with the inf. *to haue* in B123–6, indicate unvoiced consonant [v], but this might be scribal.

(2) Initial OE *ġ* is written as *ȝ* in *ȝare, ȝe, ȝere* but is otherwise *g*. Medially and finally it is *y* after OE *æ/e/i* (e.g., *body, awey, may*) and *x* (from OE *g-s*) in *buxum*. OE final g appears as *w* in *lawe, sorow*.

(3) OE *-ht* is invariably rendered *-ght*.

(4) OE *lc* becomes *lk* (*folk, ilk*). OE *-līce* is always *-ly* (but cf. *apertely* with additional *e* possibly from spelling of the adj.); OE *-ig* is always *-y*.

(5) OE *sc* is represented mostly by *sch*, e.g., *schal* (B13), *sche* (B45), *schul* (B76), *scharply* (B117), and once, inconsistently, by *sc*: *scyneth*, B134 (cf. *schinest*, B135).

(6) Aphesis of *s* occurs in *baptim* (B131).

(7) The initial spelling of words earlier beginning with *hw-* is invariably *wh-*, e.g., *whan, whennes, whom*. There is no indication of voicing one way or the other (but see further on dialect below). The graph *w* is employed not only to represent OE initial *w*, as is usual, but in diphthongs and as a spelling variant, both for vowels and consonants, e.g., representing OE *ag* (*owen* B28), OF *ou* (*jewel, stowre*) and *au* (*cawte*), and ON *ú* (*dowfe*).

C. Features of Accidence:

(1) For what must surely be a late fourteenth-century text, this later witness is not heavily inflected. There is consistency in the use of historically expected final *-e* in inflexions for plurals, infinitives and for all cases but the nominative, together with subjunctive and imperative modes. Generally the rhyme words written without final *-e* point to its redundancy in those that carry it, e.g., *birthe ↔ myrth* (B82–3), and *wys ↔ price, ryse, þis* (B85–91). Superfluous final *-e* appears on nom. *frende* (B71) and *stone* (B42), in each case probably indicating the longer sound, and on *rekynde* (B116) where an original inflexion such as OE *-od* might have made a trisyllabic form. It can be assumed that most of these inflexions were not sounded unless the metre required it, so, e.g.: *doutë þe nought* (B5), *þat ilkë swete wight* (B49), but *tak⟨e⟩ it in thoght* (B7).

(2) The sound in unstressed syllables is primarily written as *e* before final *-d*, as in *conceyued, jugged, neghed*, but cf. the variants in *i* or *y*, as in *callid, callyd, loutid*. OE *o* before final *r* is predominantly found as *i*, e.g.: *brothir, neythir, sekir*, but cf. *doghter, moder*.

(3) In nouns, the pl. and poss. endings are nearly always *-es*, as in *bales, Goddes, hawes*; but *-s* is found in *cosyns, foos, maners*.

(4) Pronouns are variable in spelling but apparently consistent in sound: 2 sg. nom. appears as *thow, þou, þow*; the acc./dat. is always *þe*, and the poss. *thi, thy, þi*; 3 sg. nom. is always *he* and *sche*; the neuter is always *it*; the acc., dat. is always *hym, here* and the genitive always *his, here* (pl. *thei, þei; hem, þem*).

(5) In verbs the fully inflected inf. is found only twice in *neuen* and *listen*. Primarily it ends in *-e*, as in *conceyue, blede, craue*, with only one other variant, the uninflected *discry*. The pr. p. ends in *-and* once in *borionand*, and in *-yng* in *drynkyng, dwellyng, sittyng*. The verbal n. ending is *-yng*, as in *blomyng, frestyng, prechyng*. Pr. 2 indic. is *-(e)st* in *hast, schinest*. Imperatives (all sg.) are in *-e*, as in *bringe, fende, kepe, neghe*, and are only uninflected in *doubt, prey, stand*. The pr. 3 sg. ending is *-eth*, and occurs only twice (*liketh, scyneth*). Pa. 3 sg. predominantly ends in *-d(e)*, as in *tolde, stode, wonde*, but uninflected endings (e.g. *fel, gan*) are nearly as common, and the metre demonstrates that final *-e* is redundant on, e.g., *gane, sawe, chese, come*; rarer are the endings in *-t(h)(e)* of *broght, cawte, soghte, wrote*. The pr. pl. occurs in *mys, knowe*. There are no strong past participles with prefix; and every other variation occurs, as in *bare, born, bourn, comen, broght*. Weak verbs in conjugation and in past participles generally end in *-(e)d* (e.g., *neuend, wanted*), *-id, yd* (*restid, peryd*), or *-t(t)*, as in *baptist, grett, kist, sett*.

(6) OE/ON adv. endings appear as *-ly*, as in *al-holy, lufly, pertly*, and *-ely* in *apertely, godely*; this could be when the A-scribe appends an adj. with terminal *-e* (cf. *gode* B100), and so not necessarily sounded.

Vocabulary and Syntax

There are 944 words in the text, and, excluding proper names, a total vocabulary of 380 words, an unusually high ratio. A sizeable portion (3 per cent) of the vocabulary is biblical, Semitic, Greek and Latin, particularly in proper names. The Latinate component (*conceyued, incarnacioun*) pertains to the sacramental content, and is not a feature of an aureate style. About 77 per cent of the vocabulary is of Old

English origin, 15 per cent is of French derivation (cf. the approximate 27 per cent of *SGGK*), and 6 per cent derives from Old Norse, including 13 common etymons (e.g., *bothe*, *callid*, *fro*, *meke*, *semly*, *take*, *þai*), the nonce word, *blomyng*, and the unusual *frestyng*; this can be compared with, e.g., the 9 per cent in works of the *Gawain*-poet. The OF lexis is a clear constituent (e.g., *borionand*, *discry*, *poyntil*, *roser*) though not otherwise distinctive; nearly all of it descends into Modern Standard English. Adjectives and adverbs are used sparingly and in commonplace collocations. The archaic alliterative vocabulary and collocations are commonplace. As in *Katherine*, the most complex words are adverbs such as *apertely*, *lawfully*, *stedefastly*, compounds such as *wildirnesse*, *honycomes* and inflected words such as *betokenith*, *borionand*, *conceyued*. A somewhat exotic vocabulary of romance, biblical and eastern origin (e.g., *Gabriel*, *camel*, *deyse*, *Herodias*) must of necessity be employed in the retelling of the Baptist's legend. Nearly a quarter of the vocabulary is substantive (cf. the one in six words of the vocabulary of *Evangelist*).

Dialect of Scribe and Author

LALME ascribes the scribal dialect to an area around the Soke of Peterborough or possibly north-west Ely, an area close to that of the *Katherine* scribe;[91] but the recovered rhymes of *Baptist* give sure indication of Northern origin, much closer to the language of *Evangelist*, and quite unlike Spalding's Lincs dialect. Customarily scribal provenance would be seen in the pr. 3 sg. *-eth* ending and some other features of orthography generally associated with Southern provenance, such as endings *-ed*, *-es*, and pervasive use of non-etymological final *-e*; while the main pointer to a Northern authorial origin is in the rhymes, e.g., *lawe*, *sawe* rhyming with MS *blowe*, *knowe* (B72–8) and *haast* in rhyming position with MS *moost* (B109 and B112). Further evidence of Northern relics includes pr. p. *-and* (B90) and pron. 3 pl. *þei*, *þai*. The MS prep. *to* (B105) must be a substitution for an authorial Northern *til(l))*, rhyming with *wille*, *fulfille*, *stille* (B100–6). Further analysis might restore more evidence of Northern authorship: in several instances alliteration would be reinstated if some Northern vocabulary were to be substituted for certain words in verses with defective alliteration, e.g., *kenned* for *wist* (B61); and a restored rhyme in B77 gives a Northern pl. *hende*, from

[91] LALME, I, 236, *s.v.* 'Associated Literary Documents'. There is no linguistic profile.

an ON derivative. As with *Evangelist* and *Katherine*, reflexes of West Saxon forms never occur, and there is no discernible South West Midland or Scots element in dialect; but the significant Norse element in the vocabulary and many parallels in vocabulary with the Towneley and York plays point to a broad radius around York. Although this text has no profile in LALME, Margaret Laing has most kindly examined a LALME questionnaire for this edition and suggests a radius of about 30 miles, and, very tentatively, marginally towards the Wakefield area.[92] There are no unequivocal dialect words in the text that could indicate a more definite locality.

The presumption of a Northern archetype is based largely on the rhyming of OE long *ā* with OF *haast*. However, many of the ME long *o* to long *a* forms could be editorially emended but then cease to rhyme with 'John'. It is thus clear that the poet's rhyming was loose, and perhaps originated from a place where both sounds would be recognized, especially for the purposes of rhyme (for the same in *Evangelist*, see pp. liv–lv).That the scribe apparently started copying a dotted *p* = *þ/y* graph in B6, and apparently corrected himself thereafter, indicates that the exemplar was almost certainly a Northern witness in which they were indistinguishable.

PROVENANCE AND DATES

Katherine

Circumstantial evidence suggests that *Katherine* was composed by a Carmelite friar, Richard Spalding, of the Stamford convent in South Lincolnshire, most likely around the year 1399. It may have been connected with Stamford's Parish Guild of St Katherine, possibly for a guild occasion. Clues to this are in the acrostics of both texts on Bodley Rolls 22 (see p. xi), the obvious dating limits of the illumination, hands and language, the dialectal boundaries of the texts, and a discernible clue in the first text, the word 'giyld', as found in K267–68: *I grete þe, most gracyous to governe hem al / þat geder þe to hir giyld, hem for to gyde.*[93]

---

[92] As in n. 90.

[93] See Kennedy, 'Alliterative Katherine Hymn', pp. 39–64, and 'Spalding's *Alliterative Katherine Hymn*: A Guild Connection from the South East Midlands?', forthcoming in *Viator*, 35 (2004). The historical and topographical part of this work draws heavily on *The*

The manuscript undoubtedly belongs to the fifteenth century; and the broad dialectal area of both texts covers only the East Midland counties, but the phonology of rhymes in *Katherine* (see 'Language', above) indicates no difference between the scribal dialect and that of the composition, and both appear to be extremely close to that of the Spalding area of Lincolnshire. A fifteenth-century scribe or poet who originated from these fenland settlements may well have been connected with any religious foundation, trade or parish guild dedicated to this saint, or with the house of a local patron, such as the Beauforts, Wells, Beks, Willoughbys, etc.[94] Along with this dialectal placing, it can be postulated that, although the wider range must be *c.*1350–1450, the vocabulary and usage of *Katherine* is closest in nature to that of the 1390s–*c.*1415; there is no aureate language or distinctly fifteenth-century quality in the verse.[95]

Candidates for authorship are few, but a 'Frater Ricardus Spaldyng', Carmelite of Stamford, ordained acolyte at Lincoln in the summer of 1399, seems a possible author.[96] Fourteenth-century Stamford was indubitably of consequence as a great military, ecclesiastical, and trading centre with at least thirty religious foundations including eight academic halls. The most important of the schools in medieval Stamford was that of the Whitefriars, which stood only yards from the meeting place of St Katherine's Guild. This was in a loft of the Parish Church of St Paul, now the chapel of Stamford School. The remains of a staircase to this loft can still be seen in the south wall.[97] Parish guilds are not recorded in the 1389 Crown returns, but the well-documented guild of St Katherine was one of a known total of five such guilds in Stamford—a town which

Town of Stamford, Royal Commission on Historical Monuments England (London, 1977), and on the work and help of *The Stamford Survey Group* and its fine publication, *The Religious Foundations of Medieval Stamford*, ed. J. S. Hartley and A. Rogers (Nottingham, 1974).

[94] See n. 99 and pp. lxxi–lxxii.

[95] Striking correspondences to the language of *Katherine* can be seen in the cognate phrases of late Midland works found in MED and OED, ranging through texts such as the late fourteenth-century *Cleanness* and *Hilton's Scale of Perfection* and the Wycliffite texts of the 1380s and 90s, but there are also striking similarities to the language of the fifteenth-century East-Anglian drama and early *Paston Letters* (see 'Notes', e.g. to K3 and K18).

[96] Lincoln Archives Office, *Register XIII: Henry de Beaufort, 1399–1405*.

[97] In 1268 the Whitefriars were building their church adjacent to St Paul's, and, in the early fourteenth century, the Oxford secessionists' 'Brazen-nose College' stood directly opposite. The Stamford convent hosted three general chapters, and in 1392 it hosted a significant anti-Wycliffite convention; see Bodleian Library MS e Mus. 86; see also *Fasciculi Zizaniorum Magistri Johannes Wyclif cum Tritico ascribed to Thomas Netter of Walden*, ed. W. W. Shirley (Rolls Series 5, London, 1858), p. 356.

has no record of craft guilds.[98] Of the seventy-nine members in 1480, no fewer than eighteen members of the town council belonged to this guild, which attracted to its rank a few of the neighbouring gentry, nobility and clergy, and the abbots of Crowland, Bourne and Spalding.[99] The guild ordinances indicate some connections between the Carmelites and the Guild of St Katherine,[100] and these may have been similar to those in Coventry, where, in 1450, 'the Carpenters Company had a collation at the White Friars'.[101]

The acrostic, *p i p w e l*, in the second text on the Bodley Rolls 22 (see 'The Manuscripts' and Plate II, pp. xo–xii above) can be linked with the place name Pipwell in Holland, Lincs, a Cistercian grange of Pipewell Abbey, Northants. Alienated in 1562, it later came into the hands of the Duchy of Lancaster and no traces of its chapel to the Virgin Mary (suggestive in relation to the Marian poem) now remain.[102] The Northants and Lincs pronunciations of the name are different today (diphthong [ai] and short *i* [i] respectively), and

---

[98] See Hartley and Rogers, *Religious Foundations, passim*, and also A. Rogers, 'Late Medieval Stamford: A Study of the Town Council 1465–1495', in *Perspectives in English Urban History*, ed. A. Everitt (London, 1971), pp. 16–38, at p. 33. The guild records are PRO C47/38–46 and Cambridge Gonville and Caius MS 670/266. The guild register from the years 1480–1534 also survives. See also *English Gilds*, ed. Lucy Toulmin Smith, (EETS, os 40, 1870), and H. F. Westlake, *The Parish Gilds of Mediaeval England* (London, 1919).

[99] The guild members in 1502 included Margaret Beaufort, who lived close to Stamford at Collyweston, and Cecily Welles, the daughter of Edward IV, who was a guild member in 1504. However, each of these ladies may have been honorary members for, in turn, they were each seigneur of the town (Gonville and Caius MS 670/266, f. 52ʳ). At the Dissolution the assets of the Stamford Whitefriars went to the Cecils at Burghley, just outside Stamford, but the Burghley House archive is not available to scholars.

[100] See Gonville and Caius MS 670/266, ff. 47ʳ–48ʳ.

[101] Quoted without source reference in P. R. McCaffrey, *The White Friars: An Outline History* (Dublin, 1926), p. 243.

[102] Hundred Rolls 1275, I, 271; also Sir William Dugdale, *Monasticon anglicanum: A History of the Abbies and other Monasteries, Hospitals, Frieries, and Cathedral and Collegiate Churches with their dependencies in England and Wales, etc.*, ed. John Caley, Henry Ellis and the Rev. Bulkeley Bandinel, 8 vols (London, 1846), quoting *Valor Eccl. Henry VIII*: 'Oblacio*n*ibus in capella be*a*te Marie Virginis de Pipwell in Hollande comu*n*ibus annis 01. 10s. od', V, 438. This is almost certainly the latter chapel that William Stuckley refers to, in his *Itinerarium Curiosum* (London, 1724), p. 20: 'a chapel dedicated to the virgin Mary at Holbeach hurn, standing 1515. . . . . Another in the fen ends'. The chapel at Holbeach Hurn has some documented history, but is about three miles from Pipwell Manor. It seems that grange chapels were invariably situated in the farm courtyard; see C. Pratt, *The Monastic Grange in Medieval England: A Reassessment* (London, 1969), *passim*. Pipwell Manor is very close to Moulton Seas End (? = 'fen ends'). It was subsequently let to a member of the dissolved monastery of Pipewell (Calendar of Patent Rolls, 5 Elizabeth 9, 1562, 995, memb. 2). For the poem see pp. xi–xii and n. 5.

the spellings started to differ in the Middle Ages, with a preponderance of the Northants notations employing a medial *e*, a preponderance of the East-Anglian spellings omitting it. From Pipwell, today's
inhabitants look west to Spalding for a centre, just as medieval
Spalding looked west (or up river) to Stamford. It seems likely that
the acrostic, *p i p w e l*, was interwoven as autograph by the second
poet, who attempted to emulate *Katherine*, starting off in a bravura
attempt at strong-stress style on this blank space at the bottom of
the roll:

> Myldyste of moode   and mekyst of maydyns alle,
> O modyrs mercyfullyst,   most chast þat euer was wyfe[;]

but who, within the first few lines of his composition, reverted to a
homomorphic pentameter, as in l. 8:

> Wythyn þi chest hath chosyn a ioyful place.

His family may have originated from this hamlet of Pipwell, just as
Richard Spalding's must originally have come from Spalding, in
which case his acrostic helps to anchor the texts in the Stamford or
Spalding area rather than further south in Northamptonshire where
the name, Pipewell, was already established. It is possible that he too
was a Carmelite in Stamford, though, from the evidence of extant
registers, one who did not take orders. It is also possible that the roll
never reached its designated owners, for the blank space that the short
poem occupies is incongruous for a finished product, but is exactly
the right-sized space for some armorial shields or other signs of
dedication that characteristically might have terminated the work of
art which this 'St Katherine' roll was surely intended to be.

Katherine may have been written for a guild event, but it is not
easy to imagine its reception unless for a competition.[103] However, it
is conceivable that, as a form of prayer roll (see further below), it may
have been written for public display, perhaps to accompany a series of
pictures, or for a member of the confraternity—and perhaps by the
guild chaplain. It is possible that the late fourteenth-century poem
was rediscovered at a renewal of guild activity such as the ordinances
relate happened in 1492, and was then reinscribed (neatly but with

---

[103] On this, see Anne F. Sutton, 'Merchants, Music and Social Harmony: the London
Puy and its French and London Contexts, circa 1300', *The London Journal*, 17 (1992), 1–
17, and Helen Cooper, 'Sources and Analogues of Chaucer's Canterbury Tales: Reviewing
the Work', *Studies in the Age of Chaucer*, 19 (1997), 183–210.

much misreading) for a lady patron or guild occasion—for the nature of the hand undoubtedly post-dates the nature of the language.

It seems likely that LALME's Linguistic Profile of *Katherine* results in an accurate grid position.[104] The profile's theoretical location of scribal provenance is about five miles to the east of Crowland Abbey, in south-east Holland, Lincs. This is about ten miles due east of the midway point on the road between Spalding and Stamford, and ten miles due south of Pipwell, Holland. Such localization apparently supports the above propositions about provenance and authorship, and it can be borne in mind that the authorities consulted on Bodley Rolls 22 (see p. xiii) agree that the somewhat provincial appearance of the bookhand and illumination would fit a Stamford composition and production.[105]

If it could be proved that the author was the Carmelite friar, Richard Spalding of Stamford, and if he was ever chaplain to the guild across the road, or commissioned to write for it, it would be satisfying to demonstrate that all three late Middle English verse legends of St Katherine were composed by mendicant writers, Capgrave, Bokenham and Spalding, though the last cannot be firmly proved.

Evangelist

Despite accomplished individual editions and studies, we are still without full investigations of the codices, and of the provenance of the many Thornton texts in both of his compilations. However, it is not difficult to deduce that most of Thornton's collection is material originally composed in Northern dialects. There are no Chaucerian pieces or works of familiar South East Midland provenance, as has often been noted. The alliterative language and, more important, the rhymes of *Evangelist* (see 'Language', above) clearly point to a proximate authorial dialect, but there are no ready clues to provenance or authorship, in either the compilation or the text. Of the religious pieces in both anthologies, Catterick's rhythmical and

---

[104] This is despite some erroneous readings of the text that suggest dependence on earlier editors; on this see T. L. Burton, 'On the Current State of Middle English Dialectology', *Leeds Studies in English*, n.s. 22 (1991), 167–208, and Kennedy, 'Alliterative Katherine Hymn', p. 140 and Fig. 140a. The linguistic profile appears in LALME, III, LP 912 (p. 295), and, on the National Grid, hand *a* of Bodley Rolls 22 has been placed at 524:323.

[105] It has been suggested that Stamford might have been the centre at which the Luttrell Psalter was produced. See Michael Camille, 'Labouring for the Lord: The Ploughman and the Social Order in the Luttrell Psalter', *Art History*, 10 (1987), 423–54, at p. 446.

alliterating sermon of 1357 (Lincoln f. 213^v) was clearly composed in York,[106] and the poem on the Trinity (Lincoln f. 189^r) which has long been attributed to William Nassington, a secular canon and proctor of York Minster (*fl.* 1375), shows a distinct localization of attribution.[107] Thornton evidently wanted to copy a quantity of the work of Richard Rolle, born in Thornton Dale only about twelve miles to the east of York. Although Rolle soon fled to South Yorkshire, his works had become famous in the three-quarters of a century that followed his death, and possibly nowhere more than in his family's locale. Indeed *Evangelist* is embedded in the devotional section of the anthology where Rolle's works, canonical or not, are prominent. However, from the immediate matrix of *Evangelist*, one or two inferences about intent can be drawn.

The four texts in this gathering comprise two Hilton prose texts, *Evangelist* and a Rollean prose text, in sequence: the end part of Walter Hilton's short English prose tract, *Of Mixed Life*; a treatise *An Epistle of Salvation*; *The Alliterative Evangelist Hymn*; and a treatise *On Prayer*.[108] The tone of much of these resonates with that of *Evangelist*, and it is possibly to these writers that we should look for clues to authorship.[109]

[106] For the name see BL MS Arundel 507: 'John de Caterick'. This was pointed out by A. I. Doyle in 'A Survey of the origins and circulation of theological writings in English in the 14th, 15th and early 16th centuries with special consideration of the part of the clergy therein' (Unpublished Ph.D. thesis, University of Cambridge, 1953), p. 31, n. 2. The place is about thirty-five miles from East Newton; the person was almost certainly a member of the York clergy. For the text see Brewer and Owen, *Thornton Manuscript*, ff. 213^v–219^r, valuable for observation of the punctuation of the strophes, uncharacteristic of Thornton, and no doubt from the examplar. It is edited as 'Dan Jon Gaytryge's Sermon', in Perry, *Religious Pieces*, pp. 1–15, and *The Lay Folks' Catechism*, ed. T. F. Simmons and H. E. Nolloth (EETS, OS 118, 1901). See further Lawton, 'Introduction', in *ME Alliterative Poetry*, p. 16; Doyle comments that 'The title *Lay Folks' Catechism* given by the editors is a double misrepresentation' (see 'A Survey', p. 32). See also R. N. Swanson, 'The Origins of the Lay Folks' Catechism', *Medium Ævum*, 60 (1991), 92–100, and Anne Hudson, 'The Lay Folks' Catechism: A Postscript', *Viator*, 19 (1988), 307–9.

[107] See edited text in Perry, *Religious Pieces*, pp. 63–75. Note Thornton's incipit which suggests he was sure of his author: 'tractatus Wille*m*i Nassyngton, quonda*m* aduocati [*sic*] cur*ie* Ebor*aci*' (f. 189^r). Doyle, in 'A Survey', p. 43, writes of him: 'probably beneficed but not occupied as a parish priest, anxious to further popular evangelization in the manner developed during the previous century or so by the mendicant friars, the poetic homily or didactic "romance"'. There are many references to him in York records.

[108] Titles of prose works taken here from Brewer and Owen, *Thornton Manuscript*.

[109] See G. G. Perry, *English Prose Treatises of Richard Rolle de Hampole* (EETS, OS 20, 1866; rev. ed. 1921), pp. 19–42; Horstmann, *Yorkshire Writers*, I, pp. 270–92; S. J. Ogilvie-Thomson, *Walter Hilton's On Mixed Life: edited from Lambeth Palace MS 472* Salzburg Studies: Elizabethan and Renaissance 92:15, Salzburg, 1986). Perry edits the whole tract, supplying the missing text from BL MS Royal 17 C. xviii. It should be noted that this

The second of the four texts in the quire, the *Epistle of Salvation*, is a short instructional prose letter on sin and salvation that was one of the texts gathered with others such as *Our Daily Work* and the *Three Arrows of Doomsday* into a collection known as þe *Holy Boke Gracia Dei*, which has associations with the Carthusian house of Mount Grace, north of York, and may have been compiled before the period 1390–95.[110] It was originally part of Hilton's *Scale of Perfection*, Book I, chapter 44,[111] a chapter on devotion to the Holy Name of Jesus, citing the Gospels very much as the *Evangelist*-poet does: 'As if oure lorde said one þis wyse: "3e þat er my derlynges and noghte anely kepid my commandementis bot also of 3owre awene fre will fulfillede my consailles"'.[112]

George Keiser has made some most interesting connections between Robert Thornton, the Ingelby family who owned one of the *Gracia Dei* texts, and Mount Grace, giving us leads to Ripley Castle, Harrogate and the Stapleton, Roos and Gascoigne families, and also to Carthusian houses at Kingston and at Beauvale, Nottinghamshire.[113] These are all suggestive lines of consideration with regard to the provenance of the poem. In general, *Evangelist* can be contextualized as one of a body of religious pieces on how a state of grace can be obtained by the busy lay person (perhaps an administrator) who takes particular pains with a mild type of religious contemplation. If it was first written in Yorkshire with the secular clergy in mind, with an exemplar in an apostle-bishop, then it is logical that it might later be taken up by a compiler with Thornton's profile.

latter MS shares works with the 'Wheatley Manuscript'. See also R. Birts, ' "The Scale of Perfection" by Walter Hilton Canon at the Augustinian Priory at Thurgarton, Book i, Chapters 38–52' (Unpublished B.Litt. thesis, University of Oxford, 1952); *Walter Hilton: The Scale of Perfection*, ed. Thomas H. Bestul (Kalamazoo, 2000); and forthcoming EETS editions by Michael Sargent and S. S. Hussey.

[110] Edited as 'The Virtue of Our Lord's Passion', in Perry, *Prose Treatises*, 44–7, and 'An Epistle on salvation by loue of the name of Iesus', in Horstmann, *Yorkshire Writers*, I. 293.

[111] Woolley, in his *Catalogue*, erroneously describes it as Book II, Chapter 3 of the *Scale*. Neither Brewer and Owen nor Thompson repeat this, but do not attempt an attribution. The correct attribution was made in 1984 by George Keiser, in ' "To Knawe God" ', p. 120. The confusion was almost certainly caused by the problem of the independence of other Holy Name pieces in Hilton MSS.

[112] f. 230ᵛ (Horstmann, *Yorkshire Writers*, I, 294–5).

[113] Now Huntingdon Library HM 148. See Keiser, 'The Holy Boke', pp. 308–14. See also Jonathan Hughes, *Pastors and Visionaries: Religion and Secular Life in Late Medieval Yorkshire* (Woodbridge, 1988).

On the matter of dating, Keiser summarizes the evidence that Thornton reached his majority in 1418 and died in 1469;[114] and MED settles on the rough date of *c*.1440 for the Thornton MSS. Most of Thornton's copies are of late fourteenth-century compositions, conservative, not the latest innovations; and, on grounds of vocabulary and style, there is little reason to date *Evangelist* later than *c*.1400. I would suggest *c*.1390.

Baptist

As discussed above (see 'Language', pp. lix–lxiv), the archetypal dialectal features in the poem show that it must have been composed by someone of Yorkshire origins, probably within a small radius of York. The scribal features of the 'Wheatley' anthology are all of basic East Midland or North East Midland dialect, yet without distinctive East-Anglian features, indicating that the compilation was possibly made by scribes from somewhere within the extensive boundaries suggested by such dialects. This area suggested extends as far as Stamford in Lincolnshire to the north and into Northamptonshire and Hertfordshire to the south. In the light of the origins of *Katherine* around Stamford, this is of some interest, but nothing can be made of the clue, except to say that the person (or association) who commissioned this small collection of pieces of largely Northern and Midland origin (either a northerner employing a scribe from the North East Midlands, or a person of North East Midland origin) was interested enough in 14-line stanza alliterative saints' hymns to include one in this neat little anthology of devotional pieces. Dialectally this area fits well with the provenance suggested (see pp. lxiii–lxiv above). If this identification could be proved, it would focus our attention on the dialectal provenance of the scribes, both of whom seem to have come from the South East Midlands. Were they in the North, copying these Northern texts for a Northern author or patron? From evidence in the binding of the codex, it seems more likely that texts that had originated there were, by the mid fifteenth century, being copied by local scribes in the Peterborough/Ely area for lay patronage.

The thirteenth-century fragments in the fifteenth-century binding, noted on p. xxiii above, are from Accounts of Expenses of the Wardrobe, mentioning the Keeper, Thomas Bek (d. 1293), and Philip de Wilueby, a kinsman who was then controller of accounts

---

[114] Keiser, *Life and Milieu*, pp. 160–3.

in the Wardrobe. The Beks and the Willoughbys of Eresby and Spilsby, to the east of Lincoln, interconnected by marriage, became two of the most influential Lancastrian families of the Lincolnshire plutocracy. Thomas Bek became Bishop of St Davids and Chancellor of Oxford, holding benefices in Wainfleet All Saints in Lincolnshire and Silkstone, near Barnsley, Yorkshire. His nephew became Bishop of Lincoln. The Willoughbys had holdings in forty-two towns, villages and hamlets, mainly in south-east Lindsey, and in 1388 the family acquired the estates of the barony of Ashby, north of Horncastle. Catherine Bertie (b. 1520), who was mother of the eleventh Lord Willoughby de Eresby, was by her first marriage Duchess of Suffolk.[115] From these fragments of binding it seems possible that the little book was made by a member of this large family, which was spread over the East Midlands, although, of course, old account rolls might have come into the hands of a fifteenth-century binder from anywhere. There is certainly some localization of dialect in the sixteenth-century scribbles of f. 2^r (see pp. xxiv–xxv) where the spelling of one of the clear words, *augth*, shows a difference from the spelling of the voiced spirants in the *Orison* text, and indeed throughout the book. This *-gth* form is a striking feature of the spelling of *Katherine* and other South Lincolnshire texts, and it is more than likely that the book was in the Lincolnshire area in the sixteenth century, or even until the time of its sale to Maggs. Its small size and its makeup of texts of mixed authorial provenance (though, apart from Maidstone's Kentish, largely Northern and East Midland), suggest that it was made for a pious lady, and the best line of future research might be in the history of Catherine, Duchess of Suffolk, a known bibliophile.[116]

Another line of inquiry is suggested by George Keiser, writing on private chapels in connection with book ownership in the East Riding of Yorkshire, who cites the inventory of Elizabeth Sywardby (of Sewardby by Bridlington on the north-east coast).[117] Owning almost every sort of devotional text that has been cited in connection with *Evangelist*, she also had two images of John the Baptist in her chapel.

[115] The above data is a paraphrase of Graham Platts, *Land and People in Medieval Lincolnshire* (History of Lincolnshire 4, Lincoln, 1985), p. 40, and DNB, *s.v.* 'Bek' and 'Willoughby'.

[116] For comprehensive information on these subjects see Carol M. Meale, *Women and Literature in Britain 1150–1500* (Cambridge, 1996), particularly the fine essays by Julia Boffey, Carol Meale and Felicity Riddy.

[117] Keiser, '"To Knawe God"', pp. 122–3.

However, a count of the images of the Baptist in medieval England would give us several thousand leads, and one was never far from a guild of the saint. This lady owned many books, but Keiser's speculation on 'whether there was a life of the Baptist in one of Elizabeth Sywardby's books and an image of the Evangelist in Thornton's chapel' (p. 122) will probably not get us far.[118] However, as Keiser points out, strong links among religious houses, and then between religious houses and common profit books soon carried a popular text about the country. Links between the efficient diocesan administrations of York and Lincoln and their religious houses appear to have been particularly good around the turn of the century, though, until more substantial studies of the Lincoln and 'Wheatley' manuscripts are made, disappointingly little can be ascertained about the origin of *Baptist*.

As to dating, the poem seems to be Ricardian, or possibly slightly later. Each piece in the 'Wheatley Manuscript' appears to be a fourteenth-century composition; for example, the *Penitential Psalms* of Richard Maidstone (d. 1396), and the Hymn from the *Speculum Christiani* (found also in the Vernon Manuscript, *c*.1385). Cognate forms in the diction and syntax of *Baptist* (see 'Notes') further substantiate a date just before the turn of the century. As well as the manuscript evidence, the vocabulary and phrasing would suggest that the date of composition was similar to that of *Katherine*, just before 1400. As with *Evangelist*, nothing in this unpolished work reflects Spalding's complexity of syntax, and its bouncy but irregular rhythms sound quite unlike the imperturbable progresses of *Evangelist*. Furthermore, the late date of the witness gives very few clues about the reason for composition.

Because of the derangement of the stanzas, it is possible that they were separately inscribed on an earlier exemplar, although this does not necessarily mean that they subtitled or accompanied a picture or frieze series. As early as the fifth century artists had depicted various scenes of the life of John the Baptist, by the eleventh century a rich narrative cycle of his life was well established, and in the fourteenth century this cycle had come to include almost twenty scenes.[119] But

[118] Like the most distinguished scholars before him, Keiser was apparently unaware of the existence of the other 14-line poems. If he had been aware, he might have made more of the connection, but, until work is done on relationships between texts owned by Elizabeth Sywardby and those in the 'Wheatley Manuscript', it seems of little use to stress it in this instance.

[119] See, e.g., the baptistry doors in Florence and the frescos of Brunswick Cathedral. On

Stanzas 2 and 10 of *Baptist* are supplicatory and include no graphic representations of the *vita*, and Stanza 9, for example, covers events that normally might take four pictures, whereas the naming of the child is given two whole stanzas (5 and 6). However, the possibility that the text accompanied visual material remains. Other likely circumstances for composition might have been for a patron's saint's day, perhaps with guild connections, or for the dedication of a chapel or altar. In the 'Wheatley Manuscript', three short poems begin on f. 57ᵛ, the incipits of which are, respectively: 'God þat madist al þing of nouȝt', 'Marye Goddis modir dere' and 'Seynt Iohn [the Evangelist] for grace þou craue' (followed by the highly popular prayer to the Virgin from the *Speculum Christiani*).[120] The prayer to 'Seynt Iohn' consists of six lines asking the Evangelist—because of his closeness to Christ's breast—to help gain grace to make a good end.[121] Although this prayer is dissimilar in form to *Baptist*, there might be one frail lead in this respecting the special devotion of a patron to the Virgin as well as to both the Baptist and the Evangelist. Mabel Day, the first editor of *Baptist*, presented a list of phrases common to both of the 'John' hymns,[122] but these are formulaic phrases, and her proposal of common authorship is not supported by contrary evidence from a study of the language and metre.

As a brief conclusion to this discussion of the provenance of all three hymns, it can be noted that we have here three associated alliterative poems, two almost certainly written in North Yorkshire and one in South Lincs. It is well known that *The Blacksmiths* may have a London or East-Anglian provenance.[123] Two recent investigations in the alliterative tradition ascribe the *Lament for John Berkeley*-poet (perhaps named Turnour) to Leicestershire, and John Tickhill, who composed 'A Bird in Bishopswood', to London.[124] The easterly

this subject see, e.g., G. de Saint-Laurent, 'De l'Iconographie de St. Jean-Baptiste', *Revue de l'art chrétien*, II (1867), 23–30, and M. A. Lavin, 'Giovannino Battista: A Study in Renaissance Religious Symbolism', *The Art Bulletin*, 37 (1955), 85–100. For the iconography of Mary and Elizabeth, see Ilse Falk, *Studien zu Andre Pisano* (Hamburg, 1940).

[120] BR 985, 2101, 2924, 2118, respectively. See Day, *Wheatley MS*, pp. 73–4. No other witnesses of these have come to light.

[121] Judging by the unmetrical first line, this has lost something in transmission; *Iohn* was perhaps an original *Iohan*.

[122] Day, *Wheatley MS*, p. xi.

[123] See Elizabeth Salter, 'A Complaint Against Blacksmiths', *Literature and History*, 5 (1979), 194–215.

[124] See *The Lament for Sir John Berkeley*, ed. T. Turville-Petre, *Speculum*, 57 (1982),

location of the alliterative saints' hymns, together with such minor alliterative texts and some of the verse of the East-Anglian drama (see further pp. xci–xciv below) should help to counterbalance the outdated notion that the alliterative tradition is a purely West Midland phenomenon.[125]

SOURCES AND AFFILIATIONS

The 'John' poems have sources in the Bible and late antiquity; the story of Katherine of Alexandria appears to have a basis in the near East from about the ninth century. The basic outlines of all three stories were widely known in fourteenth-century England, but more specific literary sources can be traced (see also 'Notes').

Katherine

From about 1100 the main elements of the 'matter of Katherine' had developed into a sequence that began with a Christian virgin of noble birth, beauty and piety who dared to upbraid the Roman despot in Egypt for loud pagan sacrifice. He imprisoned her and forced her to contest her faith with fifty rhetoricians; but Katherine not only confuted their arguments, but also converted them; they underwent martyrdom by a fire which miraculously left them unburnt (though dead). The tyrant then attempted to convert the girl by means of starvation and flagellation, offers of sovereignty, and, finally, torture by huge spiked rotating wheels, but each attempt was confounded by Christ and his angels, the last by a downward-driving angel who broke the contraption with such force that the fragments killed thousands of heathen bystanders. Such faith converted both the tyrant's queen and his chief adviser, who were also martyred.

332–9, and '"A Bird in Bishopswood": Some Newly-Discovered Lines of Alliterative Verse from the Late Fourteenth Century', ed. Ruth Kennedy, in *Medieval Literature and Antiquities: Studies in Honour of Basil Cottle*, ed. Myra Stokes and T. L. Burton (Cambridge, 1987), pp. 71–87. Tickhill almost certainly came from the place of that name near Doncaster, but is recorded as chantry priest in London for seventeen years.

[125] As far as I am aware, it was Elizabeth Salter who first pointed out that the Alliterative Revival was not confined to West Midland locations; see 'Mappings', Chapter 3 in Elizabeth Salter, *Fourteenth-Century English Poetry: Contexts and Readings* (Oxford, 1983), pp. 52–86. This point has been further argued by Ralph Hanna, 'Alliterative Poetry', in *The Cambridge History of Medieval English Literature*, ed. David Wallace (Cambridge, 1999), pp. 488–512, *passim*.

Katherine's death was finally effected by decapitation, but angels carried her body to Mount Sinai, from where her relics procured healing miracles. Although she was said to have died in AD 320, the legend arose around the ninth century, from when the first documentation dates.[126] Embroidery of the legend took place largely in northern France where the cult was vigorous, having been introduced to Rouen supposedly by a monk of Sinai in 1030. It was carried to England by the Normans and Crusaders, and sundry Latin legendaries circulated throughout Europe.[127]

This early hagiography with its *vulgata* versions shaped the *vitae* and *passionaries* of the liturgies, and the wording of the *sanctorale* versions based on them would be heard yearly by any cleric, as can be if the text of the *vulgata* is compared with the wording of breviary texts.[128] The inclusion by Spalding of one of the *Passio* motifs (the weeping maidens and matrons) indicates that he indeed knew it.[129] In non-liturgical manuscripts the *Passio* took two main forms: a full and an abbreviated version. Its full text was certainly the Latin source of the first Englishing in the early thirteenth-century West-Midland 'Katherine Group', and certain Late Middle English prose lives. The West-Midland 'Katherine Group' text has been exhaustively dealt with by recent commentators, and was fully re-edited in 1981, when the Latin source manuscripts were collated and presented in a critical edition, *Seinte Katerine*, for the first time.[130] It might be posited that

---

[126] This is the Greek *Menologium Basilianum*, now in the Vatican. For all references to the development of the legend in antiquity, see the standard studies: Herman Knust, *Geschichte der Legenden der heiligen Katherina von Alexandrien und der heiligen Maria Aegyptiaca nebst unedierten Texten* (Halle, 1890); H. Varnhagen, *Zur Geschichte der Legende der Katherina von Alexandrien* (Erlangen, 1891); G. B. Bronzini, 'La leggenda di S. Caterina d'Alessandria: passioni greche e latine' (Atti della Accademia nazionale dei Lincei. Memorie, Classe di scienze morali, storiche e filologiche, ser. 8, vol. 9, fasc. 2, 1960), 257–416.

[127] For the evolution of the tradition in England see Katherine J. Lewis, *The Cult of St Katherine of Alexandria in Late Medieval England* (Woodbridge, 2000).

[128] See *Bibliotheca hagiographica latina antiquae et mediae aetatis* (Brussels, 1898–1911). The terms *vulgata* and *Passio* are employed here for the well-known and established passion of this saint that belonged to this canon. (This does not include the story of her early life and espousal by Christ—which formed a separate and later tradition, the *vita*.)

[129] Compare, e.g., the Use of Sarum's Katherine legend with the *Legenda Aurea* and the Latin long and short *passio*; see *Breviarium ad usum insignis ecclesiae Sarum*, ed. F. Procter and C. Wordsworth, 3 vols (Cambridge, 1886), pp. 1102–18; *Iacopo da Varazze, Legenda Aurea*, ed. Giovanni Paolo Maggioni (Millennio Medievale 6, Testi 3, Florence, 1998), Cap. CLXVIII: 'De sancta Katherina', pp. 1205–50; *Seinte Katerine*, ed. S. R. T. O. d'Ardenne and E. J. Dobson (EETS, ss 7, 1981). For this subject in general see *Catholic Encyclopedia*, s.v. 'Sanctorale Cycle'.

[130] See d'Ardenne and Dobson, *Seinte Katerine*, pp. 132–43. For texts and comment on

the alliterative nature of the 'Katherine Group' text must show some affinity with Spalding's treatment, but it shows no affinity, in either rhythm or collocations; it simply happens that both are part of a diffuse alliterative tradition, separated by two centuries. It is unlikely that Spalding was particularly influenced by any extant vernacular version. In general the English accounts of the explicit legend are surprisingly disparate in their expression.[131] They are listed in Severs' *Manual*, and only one detail from the more obviously pertinent composition, Bokenham's *Lyf of S. Kateryne*, will be discussed here (see further below).[132]

The two extant Anglo-Norman verse treatments have a poetic and dramatic nature not matched in Middle English until Spalding's poem, but they do not furnish material suggestive of a distinctive source.[133] There were always sundry Latin legendaries in circulation in the Middle Ages, but by around the year 1400 in England the overwhelmingly popular one-volume compilation was the *Legenda Aurea* of the archbishop of Genoa, Jacob of Voragine, written around 1258 and based closely on three earlier tellings: the *Abbreviatio in gestis sanctorum* of Jean de Mailly (*c.*1225), the *Speculum Historiale* of Vincent de Beauvais (*c.*1244) and the *Liber epilogorum in gesta sanctorum* of Bartholomew of Trent (1245–51).[134] All four of these 'auctors' were Dominican friars. From a comparison of the texts it can be seen that these retellings were close to those of the *vulgata* 'acta sanctorum', and that Voragine's more compact versions spoke with a

such legends divided into *lectiones*, see Bronzini, 'Leggenda', 376–84. In their critical edition of the Latin sources, appended to *Seinte Katerine*, d'Ardenne and Dobson use twenty-four early manuscripts of this *Passio S. Katerine*, mentioning its possible liturgical use of the text. References to the *vulgata* and *Passio* are to this appended Latin text.

[131] For example, no resemblance in style can be detected between the 'Katherine Group' version and the South English Legendary version or between the Northern Homily Cycle and Scottish Legends of the Saints versions; no other representation in verse or prose throws light on Spalding's poem, though the fifteenth-century tail-rhyme version (Longleat MS 55, ff. 55ʳ–65ʳ) is as lively and vivid. I am indebted to Jacqueline Johnson for a text of her forthcoming edition of this work.

[132] *Osbern Bokenham: Legends of Hooly Wummen*, ed. M. S. Serjeantson (EETS, os 206 1938); 'Lyf of S. Kateryne' at ll. 6312–7377.

[133] See *The Life of St. Catherine by Clemence of Barking*, ed. W. Macbain (Anglo-Norman Text Society 18, 1964). For the other seven versions see E. C. Fawtier-Jones, 'Les Vies de Sainte-Catherine d'Alexandrie', *Romania*, 56 (1930), 80–104.

[134] See n. 129. For sources see Jean de Mailly, *Abrégé des Gestes et Miracles des Saints*, trans. A. Dondaine (Bibliothèque d'Histoire Dominicaine I, Paris, 1947), St Katherine at pp. 497–502; Vincentii Bvrgvndi, *Speculi Maioris*, 4 vols (Venice, 1591), Vol. 4, XIII, V, and *Bartholomew of Trent: Liber epilogorum in gesta sanctorum*, ed. Paoli Emore (Edizione nazionale dei testi mediolatini, Serie I, 1 (2), 2001).

new verve that appealed to later vernacular writers. About seven hundred manuscript witnesses to the Latin *Legenda Aurea* survive, and a score or so of full texts now in British libraries. Most of the later ME saints' lives appear to have been 'translated' from it, and Spalding would have known the story largely through such a tradition.

If the author of *Katherine* was a Carmelite friar of Stamford, then another likely source of material would have been the lives of the saints incorporated as *lectiones* in the very text of the breviary in its various versions, including the *Usus Carmelitarum*.[135] In such rare liturgical texts as are extant the *sanctorale* carries, if any, a brief and unexceptional version of the *Vulgata* legend, but all mendicant orders had access to various lives of the saints in Latin through their excellent libraries: one reason for the popularity of hagiography was the basis it provided for graphic illustrative sermons.[136] There are almost no works in English in the inventories of mendicant houses, but it can be seen, from the evidence of the friars Capgrave and Bokenham alone, that Englishing of hagiographical material into verse was an act sanctioned as a service to the lay public, and perhaps also as pious recreation.[137] It is now known that even the library at Merton, the largest in Oxford, was small and inadequate compared with those of many mendicant houses, and it must be assumed that, if *Katherine* originated at the Stamford house (see pp. lxiv–lxviii,

---

[135] See Oxford, University College MS 9 (a late fourteenth-century breviary and short missal), the 'Kilcormie Missal' (Trinity College Dublin MS 82), dated 1458, and the British Library's rare printed *Missale Factum ad Usum Fratrum Carmelitarum*, 3 vols (Venice, 1504). The Venice and Kilcormie books carry unexceptional versions of the *Passio*, which sweep naturally into hymns and prayers.

[136] There are only two extant catalogues of Carmelite libraries prior to 1440: an inventory of *c.*1365 of the books of Hulne, Northumberland (see *Catalogi Veteres Librorum Ecclesiae Cathedralis Dunelm.*, ed. J. Raine (Surtees Society 15, 1838), 128–31), and that of the conventual library at Florence in 1391; see K. W. Humphreys, *The Book Provisions of the Medieval Friars* (Studies in the History of Libraries and Librarianship 1, Amsterdam, 1964), 123–31, and *The Library of the Carmelites of Florence at the end of the fourteenth century* (Studies in the History of Libraries and Librarianship 2, Amsterdam, 1964). Both libraries contained hagiography.

[137] From the documentation of their houses (Lynn and Stoke Clare), there can be no dispute that both Capgrave and Bokenham belonged to the mendicant order of the Hermits of St Augustine, i.e. they were Austin Friars, not Austin Canons, as has been variously and erroneously assumed (see C. d'Evelyn and F. A. Foster, 'Saints' Legends', in *A Manual of the Writings in Middle English 1050–1500: Based upon A Manual of the Writings in Middle English 1050–1400, by John Edwin Wells . . . and Supplements*, ed. J. Burke Severs and Albert E. Hartung, 9 vols (New Haven, 1970), II, v, 410–40 and 553–645, at p. 435).

above), there would be no scarcity of narrative material from which any forgotten particulars of the story could be derived.[138]

One specific feature that Voragine and Spalding have in common is that the emperor's attempted corruption of Katherine by offering her sovereignty is placed *after* the martyrdom of the fifty philosophers, whereas the older *Passio* has this motif at the opening of the story, when the emperor first takes Katherine into custody. Little can be deduced from this shared chronology, and for our purposes analysis of 'sources' need not be the most vital concern of a study of this text which does not purport to be a *legenda* so much as a lyrical ode and petition to a propitious saint. However, there are two quirks in Spalding's version that might continue to attract scholarship: first, that Spalding inserts the confession and subsequent martyrdom of the queen and Porphiry at an earlier point in the narrative than is found in virtually every other version, since normally their martyrdom takes place after the angel has destroyed the wheel;[139] and second, that the late East Midland writers, Richard Spalding, and the friar, Bokenham (writing in Suffolk about forty years later), both employ an image that is not found in any other easily available Latin or English version, that of the tyrant *starting up* in his rage as if wounded with a spear:

> þan sprong þat cursed kayesere as spere in hert sprunge
>
> (Spalding, KI13)

and:

> þe tyraunth up sterte
> As hastyly as he had woundyd be
> Wyth a spere.
>
> (Bokenham ll. 7220–2)

The vulgate *passio* and the *Legenda Aurea* each have the image of the tyrant roaring as if injured by a wound; see also Note to KI13. The conventional idea of being wounded in the *heart* (though not by a

[138] Humphreys, *Book Provisions*, 129–31. See also p. lxxviii, and Lewis, *Cult of St Katherine*, pp. 23–5.

[139] I am indebted to Jane Cartwright and Catherine Byfield for the information that the Welsh Katerine, or 'Cathel', legends share this unusual chronology, as does the *Speculum Sacerdotale* and a version in 446 lines of rhyming couplets in Cambridge University Library MS Ff. ii. 38 (see 'S. Kateryne', ed. Horstmann, in *Altenglishe Legenden*, pp. 260–640). The Cambridge text has a scribal layer of West Midland dialectal features (*hur* 'her', *angur* 'anger', *the todur* 'the other', *thedur* 'thither', *pepull* 'people', etc.). *Katherine* shares some of these features (see 'Language', pp. xlv–xlvi), but to a lesser degree, and little can be made of these shared characteristics. Evidence from rhyme, however, is inconclusive, for defects such as *moche/stylleche* or *tryppe/wepe* muddy the waters. There is no South West Midland dipthongization.

spear) by the actions of a person hitherto dear to one is taken up by
Capgrave, writing probably slightly earlier than Bokenham:

> These woordis of pophirye, thei arn a wounde
> On-to Maxcens-is herte.   (ll. 1597–8)[140]

But none of these has the dramatic starting-up—which is also
suggestive of the tyrants of the drama.

Two other reservoirs of material must inevitably have fed the
genesis of a guild poem in celebration of this saint: the Latin hymns in
her honour and the popular folklore surrounding her cult. Despite
the relentless narrative impetus of *Katherine*, which comes directly
from its prose source material, the last four affective stanzas render it
closer in feeling to a hymn than to any other form of expression, and
its emotional impulse may derive ultimately from the myriad Latin
hagiographic hymns and prayers in which narrative, praise and
petition were intermingled. Dreves and Blume print a total of 169
prayers and hymns to the saint, the best known of which are the
'Ave', 'Pange lingua' and 'Salve' hymns of missal and breviary
liturgies.[141] That our alliterative text has this elementary affiliation
with diverse Latin lyrical compositions can be seen from four of their
main features: they generally embody praise, some narrative, and
petition, and five also have acrostics (though on stanza openings,
rather than line openings as in *Katherine*).

The acrostic is a formal literary contrivance whereby the initial or
end letters of certain lines of a verse composition make up words.[142]
Although some of the Hebrew psalms had an abecedarian arrangement, and although the first recorded acrostic is Greek *c.*180 BC, this
kind of word-play flowered with the rise of Christianity. Of the five
extant Latin acrostic hymns one is an aureate composition, opening
'Karismalis Dei cella, Virginalis tu puella' which appears to have

[140] *The Life of St. Katharine of Alexandria by John Capgrave, D. D.*, ed. C. Horstmann
(EETS, OS 100, 1893).

[141] See *Analecta Hymnica Medii Ævii*, ed. G. M. Dreves and C. Blume, 55 vols
(Leipzig, 1886–1922); *Repertorium Hymnologium*, ed. U. Chevalier, 6 vols (Louvain-
Brussels, 1892–1921); *Lateinische Hymnen des Mittelalters*, ed. F. J. Mone, 3 vols (Freiburg,
1855); Proctor and Wordsworth, *Breviarium ad usum Sarum, passim.*

[142] *Acrostic* [Greek *akron* 'end', *stikhos* 'row, line of verse']. For the acrostic see
H. Leclercq, *Dictionnaire d'Archéologie Chrétienne et de Liturgie* (Paris, 1903), pp. 365–
72; *Lexicon der Marienkunde*, ed. K. Algermissen *et al.* (Regensburg, 1957–), *s.v.*
'Akrostichis'; R. Knox, *A Book of Acrostics* (London, 1924); for a very useful study of
the acrostic and encryption of names, see E. J. Dobson, *The Origins of Ancrene Wisse*
(Oxford, 1976), pp. 327–43.

concluded a 'legenda S. Katharinae'.[143] Part of another gives perhaps
the best picture of the 'narrative' lyric tradition that lies behind our
alliterative text:

> Horrendo spectaculo subdena rotarum,
> Virgo Deum invocas, qui opus earum
> Confregit et populum stravit tenebrarum,
> Mihi planctum impetra pro culpis amarum.[144]

It can be noted that certain vernacular prayers and lyrics are close
translations of Latin hymns. One in Latin, 'a prayer' inscribed at the
bottom of a prose life, is followed by the words: 'the same prayere in
englysshe' (Lydgatean English).[145] St Katherine, next to the Virgin
Mary, was the most popular of female saints, almost certainly because
of her powers of intercession with Christ, her 'spouse', and her
ability, if remembered at the moment of death, to confer spiritual
benefits.[146] On account of this special power, she was especially
solicited at the moment of death, as in this brief quatrain:

> O pia regina, laesi cordis medicina,
> Cernere divina concede mihi, Katharina,
> Ut de sentina vitiorum carne supina
> Elever ad trina, quo mortis nulla ruina;[147]

and it is such simple solicitations that make up much of the body of
literary expression of the cult.

The use of the scroll to record certain writings prevailed for many
years after the establishment of the folio,[148] but, as far as we know,
Katherine is the only alliterative text that was professionally inscribed

---

[143] Codex St. Peter's Salzburg b.VIII 1 (*Analecta Hymnica*, 33/135).

[144] Codex St. Peter's Salzburg b.VIII 1 and Codex Monaco Clm. 7818 (*Analecta Hymnica*, 33/134).

[145] See *The Life and Martyrdom of St Katherine of Alexandria*, ed. H. H. Gibbs for the Roxburghe Club (London, 1884), pp. 65–6.

[146] See *Passio* 1107–31, and *Leg.Aurea*, 1211.127–32.

[147] Fifteenth-century Codex Parisin 11343, *Analecta Hymnica*, 33/138.

[148] Many brief lyrics and some longer works, including non-cycle play fragments, have been composed or copied by clerks on blank portions of their parchment account rolls; see Turville-Petre, 'Lament', p. 332, and Kennedy, 'Bird in Bishopswood', pp. 71–81. But the presence of these short alliterative poems is 'accidental' and thus rather different from the considered inscription of MS Bodley Rolls 22. More germane is, e.g., the bequest of Sir Thomas Cumberworth, sheriff of Lincolnshire in 1415 and 1431, of books such as 'Active Life' and a 'Vita Christi' to the Carthusians, '& þe reclus of þe grese fote at lincoln my roll of prayers' (*Lincolnshire Diocese Documents 1450–1544*, ed. A. Clark (EETS, os 149, 1941), p. 44).

and illuminated on a parchment roll.[149] Until the seventeenth century, alchemical texts, statutes and historical and genealogical
chronicles were commonly inscribed on large rolls because, with
the help of illustration on the ampler space of the roll, the linear
nature or connecting links of such subject matter could be more
clearly understood. Of literary texts formally inscribed on prepared
scrolls, three main divisions can be determined: first, private prayer
and amulet rolls; second, scrolls inscribed with various sorts of texts
for public exhibition and edification; and, third, a small number of
literary texts that have been copied on to rolls rather than folios for
other reasons. Although *Katherine* appears to belong to this last
category, by far the largest group is the first, and, as with *Katherine*,
the plea to turn aside harm is inherent in the productions of this first
large category until the Renaissance.

There is a consistent affinity between the two texts of MS Bodley
Rolls 22 and the contents of such private manuscripts as the 'Arma
Christi' rolls, and rolls with similar verse compositions of private
prayer.[150] Here, as in all of the indulgence rolls, is the same
combination of narrative description followed by petition that appears
to be unconsciously followed, though in a far more sophisticated way,
in *Katherine*. In the sophisticated milieu of late fourteenth-century
England the elemental plea for intercession and petition as means for
survival of the soul became part of an institutional framework, where
a guild membership allowed one to ask for the 'frenchip' of a
particular patron saint in return for minor sacrifice and obligation.
Such a setting, or indeed guild festivities, may have provided many
models for the genesis of *Katherine* (see 'Provenance and Dates' above)
and perhaps also of the 'John' hymns (although there is no tangible
evidence of guild association in the case of these hymns).[151] The
professional production and illumination of *Katherine* suggest rather
that there was a pertinent reason for its roll format, and this could

---

[149] For more detailed reference on the subject of the roll and other formats, see further
C. F. Bühler, 'Prayers and Charms in Certain Middle English Scrolls', *Speculum*, 39
(1964), 270–8; also R. H. Robbins, 'The "Arma Christi" Rolls', *Modern Language Review*,
34 (1939), 415–21, and 'Private Prayers in Middle English Verse', *Studies in Philology*, 36
(1939), 466–75.

[150] The 'Arma Christi' prayers are witnessed on sixteen MSS, not all rolls. For edited
texts with illustrations reproduced, see *Legends of the Holy Rood*, ed. R. Morris (EETS, os
46, 1871).

[151] For a recent exploration of this, see 'Reading St Katherine in the Parish: The
Acquisition of Knowledge and Power', Ch. 3 in Lewis, *Cult of St Katherine*, pp. 111–74.

have been either because the work was intended for a guild exhibit, or intended for private meditation—possibly by a guild member.

Friars were instrumental in the composition and dissemination of early Middle English lyrics and late Middle English hagiography, and, with the evidence of Spalding's identity presented above (see pp. lxiv–lxviii), some tentative examination of their possible fugitive compositions of the Alliterative Revival.[152] As their positions in society became, in certain areas, consolidated and respectable, mendicants continued to compose—indeed, to be chosen as versifiers, as was the Carmelite Robert Baston, taken by Edward I and Edward II with their armies to commemorate the battles with the Scots.[153] *Ancrene Wisse* is possibly of Dominican origin, and the appearance in the fifteenth century of the long, 'Lydgatian' works by the Austin Friars Capgrave and Bokenham, including, as they do, lives of St Katherine, show that by this late date, at least, the composition of verse hagiography was a distinctive part of the output of such literary friars. Hitherto there have been no patent mendicant connections with the alliterative tradition, but it can be borne in mind that Maidstone's Penitential Psalms, sporadically alliterated, though not in strong-stress metre, appear in fourteen manuscripts, mostly devotional; these codices typically contain alliterative verse.[154] Bodleian MS Digby 102 contains the partially heteromomorphic *Fifty-Two Follies of Flanders*,[155] as well as typical associates of stanzaic alliterative verse such as a C-text of *Piers Plowman* and Maidstone's Penitential Psalms. In the East-Midland 'Wheatley Manuscript', Maidstone's psalms appear directly after *Baptist*. There can be few objections to the idea that a friar may have composed this hymn in honour of a guild saint, employing the metres and formulae of the Revival.

[152] For a recent and useful overview of mendicant literary connections, see John Fleming, 'The Friars and Medieval English Literature', in *The Cambridge History of Medieval English Literature*, ed. David Wallace (Cambridge, 1999), pp. 349–75.

[153] For Misyn and other Carmelite writers such as Richard Lavenham, see Johan Bergström-Allen, ' "Heremitam Et Ordinis Carmelitarum": a Study of the Vernacular Theological Literature Produced by Medieval English Whitefriars, particularly Richard Misyn, O. Carm' (Unpublished M.Phil. thesis, University of Oxford, 2002). See also *The Fire of Love & The Mending of Life or The Rule of Living*, ed. Ralph Harvey (EETS, os 106, 1896). Baston appears to have written only in Latin; see *Scotichronicon by Walter Bower in Latin and English*, ed. D. E. R. Watt *et al.*, 9 vols (Aberdeen, 1991), VI, 366–75.

[154] See *Richard Maidstone's Penitential Psalms*, ed. Valerie Edden (Middle English Texts 22, Heidelberg, 1990).

[155] See n. 49. See *Fifty-Two Follies of Flanders*, ed. Ruth Kennedy, in *Medieval English Measures*, pp. 152–5.

Evangelist

Evangelist first recounts details of John's life as found in the gospels and Acts 3:12–23, 4:13, 19–22 and 8:14, 25. The 'Commandment to Love' is found in 1 John 4:7–11. The final biblical reference is to Revelation 1:9. Jerome's translation of Eusebius in the early third century and the descendant writings of Isidore of Hispal were fairly well-known, to the regular clergy at least,[156] and fanciful elements of the legend accrued from this time until the sudden flourishing of hagiography in medieval Europe around the tenth century. However, many of these elements must be based on the apocryphal and much discredited fifth-century Greek *Acta Johannis*.[157] It is not easy to trace the development of the widely-known story beyond the probable twelfth-century sources of the *Legenda Aurea*,[158] but such Latin *vulgata* sources appear to have provided some of the material for a medieval legend that describe the saint as surviving immersion in scalding oil, turning sticks into gold, raising the dead, writing Revelation on the island of Patmos, and finally ascending into heaven.[159] Certain parts of the accumulated legend are absent from *Evangelist*, notably John's distinctive death-scene and assumption, but also some of the well-known stories, such as the destruction of the temple of Diana, John's pursuit of the felonious young man, and tale of the partridge and young man, all present in other Middle English versions. As there may have been a stanza lost from *Evangelist* in the manuscript tradition it is not easy to deduce which specific story it may have covered, but it is most likely that it is part of the rich young men story; see Notes to E168–9. However, the *Evangelist*-poet has followed the *Legenda Aurea* very closely in parts, and this source does seem to be the most probable basis of the composition. The Evangelist was not literally a martyr, but was considered as good as one in that he was put to the test in a vat of boiling oil. The poet assumes in his readers an everyday knowledge of the legends surrounding the

---

[156] See n. 159.

[157] For the apocryphal legends, see *Acta Johannis*, ed. Eric Junod and Jean-Daniel Kaestli, 2 vols (Corpus Christianorum Series Apochryphorum I, Turnhout, 1983); this edition supersedes that of M. Bonet (Paris, 1898). See further in 'Notes'.

[158] See pp. lxxvii–lxxviii and notes 129 and 134. For the Evangelist in the *Leg.Aurea* see 'De sancto Iohanne euangelista', and 'De sancto Iohanne ante portam latinam', *Leg.Aurea*, pp. 87–96 and 471–2.

[159] The main sources are Jerome and Isidore; see *S. Eusebii: Hieronymi opere omnia* (PL 22–30), and *Isidori: Vita et Morte* (PL 81–4). For more precise references to some of these sources see 'Notes'.

apostle;[160] they are well recounted in two different stories of the *Legenda Aurea*: *De sancto Johanne apostolo et evangelista* and *De sancto Johanne ante portam latinam*. This last is a separate legend (because of its separate feast date) that commemorates the saint's ordeal by boiling oil outside the walls of Rome.

The poet honours John, son of Zebedee the fisherman and brother of James, the disciple acknowledged as the one Christ loved best, to whose care Christ consigned Mary at the Crucifixion,[161] and who later went into Asia to propagate the Christian message, becoming the first bishop at Ephesus.[162] Because medieval culture unequivocally took this John to be the author of the Fourth Gospel, the Epistles of John and the Apocalypse or Book of Revelation of St John the Divine, he was variously called the Evangelist, the Apostle or the Divine.[163] In iconography John is figured with his gospel emblem of the eagle, with chalice and viper (signifying the poisoned cup (see Stanzas 16 and 17)), with open book that signifies his authorship of Revelation, or occasionally being fed by ravens on Patmos; but his role as custodian of Mary after the Crucifixion was more affectively appealing than all of these, and furnished the familiar two figures of John and Mary regarding Christ crucified, seen widely in medieval iconography, and especially on rood screens.

There are few medieval Latin hymns dedicated to the saint.[164] Several metrical hymns to John the Evangelist in fourteenth-century

---

[160] From the time in Ephesus to his legendary death and ascension, this part of John's life, as told by Jacob of Voragine, must come from the *Acta Johannis*. The oil story is explained painstakingly in the fifteenth-century *Speculum Sacerdotale*: 'And then bi the grace of God that hym defendid he passid oute of the vessel as vnhurtyd with the fyre as he was vnfouled with flescheliche synne. Neuertheles in þat in hym was and for his good wille he was a marter. And therefore is this feste of hym as þou3 he hadde suffrid marterdom lyke to other. And þerfore in that place is made a chirche by Cristen peple, and that same day is worschipid and solempnied as for day of his marterdom', *Speculum Sacerdotale*, ed. E. Weatherly (EETS, 200, 1936), p. 153.

[161] There are six references to this at John 13: 23–26, 19: 25–27, 20: 2–10 and 21: 7, 20–24.

[162] The main source of this record of the early history of the Church is Jerome's *Eusebius* (see n. 159 above), and later patristic writers, primarily Irenaeus (see *Irenaeus: Aversus Haereses* (PG 7, 2–22, 5)) who states that he heard these facts from Polycarp of Smyrna, who actually knew John. The tradition was that John was a prisoner on Patmos late in the reign of Domitian (AD 81–86) and wrote the Apocalypse (or Revelation) there. Early in the reign of Trajan (AD 98–117) he was said to have been the first bishop at Ephesus in west Turkey, where he wrote the Gospel of John and the Epistles.

[163] Modern scholarship is still not decided on these matters; for a discussion and summary bibliography see *Catholic Encyclopedia*, *s.v.* 'John the Apostle'.

[164] *Analecta Hymnica*, 1/292, 2/325–6.

English are extant, but none would appear to have influenced our poet, who writes in a more sophisticated alliterative mode.[165] The *Cursor* text is curious in that it embodies a metrical apostrophe to John which has some similar vocabulary, though the metre is very different.[166] No extant English version furnishes a distinctive source. The version in the *Scottish Legends of the Saints* must be fairly contemporary with this stanzaic hymn, but offers few striking similarities apart from shared rhyme in one passage.[167] Much of the vocabulary is similar to that of the York and Towneley playwrights (see 'Notes', *passim*).

The pseudo-Bonaventuran *Meditationes Vitae Christi* (which were to be translated and adapted in Nicholas Love's *Mirrour of the Blessed Lyf of Jesu Christ*) were clearly influential, specifically on the affective tone of the Crato and Drusiana stories.[168] Others might well have been the instructional literature composed, sometimes for women, by writers such as the *Ancrene Wisse* author, Richard Rolle and Walter Hilton. Medieval piety emphasized John's chastity and virginity. As the youngest disciple and the one that Christ loved best, he was the male virgin *par excellence*, the Galahad of the order of the saints. The prose treatises that precede Thornton's unique witness of *Evangelist* provide some provocative resonances here. Hilton is known to have written for a female recluse, although not so much is known of her as

[165] See, e.g., BL MS Harley 4196, the 'North English Legendary' (edited as 'De sancto Johanne euangelista', in Horstmann, *Altenglische Legenden*, pp. 35–42).

[166] See *Cursor Mundi*, ed. R. Morris, 7 vols (EETS, os 57, 59, 62, 66, 68, 99, 101, 1874–93), e.g., 'He did miracls, sa wel he moght / O treind wandes gold he wroght / O grauel bi þe se side / Stanes precius o pride / And efter-ward wit crists main / þam turnd to þair kind egain. / He raisd þe widue drusian / þat was ded, and a yongman' (III, 1413); see also Notes to E61–70, E121–263, E169–82.

[167] See Note to E151–54.

[168] The *Meditationes* are found in over two hundred MSS in Latin and the vernacular. Introduced to England by the Franciscans, they were copied widely and found in many religious houses. See also *S. Bonaventura: Opera Omnia*, ed. A. C. Peltier, 12 vols (Paris, 1868), XII. The writer was identified as Johannes de Caulibus of S. Gimignano by P. L. Oliger in 'Le "Meditationes Vitae Christi" del Pseudo-Bonaventura', *Studi francescani*, n.s. 7 (1921), Numero Speciale, 143–83. They were also used as source material for much popular vernacular literature and affective iconography, e.g., the *Southern Passion* (ed. Beatrice Daw Brown, EETS 169, 1927); see, e.g. ll. 1695–705. There is an English translation illustrated with scenes from a French MS in *Meditations on the Life of Christ*, ed. Isa Ragusa and Rosalie B. Green (Princeton, 1961). For Love see *Nicholas Love's Myrrour of the Blessed Lyf of Jesu Christ*, ed. Elizabeth Salter (Analecta Cartusiana 10, Salzburg, 1974); *The mirrour of the blessed lyf of Jesu Christ: Nicholas Love*, ed. James Hogg and Lawrence F. Powell, 2 vols (Analecta Cartusiana 91, Salzburg, 1989); *Nicholas Love's Mirror of the Blessed Life of Christ*, ed. Michael G. Sargent (Garland Medieval Texts 18, New York, 1992).

of Rolle's Margaret Kirkby, and it is possibly significant that Thornton's witness to *Of Mixed Life* has different pronouns from the others; for example, Vernon's occasional 'mon' is, in Thornton's witness, '(A) man (or a woman þat is lettered and has vndirstanyng in haly writt)' (f. 225ʳ). The texts that Thornton has copied immediately before and after *Evangelist* suggest that the stanzaic, alliterative mode was congenial to the same audience who were pleased with the instructional prose and verse pieces most associated with Love and Hilton and possibly disseminated by Carthusian houses, as suggested on p. lxx above.

The text of the poem as it survives seems a diffuse exercise, employing clichéd collocations, tags and line-fillers. There is the likelihood of an extended conceit in Stanza 2, slightly marred for us by the probable error in E15 (see 'Notes'). The occasional phrase is touching in its rhythmic simplicity, as, e.g., E237–38: 'Luke þat ȝe lufande be, Ilkone to oþer', but it is not easy to discern any specific literary influence.

Baptist

As with the other two hymns, many versions of the story occur, and none extant renders a distinctive source for this alliterative version. The major sources, other than the Gospels, appear to have been the *Legenda Aurea*[169] and, as with *Evangelist*, the pseudo-Bonaventuran *Meditationes Vitae Christi*, especially for the expansion of the narrative in the cousinship of Mary and Elizabeth, and the ministering of Mary to the newborn John.[170] However, the *Baptist*-poet does not touch on the elaborate fables of John's infancy that are such a feature of, for example, the OF *La vie Saint-Jehan-Baptiste* which descended from the second-century *Book of James* (also known as the 'Protevangelium').[171] These do not form the basis for much English

---

[169] See 'De sancto Iohanne baptista', and 'De decollatione sancti Iohannis baptiste', Chapters LXXXI and CXXI in *Leg.Aurea*, pp. 540–51 and 873–85. Voragine authorizes the first of these with historical and scholastic sources such as Eusebius, Ambrose and Peter Comestor.

[170] For the pseudo-Bonaventuran *Meditationes Vitae Christi* and Love's English version see p. lxxxvi and n. 168.

[171] 'Protevangelium Jacobi', ed. in E. Hennecke, *New Testament Apocrypha*, ed. W. Schneemelcher, 2 vols (Cambridge, 1965), I, 421–38. Of Eastern influence, these writings include stories such as a flight from Herod of Elizabeth, Zacharias and John into a desert, a mountain opening to receive them, later meeting of John's family with the Holy Family, Jesus and his mother teaching the infant John how to live in the desert, meetings in Galilee and so on. For the OF legend from the two MSS in the BN (Fr. 3719

literature or art, and would not normally be found in an English life or hymn.

Behind significant scribal corruption, this short text can be reconstructed to give a buoyant and outgoing poem, replete with numerous clichéd collocations and tags. As with *Katherine* and *Evangelist*, aspects of its diction are reminiscent of the declamations of the early drama, yet the repetition of the word 'Blessed' that opens each of the ten stanzas of *Baptist* makes it the most explicit 'hymn' of the three. The poet hails and invokes John, the forerunner of Christ, and recounts details of the story as found mainly in Luke 1:5–25, 36–45 and 56–80, and Luke 3:1–22, but also in Matt. 3, Mark 1:1–11, and John 1:6–34. There is as much focus on the naming episode as on the ministry but it is not easy to conjecture why. The penultimate stanza refers to John's outspoken preaching against Herod's taking his brother Philip's wife, Herodias (Mark 6:17–18), for which Herodias ensured that her daughter, the apocryphal Salome, asked for John's head on a plate (Matt. 14:3–11 and Mark 6:19–28). The MS stanza-order up to B69 gives a jumbled version of the Elizabeth and Zacharias story, which is much improved by the reversal of MS stanzas 3 and 5. This miscopying suggests that the poem was once written with one stanza to a loose leaf, and this suggests that it might have been copied from the words accompanying a series of pictures. The present edition puts right the disarranged stanzas and attempts in as many ways as possible to restore coherence to the composition (see 'Treatment of the Texts', below).

A more significant source for the early part of the legend is the tradition of the life of Mary.[172] Of course most of the features concerning the meeting of the cousins, and the salutation by the unborn John, are fundamental, but for some specifics see Note to B49. This Northern poet was certainly not working from such material as, for example, the South English Legendary accounts, but appears to have been acquainted with the fragments of the legend in the Northern *Cursor Mundi* and Northern Homily Cycle with their homely diction.[173] See also Nassington's poem in the Thornton

---

and Nouv.acq. Fr. 7515) see *La vie Saint Jehan-Baptiste: a critical edition of an old French poem of the early fourteenth century*, ed. Robert L. Gieber (Beiheft zur Zeitschrift für romanische Philologie 164, Tübingen, 1978).

[172] See *The Lyf of Oure Lady*, ed. Sarah M. Horrall (Middle English Texts 17, Heidelberg, 1985).

[173] *Cursor Mundi*, vols II and III.

Lincoln MS, ff. 189ʳ–191ᵛ. In the incipit Thornton appears to assume that this is the 'Tractatus on the Trinity' that was attributed to Nassington.[174] In the 432 lines in octosyllabic couplets the simple hymn addressed to Christ retells the gospel story in a similar register:

> Thow wald nowthir in purpure ne byse
> Be lappede, ne in nan oþer clothes of pryce[.]   (ll. 147–8)

On the other hand, a comparison of octets of the 14-line stanza *Baptist* (lines 44–50) and the 13-line stanza *Truelove* yields more lexical and stylistic parallels:

> Now þis ilk secounde lefe, for [owr] lufe maste,
> Lighte in [þat Lady] þat gabryel grett,
> With-owtten any treson so trewe for to trayste,
> With myrthe in a mayden es god and man mett.
> It es þe Fadir and þe sone and þe haly gaste,
> Thre leues of lufe with-owtenn any lett[.]
>
> *(Truelove, 131–36 Thornton text)*

Apart from the shared vocabulary, each extract shows the same common rhythmic structure of the b-verse (largely expressed in formulas) and similar patterns of alliterating stressed words.

Even more striking is the similarity to the hymn 'Heil be þou, marie, þe modir of crist / Heil þe blessidist þat euere bare child', found in Lambeth MS 853 f. 24ʳ, in which each of the seven-line stanzas with Latin refrain start with the word 'Heil'.[175] What makes this poem more comparable with *Baptist* than with others that open in a similar way is its tripping metre which moves in and out of a strong accentual mode throughout; this, with its occasional strong caesura, could be said to exhibit the unusual b-verse found often in *Baptist*: ~xx/x/(x) (see B13, 20, 22, 28).

Further Middle English Affiliations with the Saints' Hymns

It is notable that, apart from the works of the early 'Katherine Group', written in 'alliterative prose',[176] there are no Middle English

---

[174] The *tractatus* proper is actually a prose translation of Waldby's Latin tract on the Trinity and Unity. For Nassington see p. lxix. Perry's title, 'Religious Poem', is merely generic (Perry, *Religious Pieces*, 63–75).

[175] See *Hymns to the Virgin & Christ, The Parliament of Devils and other Religious Poems*, ed. F. J. Furnivall (EETS, os 24, 1867), pp. 4–5. The MS is dated about 1430.

[176] But note the 'rhythmical system' of, e.g., Ælfric's *Life of Saint Edmund* discussed in Angus McIntosh, 'Early Middle English Alliterative Verse', in Lawton, *ME Alliterative*

alliterative hagiographical poems apart from our three 14-line stanza hymns, *St Erkenwald*,[177] and, possibly *Joseph of Arimathea* (a 'saint' by acclaim, though with no place in the calendar).[178] It is also notable that there are effectively no extant treatments of apostrophe in alliterative verse apart from the treatments in these three hymns (though we might include the first few lines of Pipwel's 'Saint Mary' (see pp. lxvi–lxvii)). So, it can be argued that, as a class, our three hymns stand quite alone within the alliterative tradition.

The unrhymed *Joseph of Arimathea* is clearly one of the earlier productions of the Revival, and, with its broken metrical patterning and alliteration, its single witness is evidently not a sound one. Despite its religious subject, in treatment of the material and in language the poem can be seen to belong to the genre of alliterative Arthurian romances of the 'High Revival', and nothing in it, apart from the exciting 'romance' element of 'legend', suggests a remote ancestry for the saints' hymns. *St Erkenwald* is different again. Although written by an author with North-Western affiliations, the whole manner of this occasional 'London poem', from its Saxon sources, patristic influence, measured narrative quatrains and judicious moderation of tone, could hardly be more different from the springy vociferation of the three stanzaic hymns with their 'oriental' hagiological sources, and ebullient discourse.

However, what is clear is that, in some aspects of style, our texts do resemble other alliterative texts which present religious stories in dramatic or iconographic form. In cadence, rhythm and general tone, it is easy to detect a resemblance to some of the 13-line stanza poems. This is not surprising, as the moral tone and metrical patterns seem to be common to both. *Susannah* is a work that is religious, moral, iconographic and is about a wronged, virtuous woman.[179] In one way its apparent goal is similar to that of *Katherine* and all female hagiography: to set up a righteous woman as moral exemplar. We can hear verbal, rhythmic and syntactic resonances (though more with the 'John' hymns) in one of its simplest stanzas, that, for example, describing Susannah's imprisonment at ll. 170–82:

Poetry, pp. 20–33, and example at p. 31. See also Lawton, 'Introduction', in same volume, *passim*, and Ralph Hanna, 'Alliterative Poetry', in Wallace, *Cambridge History*, pp. 488–512, at pp. 489–90 and *passim*.

[177] *St Erkenwald* is best edited in Turville-Petre, *Alliterative Poetry*, pp. 101–19.

[178] See *Joseph of Arimathea*, ed. David Lawton (New York, 1983).

[179] Best edited as 'A Pistel of Susan', in Turville-Petre, *Alliterative Poetry*, pp. 120–39.

Hyr kynrede, hir cosyns and alle þat hire knewe
Wrong handes, iwis, and wepten wel sare . . .[180]   (ll. 170–1)

Such writing might have been an influence on Spalding and the
poets of the 'John' hymns, and indeed one of the *Susannah* witnesses
(Pierpoint Morgan MS M 818, ff. 1ʳ–5ʳ) evidently was copied by a
scribe from around Swineford, near the Holland fens, and very close
to the scribe of *Katherine* (see LALME profiles (Grid 507:345)). But
it becomes apparent that the stanzaic verse that is closest in flavour to
the alliterative saints' hymns is not so much these individual verse
compositions as that found in the alliterative verse of the guild cycle
and non-cycle dramas. The diction (if not the syntax) of Spalding's
Katherine consistently resonates with that of the vaunting speeches of
the villains of the many of the East-Midland and Northern plays,
even when they are not dealing with this particular tyrant. Much of
this has to do with the virtually identical strong-stress metre and
employment of rhyme, and there are lexical similarities, too. The
well-known speeches of Herod in the N-Town pageants (perhaps of a
Lincoln or Norwich or moveable East-Anglian cycle—a matter still
undecided by the most recent scholarship) will spring to mind.[181] But
Satan's words in *The Second Trial before Pilate*, from the same cycle,
are equally resonant:

> Thus I reyne as a rochand with a rynggyng rowth!
> As a devyl most dowty, dred is my dynt!
> Many a thowsand develys, to me do þei lowth,
> Brennyng in flamys as fyre out of flynt!   (ll. 466–9)

In the light of the Yorkshire provenance of the 'John' hymns, it is
pertinent to compare the language of all three poets of the saints'
hymns with that of the York cycle. A careful reading of the York
plays yields many alliterative lines, the diction and syntax of which
are particularly redolent of *Evangelist* (see also 'Notes' to *Evangelist*),
not so much in the two 14-line York plays, but most noticeably in the
York Barkers 13-line stanza pageant, 'The Fall of the Angels'.[182]

The poetry of the drama from the more westerly provinces (i.e. the
cycles of Chester and Wakefield, and the two remaining Corpus

---

[180] Turville-Petre, *Alliterative Poetry*, p. 131.
[181] See *The N-Town Play*, ed. Stephen Spector (EETS, ss 11, 12, 1991).
[182] See *The York Plays*, ed. Richard Beadle (London, 1982), pp. 49–53. Echoes of all
three hymns here are too numerous to cite. For the two 14-line pageants in the York cycle,
see Kennedy, 'Strong-Stress Metre', pp. 129–30, 135–6, 147–8.

Christi plays from Coventry) yields virtually nothing in language cognate with that of the hymns, but the language of the drama that sounds more like Spalding's Lincolnshire composition is, unsurprisingly, that of the extant East-Anglian plays: the N-town cycle, *Dux Moraud*, the *Castle of Perseverance*, and others. See, for example, from lines 167–69 of the East-Anglian fragment, the 13-line stanza *Dux Moraud*, dated *c.*1400:

> I am comly and curteys and crafty of kynd,
> I am comly castyn fro knottys of care.[183]

Naturally, this begs the question about the place of the verse of the drama in the 'Alliterative Revival' and it is surely time for parameters to be redrawn (see also pp. xxix–xxxi above). It would be over-ingenious and too tempting to conjecture that Spalding was influenced by the language of plays that he may have seen performed in Lincoln, Norwich, or indeed Stamford,[184] or that the *Evangelist* and *Baptist* poets were influenced only by the York (and possibly Beverley or Wakefield) cycles, and that this was what gave their verse its characteristic directness and vitality, but it is far from unlikely that the alliterative language so often employed by the local writers who must have shaped the plays would be an element of a literary milieu that the poets of our hymns were well acquainted with. Oakden dates *Evangelist c.* 1375–1400,[185] and my re-editing bears this out, dating all three hymns *c.*1399. On the other hand, most modern editors agree that the evidence from the records of the drama is that specifically *alliterative* measures of long lines were adopted in rewritings that took place almost certainly well into the fifteenth century. From this late dating of the alliterative redactions of the medieval drama, it appears rather that the rewriting was influenced by a new interest in the works of the Alliterative Revival, perhaps such individual stanzaic compositions as *The Awntyrs* and *The Truelove*, though, more likely, many lost texts. Yet a date before the early 1380s is possible for *Susannah*,[186] and

---

[183] See *Non-Cycle Plays and Fragments*, ed. Norman Davis (EETS, ss 1, 1970), pp. 106–13.

[184] Apart from the N-Town cycle and the East-Anglian fragments, cathedral, church and guild records indicate plentiful dramatic activity in Lincolnshire, including cycles at Lincoln, Boston, Louth and Stamford and pageants, parish plays and guild plays in other towns of importance. See S. J. Kahrl, *Records of Plays and Players in Lincolnshire 1300–1585* (Malone Society VIII, 1974).

[185] Oakden, *Alliterative Poetry*, vol. i, p. 232.

[186] It appears in the Vernon MS (Bodleian Library MS Eng. poet. a. 1) with its sure dating in the 1380s.

much of the stanzaic alliterative material appears to have been composed well within the fourteenth century. It is curious that the 13-line stanzas of the very late East-Anglian *Castle of Perseverance* sometimes seem to echo those of the much earlier Northern romance, *The Awntyrs off Arthure*. We can only assume that the persons employed to write or rewrite such plays were local men who, for some reason, enjoyed the alliterative mode. This would suggest that their influence on the drama of the eastern counties shows something of the geography of the alliterative tradition. It is thus possible to make a tentative hypothesis that there was some flowering of the Revival in the early fifteenth century in the East Midlands (one which can be clearly seen to have made its way into Scotland by the mid-fifteenth century), largely witnessed by the alliterative lines in the plays, but perhaps influenced by a surge of stanzaic alliterative verse of which our hymns are a small surviving example. However, in this matter there can be no certainties. If we assume a later rather than earlier date for *Katherine*, the more easily acceptable fact might be that Spalding in particular *was* influenced by the commonplace, rewritten alliterative tyrant speeches of the guild cycles. If we assume an earlier dating for *Katherine* (say in the 1390s) it may still be that the original tyrant speeches of the fourteenth century that were spontaneously alliterative, though not 'rewritten' in stanzas of the alliterative long line, provided that impetus. We know, from Chaucer's *Miller's Tale* that Herod was acted on a scaffold as early as in the 1380s,[187] and in the early alliterative vaunting speeches from the earliest surviving 'moral play', *The Pride of Life*, which can be dated about 1350, the king speaks thus in his boastful pride: '[I] schal wirch ʒu wo with werkis of wil / And doun schal ʒe drive, be ʒe neuer so dere'.[188] When Spalding composed his lines K117–120, the *Evangelist*-poet his lines E113–17, or the *Baptist*-poet his lines B19–22, were they unconsciously replicating such rudimentary bombast?

The relationship between the language of the drama and that of other Middle English verse compositions—especially in the matter of alliterative works—is not one that has been closely examined. In the light of the preliminary observations made above, and bearing in mind the devotional nature of both genres (the saints' hymns not

---

[187] See *The Riverside Chaucer*, ed. Larry Benson *et al.* (Boston, 1987), *CT* l. 3384.

[188] Lines 119–20, and see the entire speech, in *Non-Cycle Plays and Fragments*, ed. Norman Davis (EETS, ss 1, 1970), pp. 93–4.

noticeably private) it would seem that it is a field worth investigating in more detail.

TREATMENT OF THE TEXTS

Spelling has not been normalized, but initial double *ff* is treated as a capital except in its one mid-line appearance in K2, when it is replaced by *f*. Consonantal *i/j* is employed erratically by the *Katherine* and *Baptist* scribes which presents problems in alliterative texts. It has been normalized in the name 'John' which is always in metrically stressed position, and when in alliterating position with palatal *ch* and *g*, as in, e.g., K259, K260 and B72, but has not been normalized in, e.g., *Jhesu, Ihesu, Iordan* (B50, B101, B102). In the acrostic that parallels K235 an *i* graph is placed against the poem's *I/J*, and at K259 and K260 (a couplet which scribally alliterates on *I/J, i* and *ch*), *p = y* parallels the poem's *I/J*. A logical step from this would be to modernize *y* as vowel to *i* and transcribe all apparent *j* graphs as *i*, but this would leave the problem (albeit a visual one) of *i/I* alliterating with affricative *ch* and *g*. I have chosen a compromise which I think fits best in the circumstances.

Punctuation is editorial, cognizance having been taken of the manuscript punctuation; all three scribes have careful method as regards capitalization. Word division has generally been regularized to conform with the usage of MED, and that of previous editors has been disregarded. The *Katherine* MS has twelve instances of uneven notation (e.g., K173: *fulsone*; K251: *a sent*)—all unproblematical and regularized. The *Evangelist* MS presents forty-one cases of Thornton's characteristic spacious word division, e.g., *be kende* (E98), *euer ilk a* (E139). Of these, thirty-six have been regularized, and, for varying reasons, several have been hyphenated: *ay-whare* (E24); *by-dene* (E25, E50, E51); *in-with* (E52); *for-sothe* (E176); and *vpe-ryghte* (E192); see further 'Notes'. The *Baptist* MS has fifteen instances of unusual word division, largely due to scribal misreading, e.g., *borion and* (B90), *fulworthy* (B127). However, in five instances, some of the idiosyncratic prepositions or prefixes have been subjected to editorial hyphenation : *al-holy* (B30); *many-folde* (B38); *a-plight* (B47); *be-[f]orne* (B53); *on-one* (B67); see also 'Notes'.

The graphs for *n* and *u* are indistinguishable in the manuscripts, as are *þ* and *y* in *Katherine* except in two places (see n. 9). Where this is problematic in interpretation the issues are discussed in the 'Notes'. *Baptist* has many instances of indistinguishable þ and *y* graphs, but also some gradations of *y* graphs towards a full secretary *y*. This has not led to any problems in interpretation. ȝ is expanded throughout. þ*ᵉ* is given its common value. þ*ˢ* and *w*ᵗ are expanded to þis and *with* in conformity with the full forms (in *Katherine* the occurrence of the *i*-form, together with the word *wi*ˢ, written in error in K115, gives enough support for an expansion of the abbreviated *w*ᵗ to *with*). þᵗ is expanded to þat in accordance with the phonology of all three texts. In *Baptist*, MS þᵘ (12 times) is expanded in accordance with the orthographically more Northern þou, not with MS full forms *thow*/ þow (14 times), as these are almost certainly East Midland scribal.

Letters in square brackets indicate editorial emendations to the text.

The apparatus, which refers to line numbers, indicates MS readings that have been emended in this edition. Words within a lemma are taken from the text. The square brackets from the text are omitted within the lemmas. Emendations adopted from those of previous editors are indicated by the italicized initials *P* (Perry, 1861, rev. 1914), *Hs* (Heuser, 1907), *Hlt* (Holthausen, 1937) and *D* (Day, 1921).

Some points on issues of the individual manuscripts follow.

Katherine

There are no reasons for thinking that the crossed *ll* is a flourish, as often in other MSS, because *alle* is found as a full form in six of its seven occurrences, and *all* does not seem to occur in Middle English. The fully written ending ~*sse* is not found, but, as uncrossed ~*ss* is not employed in the MS either (cf. *blis* K274), it is assumed that the scribe was as consistent with *ff* as with ~*ll*, and the traverse crossing has been expanded to ~*e* throughout. Barred nasals are problematic. They occur over long *n* in **Qweñ*, K7; **maydeñ*, K145; *orisoñ*, K170; *faunchoñ*, K185; *prisoñ*, K212; *resoñ*, K214; **ameñ*, K281; over short *n* in *gyñ*, K150; *soñbeem*, K252; *kateryñ*, K265; **kyñg*, K273, and over *m* in *lym̃*, K162. A certain sign that the bar is a flourish is its employment in the final *Amen*; in three other instances (marked * above) expansion is not legitimate. Furthermore, terminal long *m* is *not* barred, in *hem* ('Frontispiece', l. 21), *adam* K227, *Quan* K149 and *mayden* K186. Thus the barred nasal has not been expanded in any instance. *Hs* and *Hlt* expand in *orisoñ*, *faunchoñ*, *prisoñ* and *resoñ* to ~*oun*. From the evidence of this MS, there are no palaeographical grounds for such an expansion. The expansion of the terminating ~ñ to ~*un* in, for example, *resoñ* (K214), contradicts the three other spellings of the full form: *reson* (K14, K15 and K45). The ~*on* spelling is equally common in Middle English, and indeed the concurrent *prisonere* appears in K183. Previous editors are not necessarily wrong here, though their readings could be correct but ill-founded, in that an exemplar with terminal *ū* = *un* on these words may have been copied as terminal long *ñ*. However, there is neither phonological nor palaeographical evidence in this MS that terminal OF ~*on* should become ~*oun*, and the barred *n* is not here expanded in these OF derivatives. Previous editorial decisions as regards *i/j* and *u/v* are disregarded. The latter would show Holthausen's rationalization of the text against clear manuscript evidence, an intention seen also in his substitution of the fricative ending -*ht* for -*th* throughout; this does not help us note that terminal -*ht* (either scribal or earlier) is employed once at in *myht* (K10).

Evangelist

The seventy-two nasal bars are read as otiose because otiose bars over the *n* of *Jhoñ* in E14 and *Ameñ* in E266 indicate that its employment elsewhere is probably a flourish. Thornton is inclined to spell rhyming words with the same number of minims, and the evidence of such rhyming words (as in, e.g., E183–89) shows that the nasal bars are otiose. Because Perry's edition was revised in 1914, Horstmann's edition can now, in effect, be seen as the earliest. Horstmann expanded seventy of the seventy-two nasal bars in the MS, giving readings such as *manekynde* (E1), *pene* (E132) and *Amene* (E266). There are two instances where Horstmann does not expand, but edits with a printed nasal bar: *lurdañs* (E117) and *delfyñge* (E156); the latter reading is rational, but Horstmann's reluctance to read *lurdane* in the presence of *Ephesyme* and *Amene* is inexplicable. His seventy -*me* and -*ne* readings are not included in the apparatus of the edited text. Perry evidently sees some of the nasal bars as meaningful and expands to: son*n*es, E35; lym*m*e, E113 (Perry l. 111); com*m*es, E154 (Perry l. 152); bewan*n*e E183 (Perry l. 181); son*n*e, E200 (Perry l. 198); command-me*n*t, E243 (Perry l. 241). In the matter of final -*e*, Perry adds an *e* to *ilk*, E60 (Perry l. 58), perhaps because Thornton usually does; there is no *e* in the MS, and no sign that *k* carries an indicator of curtailment. In the case of *wirchip* (E254) Horstmann and Perry (both at their edited l. 252) read the pen slip from the diacritic on the second *i* as some sort of abbreviation mark. Conversely, Perry does not read either the clear, fully written, round terminal -*e* in *childe*, E63 (Perry l. 61), or in *wepede*, E197 (Perry l. 195).

Baptist

The rearrangement of two stanzas and some lines (see textual apparatus and 'Notes'), recovers more of the narrative that is embedded in the disordered witness. There are eight ambiguous flourishes which may indicate final -*e*, as on *stan'* (B70), but neither the phonology of a late Northern text nor the heteromorphic metre demand expansion, and the flourish on MS *lawe'* (B36) shows that they may well all be superfluous. The phonology of the rhymes might give cause for concern that the text has not been restored to something closer to its evident Northern original. The problem with starting such a venture would be in deciding where to stop, and, as this is the first critical edition with line and stanza order restored, it establishes a basic profile of a Northern archetype with a strong East Midland layer in the transmission of the single witness. Further editions will undoubtedly ensue.

SELECT BIBLIOGRAPHY WITH ABBREVIATIONS USED IN THIS EDITION

TEXTS AND EDITIONS

Acta Capitulorum Generalium Ordinis Fratrum B.V. Mariae de Monte Carmelo, 2 vols (Rome, 1912, 1934).

Acta Johannis, ed. M. Bonet (Paris, 1898); ed. K. Schäferdiek, in R. McWilson, ed., *Acts of John* in E. Hennecke, *New Testament Apocrypha*, ed. W. Schneemelcher (London, 1965), pp. 188–259; ed. Eric Junod and Jean-Daniel Kaestli, 2 vols (Corpus Christianorum Series Apochryphorum I, Turnhout, 1983).

Acta Sanctorum Bollandi (Antwerp, 1643–1940).

Analecta Bollandiana (Brussels, 1882–).

Analecta hymnica: Dreves, G. M., and Blume, C., *Analecta hymnica Medii Ævi*, 50 vols (Leipzig, 1886–1922).

Awntyrs: *The Awntyrs of Arthure at the Tern Wathelyn*, ed. F. J. Amours, in *Scottish Alliterative Poems in Riming Stanzas* (STS 27, 38, Edinburgh, 1892, 1897), pp. 116–171; *The Awntyrs off Arthure at the Terne Wathelyne*, ed. R. J. Gates (Philadelphia, 1969); *The Awntyrs off Arthure at the Terne Wathelyn*, ed. R. Hanna III (Manchester, 1974).

Baptist: *The Alliterative Hymn to St John the Baptist*; ed. Mabel Day as 'Hymn to St. John the Baptist', in *The Wheatley Manuscript: Middle English Verse and Prose in British Museum MS. Additional 39574* (EETS, os 155, 1921 (for 1917)), pp. 15–19; ed. Ruth Kennedy, in 'The Alliterative Katherine Hymn: A Stanzaic Poem of the Late Fourteenth Century' (Unpublished Ph.D. thesis, University of Bristol, 1991), Appendix, pp. 418–446.

Bibliotheca hagiographica latina antiquae et mediae aetatis (Brussels, 1898–1911).

Bokenham: *Osbern Bokenham: Legends of Hooly Wummen*, ed. M. S. Serjeantson (EETS, 206, 1938).

Capgrave: *John Capgrave: The Life of St. Katharine of Alexandria*, ed. C. Horstmann with forewords by F. J. Furnivall (EETS, os 100, 1893).

Cursor Mundi, ed. R. Morris, 3 vols (EETS, os 57, 59, 62, 68, 99, 101, 1874–93).

Digby: *The Digby Plays: The Late Medieval Religious Plays of Bodleian MSS.*

Digby 133 and E. Museo 160, ed. D. C. Baker, J. L. Murphy and L. B. Hall (EETS, 283, 1982).

Eusebius: Historia Ecclesiastica, ed. K. Lake, 2 vols (London, 1927), Books IV and V; ed. D. Vallarsi, *A Translation of Eusebius's Chronicles with Jerome's Additions*, 11 vols (PL 22–30).

Evangelist: The Alliterative Hymn to Saint John the Evangelist; ed. C. Horstmann, 'Of Sayne Johne þe euangelist', in *Altenglische Legenden: Neue Folge* (Heilbronn, 1881), No 23, pp. 467–71; ed. G. G. Perry, 'Of Sayne Iohan the Euaungelist', in *Religious Pieces in Prose and Verse from R. Thornton's MS* (EETS, os 26, 1867, revised 1914 (for 1913)), pp. 97–105; ed. Ruth Kennedy, in 'The Alliterative Katherine Hymn: A Stanzaic Poem of the Late Fourteenth Century' (Unpublished Ph.D. thesis, University of Bristol, 1991), Appendix, pp. 360–417.

Gilte Legende: Translation of the Legende Dorée of Jean de Vignay by 'a synfulle wretche' (London, 1438) (STC 24873).

The Golden Legend, ed. William Caxton, (London, 1483).

Hilton, Walter, *Scale of Perfection*: R. Birts, '"The Scale of Perfection" by Walter Hilton Canon at the Augustinian Priory at Thurgarton, Book i, Chapters 38–52' (Unpublished B.Litt. thesis, University of Oxford, 1952); *Walter Hilton: The Scale of Perfection*, ed. Thomas H. Bestul (TEAMS Middle English Texts Series, Kalamazoo, 2000).

—— *Mixed Life: Walter Hilton's On Mixed Life: edited from Lambeth Palace MS 472*, ed. S. J. Ogilvie-Thomson (Salzburg Studies: Elizabethan and Renaissance 92:15, Salzburg, 1986).

Horstmann, C., *Altenglische Legenden: Neue Folge* (Heilbronn, 1881).

—— *Yorkshire Writers*, I: *Richard Rolle of Hampole, an English Father of the Church, and his Followers* (London, 1895).

—— 'La estoire de Euangelie', in *The Minor Poems of the Vernon MS*, I (EETS, os 98, 1892), pp. 1–11.

Isidore: *Sancti Isidori Hispalensis Episcopi, De ortu et obitu patriarcharum* (Cologne, 1617) (PL 81–84).

Jacobus de Voragine: The Golden Legend, selected and translated Christopher Stace, introduction and notes Richard Hamer (London, 1998).

Jean de Mailly: Abrégé des Gestes et Miracles des Saints, transl. A. Dondaine (Bibliothèque d'Histoire Dominicaine I, Paris, 1947), St Katherine at pp. 497–502.

Katherine: The Alliterative Katherine Hymn; ed. W. Heuser, 'Die Katherinenhymne des Ricardus Spaldyng und eine Marienhymne derselben Pergamentrolle', *Anglia*, 30 (1907), 523–48; ed. F. Holthausen, 'Ein Mittelenglischer Katharinenhymnus von Richard Spalding', *Anglia*, 60 (1937), 150–64; ed. Ruth Kennedy, 'The Alliterative Katherine Hymn: A Stanzaic Poem of the Late Fourteenth Century' (Unpublished Ph.D. thesis, University of Bristol, 1991).

Katherine Group: *The Life of Saint Katherine, from Royal MS. 17 A.xxvii*, ed. E. Einenkel (EETS, os 80, 1884); *The Lives of Women Saints*, ed. C. Horstmann (EETS, os 86, 1886); *Seinte Katerine*, S. R. T. O. d'Ardenne and E. J. Dobson (EETS, ss 7, 1981).

Kurvinen, A., 'The Life of St. Catherine of Alexandria in Middle English Prose' (Unpublished Ph.D. thesis, University of Oxford, 1961).

Lavynham, Richard, *A Litil Tretys on the Seven Deadly Sins, by Richard Lavynham, O. Carm.*, ed. J. P. W. M. Van Zutphen (Rome, 1956).

Leg.Aurea: *Iacobo da Varazza: Legenda Aurea*, 2 vols, ed. P. M. Maggioni (Florence, 1998).

Liber Quotidianus Contrarotulatoris Garderobae, anno regni Regis Edwardi primi vicesimo octavo (London, 1787).

Love, Nicholas, *Nicholas Love's Myrrour of the Blessed Lyf of Jesu Christ*, ed. Elizabeth Salter (Analecta Cartusiana 10, Salzburg, 1974); *Nicholas Love: The mirrour of the blessed lyf of Jesu Christ*, ed. James Hogg and Lawrence F. Powell, 2 vols (Analecta Cartusiana 91, Salzburg, 1989); *Nicholas Love's Mirror of the Blessed Life of Christ*, ed. Michael G. Sargent (Garland Medieval Texts 18, New York, 1992).

Lydgate: *John Lydgate: Minor Poems*, ed. H. N. MacCracken (EETS, 192, 1934).

The Lyf of Oure Lady, ed. Sarah M. Horrall (Middle English Texts 17, Heidelberg, 1985).

Maidstone: *Richard Maidstone's Penitential Psalms*, ed. Valerie Edden (Middle English Texts 22, Heidelberg, 1990).

Mirk's Festial, ed. T. Erbe, Vol. 1 (EETS, es 96, 1905), [Vol. 2 not published].

Misyn, Richard, *The Fire of Love and The Mending of Life or The Rule of Living . . . from the De Emendacione Vitae of Richard Rolle*, ed. Ralph Harvey (EETS, os 106, 1896).

The Northern Homily Cycle, in C. Horstmann, *Altenglische Legenden*, pp. 1–208.

N-Town: *The N-Town Play*, ed. Stephen Spector (EETS, ss 11,12, 1991); *The Mary Play from the N. Town Manuscript*, ed. Peter Meredith (London, 1987); *The Passion Play from the N. Town Manuscript*, ed. Peter Meredith (London, 1990).

Non-Cycle Plays and Fragments, ed. Norman Davis (EETS, ss 1, 1970).

The Parlement of the Thre Ages, ed. M. Y. Offord (EETS, 264, 1959).

Passio: 'Passio S. Katerine: Vulgate Version', in *Seinte Katerine*, ed. S. R. T. O. d'Ardenne and E. J. Dobson (EETS, ss 7, 1981), pp. 132–203.

Pipwel's St Mary: ed. W. Heuser, 'Die Katherinenhymne des Ricardus Spaldyng und eine Marienhymne derselben Pergamentrolle', *Anglia*, 30 (1907), 523–48; ed. F. Holthausen, 'Ein Mittelenglisches Gedicht über die Fünf Freuden Marias', *Anglia*, 59 (1935), 319–21; ed. Carleton

Brown, 'The Five Joys of Our Lady, with Acrostic', in *Religious Lyrics of the Fifteenth Century* (Oxford, 1939), pp. 55–6.

PG: *Patrologiae cursus completus: . . . Series graeca, &c.*, ed. Jacques Paul Migne, 166 vols (Paris, 1857–1883).

PL: *Patrologiae Cursus Completus. Elucidatio in 235 tabulas Patrologiae Latinae Auctore Cartusiensi*, ed. Jacques Paul Migne, 235 vols (Paris, 1800–1875).

Sc.Leg.Saints: *Legends of the Saints in the Scottish Dialect of the Fourteenth Century* (*MS. Cambr. Univ. Gg II.6*), ed. W. M. Metcalfe, 3 vols (Scottish Text Society, 23, 25, 35, 37, Edinburgh, 1896).

SGGK: *Sir Gawain and the Green Knight*, ed. J. R. R. Tolkien and E. V. Gordon, 2nd edn rev. Norman Davis (Oxford, 1967).

Speculum Maioris Vincenti Bvrgvndi, 4 vols, Vol. IV, *Historiale* (Venice, 1591).

Spec.Sacer.: *Speculum Sacerdotale*, ed. H. E. Weatherly (EETS, 200, 1936 (for 1935)).

Susannah: 'The Pistill of Susan', in *Scottish Alliterative Poems in Riming Stanzas*, ed. F. J. Amours (Scottish Text Society 27, 38, Edinburgh, 1897, 1892), pp. 190–245; *Susannah: An Alliterative Poem of the Fourteenth Century*, ed. Alice Miskimin (Yale Studies in English 170, New Haven and London, 1969); 'A Pistel of Susan', ed. Thorlac Turville-Petre, in *Alliterative Poetry of the Later Middle Ages: An Anthology* (London, 1989), pp. 120–139; 'The Pistel of Swete Susan', ed. Russell A. Peck, in *Heroic Women from the Old Testament* (TEAMS Middle English Texts, Kalamazoo, 1991), pp. 73–108.

TowneleyPl.: *The Towneley Plays*, ed. Martin Stevens and A. C. Cawley, 2 vols (EETS, ss 13, 1994).

Truelove: *The Four Leaves of the Truelove*, ed. W. de Worde, *The iiij leues of the trueloue* (London, c.1520) (BL Huth 102; STC 15345); *The Quatrefoil of Love*, ed. I. Gollancz and M. M. Weale (EETS, 195, 1935 (for 1934)); 'The Literary and Textual Context of *The Quatrefoil of Love*', ed. Richard Higgins (Unpublished MA thesis, University of Bristol, 1987), pp. 63–102; 'The Four Leaves of the Truelove', in *Moral Love Songs and Laments*, ed. Susanna Greer Fein (TEAMS Middle English Texts, Kalamazoo, 1998), pp. 161–254.

Uses: *Ordinale Exoniensis*, ed. J. N. Dalton, 4 vols (Henry Bradshaw Society, 37, 38, 63, 79, London, 1909–40); *The Hereford Breviary*, ed. W. H. Frere and L. E. G. Brown, 3 vols (Henry Bradshaw Society, 26, 40, 46, London, 1904–15); *Breviarium ad usum insignis ecclesiae Sarum*, ed. F. Proctor and C. Wordsworth, 3 vols (Cambridge, 1879–86); *Breviarium ad usum insignis ecclesie Eboracensis*, ed. S. W. Lawley, 2 vols (Surtees Society 71, 75, 1880–82).

Vulgate: *Nova vulgata Bibliorum sacrorum editio minor*, Sacrosancti Oecumenici Concilii Vaticani II ratione habita iussu Pauli PP. VI recognita auctoritate Ioannis Pauli PP. II promulgata (Vatican City, 1979).

WarsAlex.: *The Wars of Alexander: an Alliterative Romance translated chiefly from the Historia Alexandri Magni de Preliis*, ed. W. W. Skeat (EETS, ES 47, 1886); *The Wars of Alexander*, ed. H. N. Duggan and T. Turville-Petre (EETS, SS 10, 1989).

WEV/WLV: *The Wycliffite Bible, Early and Late versions: The Holy Bible with the Apocryphal Books, in the earliest English versions made from the Latin Vulgate by John Wycliffe and his Followers*, ed. Josiah Forshall and Frederic Madden, 4 vols (London, 1850).

Yk.Pl.: *The York Plays*, ed. R. Beadle (York Medieval Texts, second series, London, 1982).

OTHER WORKS

André, J. L., 'St. Katherine in Art, Legend and Ritual', *The Antiquary*, xxxvi (1900), 235–41.

Bale, John, *Index Britanniæ Scriptorum* (Basle, 1559).

Borroff, Marie, *Sir Gawain and the Green Knight: A Stylistic and Metrical Study* (Yale Studies in English 152, New Haven, 1962).

Boyce, James, O. Carm., 'The Liturgy of the Carmelites', *Carmelus*, 43 (1996).

Brewer, D. S., and Owen, A. E. B., *The Thornton Manuscript* (Lincoln Cathedral Library MS. 91) (London, 1975, reprinted with Introductions revised, 1977). (*St. John Evangelist* at ff. 231^r–233^r).

Briquet: Briquet, C. M., *Les filigranes: dictionnaire historique des marques du papier, des leur apparition vers 1282 jusqu'en 1600*, 4 vols (Leipzig, 1923 (2è ed. 1966)).

Bronzini, G. B., 'La leggenda di S. Caterina d'Alessandria: passioni greche e latine' (Atti della Accademia nazionale dei Lincei. Memorie, Classe di scienze morali, storiche e filologiche, ser. 8, vol. 9, fasc. 2, 1960), 257–416.

Butler's Lives of the Saints, ed. Herbert Thurston and Donald Attwater, 4 vols (London, 1956), Vol. IV, 623.

Cable, Thomas, *The English Alliterative Tradition* (Philadelphia, 1991).

Copsey, Richard, O. Carm., 'The Carmelites in England 1242–1540: Surviving Writings', *Carmelus*, 43 (1996), 175–224.

—— 'The Carmelites in England 1242–1539: Surviving Writings. Additions and Corrections 1', *Carmelus*, 44 (1997), 188–202.

Daniel, H. A., *Thesaurus hymnologicus*, 5 vols (Leipzig, 1886–1922).

d'Evelyn, C., and F. A. Foster, 'Saints' Legends', in *A Manual of the Writings in Middle English 1050–1500*, ed. J. B. Severs (Connecticut, 1970), Vol. 2, v., 410–40 and 553–645.

Doyle, A. I., 'A survey of the origins and circulation of theological writings in English in the 14th, 15th and early 16th centuries with special consideration of the part of the clergy therein' (Unpublished Ph.D. thesis, University of Cambridge, 1953).

—— 'The Manuscripts', in *Middle English Alliterative Poetry: Seven Essays*, ed. David A. Lawton (Cambridge, 1982), pp. 88–100.

—— 'The Shaping of the Vernon Manuscript', in *Studies in the Vernon Manuscript*, ed. Derek Pearsall (Cambridge, 1990), pp. 1–14.

Dugdale, William, Sir, *Monasticon anglicanum*, ed. John Caley, Henry Ellis and the Rev. Bulkeley Bandinel, 6 vols (London, 1846).

Duggan, H. N., 'The Role of Formulas in the Dissemination of a Middle English Alliterative Romance', *Studies in Bibliography*, 29 (1976), 265–88.

—— 'Alliterative Patterning as a Basis for Emendation in Middle English Alliterative Poetry', *Studies in the Age of Chaucer*, 8 (1986), 73–105.

—— 'The Shape of the B-Verse in Middle English Alliterative Poetry', *Speculum*, 61 (1986), 564–92.

—— 'The Authenticity of the Z-Text of "Piers Plowman": Further Notes on Metrical Evidence', *Medium Ævum*, 56 (1) (1987), 25–45.

—— 'Notes Towards a Theory of Langland's Meter', *Yearbook of Langland Studies*, 1 (1987), 41–70.

—— 'Final -e and the Rhythmic Structure of the B-Verse in Middle English Alliterative Poetry', *Modern Philology*, 86 (2) (1988), 119–45.

Egan, K. J., 'The Establishment and Early Development of the Carmelite Order in England' (Unpublished Ph.D. thesis, University of Cambridge, 1965).

Fawtier-Jones, E. C., 'Les Vies de Sainte-Catherine d'Alexandrie', *Romania*, 56 (1930), 80–104.

Fein, Susanna Greer, 'Twelve-Line Stanza Forms in Middle English and the Date of *Pearl*', *Speculum*, 72 (1997), 367–98.

—— *Moral Love Songs and Laments* (TEAMS Middle English Texts, Kalamazoo, 1998).

Fleming, John, 'The Friars and Medieval English Literature', in *The Cambridge History of Medieval English Literature*, ed. David Wallace (Cambridge, 1999), ch. 13, pp. 349–75.

Gibson, Gail McMurray, *The Theater of Devotion: East Anglian Drama and Society in the Late Middle Ages* (Chicago, 1989).

Halliwell, J. O., *The Thornton Romances* (The Camden Society 30, London, 1844).

Hartley, J. S., and Rogers, A., *The Religious Foundations of Medieval Stamford* (Stamford Survey Group Report 2, Nottingham, 1974).

Hooper, A. G., 'The Lambeth Palace MS of *The Awntyrs off Arthure*', *Leeds Studies in English*, 3 (1934), 37–43.

Hanna, Ralph, III, 'Defining Middle English Alliterative Poetry', in *The*

Endless Knot: Essays on Old and Middle English in Honor of Marie Borroff, ed. M. Teresa Tavormina and R. F. Yeager (Cambridge, 1995), pp. 43–64.

—— 'Booklets in Medieval Manuscripts', in *Pursuing History: Middle English Manuscripts and Their Texts* (Stanford, 1996), pp. 21–34.

—— 'Alliterative Poetry', in *The Cambridge History of Medieval English Literature* (Cambridge, 1999), Chapter 18, pp. 488–512.

Hughes, Jonathan, *Pastors and Visionaries: Religion and Secular Life in Late Medieval Yorkshire* (Woodbridge, 1988).

Humphreys, K. W., *The Book Provisions of the Medieval Friars* (Studies in the History of Libraries and Librarianship 1, Amsterdam, 1964).

Jacobs, Nicholas, 'The Processes of Scribal Substitution and Redaction: A Study of the Cambridge Fragment of *Sir Degarre*', *Medium Ævum*, 53 (1984), 26–48.

Jolliffe, P. S., *A Check-List of Middle English Prose Writings of Spiritual Guidance* (Toronto, 1974).

Jordan, R., *Handbook of Middle English Grammar: Phonology*, trans. and revised by E. J. Crook (The Hague and Paris, 1974).

Kaluza, M., *A Short History of English Versification* (London, 1911).

Keiser, G. R., 'Lincoln Cathedral Library MS. 91: Life and Milieu of the Scribe', *Studies in Bibliography*, 32 (1979), 158–78.

—— 'þe Holy Boke Gratia Dei', *Viator*, 12 (1981), 289–317.

—— 'More Light on the Life and Milieu of Robert Thornton', *Studies in Bibliography*, 34 (1983), 111–18.

—— ' "To Knawe God Almyghtyn": Robert Thornton's Devotional Book', in *Spätmittelalterliche Geistliche Literatur in der Nationalsprache*, ed. James Hogg (Analecta Cartusiana 106, Salzburg, 1984), 2103–29.

—— ' "Noght how lang man lifs; bot how wele": the Laity and the Ladder of Perfection', in *De Cella in Seculum: Religious and Secular Life and Devotion in Late Medieval England*, ed. Michael G. Sargent (Cambridge, 1989), pp. 145–60

Kennedy, Ruth, 'New Theories of Constraint in the Metricality of the Strong-Stress Long Line, Applied to the English Rhymed Alliterative Corpus, *c.*1400', in *Métriques du Moyen Âge et de la Renaissance*, ed. Dominique Billy, afterword by Marc Dominicy (Paris, 1999), pp. 131–44.

—— 'Strong-Stress Metre in Fourteen-Line Stanza Forms', in Kennedy, *Medieval English Measures*, pp. 127–55.

—— 'The Evangelist in Thornton's Devotional Book', forthcoming.

Kennedy, Ruth, ed., *Medieval English Measures: Studies in Metre and Versification* (*Parergon*, n.s., 18.1, Special Issue, 2000).

Ker, N. R., *Medieval Manuscripts in British Libraries*, 3 vols (Oxford, 1977).

Knowles, David, *The Religious Orders in England* (Cambridge, 1948).

Knust, Herman, *Geschichte der Legenden der heiligen Katherina von Alexandrien und der heiligen Maria Aegyptiaca nebst unedierten Texten* (Halle, 1890).

Kurvinen, A., 'Caxton's "Golden Legend" and the Manuscripts of the "Gilte Legende"', *Neophilologische Mitteilungen*, 60 (1959), 353–75.

Lawrence, R. F., 'Formula and Rhythm in "The Wars of Alexander"', *English Studies*, 51 (1970), 97–112.

Lawton, David A., ed., *Middle English Alliterative Poetry: Seven Essays* (Cambridge, 1982).

Lewis, Katherine J., *The Cult of St Katherine of Alexandria in Late Medieval England* (Woodbridge, 2000).

Lickteig, F. B., *The German Carmelites at the Medieval Universities* (Rome, 1981).

Lincoln Cathedral Library, *Catalogue of the Manuscripts in Lincoln Cathedral Chapter Library*, ed. Reginald Maxwell Woolley (London, 1927).

Luick, Carl, 'Die englische Stabreimzeile im XIV, XV, und XVI Jahrhundert', *Anglia*, 11 (1889), 392–443, 553–618.

—— 'Englische Metrik: Geschichte der heimischen Versarten', in *Grundriss der germanischen Philologie*, ed. H. Paul, 3 vols (Strasbourg, 1900–1905), II, 2.

—— *Historische Grammatik der englischen Sprache*, 2 vols (Leipzig, 1914–21, 1929–40).

Macbain, William, ed., *The Life of St. Catherine by Clemence of Barking* (Anglo-Norman Text Society 18, 1964).

McCaffrey, P. R., *The White Friars: An Outline History* (Dublin, 1926).

Macray, W. D., *Catalogi Codicum Manuscriptorum Bibliothecæ Bodleianæ, Part V, fasc.1* (Oxford, 1862).

McCully, C. B. and J. J. Anderson, eds, *English Historical Metrics* (Cambridge, 1996).

MacDonald, G. W., *Historical Notices of the Parish of Holbeach in the County of Lincoln with Memorials of its Clergy from A.D. 1255 to the Present Time* (King's Lynn, 1890).

Madan, Falconer *et al.*, *A Summary Catalogue of Western Manuscripts in the Bodleian Library at Oxford which have not hitherto been catalogued in the Quarto series*, 7 vols in 8 [Vol. II in 2 parts] (Oxford, 1895–1953; reprinted with corrections in vols I and VII, Munich, 1980).

Marnfke, W., *Der älteste englische Marienhymnus* (Leipzig, 1907).

Matonis, Anne, 'A Reexamination of the Middle English Alliterative Long Line', *Modern Philology*, 81 (1984), 339–60.

—— 'Non-*aa/ax* Patterns in ME Alliterative Long-Line Verse', in *English Historical Metrics*, ed. C. B. McCully and J. J. Anderson (Cambridge, 1996), pp. 134–49.

Mone, F. J., *Lateinische Hymnen des Mittelalters aus Handschriften herausgegeben und erklärt, etc.*, 3 vols (Freiburg, 1853–5).

Mustanoja, T. F., *A Middle English Syntax: Part I. Parts of Speech* (Mémoires de la Société Néophilologique de Helsinki 23, Helsinki, 1960).

Oakden, J. P., *Alliterative Poetry in Middle English*, 2 vols (Manchester, 1930, 1935).

Ogden, Margaret S., ed., *The Liber de Diversis Medicinis in the Thornton MS* (EETS, 207, 1938 (for 1936)), Introduction, pp. viii–xvi.

Peck, Francis: *Academia Tertia Anglicana; or, the Antiquarian Annals of Stamford by Francis Peck* (*London, 1727*), with a new introduction by A. Rogers and J. S. Hartley (London, 1979).

Poskitt, Margaret, 'The English Carmelite Province: 15th Century', *Aylesford Review*, 1 (1956), 98–100.

—— 'The English Carmelites: Houses of Study and Educational Methods', *Aylesford Review*, 5 (1963), 226–37.

Ramsay, W. M., *The Church in the Roman Empire before A.D. 170* (London, 1903).

Robinson, Pamela R., 'The "Booklet": A Self-Contained Unit in Composite Manuscripts', *Codicologia*, 3 (1980), 46–69.

Rolfe, J. C., ed., *Suetonius*, 2 vols (Loeb Classical Library, London, 1913, 1914).

Rogers, A., *The Making of Stamford* (Leicester, 1965).

Rushe, J. P., 'The Origin of S Mary's Gild in Connection with Corpus Christi College, Cambridge' (Proceedings of the Cambridge Antiquarian Society, n.s. 16 (1), 1912), 20–52.

Sargent, Michael, 'The Transmission by the English Carthusians of Late Medieval Spiritual Writings', *Journal of Ecclesiastical History*, 27 (1976), 225–40.

Smet, J., *The Carmelites: A History of the Brothers of Our Lady of Mount Carmel ca.1200 A.D. until the Council of Trent* (Rome, 1975).

Stern, Karen, 'The London "Thornton" Miscellany: A New Description of British Museum Manuscript 31042', *Scriptorium*, 30 (1976), 201–18.

Thompson, J. J., 'Robert Thornton and his Book Producing Activities: Aspects of the Transmission of Certain Late Medieval Texts in the Light of Their Present Context in Thornton's Manuscripts' (Unpublished D.Phil. thesis, University of York, 1983).

—— 'The Compiler in Action: Robert Thornton and the "Thornton Romances" in Lincoln Cathedral MS 91', in *Manuscripts and Readers in Fifteenth-Century England*, ed. Derek Pearsall (Cambridge, 1983), pp. 113–24.

—— *Robert Thornton and the London Thornton Manuscript* (London, 1987).

Thompson, R. M., ed., *Catalogue of the manuscripts of Lincoln Cathedral Chapter Library* (Cambridge, 1989).

Toulmin Smith, Lucy, ed., *English Gilds* (EETS, os 40, 1870).

Turville-Petre, Joan, 'The Metre of "Sir Gawain and the Green Knight"', *English Studies*, 57 (1976), 310–28.

Turville-Petre, Thorlac, *The Alliterative Revival* (Cambridge, 1977).

—— 'Emendation on Grounds of Alliteration in *The Wars of Alexander*', *English Studies*, 61 (1980), 302–17.

—— *Alliterative Poetry of the Later Middle Ages: An Anthology* (London, 1989).

Varnhagen, H., *Zur Geschichte der Legende der Katherina von Alexandrien* (Erlangen, 1891).

Vriend, J., *The Blessed Virgin Mary in the Medieval Drama of England* (Purmerend, 1928).

Waldron, R. A., 'Oral-Formulaic Technique and Middle English Alliterative Poetry', *Speculum*, 32 (1957), 792–804.

Wallace, David, *The Cambridge History of Medieval Literature* (Cambridge, 1999).

Westlake, H. F., *The Parish Gilds of Mediæval England* (London, 1919).

Wilson, R. M., 'Some Lost Saints' Lives in Old and Middle English', *Modern Language Review*, 36 (1941), 161–72.

—— *The Lost Literature of Medieval England*, 2nd edn (London, 1970).

Zimmerman, R. P. B., ed., *Monumenta Historica Carmelitana* (Levins, 1907).

ADDITIONAL ABBREVIATIONS

AN	Anglo-Norman
ASD	*Anglo-Saxon Dictionary* and Supplement, ed. Bosworth and Toller
BL	British Library
CUL	Cambridge University Library
DNB	Dictionary of National Biography
EETS	Early English Text Society (os/es/ss: Original Series/Extra Series/Supplementary Series)
L	Latin
LALME	McIntosh *et al.*, *A Linguistic Atlas of Late Mediaeval English*
ME	Middle English
MED	*Middle English Dictionary*
OE	Old English
OED	*Oxford English Dictionary*
OF	Old French
OI	Old Icelandic
ON	Old Norse
STC	*Short Title Catalogue of Early Printed Books*

Summ.Cat.   *Bodleian Library Summary Catalogue of Western Manuscripts*
Vulgata   Vulgate *Passio* of St Katherine of Alexandria

The abbreviations for grammatical forms are those recommended by EETS and listed in, for example, *The Ayenbite of Inwyt*, ed. Pamela Gradon (EETS, 278, 1979), p. 235.

THE ALLITERATIVE
KATHERINE HYMN

I

Katereyn, þe curteys of alle þat I know,
  cumlyest kepyng kaytefs fro kare,
Of lyth þou art lanterne to leche hem below,
  to leede hem þat þe loue fro bales ful bare.
For no throng of no threte þou woldest not ouerthrow,   5
  bot tholyd thykly, thank of vs, care;
Qwen þe tyraunt trayfoly walde turne þe, I trow,
  with towchyng of turnement he tynt [þe] to spare.
To spare þe he tynt þere,
Qwen he his myht mynt þere,   10
To momyl on his mawment;
And, for þou styfly stynte þere,
As fyre doth of flynt þere
þi resons hym rent.

2

Katereyn with hyre resons þat rwd þus sche rent;   15
  sche rowth not of his rialte, hir rewle was so rithe;
And so þat bostful belamy þat beerd so bent
  þat neþer bewte ne bonchif abode in his bythe.
þan to seke schofferes his sergauntes he sent,
  to se qwo schuld scort hyre sawes in his sythe.   20
Fyfti fyne retorikes in hast þei hem hent;
  of clargy in kyngdames þe hyest were hythe.
Heyest were þei hythe þan,
And most made of myth þan,
Clergi to kepe.   25
He, þe beerde bryth, þan,
Soche poyntes hem pyth þan
To her lore þei lepe.

K8 þe] not

3

Katereyn þus ful lufly sche lawth to here lore
　　lythly fyfty retorikes to lede in hyr lees.　　　　　　　30
Alle þei bowed hir blely and blessed hire ibore,
　　and bonde hem to hire biddyng before al þe prees.
þan þat cursud cay[tef], was kyng þere icore,
　　commaund his commyneres, cantly in rees,
To forme a fyre ferly, his face þere before,　　　　　　　35
　　alle þo fyfty fe[l]a[w]ys in fyre to fees.
In fyre he wolde fees hem,
But al dyd hit plese hem,
For hurt hade þei none.
And for þei to-ches hem　　　　　　　　　　　　　　　40
No paryng to p[r]es hem
Was of on here alone.

4

Katereyn, wyttily þus þou wit wanne
　　qwen þo wyȝthes at þi wyl here wordes had wonne;
þo þi rial resons to ryth so þei ranne,　　　　　　　　　45
　　þer now þe[i] reygn rially þat rewly haue ronne.
In mankynde so mytthyly was neuer mane
　　haþ fyfty wyȝthes be his worde so wittily wonne;
Qwerefore þat thef thankles thyrsted þe þane
　　and bad throw þe in a t[h]rowe thyk fro þe sonne.　　　50
Thyk in a t[h]rowe þus,
He made his wow þus,
þe t[welue] dayes to sitte;
To hym þe to low þus,
No mete he wil alow þus,　　　　　　　　　　　　　55
To turne þi witte.

5

To turne þi witte hym tarying þe tredyd þat traytour
　　qwen þou were throw throghe; but Trewþe þer þe tente

K31 blessed] second s superimposed on a previously-written t in an original blest.
K33 caytef] Hlt capfte　　　　K36 felawys] Hlt fesawnt'ps　　　　K41 pres] Hlt ples
K46 þei] Hlt pe　　　　K50 throwe] Hlt trowe　　　　K51 throwe] Hlt trowe
K53 twelue] Hlt too

Qwen a dentywos dowf made þe to dewre,
  and dyth þe fro derknes and solace þe sente.   60
Solace sothe þe soþly of oure sauyour,
  qwen he saw þe in sorowes, to save þin entent,
And schewd þe þe salf of his sokour,
  qwen he seyed seemly, 'For me þou schalt be schente;
For me þou schalt be blamyd;   65
Be not þerfore aschamyd
þe deth for to take;
And, for þou schalt be famyd,
Fayre haue I framyd
A crowne for þi sake.'   70

6

Katereyn for þi sake þe sothe þan, for to sene
  þe solas of þat savyour þat schap þe to schame;
Qwen pertly to Porfiri presed þe qwene
  and prayed hym plese þe porter to se Katereyn same,
þere þei com to Katereyn, comly and clene,   75
  to commen with þat curtays and knowen of hyre game,
Al bemus of briȝtnes abowt hyre þer beene,
  and with hire bawmyng of blis þo briddus sche brogth
    tame.
þo briddes brogth sche tame so,
Bothe queen and knyȝt be name so,   80
To cristen beleue;
Qwen grace was hir game so,
No grymme myth hem grame so,
So dethe was hem leue.

7

þat deth þat is derue here to dye not þei dowte   85
  qwen þei departe fro þat dere, sche drof [h]e[m] fro drede.
No lenger sche þat was lost to hire lo[rd]e þan wold lowte,
  bot longly la[b]owrid him with al his gret lede.
þan stode he astonyd, sturdy and stowte;
  he stranglyd hymselue so he strof, almost, in dede;   90

K86 hem] *Hlt* þe   K87 lorde] *Hlt* lowe lowte] þei lowt   K88 labowrid] *Hlt* lagowrid

And, for his qween schortly schamed not his schowte,
    he schope hir to schrynk qwen sche schuld blood schede.
Her blod sche did schede þo
Qwen þei vnwrapped hir wed þo,
Hir pappes for to kerf.   95
Here my[nd] was on hir mede þo,
þe swerde sche myth not fre[de] þo,
þat hir hede schuld sterf.

8

þus sterved þe qween strongly of hym þat was sterne,
    and now sti[rt] may sche not so stytly sche stode;   100
þan Porphyri litthly, as loue gane hym lerne,
    he wonde hire wowndyd in a wed and grof hire ful goode.
þere dredles þe deueles lym wax wondur derne
    and dispised dedly, to deel þer hys mode:
'Qwat bachilere was so bold awey hir to berene,   105
    eyþer to beryen hir bones or hyr blode?
Hir bones and hir [blode] als,
With mytthynes of mode als?'
Porphiri sayde:
'þat dede dyd I good als.   110
For I schuld feel hir fode als,
In graue I hir layede.'

9

þan sprong þat cursed kayesere as spere in hert sprunge;
    he spared no speche to þe pepul fast for to spende;
He seyde, his tene wi[th] hi[m] for to tempure and to
        tellen with tunge,   115
    as þat his trw tutor wold not entende:
'Allas!' sayd þat caytyf, 'Qwat woo hath þe wrunge?
    To wirkyn aȝens me neuer I þe [w]ende!
þou schalt for þi traytury to turment be slounge,
    to fecchen alle þi ferys, fro foly hem to fende!'   120
Fro foly þere he fende hym
With mekenes to mende hym

K96 mynd] *Hlt* mpth   K97 frede] *Hs* fre   K100 stirt] stif   K107 hir
blode] *Hs* hir   K115 with him] *Hlt* wi^s hir   K118 wende] *Hlt* reende

To þe deth qwen he went;
Euer Porphiri wende hym
Goddys merci to mende hym,   125
For his heed was hi[m] rent.

10

þan was lufly Katereyn lyft vp oloft
    and laȝgth fro þat low lake, þat lurdeyn to lef.
He sayd to þat semly, her sorowes for to soft,
    'And send our syre þi sacrifice, no schame schal þe gref   130
And I schal crowne þe in þe court of our goddesse croft,
    and after my first chosyn I chese þe þe chef.
And, bot þou folow þis fast, faynt schalt þou oft
    qwyles any fresch freye may feel þe to mef:
Qwyles þat þou meue mayst   135
And feel any greue mayst
With punchyng of peles,
Siþ not my god þou leue mayst,
Prestly þou preue mayst
Turnyng of qweles!'   140

11

Wyth wrenchis and wylys þus wrogth he his wrake
    with a wondurful cast þat wiȝth to wynne.
Al here vertuus werk for wychcraft was take,
    for sche wrogth not his wille, for sleyȝt ne for gynne.
þan made he þat mayden, hi[r] mynde for to make,   145
    to medyl hire with mischef, hir myȝth for to mynne.
So slely þat sleyȝth so deuly was schake
    þat four thowsand of þat thref thyrst were ful thynne.
Qwan þat throng was thyn þan
Disjoyned was þat gyn þan,   150
Selcouyth in syȝth!
Matrones more and [myn] þan,
With maydens, wold not blyn þan
To wepe for þat wyȝth.

K126 him] *Hlt* his   K145 hir] *Hlt* his   K152 myn] *Hlt* manp

12

þan þat beerde briʒthest brast on a breyd;   155
   to þo buntiful beerdes abooue sche hem bilde;
To haue no pyte on hir peyne, prestly sche preyd;
   So al hir pert pouste in payn[i]e hit was pilde.
þan þat sory senatour sodanly seyd,
   for sche so þo feres freschely had fylde,   160
Liʒthly with a swerd hire lyf schuld be leyd.
   To lawnch þat lym lusty hir nek was ful milde.
As feythful to fynde here,
And comly ful kynd here,
Sche prayed for hir frendys,   165
þat qwoso wold [hem bynde] here
To haue hire in mynde here
To fende hem fro fendys.

13

An heylyng ful hendly Katereyn þer hente
   qwen he þat was hyʒest hyr orison herde,   170
And seyd, 'My dere derlyng, to Trewth take entent,
   for þei schal lif at þi lust on þi loue haf lerede.
To save þe ful sone I am at asent,
   to fende þe fro fyendys wald make þe aferde,
For alle þe meyne of myrþe hely haue mente   175
   to myrthe þe with melody qwen myth hath þe merde.
Qwen merde haþ þe myʒth þus,
þe schal I lyʒth þus
Ful hyʒe vp in heuen;
As semly in oure siʒth þus   180
Schalt þou rest oriʒth þus
þour stiffenes of steuen.'

14

þan prestly þat prisonere hir nek forth sche pytte
   and preuyd hirself purly qwen peyne did hir prik.
Fersly with a faunchon þat comly was kitte   185
   þat milk fro þat mayden throng þere ful thik.
þus was þe cors knytt of a kaytyf vnknyit

qwen sche was woundid vnworthi, as woful and wik.
And as fresch fesaunt to hire fere þan sche flyit,
    qwen fayntly sche foundyed as a flayn flik,   190
þan þat flik flayn newe
Angeles ful fayn newe
Hir body þei fett.
With my3th and with mayn newe
Hir þat was slayn newe   195
In Syna þei sett.

15

To Syna ful scherply sothly þei flye,
    qwen þei hadd fet þat fe[iþ]ful, farly to feel.
To Crist for þat curteys comly þei crye,
    for þei knewe wele þat Katereyn our karis schuld here
      keel.   200
My3tthily o þat mount with melodye
    þei mynt for to myrthe vs at euere-ilka meel.
þerefore thanke hyre to herbor[o]gh hye
    qwer, fro hire, realy, oyl-riueres reel.
Oyl releþ oft so   205
Fro hir vp oloft so
Sekenes to socure;
þus salf fro hir soft so
Commeth fro hir croft so,
Hir to honoure.   210

16

þis peyne þat sche preuyd I rede þou it pondur,
    þat sche put þe fro prison qwere peyne is ful prest.
For alle þat hire worchipes sche wardeþ hem with wondur
    and reuleþ hem be reson þat recheþ hem to rest.
Qwen þou tretest in tempest of hayl or of thondur   215
    sche koueres þe kyndly fro kares þe to kest,
And sendys þe surauns, þi sorowes for to sondur,
    and brynges þe to bonchef, þi bales to brest.

Lines K188 *and* K190, *which are adjacent in the MS, have been interchanged.*
K198 feiþful] *Hlt* fepiful   K203 herborogh] herborgh   K204 oyl-riueres]
Hlt oyl riueres reue*res*

Fro balys to blysse þor
Wytty sche wysse þor   220
þat haue hire in mynde.
No myȝth may sche misse þor,
For Crist graunt hir þisse þor,
Qwere sche was pynde.

17

k   Kepe hem here, Katereyn, al þat þe calle,   225
    and kache hem fro kares qwen þei krepen in klay;
a   And hem þat are of Adam [heres] here, alle,
    fro þe aungeles of angwysch þou a[uert] hem ay.
t   Turne away al traytures, turtyl so talle,
    þat towchyn vs with turmentys of tene and of tray.   230
e   Euer entrik þou our enmyes to falle;
    entyr þou oure herandys to Crist euerei day.
r   Reche vs blysse blyth þer,
i   Jentyl in loue liþ þer,
    Oure foos for to fende.   235
n   Now swynk þou for vs swith þere,
a   Ay kyndnes to [k]iþ þere,
    Oure myrthys for to mende.

18

Ri   Ryal þou reyngnest qwere ryalte is ryf,
    and rewlyst hem þat be rwd and redyn on þe rent.   240
car   Carpyng of þi curtesy kep vs fro þat cnyf
    þat cursurdly karueth vs qwen we to synne sent.
d   Dyntes of deuelys dere fro vs dryue
    þat doluyn ben in derckenesse deply adent.
us   Us qwi[t]h of his vertues qwere þou art wyffe,   245
    þat wyȝthly wroȝgth al, with qwom þou art went.
    With qwom þou art went now,
    Heel þou vs hent now,
    Uirgyn so cleen.
    Her bales ma[k]yst þou blent now,   250
    To lerne þe asent now,
    Sonbeem so scheen.

K227 heres here] here   K228 auert] awtur   K237 kiþ] *Hlt* hip
K245 qwith] quich   K250 makyst] mayst

19

s Schere away charp schowres þat schap vs to schrik,
  and schaf awey chames þat schrunk be in schenchip;
pal Pales vs with pyte, and pride fro vs pik;   255
  put vs fro þis pouert and put vs to wirchip;
ð Draw vs to þi dyngnite fro þis depe dyk,
  and to þi dentiwos dool qwere deieþ euer demschip.
ȝ Joyne vs to Jesu, þat chesus hym lyk;
  chef of our jornay, we chees euer þi frenchip.   260
n Now þi frenchip to fynde ay,
g God on þe make our mynde ay,
  Oure mede to encresse.
  þo pynchars vs haf pynd ay,
  þou kille hem, Kateryn, kynd ay,   265
  And profor vs þi pesse.

20

I grete þe, most gracyous to governe hem al
  þat geder þe to hir giyld, hem for to gyde.
Fe[n]d vs, feer fa[i]þful, þat vs no foly fal,
  for [f]eynthed and freelte we feel vs besyde.   270
Saue þou our sawles synful qwen þei apere schal,
  and wi[n] vs to þi wonnyng fro þis woo wyde.
To þat kyng þat is kyndest, Katereyne, vs cal,
  þat born was our broþur, in blis we to abyde.
Katereyne to þat kyng vs   275
  þat on crosse for hyng vs,
  Vs alle mut þou wysse.
To þat b[li]sse he bryng vs
  Qwere aungeles schul syng vs
  With joye and with blysse.   280

Amen.

K269 Fend] Feed   faiþful] fapful   K270 feynthed] *Hlt* sepnthed   K272 win] wᵗ
K278 blisse]*Hlt* bilsse

THE ALLITERATIVE
JOHN EVANGELIST HYMN

OF SAYNE JOHN þE EUAUNGELIST

1

f. 231ʳ Of all mankynde þat He made þat maste es of myghte
And of þe molde merkede and mesured that tyde,
Wirchipede be þou Euaungelist with euer-ilke-a wyghte
þat He wroghte in this werlde wonnande so wyde.
Louede be þou lufely, lugede in lyghte.　　　　5
To life ay in lykynge þat lorde the relyde
That in Bedleme was borne of a byrde bryghte.
That barne brynge vs to blysse þare beste es to byde;
To byde in His blysse
Thare He es and His　　　　10
Dysciples ilkone;
Whare myrthe may noghte mysse
That waye þou vs wysse,
Euaungelist J[oh]n.

2

John, as þe gete or ge[m dere and] gente,　　　　15
As jasper, þe jowell of gentill perry,
So was þou daynte as drowry derely endent
In His dedis þat for dule endeynede Hym to dye.
þou was lufed of þat lorde þat vs lyfe lente;
þare was na lyueande lede He lete mare by,　　　　20
Ne na wyghte in þis werlde with Hym þat went;
And by thi werkes I wate þat þou was worthi.
Wele worthi þou ware
For thi werkes ay-whare
And dedis by-dene.　　　　25
Now forthir to fare

E8 blysse] *second long* s *written over previously written* e.　　　E14 John] Jhon
E15 gem dere and] germandir

Of thi mekenes mare
With mouthe will I mene.

3

In Galylee graythely gome was þou get,
As Godd of His gudnes granted þe grace.   30
Zebede, thi fadir, the fude þat the fet,
He fedd the and fosterde þat faire was of face.
þou was myldeste of mode þat euer man mett.
Thi modir highte Mary, swylk menesyng men mase,
The seet scho aste for hir sones myght hir thynk wele sett,   35
And of thaire syttynge forsothe hafe sere solace.
Solace was it to þe
The Pereles of Pousté
Called the full styll.
þou forsuke thi fadir fre,   40
Schipe and nett of þe see,
And went Hym vntill.

4

Thi modir, thi mobles, all maner of thyng
þat any man in his mynde aftir myght mene,
Of all þe welthe and þe wanes thou hade in kepynge   45
    .   .   .   .
    .   .   .   .
To cayre with þat cumly thou keste the full clene;
With þat lorde for to lende was thi lykynge
And for His lufe all lythes lefte thou by-dene.   50
By-dene lefte þou it all
þat was thyne in-with walle;
The werlde þou forsuke.
Thareby sett thou bot smalle   f. 231ᵛ
When thou com to His calle,   55
As witnese the buke.

5

Thou was witty and wyse, thi werkes vnwylde;
þou werede the fro wyrkynges wrechid þat ware;

E46, E47 See 'Notes'.

þou was methe and meke as mayden for mylde;
Thi mynde moued þou fro myse one ilk a manere;   60
Thou was faire and fayntles, with na fylthe filede,
Ne with na fanding thi flesche defoulede with na fere:
Forthi was þou chosen, chaste as a childe;
Oure cheftane He chose the, vnchangide of chere.
Thi chere was full chaste   65
Fro werkes all waste,
Noghte assentand to syn.
Full gude was thi gaste;
Na filthe had defaste
The, verray virgyn.   70

6

Thow was sybbe oure saueoure, hir syster sone
Whas semely sydis saluede oure sare,
þat was þe byrde so bryghte with birdyn ȝode bun,
And þe barne alþer beste of body scho bare.
Bathe frenchipe and faythe to frayste it bese fun   75
In þat frely fude, to folowe His fare;
Forthi with þat worthi, John, wald þou wonn,
And with Hym walke whate way þat His will ware.
Ware His will was to wende
Or Hym lyked to lende,   80
Bathe myldely and still,
þou helde þe ay with þat hende
And ferde forthe with thi frende
And wroghte at His wyll.

7

Thou was preué with þat prynce in euerilk-a place;   85
To the He publischede þe poyntis of His preuaté:
Firste when þat frely transfegurede His face
To a fone of His folke, a ferly to see;
Seþen at the supere thorghe souerayne grace
Many selcouthe syghte schewede He to þe;   90
For þou was trayste and trewe and folowede His trace
And tuke at His techyng, þat faythfull es and free.

E62 fere] fare fere (fare *canc.*)   E86 publischede] pup publischede (pup *canc.*)
E89 supere] sop supere (sop *canc.*)

Free fro thralle vs to brynge
Heghe one rude walde He hynge,
So lawe wald He lende;   95
And þou, His derlyng,
His modir in kepyng
To þe He bekende.

8

Thou was bouxsom and bayne hir body to tent,
And to His byddyng bowand to blyss þat vs broghte.   100
Thou seruede þat semly, till hir sone sent
Aftir hir Hymselfen, and sythen þou soghte.
Into Asye þe way warely thou went;
Thare worthyly werkes of wirchipe þou wroghte;   f. 232ʳ
Prechide appertely the puple repent;   105
Thorghe prikkynge of penance fra paynes þou thaym broghte.
þou broghte thaym to blysse
Thorowe mendynge of mysse;
Gret kirkes þou made.
þe Emperoure of þis   110
Was warre, as I wysse,
And hatrede he hade.

9

Domycyane, þat deuyls lyme, dedeyned at þi dede
And demyd the for thi doynge with dule for to dye.
With tyrauntез he tuk the als theefe in þat thede;   115
Thay toylede the bytwene thaym and threted the thraly—
Thase licherouse lurdans, laytheste in lede.
To Portelatyn thase laddes the ledden full laythely;
Thane the boustoure balde with barett he bedde
That thay thi body suld bare with bale for to bye.   120
To by was þou made bare
And done in a tonn thare
With oyle wellande hate.
Seþen wald þay noghte spare—
þay sett the full sare   125
One ane yren plate.

E106 Thorghe] Thor`g´ he   E115 thede] tyde thede (tyde *canc.*)

10

Of all þe dedes þay couthe doo þat derfe ware and dill
Thou dyede noghte, for thaire [dede] dide no dere vnto the.
Foulely foullede þay thi flesche ȝit felid þou nane ille:
Forthi þi famen the flemede owte of cuntré.   130
þan to Pathmos a[pa]ce passede þou vntyll;
The Apocalips in þat place, with a pen free,
Wysely þou wrate it, with witt and with will,
And for thi werke þou ware worthi wirchipede to be.
To be wirchiped with myghte   135
þou ware worthi, full ryghte,
In euerilk-a place.
Thou was witnes of lyghte
þat wysses euerilk-a wyghte.
Thi name es Goddes grace.   140

11

Grete grace was the gyffen and grauntede also
Thurghe His gudnes þat gyfes vs all gyftes of mayne.
Whils þou suggeourned in þat suyle, Domycyane, thi foo,
At a semle þat segge in certayne was slayne.
þan þou gysed the gerne, and gafe the to goo   145
Tyll Ephesym graythely þe gates þat ware gayne.
Feele folke ware thi frendes þare þou ferde froo
And for to frayste of thi fare þe toþer ware fayne.
Fayne ware þe folke free
And come rynnande to the   150
And hailsed the hame;
And saide þus vnto the:
'Blissede ay mote he be
þat comes in Goddes name!'

12

f. 232ᵛ Thane was Drucyane dede, thi derlynge so dere,   155
And sulde to delfynge be done, dredles, þat daye;
Bot þou bade thayme habyde and sett down þe bere;
Thou blyssede þe body bare þare it laye.

E128 thaire dede dide] dede *canc.*   E131 apace] aplace   E141 þe] `þe`
E156 delfynge] def delfynge (def *canc.*)

Scho sett hir vp softely with a blythe chere,
Als scho hade slepede, it semede, sothe for to saye.   160
þay hade wondir of þat wyghte, þe wyes þat þere ware,
And all wirchipede thi werke þat wente by þe waye.
By þe way þay þat went,
þay lefte landis and rent,
With the for to wende.   165
To no thynge tuke þay tent,
And sone sum of thaym repent,
By fondyng of þe fende.

13

þay ware cumbyrde in couetyse—þe caytefs had care—
For þaire knaues ware cledde in clethyng full clene,   170
And þay hade no thynge in hande as þay had hadde are,
And ware noghte halden so myghty as þay hade are bene;
Forthi wroghte þou þaire will of wandes þat ware;
Thow made golde full gude and gafe þam, I wene.
Smale stanes of þe see saynede þou þare,   175
And þay warre saphirs, for-sothe, was nane swylke sene.
Sene swylke was þare none
For fyne precyouse stone.
The wandes when þou badde
þay ware golde ylkone.   180
þou gafe thaym welthe mare wone
þan þay euer hadde.

14

When þay had welthe more wane þan þay euer bewane
þay wente home by þe waye; vnwysely þay wroghte.
A ʒonge barne in þat burghe was dede ryghte thane;   185
þat ilke body þat hym bare, to bale scho was broghte.
His modir come murnande, with hir many mane;
To the made thay thayre mane; mele myghte thay noghte;
And, for thay grett so grysely, to grete þou bygane;
To Godd of His gudnes seþen þou besoghte.   190
þou besoghte Godd of myghte;
þan þe childe rase vpe-ryghte
And tolde þam full euen:
þat lett by þi lare lyghte

And couetede þe golde bryghte   195
How þay hadd loste heuen.

15

Than thay wepede and weryede þaire werke and þaire wyll,
þat þay, for welthe of þe werlde, sulde wende vnto woo.
Thow said, 'Will ȝe suffire, sothely and still,
Seuen dayes penance?'—and sone said thay, 'Ʒoo'.   200
Thay tuke at thi techynge and traysted þartyll;
þay had forthynkyng in thoghte þat þay it fledde froo.
þe precyouse stones semly to see appon syll
And þe golde in thaire kynde agayne gun þay goo.

f. 233ʳ   Thay go agayne in degré,   205
As þaire kynde was to bee,
Stones as þay ware.
The golde turnede to wandis free.
þan þat syghte fra thay see
Myse didd þay na mare.   210

16

In þat cuntre was a clerke knawen and kende;
þay callede hym Craton þe Cunande thurgheowte clergy.
All þe lande and þat lede þat he gun in lende
With his lawes and his lare warre þay ledd by.
þat philosophir all þe folke faste he defende   215
That thay suld noghte in thi faythe, John, þam affy.
þus merrede he þe men þaire mysse for to mende,
And thurghe mawmetis he made mony a maystry.
Thurgh thaym the he soghte;
For the, John, forsothe, he wroghte   220
A puyson to profe the.
He saide, as he thoghte,
If it noyede the noghte,
þan walde he lufe the.

17

Bot, þat puyson to profe, þat prouddeste in palle   225
Profirde it two presoners was puneschede in pyne.
Als faste als þay felyd it downe dede gun þay falle,
So was it fell for to frayste, þe fylthe was so fyne.

Bot þou sauede thaym alsone, seande thaym alle,
And saynede þe coppe swetely and suppede it off syne.   230
Thow hade no harme; þat behelde þat hendeste in hall;
And to the hally þay heledide, bathe he and his hyne.
His hyne holly and he
Trewely trowede þare to þe,
Become þare thi brothire.   235
þou saide to þat menȝe:
'Luke þat ȝe lufande be
Ilkone to oþer.'

18

Thou bade thaym be free to frayste in þaire fare,
Faythefull and frendely till euerilk-a fere.   240
'What may þis mene?' quod these men. 'Mone it vs mare.
We hafe no mencyon ne mynde of þis matere.'
'It es þe comandement of Criste þat I ȝow declare:
To kepe it be connande, all mankynde clere.
Luke ȝe releue ilke a lede—þat lykes ȝoure lare;   245
To lufe ilk man as ȝoure-selfe—this lesson ȝe lere.
To lere nowe þis ryghte
Gret Godd of His myghte
Graunte ȝow þe grace.
And Ihesu, þat worthi wyghte,   250
Helpe vs all to þat lyghte
For to see His face.'

19

Wyse men and witty þat of thi werkes wyste
Weled the for wo[r]thi wirchip to welde;
To be þaire beschope blethely þay bedde the, so blyste,   255 f. 233ᵛ
For þou myghte in thaire bale beste be thaire belde.
Thay menskede the with manhede with mytir vnmyste,
And folowed thi fare freely in frythe and in felde.
Thus thow lyffede in the lande whils oure lorde lyste,
And when Hym lykede He laghte the; thi gaste þou gun
      Hym ȝelde.   260
For to ȝelde the thi mede
In heuen, for thi gude dede

E254 worthi] P wothi

When þou heþen paste,
He was redy, we rede.
To þat lyghte He vs lede   265
þat euer more sall laste.   Amen.

Explicit

THE ALLITERATIVE
JOHN BAPTIST HYMN

1

Blissed be thow, Baptist, borne and forth broght
Of a byrde baran, bales to bete.
Gabriel ful godely to thi fader soght,
And seid to þat semely sawes ful swete:
'þi wyf schal conceyue a child, doute þe nought,   5
Thorgh þe grace of grete God!'—þus he gan hym grete.
'His name schal be calde Jon; take it in thoght.
Many men in his birth with myrthe schul mete.'
With myrthe to mete
To the soule sete,   10
Nedeful to neuen!
When we awey wende   f. 13^r
þ[er] we schal long lende
He bring vs to heuen.

2

Blissed be þou, Baptist, most witty in wone.   15
Was neuer wight in þis worlde more worthi in wede
Ne neuer body better of blode ne of bone,
But Crist þat for vs his blode wolde blede;
Ne neuer non gretter on ground myght gone,
Ne no man markyd on molde more myghty in mede.   20
þow art stalworth in stowre and stedfast als stone:
Stande stifly with vs and neghe vs at nede.
Ʒe, neghe vs at nede!
And make vs at spede
Of God to gete grace.   25
He bring vs to þat blys
þer myrthes non mys
Before His owen face.

B13 þer] D þat   B22 at] and at (and *canc*.)

3

Blissed be þou, Baptist. I grete þe with good.
Al-holy my hert þow hast in þi ho[l]de.   30
þow forgoher of Crist þat restid on rood,
Bothe in wele and in wo þou wroght as he wolde.
f. 14ʳ*   þat messager þat tolde Mary with ful mylde mode
þat Goddes sone wolde be bourn of þat body bolde,
þi[s] aungel schewed þanne in þat stede þer þei bothe stode   35
And broght worde of þat bright and trewly þanne tolde.
Trewly he tolde
To þi fader many-folde
And neuend on-one;
For he wolde þe aungel noght leue   40
Ful sore it gan hym greue:
He stode doumbe as stone.

4

Blissed be þou, Baptist, roser of ryght.
When þat mekeful Mary with þi moder mett,
And sche had conceyued Crist þat [maste] is of myght,   45
þat swete ful semely here sawes sche sett.
Sche kist here cosyn pertly a-plight
And thorgh þe grace of here sone ful godely here grett.
þere sche cawte in clothes þat ilke swete wight
þat loutid to Jhesu withouten any lett.   50
Withouten any le[t]t,
Men said, or thei mett
Oure fadres be-[f]orne.
God kepe vs with wyn
And saue vs fro synne   55
þat we be noght lorne.

5

Blissed be þow, Baptist, whan þou were borne bare
Of þat buxum body þat þow within bredde,
When þou were comen to þis world and combrid with care
For sorow and for synne þat men were in stede,   60

*B29 ff. *Stanzas 3 and 5 in the MS have been interchanged (see 'Notes').*   B30 holde]
D honde   B35 þis] þi   B45 maste is of] D is full of   B51 lett] leet
B53 be-forne] be borne   *B57 ff. *Stanzas 3 and 5 in the MS have been interchanged (see
'Notes').*

Cosyns kyde of þi kyn þat wist of þi fare,
Ful many aboute þe þare þa[nne] was sprede,
For [gadrid] togedir þei busked hem ful ȝare,
As þe lawe was in land, þider were þei lede.
When þei gan hem lede   65
As thei toke to rede
þai fraynd on-one,
[þe] child for t[o] calle:
He wrote to þem alle:
'His name is callid Joon.'   70

6

Blissed be þou, Baptist, to many folk a frende;
Oure Jewel of Joy, jugged be lawe;
Faythful in frestyng, oure foos fro vs fende;
Solace to the sory, s[e]kir in thy sawe,
Serteyn to synful, socour þow sende   75
At þe dredeful day whennes bemes schul blowe,
þou þat mylde Mary helde in hir h[e]nde,
First whan þou were born, as clerkes wele knowe.
As clerkes wele knowe,
þi fader in a throwe   80
[A poyntil] hade he hent.
Thorgh myracle of þi birthe
In þat tyme of myrth
His speche was hym sent.

7

Blissed be thow, Baptist, so ware and so wys;   85
In wode and in wildirnesse was þi wonyng;
Neythir purpil ne palle, ne pelle of price
But of camel skyn þow toke þi clothyng.
Hawes þow [hent], and rotes of þe ryse,
With borionand bere in the blomyng;   90
Hony-comes [for] ryche mete—wanted þe þis;
Folk louely þow lerned vnto þi lykyng;

B61–63 (*MS ll. 33–35*) *and* B65–66 (*MS ll. 37–38*) *have been interchanged (see 'Notes').*
B62 þanne] þam   B63 for gadrid] for   B67 on-one] o none   B68 þe child for
to] A child forth þei   B74 sekir] sokir   B77 h[e]nde] *D* honde   B81 A poyntil
hade] *D* hade   B89 hent] *D* toke   B91 for] *D* and

Vnto þi lykyng,
Watir drynkyng
[N]e toke it in thoght;   95
Sydir ne wyne
Were it neuer so fyne
þou neghed it noght.

8

Blissed be þow, Baptist, bothe fere and nere,
Dwellyng in deserte with ful gode wille;   100
þow baptist Ihesu withouten any were
In þe Flume Iordan, þe faith to fulfille.
F[ro] þe incarnacion the thre[teth] ʒere,
As fel on þe twelft day, he peryd [þe vntille];
þe Holy Gost of heuene he come to þe þere,   105
And as a dowfe on þe he satt þanne ful stille.
He sat on þe ful stille
As it was his wille;
A voyce sayde in haast:
'þis is my child   110
Bothe meke and mylde
In whom me liketh moost.'

9

Blissed be þou, Baptist, for thi prechyng.
þow profet apertely þe poyntes of pees.
To Herode and Herodias, his dere derlyng,   115
Resones and right þow rekynde on ryse.
þou sayd ful scharply in þi saiyng,
And stode stedefastly and thoght not to sese:
He led hym not lawfully in his likyng,
For Philip his brothir wyf þat he to hym chese.   120
þe wyf þat he chese
Sittyng on deyse
Gretly gan hy[r] greue.
Sche made hir doghter craue
þi heued for to haue,   125
And Herod graunt hy[r] leue.

B95 Ne] he   toke it t] (t canc.)   B103 Fro] D for   the threteth] D of the thred
B104 peryd þe vntille] peryd   B105 þe] Vn to þe   B123 hyr] D hym
B126 graunt hyr] D gurant hym

10

Blissed be þow, Baptist, þi name is ful worthy.
It betokenith Goddes grace as clerkes vs [c]lere;
And o[n] many moo maners men may it discry
Whoso wil lufly listen and [l]ere.   130
Baptist for baptim, so saith þe story
Of þat worthy wight þat hath no pere.
Prophet and aungel he may be callyd holy
And lantern of light þat scyneth ful clere.
þow þat schinest so clere   135 f. 15ᵛ
Goddes darlyng so dere
As we in bokes rede;
Seint Jon þe Baptist
Prey for vs to Crist
þat heuen be oure mede.   140

B127 Baptist] Ba`p'tist   B128 clere] *D* lere   B129 on] *D* of   B130 lere] *D*
bere

NOTES TO THE TEXTS

The Notes are primarily lexical, though some lines of interest for metrical or other reasons are also discussed. Holthausen's emendations to *Katherine* (made largely, though not entirely, on metrical grounds) have been considered too numerous to comment on unless of special interest. Abbreviations of the textual references are as those in MED supplemented by those in OED; the full titles can be found in MED's *Plan and Bibliography* and *Supplement* and OED's *List of Books Quoted in Vols. I–XII.* Some editions are given their reference within the 'Notes' (generally recent publications, or texts in MS). Editions of many of these texts will be found in the 'Bibliography'. Translations from the *Acta Johannis* are from McWilson's English edition in *Hennecke, New Testament Apocrypha* rather than from the French *editio princeps*. Citations from Maggioni, *Legenda Aurea* are to page and sentence, those from the vulgate *Passio S. Katerine* are to sentence, in d'Ardenne and Dobson, *Seinte Katerine*, pp. 144–203. Citations from the Wycliffite Bible refer to the parallel text edition of Forshall and Madden, with abbreviations WEV or WLV to distinguish the early and late versions. The *N-Town Cycle* of Plays is cited as *N-Town* rather than MED's *Ludus C* and uses the text of Stevens and Cawley. Examples cited from *Wars Alex.* carry the line numbers of the critical edition of Duggan and Turville-Petre, *The Wars of Alexander*, except when one manuscript is cited, when references from Skeat's edition used in MED are indicated. For reference to texts from Bodleian MS Digby 133, see 'Bibliography', *s.v. Digby Plays*; the Mary Magdalene play is abbreviated as *Mary Magd.* Other abbreviations should be found under 'Additional Abbreviations' at the end of the 'Bibliography'.

Notes to *The Alliterative Katherine Hymn*

K1–4 The invocation refers to Katherine's specific powers of intercession in the afterlife, rendered especially effective if she was borne in mind at the moment of death or when in dire straits. See *Leg.Aurea*: "'Ihesu, rex bone, obsecro te ut quicumque passionis me memoriam egerit seu in exitu anime uel in quacumque necessitate inuocauerit tue propitiationis consequatur effectum" . . . Factaque est uox ad eam dicens: "Veni, dilecta mea, speciosa mea! Ecce, tibi celi ianus est aperta. Nam et hiis qui passionem tuam celebrauerint optata presidia promitto de celis'" (1211.128–9); see also K163–8.

K1 *curteys* superl. as n., lacking final -*t*. Forms of the superl. adj. without -*t* are found in the Ashmole manuscript of *WarsAlex*.: *grettis, fewis, proudis* (3779, 3866, 5592).

K2 *kepyng* either pr. p. used appositively (see Mustanoja, pp. 554–6), or an example of the verbal noun used with acc. rather than gen. (see Mustanoja, pp. 574–5).

   kare In the Katherine legend this is specifically 'eternal woe' (i.e. Hell). See Note to K1–4.

K3 *below* MS *be low*. A rare word in ME, and found only as adv. Neither OED nor MED register its incidence in *Katherine*. Its first (and only other) recorded occurrence is in *c*.1380 *Cleanness* 116: 'siþen on lenþe bilooghe ledez inogh', where it means 'below the high dais', and is written as one word in the manuscript; OED here gives its origins as a variant of earlier *a-lowe*, parallel to *an-high* (now 'on high'); the synonymous pair, *a-low/below* was analogous to *a-fore/before*, etc. The reading here is based on such parallel usages as *a*. 1450 *St.Etheldr*.238: 'in vrthe here alowe'.

K4 *bales ful bare* 'troubles [that are] totally unmitigated'. MED defines this occurrence as an adjectival intensive, giving 'extreme torture' (see *bar* adj.14), and does not appear to acknowledge *bar(e)* as adv., though see OED *bare* adv. †1. 'thoroughly, completely', citing *c*.1390 *SGGK* 465: 'ʒet breued watz hit ful bare A meruayl among menne'. MED classifies that example from *SGGK* as an adj.: 'exposed to view, unconcealed' (see *bar* adj.14). Analogous to this would be to read Spalding's *ful bare* as an adverbial intensive qualifying *leede* 'freely, manifestly', though Spalding's syntax is normally v.+ qualifying adv.

K5 See MED *overthrouen* v. 2 (c), 'to incline to evil', and v. 4, 'to discredit (one's reputation)', cf., *c*.1445 Pecock *Donet* 142/16: 'þei in her owne declaraciouns . . . hem silf ouer þrowen'. For intrans. forms see also v. 5 (a) and (c), and OED *overthrow* v. †5.

K6 'And suffered affliction grievously for consideration of us'; *thank of vs* is in parenthesis, and *care* is what she suffered. The a-verse of this line is metrically unusual, and a vestige of the Class II OE v. in the author's pronunciation is suspected, giving a trisyllabic *tholyed*, or possibly the dipthongization, as found in, e.g., *flyit* (K189); see *a*. 1460 *TowneleyPl*.32/53: 'he myght no thoyle afor his face'.

   thank of vs 'for our sakes', from early senses of *thank*, n. 'thought'; OED *thank* sb.2 is more explicit here than MED.

K7 *tyraunt* Later medieval forms of the legend name the tyrant as Maximinus or Maxentius, who reigned in the fourth century; there is a full and useful note in d'Ardenne and Dobson, *Katerine*, p. 204. Voragine offers 'footnotes' in *Leg.Aurea*, citing his source in Vincent de Beauvais

(1215.136–7 and 199). Here, as in most medieval legends, the oppressor is endowed with the stock characteristics of the stage tyrant. On a series of wall paintings of the life of St Katherine in the parish church of St Peter and St Paul, Pickering, Yorkshire, he is portrayed as black-skinned.

trayfoly After writing an original *u*, the scribe transformed it into a secretary *a* in the first syllable, suggesting an initial misreading of *trupfoly*, but the *lectio difficilior* makes better sense; see MED *traifoli*, adv. If the derivation is from OF *trai* 'trick, deceitful device', as MED suggests (which makes good sense), then the unusual suffix appears to come from either Old Frisian or Old High German *fol*, 'full', or it may merely be a spelling of 'fully'. Alternatively, the adv. may be a scribal misreading of whatever *trayþ(e)ly* [etym. unknown] actually means in *c.*1380 *Cleanness* 907: 'For we schal tyne þis toun and trayþely disstrye'; see also *Cleanness* 1137: 'For þenne þou Dry3tyn dyspleses wyth dedes ful sore And entyses hym to tene more trayþly þen ever'; see also Note to K3, where again *Cleanness* provides comparison with a rare word. Judging by these contexts, the word could mean something like 'grievously'.

K8 'He refrained from sparing you from the application of torture'.

turnement: 'torture'; cf. OED *torment sb.*2. Forms with medial *n* show confusion with *tournament* in its sense of 'rotation', but are also used to give a sense of deliberate corporeal injury where no rotation took place; cf. 1415 *Sat.against Lollards* 113 (in *Pol.Poems*, Rolls Series, 2, 246): '[a statue of Saint] James . . . twyes had turnement'.

he tynt þe to spare MS *he tynt not to spare*. The manuscript reading would be meaningless without a second pron. The phrase has been emended to make sense on the grounds that the acc. pron. *þe* is employed in the iteration of the next line.

tynt Holthausen suggests an *i* mutation of *tent* 'intend', which would allow for retention of *not*; but the phonology does not support this; OF/AN *e* is invariably spelt *e*, and *Katherine* has three examples of the same L and OF root, all in *-e* (*entent* K62, K171, and *entende* K116). Trans. use of v. *tinen* plus inf. is not otherwise recorded, but appears here to be a form of negative, on analogy with 'fail to . . .' / 'cease to . . .', and, coincidentally, 'spare to . . .' (see next).

K9 'He desisted from sparing you there'.

K10 *myht* This gives the only example of an *-ht* ending in the witness. Elsewhere the OE spirant is written *-(3)th*.

mynt 'thought, intended', with possible connotation of 'aimed, threatened'. Cf. 1440 *PParv*.338: 'Myntyn, or amyn towarde, for to assayen: *Attempto*'.

K11 *momyl* For a trenchant illustration of heathen 'momyling' see *Mary Magd.* (Dgb 133) 1187–97: 'Mursum, malgorum, mararo3orum, Skartum

sialporum, fartum cardiculorum, Slavndri strovmppum, corbolcorum, Sny-
guer snagoer werwolfforum [etc.]'.

K12–14 'But because you unyieldingly withstood there, [then] there—[just]
as fire [sparks out] of a [withstanding] flint—your arguments lacerated him'.
The adverbial clause of K13 qualifies *rent* in K14, not *stynte* in K12.

K12 *stynte* See MED *stonden* v. 24 and OED *stand* v. 9b. 'To remain
stedfast, firm, secure'. For the form cf. OE *standan*, common pa. *stent*, and
rarer *stynt*, as in *Maldon* 51: 'þæt her stynt unforcuð eorl mid his werode'.
Some lexical shading may come from *stinten* [OE *styntan*] 'stop', and *astinten*
[OE *astyntan*] 'to make ineffective, foil, make blunt', more cognate with OI
stynta 'stay in conflict' (see OED *stint* v. 3).

K13 *As fyre doth of flynt* A common alliterative collocation, but here the
image is of the struck, withstanding object (Katherine) from which issues
the searing fire that destroys the tyrant's might.

K17–18 Several readings are possible, but the best sense comes from *þat
beerd* [i.e. Katherine] nom., and *belamy* acc., giving a parallel construction to
sche (hym) rent in K15: 'And because of this that girl so overcame that
threatening fair friend / That neither handsomeness nor prestige inhered in
its place [in him]'. This represents Katherine's earliest dialectic triumphs
over the tyrant as described by Voragine: 'Cumque de filii incarnatione
sapienter plurima disputasset, stupefactus cesar non ualuit ad hoc respon-
dere . . . Videns autem cesar quod eius sapientie obuiare non posset'
(*Leg.Aurea*, 1206.26, 1207.47). The glossing of *beerd* as 'beard' [OE *beard* in
a lengthening group; see Jordan §59] would depend on reading *þat beerd so
bent* as a unique form of one of the common idiomatic phrases such as *shaven
his beard*, *rennen in beard* 'insult, get the better of', but I have found nothing
similar in collocation with *bent*. An adoption of this reading would give
problems with the second *þat* in the line, which would require emendation
to *his*. Another possibility would be to take *belamy* as nom. and *beerd* as acc.,
which assumes that the tyrant oppressed the maiden; but this is not so
precisely supported by the sources and analogues as the reading adopted
here. The b-verse also happens to be unmetrical; *þat beerd [sche] so bent*
would be a more typical construction.

K17 *þat bostful belamy* Cf. *a.* 1450 *Yk.Pl.*339/213–4: *Sattan (to Christ):*
'"Howe, belamy, abide, With al thy booste and bere"'. The sources illustrate
the rage and might of the tyrant, and the dramatic convention that any
villain (e.g., Satan, Herod, Caiaphas) was bound to rant and strut is used in
the poem, and this is how I have read *bostful*. However, an alternative sense
of 'menacing' is possible; cf. 1384 WEV 2 Kings 12: 31: '[David] sawede the
puple of it, and ladde about vpon hem boostful yren carris (WLV: dide
aboute hem yrun instrumentis of turment)'.

K18 *bythe* This unusual n. derives from OE *byht* 'a bend, abode' [prob. from OE *bygan* 'to bend']; see MED *bight* n. (c).

his bythe 'its place', relating to the immediately preceding nouns, and not as 'his [i.e. the tyrant's] place'; see, e.g., *c.*1376 *PPl.A(1)*(Vrn)2.6: 'Loke on þe lufthond . . . Boþe Fals and Fauuel and al his hole Meyne!'. See MED *hit* 5 (e) 'referring to a compound antecedent their'.

K19 *schofferes* The root, which is of ON origin, is often found alliterating with *scorn*, and is not recorded in English before 1390. MED cites K19 as its only example under *scoffer* n. (b): 'a railing controversialist'. *Leg.Aurea* has 'philosophers', *grammatici rhetores* and *oratores*. The more caustic sense must be based on the *pugnatura* of *Passio* 293, and on the *Katherine Group* witnesses (see d'Ardenne and Dobson, *Katerine*, p. 38), where the rhetoricians are called *moteres* 'debaters'. Despite this, MED's definition seems inaccurate, for the philosophers did not get a chance to rail. 'Detractors' would be a better gloss.

K20 *scort* This is one of the few Northern forms in the text. MED cites only meanings corresponding to 'cut short', many of these glossing L *breviatare*, or employed as corollary to ME *abregge*. However, see *Passio*, 215: 'contionatricem temerariam suis assertionibus superatam reddiderint'; ibid., 277: 'fieri potest vestris eam argumentis inclausam confutare'; and *Leg.Aurea*: 'si concionatricem uirginem suis assertionibus superarent. . . . superaueritis . . . "ut uestris argumentis penitus confutetur"' (1207.47, 54). The patent sense (from both sources and this narrative) of 'refute, render ineffectual' is a usage closer to the Latin, but not otherwise found before Shakespeare; see OED *short* v. 5, 'To make of no effect. *nonce-use*'; 1611 Shaks. *Cymb.*1.vi.200: 'I shall short my word By length'ning my returne'; and *shorten* v.3 †b. 'To render ineffectual. *Obs*'; 1605 Shaks. *Lear* IV.vii.9: 'Yet to be knowne shortens my made intent'. It would be interesting if such a meaning was intended as early as this.

K21 *Fyfti fine retorikes* There is no excuse for Heuser's *ffifti fiue*, as he knew from the sources and noted in his apparatus that it was 'Richtige zahl 50', and that letters *n* and *u* are indistinguishable in the witness. Cf. *a.* 1400 *WarsAlex.*2336: 'Send Ten fyne Philosofours to fand with my wittes'.

retorikes 'rhetoricians'—masters of the art of rhetoric, used to persuade or influence others. The alliteration would have been enhanced by a word like 'filosophers', used in collocation with *fyne* in *a.*1400 *WarsAlex.*2336 (see above), but trisyllabic *retorikes* makes for rhythmic norms, and the *Passio* here has 'quinquaginta uiros qui se in omni doctrina Egyptiorum et artium liberalium—immo in omni sapientia mundi—excellere ultra omnes mortales asserebant' (262); also: ibid.: 'rethores et grammaticos', 'pugnatura', 'magistri' and 'oratores' (211–323, *passim*).

K22 *þe* It is just possible that this is a relative pron. 'who', as in MED *the* pron. (1) 1.b (b) (an attractive idea suggested by Thorlac Turville-Petre). This would give a more elegant and interesting reading, adding yet more to the lexical and syntactic idiosyncrasies of the poem; but the usage, common in the *Katherine*-group, had generally died out by the late fourteenth century, and it seems more likely that the word is a demonstrative, and that omission of the relative pronoun in this line parallels those in K33, K172 and K174.

K23 *hythe* An alternative interpretation of a pp. from *highten* [OE *hyhtan*] would give 'prepared', as in *a.* 1387 Trev.*Higd.*2.23: 'In Brytayne beeþ hoote welles wel arrayed and i-hiȝt [L *apparati*] to þe vse of mankynde'; but collocation with *hyest* points more obviously to the rhetoricians' known status (i.e. reading ME *hoten* [OE *hātan*], pp. *hyȝt, hyghte*, giving 'called' or 'reputed'); for development of ME fricative from OE pp. *hāten*, see OED *hight v.*[1].

K25 *Clergi to kepe* 'to defend (their orthodox) doctrine'. Cf. *c.*1450 *Interpol.Rolle Ps.*(Bod 288) p. 54: 'In these articlis of bileeve [*Te Deum*] is myche fair clergie'.

K26 *He* The North East Midland form at this date is ordinarily *sche*, and this is found everywhere else in the poem (28 times). In a witness of Lincs origin the solitary occurrence of *he* for 'she' is unlikely to be a relict of a copy in which *he* occurred regularly. On the other hand, omission of *sc* from *sche* in the scribe's exemplar is not a likely scribal error. It must be concluded, therefore, that *he* is original. Occasional use of the form in this dialect is supported by its occurrence in one manuscript of Richard Rolle, *The Prick of Conscience* (London Society of Antiquaries MS 687; LALME NFK 638); see R. E. Lewis and A. McIntosh, *A Descriptive Guide to the MSS of 'The Prick of Conscience'* (*Medium Ævum* Monographs, n.s. 12, 1982), p. 85, where this manuscript is localised on dialectal evidence to 'probably north Norfolk, but just possibly east Lincolnshire'. See also *SGGK* 1872, where *he* for 'she' once replaces usual West Midland *ho*: 'When he [*MS emended by most editors to* ho] was gon Sir Gawayn gerez hym sone'.

K27 *pyth* Spelling with *h* and the phonology of the rhymes show that etymologically this word comes from ME *picchen* [obsc., possibly from OE **piccan* 'pitch']. The alliterative collocation with *poyntes* is paralleled in *SGGK* 1454: 'Schalkez . . . Haled to hym of her arewez, Bot þe poyntez payred at þe pyth þat pyȝt in his scheldez'. A figurative sense of *picchen* is found elsewhere in ME only in *c.*1426 Audley *Poems* 157/54: 'Haile! þi pete on vs þou pyȝt'. Here, at K27, there appears to be some overlapping with a *y*-form of *putten* [OE *pytan* 'put'], found in K183: 'Hir nek forth sche pytte'. This is confirmed by one ME sense of *putten* (OED *put v.* 22), as in *c.*1300

Wright *Lyric P.*xvi.53: 'To love y putte pleyntes mo'. A composite poetic meaning gives something like Modern English 'put it to them', though the sense of 'pitching' argumentative points is not otherwise recorded until the nineteenth century.

K28 *To her lore þei lepe* 'They came over to [the side of] her teaching'; see *Passio* 531: 'ecce omnes conuertimur ad Christum'. Cf. *c.*1384 Wycl. *50HFriars.*384: 'þus deede beggars, freris, lippen up to kynges powers'. MED cites K28 under *lepen* v. 4 (d), 'to make an assault,' which would give 'she, the radiant maiden, then, put such points to them, then, [that] they attacked her doctrine'. It is not easy to contradict MED's reading, as the poet does not normally repeat a narrative point, and the sense of conversion could be said to be represented subsequently in K29–32. The rhetoricians did start to question Katherine, but did not get round to attacking her doctrine because she, as ever, did all the talking and they stood speechless. My reading is based on idiomatic omission of conj., *þat* 'to the degree that', and ties in better with the subsequent adv. of manner, *þus*, in the next line, and indeed the meaning of K29–30 altogether.

K30 *lede in hyr lees* A not uncommon metaphor; cf. *c.*1430 *Pilgr.LM* IV.xl.195: 'She is prioresse, whiche leedeth alle þe cloystreres in les, bounded bi hondes and bi feet'.

K31 *ibore* 'born', pp. of ME *beren* 'to bear'; cf. 1297 *R.Glouc.*516: 'Thei he were a bast ibore'. Use of pp. as complement must mean 'blessed the fact that she had been born, blessed her birth, blessed her existence', and so, strictly speaking, *hire* in K31b is probably pron. nom., as in the first definition here, but I have glossed it as part of the acc. construction. No similar construction is recorded; this idiomatic use of the pp. may have been influenced by OE *gebyrd* 'birth'.

K33 The construction depends upon an idiomatic omission of a relative pron. 'who' before *was*. See also K172 and K174.
   cursud caytef Cf. *Mary Magd.*(Dgb 133) 631: 'O I, cursyd cayftyff, þat myche wo hath wrowth'; here there is a similar scribal error, the insertion of a misplaced *f*, as in our MS *capfte*.

K34 *commaund* An abbreviated and familiar form of pa. t. in words of AN derivation where the dentals (here of *commaunded*) are run together; so also *graunt* K223, *departe* K86.
   cantly in rees 'forcefully in violent haste'. The phrase could be part of the emperor's command, as indirect speech, i.e., 'valiantly and quickly to build a fire', but the reading here is more in keeping with *Passio* 535: 'Audiens hec, tirannus precipitibus furiis agitatus, accenso in medio ciuitatis uehementissimo igne'; see also *Leg.Aurea*: 'Audiens hec tyrannus nimio furore succensus omnes in medio ciuitatis cremari iussit' (1208.71); and Spalding would have wished to exploit this important dramatic image of the tyrant's

rage. Since elsewhere the adv. *cantly* and adj. *cant* 'valiant, dauntless' always have positive overtones (see, e.g., *c*.1340 Minot *Poems* 16/64: 'John of Aile . . . with scheltron ful schene Was comen into Cagent cantly and kene'), the poet's choice of it in the present line seems to be dictated rather by the needs of alliteration.

K36 *felawys* MS *fesawnt'ps/fesawut'ps*. Heuser's reading of *fesawntys* could possibly be defended on grounds of sense by a parallel with K78: *And with hire bawmyng of blis þo briddes sche brogth tame*; there the queen and Porphiry are referred to, like the rhetoricians, as just having been converted. Although 'birds' is a common complimentary term, one does not elsewhere find the pheasant species being singled out, except that there is a singular simile in K189: *And as fresch fesaunt to hire fere þan sche flyit*. This simile, however, illustrates rather the espousal with Christ: Katherine's youthful and feminine perfection, remade, after her hideous tortures, together with the natural homing of a creature to its mate. A metaphor based on the same creature is not as effectual with converted *retorikes*, unless the poet is referring to their being tied up in bundles ready for the fire, just as pheasants might have been for the oven. Certainly it can be argued that this poet employs similar startlingly vivid rustic imagery in the narrative sections: as in *thref* (K148), *flik* (K190) and *fesaunt* (K189). However, Holthausen's emendation to *felawys* is sensible; it stresses the group identity and martyrdom: they were colleagues as philosophers and partners in their punishment. It can be defended on grounds that MS long *s* and *l* could have been confused; however, it does not account for three graphs in the MS: *n t '*. MS reading of the b-verse can only be defended metrically if dat. *-e* of *fyre* is sounded (see pp. xxxiii–xxxvi) but, as Spalding does not elsewhere sound final *-e*, this is unlikely. An archetypal *in fyre for to fees* would be more likely.

K40 *for þei to-ches hem* ?'because they came by [for themselves]'—a rare and obsolete use of the v., giving a specific meaning distinct from 'choose', i.e. 'pick up, come by' (see OED *choose* v.B.6; cf. *c*.1320 *Cast.Love* 1317: 'Such strengþe he him þo ches þat prince of al þe world he wes'; though OED cites no illustrations of this sense after the 1380s). MED omits this signification, perhaps for lack of definitive examples. The form was almost certainly employed for metrical reasons, but intensifying prefix *to-* (as used with several ME verbs) also emphasizes the utter flawlessness of the converts' bodies in their deliverance.

K41 *to pres hem* MS *to ples hem*, emended by Holthausen; cf. *c*.1380 Chaucer *Bo*.4.pr.5.25: 'I merveile me . . . why . . . that tormentz of felonyes pressen and confounden goode folk'. A reading based on the MS sense, that this lack of injury was to their pleasure, would be trite. The self-rhyme here is also anomalous: inf. 'please' is spelt with *-e* (*plese* K74) as is the pa. 3 pl. (K38), and the witness is almost certainly corrupt. The sense 'to afflict them' is idiomatic of Spalding's apparent standpoint (cf., e.g., K230, K231, K253), and is palaeographically reasonable, in that a long *r* in an exemplar could have been mistaken for *l*.

K42–3 The stanza-linking concatenation breaks down here for the first time. The smooth running of the narrative, however, shows that there could have been no extra stanza in the archetype at this point, and the re-establishment of the concatenation between K56 and K57 shows that Stanza 4 is unquestionably where it should be in relation to the next.

K42 *Was of on here alone* 'was entirely due to her'; an unusual construction, suspect in a section of the text that has several difficult readings (see K41, above). The obvious emendation to *along* [OE *gelang*], an adj. always used with v. 'to be', would not rhyme. No parallels to the construction *of on* have come to light.

K43 *þus þou wit wanne* 'thus you overcame [established] doctrine'. Glossing of the v. is partially dependent on a probable contrast with the interpretation of *wonne* in the next line. The form may have been chosen to suit the rhyme; see also next.

K44 *here wordes had wonne* 'had dispensed, uttered their words'; one of the few formulaic alliterative collocations in the text. The philosophers had said what they could. See MED *winnen* v. 11a. (b); cf. *a.* 1400 *Siege Jerus.*(*1*) 173: 'Or þis wordes wer wonne to þe ende . . .'.

K45–6 There are no warranted grounds for emendation, but the repetition of *rial*(-) in both lines is suspect. The second appearance, in K46, though also unexceptionable in itself, may have been the result of contamination. See also Note to K46, below.

K46 *þer now* referring to the martyrs' perpetual existence, pre-eminent in Heaven. Heuser and Holthausen emend to *y* [*k*]*now* which is unsatisfactory on several counts: the reading is palaeographically straightforward (MS *p' now*); the curtailed word is precisely similar to that in K58; and in this case the dot actually looks like an apostrophe, just as it often does in the occurrences of *Kat'epn*. Early photographs may not have shown the stain of this apostrophe left by flaking ink (moreover, ultraviolet light helps to confirm *o* in *now*).

þei reygn MS *þe repgn* makes no sense. The pron. almost certainly refers to the converts, not to the 'reasons'; see *Passio*: 'felici martyrio coronati' (551); and *Leg.Aurea*: 'At uirgo ipsos confortans ad martyrium constantes effecit' (1208.72).

þat rewly haue ronne 'who grievously have run [the course of martyrdom]'; see MED *reuli* adv. [OE *hrēowlīce*]. The viable alternative reading based on MED *reuleli* adv. [from OF *reule*], 'who correctly have undergone (the Christian path)', has been rejected, on grounds that this adv. is uncommon and used mostly of the religious rule and ordered daily living. An indication of the rewards for the *physical* afflictions of martyrdom is more appropriate at this point.

haue Heuser and Holthausen inexplicably read the tolerably clear MS *haue* as *haþ* and *haf* respectively.

K47 *mytthyly* Probably adj.; see MED *mightili* and *mightli* adj.; cf. *hendly* (K169).

K49 *thankles* Found in ME otherwise only in Gower *CA* 7.2134 and *Paston* 1.589.

thyrsted A metathesized form of Early ME *þrusten*, ON *þrȳsta* 'to press, force'; see also Note to K148.

K50 *throwe* MS *trowe*. The *Passio* and *Leg.Aurea* give 'in carcere tenebroso' and 'caesam in obscurum carcerem', which other late ME versions render as 'prison'. Heuser retains the manuscript reading (presumably OE *trog, troh*, strictly 'vessel' or 'cistern', here perhaps 'sepulchre-like cell'), but this lacks lexical support, and the emendation restores alliteration.

K53 *twelue* MS *too*. The sources and all other vernacular versions unanimously state that Katherine was incarcerated for twelve days. Reflexes of OE/ON final *-f* are divided equally between *-f* and *-ue*, as they are after *-l* (*salf* and *-selue*), and Holthausen emends to *twelf*. However, OE *-elf* gives *-elue* in *-selue*, and this spelling would conform with the only two adjectives from OE *-f* in the text, *leue* (K84) and *derue* (K85).

K54 *To hym þe to low þus* 'in order to humble you to him by these means'. This unusual and complex construction involves the less usual trans. sense of *louen* 'to humble someone', to which is added dat. pron. *hym*, giving 'to humble someone to someone else'; cf. *c.*1420 Lydg. *TG* 440: 'For vnto ȝow his hert I shal so lowe . . . That he ne shal escape'.

K56–7 *turne þi witte* 'subvert/undermine your (way of) thinking/conviction' [i.e. 'make you change your mind']; see OED *wit sb.* †13. The phrase does not have Modern English connotations of turning someone's head or driving someone mad. Metrically the line lacks a long dip which could be restored by emending to *For to turne þi witte*, with *-e* in *turne* unsounded, giving the same rhythmic pattern as the final lines of Stanzas 2 and 7 (K28 and 98), or by assuming a sounding of the inf. inflexion, as read here.

K57–8 Properly this should be a subj. construction: 'In order to subvert your conviction through [his] harrassing [of] you, he would have trampled you down, if it were not for the fact that Truth attended you there'. It is here glossed slightly differently: 'To subvert your convictions [for] provoking him, that treacherous one trampled you [down] / when you were thrown [down] to the utmost [depth]. However, Truth attended you there'.

K57 *hym tarying* 'with him harassing you'; see MED *tarien* v.2. and OED *tary v.*; cf. 1325 *Cursor* (Vsp) 28153: 'I womman haue vn-buxum bene And tarid myn husband to tene'.

K58 *throw throghe* 'imprisoned fast'. Holthausen emends to *throw[n in a] throghe* (the latter referring back to the cell (*trowe*) of K50–1), but the MS reading, though odd, sounds idiomatic of Spalding and is a typical construction in the text, where pp. is so often followed immediately by adv.

    throw 'constrained, imprisoned'. For this rare pp. form, see MED *throuen* v. 2 (c), and the suggestive OED *throwen v.*[1] †4 †b 'to constrain'.

    throghe 'altogether, entirely, tightly'. Neither the significance nor etymology is straightforward, and the spelling is also unusual. I read the word as a derivative of Late OE *þuruh*, ON *þrā*, the vowels of which are both written as *o* in this text; cf. *c.*1470 *Golagros & Gaw.* 60: 'The berne bovnit to the burgh . . . and thrang in full thra'; see MED *thrō* adv. and OED *thorough, prep.* and *adv.* and *through, prep.* and *adv.* Taking extended meanings of *throw* and *throghe*, the most satisfactory gloss is 'imprisoned fast'; cf. *c.*1325 *Cursor* (Trin-C) 16560: 'Ʒitt þe kyng hem helde ful þro For wolde he not lete hem go'.

    but 'yet, however', possibly introducing a subj. construction; see Note to K57–8, above.

    Trewþe 'Truth [i.e. God, Christ]'; cf. *c.*1387 *PPl.B.*(Trin-C) 1.12: 'The tour upon the toft . . . Truthe is therinne . . . he is fader of feith and formed you all'.

    þe tente 'rendered service to you', 'looked after you', or 'was near you', an aphetic form of *attenden*, employed for metrical regularity, as with *dewre* in the next line.

K59 *dentywos dowf* See *Passio* 824 and *Leg.Aurea* 85. Katherine's personal relationship with Christ is constantly articulated. Thus Christ himself sent the food; it was transmitted by a white dove; this dove was seen as a heavenly messenger, and was not the Holy Spirit, so *Leg.Aurea*: '"Christus me per angelum enutriuit"'(1209.88).

    dentywos The spelling with *e* is a normal reflex of OF *ai* in this text (as in *pesse, ples(e)*), and *w* is a normal reflex of OF *u/v* (as in *labowrid, wow*), pointing to a development from OF *daintive*. Holthausen emends to *deintyows* unnecessarily.

    dewre as with *tente* in K58, this is an uncommon aphetic form of *enduren* 'endure', employed for metrical reasons. The sense here is analogous to 'bear up'.

K60 *derknes* not so much the 'darkness' of desolation or despair that might have overcome Katherine, who was more than steadfast enough in her faith ever to experience this; the sense of a literal radiance is adequate; see *Passio* 669–71: 'Sed ne in his Christus famulam suam deseruit; adsunt illi angeli de celo, confortantes eam et inestimabili claritatis fulgore locum penitus irradiantes'.

K61 *Solace sothe þe soþly of oure sauyour* 'Solace visited/attended you, truly, from our saviour'. The line makes good sense and is entirely in Spalding's common idiom of v. + adv. when *sothe* is read as v. pa. 3 sg. [from OE *secgan, soȝt*] with the scribe's characteristic *-th* for the spirant + *t*, as also at K71; see MED *secchen* v. 10, and OED *seek* †5b. 'visit the soul'. Cf. the verbal n. in *a.* 1450 *LDirige(1)* 93: 'þou cloþedest me with flesch and skyn . . . Lyf and mercy ȝaf me withyn . . . þy sechyng haþ kepyd my gost with wyn'. For the metre see Note to K63.

K62 *entent* 'frame of mind'; see MED *entente* n. 4.

K63 *sokour* Holthausen emends to [*saving*] *sokour* on metrical grounds, following the triple measure that is evolving in these rhymed long lines. It could be asked why he did not do the same for K61. Here, as there, the MS reading has been retained in view of the b-verse archetypal metre with both clashing stresses within a final disyllabic word ($\sim$xx//), as in, e.g., *Awntyrs* 107 and 238: '$\sim$as a womane'; '$\sim$at þi weting', and *Susannah* 18, 136 and 305: '$\sim$of heore langage'; '$\sim$ben vr lemmone'; '$\sim$in þe dismale'.

K63 *schewd* Both previous editors have *shewd*, indicating that Holthausen probably used Heuser's edition with this published error as his copy text, and transmitted it again. The *c* graph is perfectly clear and the reading of graph *e* is substantiated by its identical form in *hymselue* at K90.

K68 *for* Read as 'in order that' (emphasizing Christ's control of events) rather than as conj. 'because' as in K91 and K111.

famyd 'celebrated'. MED cites the v. in this passage as an aphetic form of *defamen* [OF *defamer*] and there are parallels that would suggest a common collocation of *aschamen* and *defamen*, as in e.g., *c.*1303 Mannyng *HS* 6569: 'For to make hym be ashamed þat he shulde be so defamed'. However, as in this last quotation, *defamer* and its derivations have the precise connotation of slandering, and being slandered was to be the least of Katherine's afflictions. For the same reason the sense 'starved', from OF *afamer*, can be discounted, despite the saint's undergoing the twelve days of privation at this juncture. It would seem more likely that Christ's words in the *vulgata* versions, 'Constans esto et ne paueas, quia ego tecum sum nec te desero; est etenim non parua turba hominum per te nomini meo creditura' (*Passio* 829–31), provide a sounder basis for a gloss of 'acclaimed'.

K71–8 'For your sake, Katherine, [it] sought you then, in order to behold the consolation of the saviour who destined you to a shameful fate; / When unhesitatingly the queen hurried to Porphiry / and begged him to propitiate the porter in order that they might see Katherine together, / they come there to Katherine, in a fitting and seemly manner, / to converse with that gracious [one] and find out her way of behaviour, / Beams of radiance are entirely all about her, / And [so] with her effusion of holiness she rendered those fledglings tame'. Editorial punctuation indicates only one of many possible readings of the sentence structure.

K71 *þe sothe þan for to sene sothe* is read as a preterite of *secchen*, in collocation with 'solace', as in K61 (see Note).

K72 *þat schap þe to schame ?* 'who destined you to a degrading fate [in order that you would eventually bear the crown of martyrdom]'. Cf. 1340–1370 *Alex. & Dind.*809: 'þat schullen schamely be schent & shapen to paine'.

K73 *Porfiri* Porphirius, or Porphiry, the legendary adviser to the tyrant, captain of his guard, and here also his 'true tutor' (see K116 and Note, and also p. lxxv).

K74 *plese* 'propitiate, bribe', best illustrated by the verbal substantive in, e.g., *c.*1387 *PPl.B.*(Trin-C) 3.231: 'Prestis & personis þat plesyng [vrr. plesynges, presentz, penys] desyreþ . . . taketh mede & money for massis þat þei synge'. MED *plesen* v. does not include what seems like Spalding's definitive example; the Latin is fairly unmistakable: 'quid restat nisi ut custodes carcens mercede ad consilium nostrum inflectamus . . . Nec mora: Porphirius ad consensum custodes emolliuit' (*Passio* 724–7).

to se 'in order that they might see'.

same 'together' [OE *samen*]. Heuser's and Holthausen's transcriptions of *fame* (presumably reading *Katereyn* as gen. of respect without *s*) are without foundation; the initial long *s* is like all others in the text.

K75 *com* this v., with *beene* in K77, *dowte* in K85, and possibly *departe* in K86 (see Notes), form a cluster of pr. historic tenses at this point of the story where action and concrete detail are abundant.

comly and clene the force of the phrase seems to be adverbial of manner, as is idiomatic in the text.

K76 *commen with* 'converse, enter into discussion with'; see MED *commŭnen* v. 3 (a).

hyre game 'her mode of being, way of acting'. Cf. *c.*1390 *Deus caritas* 42: 'Charite I rede þat we beginne As bi-fore alle oþer games'. See also K82.

K77 *Al bemus Al* here must be an adverbial emphatic 'entirely', qualifying *beene*. There appears to be no parallel to Spalding's knotty syntax, with this adv. just preceding a n.; but cf. the more common expressions, e.g., *c.*1400 *WarsAlex.*103: 'Clede hym all as a clerke'.

K78 *bawmyng* 'infusion, application', verbal n. [from OF *ba(s)mer*]. As the verb itself was not employed figuratively until the sixteenth century, it is remarkable that Spalding's figurative use of the verbal n. appears to be unique before its use by Dickens in 1844. The verbal n. is used in a literal sense in Trevisa's medical work, *c.*1387, and Lydgate uses n. *bawme* in a similar figurative way (see 1439 Lydg. *FP* 4.1133: 'Philosophie dede hir besi peyne To yiye hym . . . The soote mylk of hir brestis tweyne . . . bawme is non . . . Of worldli richesse may be therto compared').

briddus In the fourteenth century the literal sense of *brid* was a *young* bird or the young of any species, leading to its use as a term of endearment, as in, e.g., *a*.1325 *Cursor* (Göt) 9811: 'Qua-so on suilk a brid [i.e. Jesus] wilde thinck'. Spalding gathers in this sense because the queen and captain are so much approved of by this point. The sense is thus something like 'gentle novices'.

brogth tame 'brought to be tame', i.e., 'brought to a condition of receptivity [to the Christian faith]'. See OED *bring* v. 8: 'to cause to come to, into, etc., a certain state or condition'; cf. the only analogue: *a*.1400 *Destr.Troy* 74: 'Cornelius . . . brought it [book on Trojan war] so breff, and so bare leuyt, þat no lede might have likyng to loke þerappon'.

K80 *be name* Several interpretations of the phrase can be substantiated: 'indeed', 'individually', 'each of the aforementioned' or 'especially', but I have read it as 'by title', indicating how the high rank of the two converts redounded to Katherine's prestige; see MED *name* n. 1c.

K82 *hir game* 'her objective'; see also Note to K76. There is some case for reading *hir* as 'their', as in K268, understanding that the queen and Porphiry were so intent on their pursuit of grace that death was dear to them; but the *Passio* wording indicates that it is Katherine's expertise in Christian grace that was being spoken of (see Note to K85–6, below).

K83 *grymme* 'wrathfulness, savagery', not common in substantive use; cf. 1462 Hardyng *Chron.B.* p. 264: 'The Sarasyns . . . he slewe with much gryme'.

K85–6 *Passio* 801–4: 'Iam leti de ciuium supernorum presenti uisione et beate uirginis consolatione, regina simul et Porphirius procedunt de carcere, parati ad omnia que tortor insanus poterit inferre pro Christi nomine sustinenda'. The tortured syntax here is best understood if the four clauses are read in inverse order, meaning: Katherine had *so* driven her visitors from fear that, when they were to part from her, they did not dread to die the terrible death, so 'They do not fear to die that death that is dreadful here / when they part from that precious one, she had so driven them from terror'.

not þei dowte 'they do not dread' (see also Note to K75).

K86 *departe* probably a contracted form of a preterite of French derivation, employed to cut the second dip of the a-verse to a more acceptable three rather than four syllables (see also *commaund* and *graunt*, K34 and 223 and Notes); cf. the pp. in *c*.1338 Mannyng *Chron.Pt.1* 7634: 'deþ hadde departe [vr. departed] þer lyf'. Alternatively the v. is possibly either pr. historic (see Note to K75), or subjunctive: 'when they would part from' (seven of the ten subjunctives in the text are uninflected, see 'Language', p. xlviii).

hem MS *pe* makes no sense, and addition of a final *-m*, on grounds that a nasal bar was probably missed, is relatively straightforward, giving acc. pron. *þem*. Palaeographically the form *þem* would be preferable, and dialectically it would be understandable, when the nom. is always *þei* (21 times), but *þem* is not found in this MS, and *hem* is found 26 times. Because there is already some corruption in this vicinity (as there is not in the similar instance of one anomalous pron. in K26 (see Note to K26)), this word should probably be emended to the regular pron. acc. pl. It can then be assumed that an earlier exemplar had an *h* with a long downstroke, resembling *þ*. Cf. *Passio* 753–62, 801–4: (Katherine talking) "'Ne ergo mementanea penarum genera formides, quia non sunt condigne passiones huius temporis ad interminabilem gloriamque talibus pro Christo penis emercatur; ne ergo uerearis regis temporalis aut mortalis sponsi." Iam leti de ciuium supernorum presenti uisione et beate uirginis consolatione, regina simul et Porphirius procedunt de carcere, parati ad omnia que torto insanus poterit inferre pro Chrisi nomine sustinenda'. There is no mention of this emboldening in *Leg.Aurea*.

K87 'No longer would she [the queen], who was [now] lost / doomed, bow to her lord [and master]'. MS: *No lenger sche þat was lost to hire lowe þan wold þei lowte*. In isolation the MS reading would appear to make good sense in that the queen was now a lost cause since she had embraced the Christian faith, and so *þei*, the court retinue, would no longer make obeisance to her. When the line is placed in conjunction with the subsequent one (MS: *bot longlþ lagowrid him with al his gret lede*), and, indeed, with K89 (see below), it is clear that this whole area of the witness is corrupt, perhaps due to the state of an exemplar; note also the irregular and non-metrical b-verse. Some judicious emendation makes so much *good* sense that it would appear perverse to twist the MS readings into *some* kind of sense. It could be inferred that the emperor was the lost one because he was, as a sinner, doomed—and this is how Heuser apparently read the line—but this incidental observation cannot weigh against the characteristic fluent flow of the narrative, or the fact that we are now into the 'queen' section of the story; furthermore, such a reading would require emendation of *sche* to *he*. That latter reading is quite possible if MS *langowrid him* is adopted later— or even a sense that the king *labowrid* the queen. However all this makes one complex explanation, and it is more straightforward to remain consistent with the facts of the legend. Further, the king would not stand 'astonyd' (see K89) after his own berating, but surely would do after his queen's sudden attack on him, as happens at the latter end of the source legends. Spalding identifies the queen's attitude from that latter part of the legend where, having just witnessed the event with the wheel, the queen descends from her vantage-point and berates her husband; so *Leg.Aurea*: 'Regina autem que desuper hoc adspiciebat et usque tunc se celauerat statim descendens imperatorem de tanta seuitia durius increpauit. Rex autem furore repletus, cum regina sacrificare contempneret' (1210.105, 106); and *Passio*: 'Erat dudum regina desuper spectans diuine ultionis prodigiale signum; et que prius se occultabat propter metum uiri sui, nunc, arrepto itinere, se in conspectu belue seuientis constanter immersit, "Quid tu," inquiens, "miserande coniunx, contra Deum eluctaris? Que te insania, o crudelis belua, aduersus factorem tuum insurgere cogit? [etc.]"' (970–5). It is clear, then, that Spalding has not invented a new episode where the emperor gives his wife general misery before torturing her; neither of the two main sources supports this; in each case the queen is taken straight off to torture.

lorde Holthausen's apt emendation of MS *lowe* has been adopted here. The scribal error is understandable in that the collocation of *louten* and *loue* was so familiar; and it is palaeographically sound in that a long *Anglicana r* plus *Anglicana* curled *d* could easily have been misread as *Anglicana w*. With some hesitation the pron. *þei* has been removed from the end of the line, because it is metrically and grammatically superfluous and presents the appearance of a typical insertion to help a scribe clarify the other misreading in the line. The alternative possibility would be to emend MS *þei* to *sche* on the grounds that there is so much carelessness with pronouns throughout the witness. That would give an idiomatic repetition of the pron. nom. fem.: *No lenger sche þat was lost to hire lo[rd]e þan wold [sch]e lowte.*

The sense is thus more satisfactorily established, but this reading still leaves the b-verse with two long dips. Alternative readings would depend upon one's trust of the poet's metrical usage and sounding of final -*e*. If, together with MS *þei*, the word *hire* is removed, the b-verse can be read as a metrical -*to lorde þan wold lowte* (x/xx/). This is fairly idiomatic of Spalding, though the omission of adj. poss. is a perceptible loss. A harder case to argue (especially to habitual readers of Chaucer, unaccustomed to the rare, harsh xx/x/ b-verse) would be for -*to hire lorde wold lowte*—with no sounding of final -*e* on *lorde* (as would be consistent with the date and provenance suggested, even on a dative). But this would mean that both *þan* and *þei* would have been scribal insertions. The final reading is what seems to be the most fitting, though far from ideal, compromise of witness testimony, sense and metricality.

K88 'But lengthily upbraided him and all his great retinue'. For the reasons given above, *lagowrid* can be emended to *la[b]owrid* (see MED *labor* v. 4 (b), 'oppress, vex, harass'), and it can reasonably be assumed that the queen was the one doing the berating. That having been established, the pron. problems of K87–8 fall somewhat into place, and the myriad possible permutations of them can, to a large extent, be resolved. MED suggests an emendation of MS *lagowrid* to *la[n]gowrid* (s.v. *langouren* v. 'languish, suffer, endure'), requiring emendation of both feminine pronouns in K87 to masculine. For all the reasons given for previous lines and this, it seems to the present editor that the reading offered is more satisfactory. Palaeo-graphically it relies on scribal substitution of *g* for an exemplar's *b*. If an original *Anglicana b* were slightly dropped it could come to resemble an *Anglicana g*.

K89 *þan stode he astonyd* This straightforward line provides almost certain evidence that the king had done neither the harassing nor the berating (see Notes to K87 and 88, above). The king would not be stunned after his own berating, but surely would be after his queen's sudden attack on him. See *Passio* 970–1003 and *Leg.Aurea* 100.

K90 'He rampaged to such a degree that he almost choked himself, indeed.' The line is problematic both metrically and because the meaning of the last three words is ambiguous. Without the word *almost* the line would scan regularly with alliterative stress, aa/ax, on *stranglyd*, *selue*, *strof* and *dede*. It seems that the poet has desperately crammed in the necessary qualifier, *almost*, and made a mess of his line in so doing, simply because there is no possible synonymous qualifier to alliterate on *d* with the rhyming *dede*. With the inclusion of *almost*, the caesura might come after *strof*, and the line then scan aa/xx on *strangyed*, *strof*, *al* and *dede*. Problems then arise with the phrase *in dede*, which could, with phonological consistency, mean 'unto death' or 'indeed'. I have read the latter because no precedent comes to light for the prep. of motion, *in*, being used with 'death', though this may have been Spalding's meaning (see Lindesay, below).

The v. *stranglen* was more commonly used of choking or suffocating than of strangulating, and was occasionally used in a near figurative manner; cf. *a.* 1578 Lindesay *Chron.Scot.*(S.T.S.(Pit)) I.407: 'Or they come he was near-hand strangled to death be the extreme melanchollie'. Some precedent of an extravagant usage exists from stage villains and sundry beasts and devils in literature; cf. *c.*1386 Chaucer *CT.Pars.I.*768: 'They been the develes wolves that stranglen the sheep of Jhesu Crist'. There is no distinctive source of our tyrant's self-choking or killing with rage, but a similar sense comes from other parts of the sources, as when he hears of Porphiry's 'treachery' at *Passio* 1042–4: 'His tyrranus, uelut alto uulnere saucius, pro planctu rugitum uelut amens altum emisit, quo tota regia pertonuit'.

so he strof 'he raged to such a degree'; cf., e.g., *c.*1387 *PPl.B.*(Trin-C) 18.368: 'I faught so, me thursteth yet'.

strof OED (*strive* v.8) illustrates an intrans. usage applied to restive animals which renders the most appropriate parallel, in 1398 Trevisa *Barth.*28/15.775: 'Whan the wylde oxe hath longe stryue and maye not delyuer hymself out of the bondes . . . thenne for indignacion he loowth full lowde'. See also MED *strīven* v. 4 (b) and (d).

K91 *for* 'because'. See also K111.

qween There is no palaeographical justification for Heuser's and

Holthausen's readings of *qwene* (as also in K99, but cf. *qwene*, K73). The bar is over a second *e* in both instances, as also in *queen*, K80.

schamed 'dreaded, respected, feared'. In this sense the word is paralleled in biblical translations; cf. *c.*1384 WEV Luke 18: 2: 'Sum iuge was in sum citee, which dredde not God, nether schamede of [Vulgate *reverebatur*] men'.

K92 *he schope hir to schrynk* 'he planned to cow her'; see the parallel construction in K253. This causative use of *schrinken* is commonly used of literal 'withering' (e.g., *a.* 1398 Trev.*Barth* 190a/a: 'An herbe þat hatte Apium risus . . . draweþ and shrinkeþ Iawes of men'); it is not used causatively of 'flinching' (cf. *a.* 1400 *Morte Arth.*(*1*) 2105: 'They scherenken fore schotte of þe scharpe arowes'); but this seems to be one more example of Spalding's enterprising use of verbs.

qwen sche schuld blood schede 'at an occasion when she would shed blood'.

K95 *kerf* cf. Lay. *Brut* 29359: 'Of cnihten he cerf þe lippes, of madenen þa tittes'.

K96 *mynd* MS: *mpth*. The emendation makes better sense of the ensuing line. The error is understandable in the presence of *myth* K97, and was almost certainly caused by eyeskip.

K97 *frede* MS *fre*. Emendation to *fre[d]* [OE *gefrēdan* 'suffer , experience'] restores rhyme and makes good sense; the final *-e* has been added to make spelling of the rhymes consistent, as it is virtually throughout the witness. Cf. *c.*1000 Ælfric *Hom.I.*544: 'Hi swurdes ecʒe ne ʒefreddon'. How an original *d* might have disappeared in copying is unclear. Possibly the original word *fred* ended in a highly curled *Anglicana d* graph that often looks like an *Anglicana e*, so that a scribe chose to spell as *fre* a word in the exemplar that appeared to him like *free*.

K98 *þat hir hede schuld sterf* 'which was to annihilate her being', reading *hede* in its common sense of 'person, being'. The v. is almost certainly used transitively (see also Note to K99, below); this is unusual, but found in, e.g., *a.* 1529 Skelton *Duke of Albany* 251: 'The fynde of hell mot sterue the!'. Because of the rarity of such trans. use, an alternative conjecture might resemble *þat sche ne schulde sterf* (i.e. that she would not die, but have everlasting life); cf., e.g., *c.*1385 Chaucer *TC* V.1844: 'And loveth hym the which . . . Upon a crois . . . First starf, and roos, and sit in hevene above'. However there are no palaeographical grounds for such a bold emendation.

K99 *sterved* the more common intrans. use of the same v. which was probably used transitively in the previous line. Although there are no other instances of exchange of trans. and intrans. senses within the concatenation or iteration, Spalding does frequently play on change of finitude, mood, tense, person and number in his use of verbs, and of case in his use of nouns, at these key points in the structural framework (see, e.g., K14–15, K92–3, K120–1, K134–5, K218–9).

qween see above, K91.

strongly Either 'bravely, with fortitude' or 'violently'. There are close parallels that give grounds for the first reading; see, e.g., 1535 *Coverdale* 2 Esdras 10: 15: 'Loke what happeneth vnto ye, beare it strongly [Vulgate *fortifer fer*]'. The latter sense, however, ties in better with the ensuing phrase in K99: *of hym þat was sterne* (*s.v. of* below). Cf. 1340 *Ayenb.*157: 'þe dyeuel yziȝþ . . . þe stat of þe manne . . . and to huet vice he ys mest bouȝinde . . . and of þo half him asayleþ stranglakest'.

of 'by means of'; cf. *a*. 1300 *KAlex.*602: 'He shal be poysond . . . Of his owen traytoures'.

K100 *stirt* MS *stif* makes no sense, and Holthausen's emendation to *stir* is little better. The word *stirt* is here proposed on grounds of sense, and because palaeographically the emendation can be justified in that an original long *r* followed by *t* in *stirt* could easily have been misread as *f*. The alliterative collocation of *sterten* (though more often in its meaning of 'leap out') with *stytly*, or *stithly* or *stiffly*, is common; see, e.g., *c*.1400 *Destr.Troy* 10977: 'And ho stithly in the stoure start vppon fote'. The sense of not flinching when withstanding injury (together with the collocation of *sterten* and *standen*) is also found in *c*.1390 *Gawain* 2286: 'For I schal stonde þe a strok and start no more'. The *i*-form is supported by the phonology, and is found, for example, in the East Midland *Promptorium Parvulorum* and Chaucer manuscripts. See OED *start v.* for a long entry on the etymology of this v. Cf. 1508 Dunbar *Tua Mariit Wemen* 234: 'Scho suld not stert for his straik a stray breid of erd'.

stytly Both previous editors emended to the more common *styfly* or *styply*, but, in fact, the Northern form is well attested, e.g., *c*.1325 *Cursor* (Vsp) 23757: 'If we stitli all wil vs ster, crist help sal be us ner'.

K101 *as* Hs, Hlt: *os*. The problem of transcription is compounded because the form *os* is dialectically a feasible variant here, and we have already seen the solitary form *he* appearing among 28 *sche*-forms (see Note to K26). Ultraviolet light and magnification now demonstrate that the first letter is an *a*, though it would be difficult to quarrel with anyone who read it as *o*; and although it does not quite match the usual *a*-graph variants, the entire word is identical to MS *as* in K116.

loue the Christian commitment that had been taught to Porphiry by Katherine. This can be specifically traced to the doctrine of the Seven Bodily Deeds of Mercy—a doctrine which arose within medieval, not early-Christian, theology, and so does not figure in the sources. See also K111.

K102 *wonde hire wowndyd* an unambiguous example of Spalding's 'gram-metrical frame' of pp. applied to the acc. immediately after a v. (see also Notes to K36 and K251).

K103 *deueles lyme* Cf. E113.

K104 *dispised* 'vituperated, blasphemed'; Spalding appears to be the only writer to have used the v. in this sense without an object, and may have been influenced by the phrases *to sinnen/sweren dedli* (see also next).

dedly 'execrably, dreadfully', an intensifier often used with such verbs as *sinnen* and *sweren*, where it means 'in such manner as to endanger one's soul'; cf. 1340 *Ayenb.* 6/24: 'Yef he zuereþ uals be his wytinde, he him uorzuerþ . . . zuerþ dyadliche'. The intent appears to be to convey the foul and blasphemous nature of the tyrant's outbursts.

deel Evidently 'deliver, give vent to', but other 'venting' usages are not recorded.

K105 *bachilere* A technical term for the class of knighthood that comes just below the ranks of the hereditary noblemen. This is exactly where Porphiry, as the captain of the emperor's guard or his 'trw tutor', would most appropriately belong.

K107–9 It is not clear who is talking in these lines, and several alternative readings present themselves. The main uncertainty is with *mytthynes of mode* of K108, which could refer to Porphiry's manner of reply, or even to the tyrant's manner of questioning, rather than to the manner of burial. But see *Passio* 1023–5: 'Porphirius . . . corpus regine et martyris, conditum aromatibus, sepeliuit'.

K107 *hir blode als* MS *hir als*. The emendation is patently needed to restore iteration, rhythm and rhyme. Heuser emends to *blod*. Following Holthausen, final *e* has been added here in conformity with *blode* in the previous line and with two of the three rhyme words.

K111 *For* either 'in order that', or, as in K91, 'because' (see next).

schuld 'ought to', used more weightily and nearer to its etymological sense 'must', and referring to his Christian duty to bury the dead; see Notes to K101 and 108. See also *Passio* 1029–33: 'Quid tu homines innoxios punirir [*sic*, but puniri?] mandasti, imperator, uelut sacrilegii reos, quos potius defensos esse oportuerat, si te nature religio humana corpora a feris et uolatilibus tollenda esse docuisset? Qua in re uesano te spiritu agitari manifestum est, qui humanis corporibus nec etiam sepulturam indulges'.

feel v. found only in Northern and North Midland texts: 'conceal', so, contextually, 'bury'; see *Leg.Aurea*: '"Ego sum qui Christi famulam sepeliui"' (1211.114); this last derives from the same Indo-European root as Northern *felen*. Cf. *c.*1375 *NHom.*(3) *Pass.*3264: 'þe body full fayn wald þai stele, O-way fra vs it for to fele'.

fode 'person, body'. See E31 and E76. The two prevalent senses of *fode*, i.e. 'food' and 'offspring, young person', here mean something like 'her young being that would otherwise be food for beasts'. Cf. *c.*1200 *St.Kath(1)* 2244: 'Hare bodies unbiburiet alle, fode to wilde deor'; and *a.* 1400 *Torrent* 1823: 'The quene wexid tho nere wood For her doughter, that gentill ffode'. Cf. also E113.

K113 See also pp. lxxix–lxxx above. The image is common. See *St.Kath.*(2)(Auch) 595: 'As þei he hadde wounded be /Wiþ swerd, wiþ spere oþer kniif'; but there could be a variation here depending on whether the v. *sprunge* means 'had struck [into]' or 'was shivering'. So, the tyrant sprang up either (1) as if a spear [had been] plunged or shot [into] his heart, or (2) as if a spear were quivering or had shattered in his heart (see MED *springen* v.5.(f)). I have read the phrase as the first, possibly more straightforward, of these, despite the collocation with 'spear' in the second (as in, e.g., *c.*1400 *Destr.Troy* 9666: 'Speires vnto sprottes sprongyn ouer heddes').

K114 *he spared no speche . . . for to spende* 'he did not forbear vehemently to expend any words/utterance'. The collocation is common, but the sense here of 'not stinting to expend' is the same as when the v. is more commonly used with *mouth* or 'the rod'. See also next.

spende The v. of the common alliterative collocation *spenden* + *speche* (as in, e.g., *SGGK* 410: 'If I spende no speche, þenne spedeȝ þou þe better'), is here employed in a context that evokes other senses such as (1) of squandering, as in, e.g., *a.* 1500 *Chartier Quad.*(2) 170/18: 'Ye waste and spende afore the hande all suche as shulde helpe yow in your grette necessities'; (2) of expressing an opinion (now found only in Northern dialect), as in, e.g., 1687 Miége *Gt.Fr.Dict.*II s.v., 'To spend his verdict, to give one's Opinion'; or (3) of hounds bellowing, as in, e.g., 1590 Cokaine *Treat.Hunting* D ij b: '. . . He will vent so oft, and put vp ouer water, at which time the houndes will spend their mouthes verie lustely'.

K115 The unmetrical b-verse could be emended to either *and tellen with tunge*, or *and to telle with tunge*.

tene 'wrath, rage'; often conceptualised as something to be 'wreaked'; cf. *c.*1200 *Orm.*19606: 'And forrþi let he takenn himm To wreken hise tene'. This brings some light to bear on *tempure*, below, and possibly *spende*, above.

with him MS reading, *wiˢ hir*, does not readily suggest a one-word adv. Holthausen emends MS *wiˢ* to *wiþ*, as if the raised *s* sign might have been an intended *þ*. The other seven uses of raised *s* in the MS simply indicate a final *s* and never a *þ*. Katherine is still imprisoned, the anger is with Porphiry, and the pron. must be emended accordingly.

tempure The usual sense is 'assuage', 'modify' or 'restrain', or even 'dispense in a measured way', but a gloss of 'wreak', i.e. 'assuage by giving vent to it', seems most applicable here in the presence of *tene*; however, there seem to be no recorded examples of such usage. Cf. MED *tempren* 6 (d).

K116 *as that* 'because'. Heuser erroneously reads *as*, with its secretary *a* and *b*-shaped *s*, as *al*, and Holthausen silently follows him—whether unconsciously or as an emendation is not clear, for Holthausen's emendations are not always indicated. This is one of several examples suggesting that Holthausen used Heuser's text as his base rather than making a new transcription. Curiously, *al that* makes a better reading, which is perhaps why Heuser unconsciously transcribed it in the first place.

trw tutor 'loyal warden'. Porphiry, as a particularly valued minister, is here regarded as the tyrant's protector and counsellor. In early usage the sense did not have today's pedagogic overtones; see OED *tutor sb.* and MED *tūtŏur* n. 2 (a).

entende MED inexplicably deserts Heuser's edition and follows Holthausen's spurious emendation, 'no[t]', in this citation. The manuscript is perfectly clear. The sources are no help with the interpretation, but ME senses 'pay heed to, listen to', meaning that Porphiry refused to listen but went right ahead with his new persuasion, give the most straightforward translation; cf. 1410 Walton *Boeth*.p.86: 'En[t]ende what I schal say'. However, see OED *intend v.*, which tracks the extensive and complex development of senses in L and OF, reflected also in ME.

K117 Spalding appears to fail to alliterate a common n. on *w* in this line. Alliteration would be very much improved by *welawey* for *allas* and *wode*, *wrecche*, *wycked* or *wyght* for some of the syllables that might have resulted in a scribal *caytef*. Howevr, there is no strong evidence of scribal substitution of concrete vocabulary in the text and no strong grounds for emendation.

woo The tyrant is thinking subjectively. Whatever religious activity has effected the change in Porphiry is the cause of, and so in his mind has become, the *tyrant's* nightmare. The best translation is probably 'dreadful thing, evil dispensation'.

wrunge 'pressed, tormented, wrested'. See OED *wring v.* 9. †d; cf. 1528 More *Dyalogue* III. Wks.210/1: 'Our harte euer thinketh the iudgement wrong, that wringeth us to the worse'. See also MED *wringen* v. 6.

K118 *wende* 'believed'; MS *reende*. The emendation (based on spelling in K124) makes better sense and furnishes an ax/xa pattern to the otherwise unusually defective alliteration in the copy. MS *reende* could be read as past tense of OE *geregnian* 'to prepare, dispose', but normally the verbal sense is 'to array'. The three possibilities alliterating on *w* are *wēnde* 'ween, believe' [OE *wēnan*], *wen(e)de* 'wend' [OE *wendan*], or *wenede* 'wean' [OE *wenian*]. Although the last has precedent in its OE sense of 'trained', which would be most germane, and would have a more appropriate rhyming vowel sound than the long sound indicated by the MS *ee*, such a sense had apparently died out by the fourteenth century, when it had come to mean something like 'weaned' (however, see ASD, *s.v. wenian*). The reflexes from *wendan*, although they also sound a short *e*, would here convey 'turned over in the mind, reflected upon', which might be appropriate for Porphiry's later deliberations (see Note to K124), but not for the emperor in this context. This leaves a reflex of OE *wēnd(e)* 'believed, imagined'. The sense is exact (see *Passio* 1046–52 and *Leg.Aurea* 116), but poses the problem that OF short *e* of *entendre* and *defendre* and the short reflex of OE *spendan* would then rhyme with long *e* (also perhaps indicated by the scribe's double *e* graph, often used for long *e* as in, e.g., *keel, meel, reel* (K200-4)). However, for rhyme of the long *e* of *wende* with *fende* and *mende* see K122–4, below, and this probably settles the decision. In conformity with spelling in K124, one MS *e* graph has been removed from the text, on the assumption that an original *Anglicana* w was read and copied as *re-*. The emended alliterative pattern ax/xa is similar to that of the following line.

K119 The rare alliterative pattern ax/xa is unique to this line, but is premised on the dubious argument that [s] and [ʃ] alliterate (see p. xxxviii and n. 77).

K120 *fecchen* There is no distinct source for the tyrant's statement. Holthausen emends to *teechen*, palaeographically plausible, and making good sense. In so doing he reduces the optimum aa/aa alliterative pattern to xa/aa, though this pattern is witnessed elsewhere, e.g., K91 and K213; the alliterating *t* of Holthausen's emendation builds upon the alliteration on *t* in the previous line, thus partially maintaining the poet's standard pattern of alliterating on one main letter throughout each of the four couplets of the octet. Such a 'recompensing' pattern can also be seen in K21–2 and K159–60. However, it should be noted that when the alliteration goes, the maintenance of couplet alliteration often breaks down altogether, as in, e.g., K213–4 and K271–2 and in the MS line here. An emendation in the same category, following Holthausen, has been made in K158, but, with some reservations, the MS reading has been retained here.

K121 Word-play on *foly* and *fende* of K120, where the tyrant's words denote the 'sin' of converting to Christianity. But, in the voice of the narrator, we are told that the captain defended himself from doctrinal transgression by going to his Christian martyrdom with extra faith and humility.

K122 *to mende hym* The sense [from OF *amender*] appears to be reflexive: 'to improve [himself]' even further in his already-won state of grace; cf. *a*.

1398 Trev. *Barth*.22a/a: 'Ʒif þe soule by resoun turneþ toward god, he is byschyned, amendid [L *melioratur*] & lmade perfite'. See also K125.

K123 This is one of the two unmetrical b-verses in the sestets (the other is the rhyming K126). It would be improved by the omission of *þe*.

K124 'Porphiry constantly believed [for] himself / [that] God's mercy would make amends to him [for his sins]'.
    wende hym 'supposed, hoped' [OE *wēnan*], rhyming, as in K118, on short *e*.

K125 *mende* This self-rhymes with *mende* K122. Holthausen substitutes *tende*, no doubt suspecting eyeskip and perhaps an involuntary entering of the common collocation with *merci*, as in, e.g., *a*. 1450 *Castle Persev*.1693: 'Mercy may mende al þi mone'. He might be correct, but there are no compelling reasons to change a fairly satisfactory manuscript reading, and there are no parallel examples of God's mercy *tending* the soul. The sense here must be a variation on *mender* as used in K122, but here with the more usual trans. meaning to 'redeem' his natural quota of sins through his martyrdom—the doctrinal logic being that, through martyrdom, he would miss out on the regular punishment of the afterlife and go straight to heaven.

K126 *him rent* 'was rent (from) him'. MS *his rent*. The manuscript reading is particularly attractive and can possibly be seen as a grim joke (it would depend upon the common interpretation of *heed* as 'being, person'; cf. 1400 *Eche man be war* 39: 'Man, not nys thyn, alle god lent . . . And Ʒut thy soule is goddis rent'; *c*.1440 *Daily Work* (Thrn) 302: 'Sacrifice askes god of mane as rent'). However, there is little theological logic in *rent* 'payment' through martyrdom, unless in the sense of paying through the blood of martyrdom. The emendation, tentatively made, gives a more straightforward reading, consistent with the tone of the whole and with the basic fact of the legend— that Porphiry was beheaded. The defective metre of the line echoes that of K123 with which it rhymes. It should be a strict b-verse pattern, as are the other 19 of the 20 fourteenth lines, and both the manuscript metre and that of the emended line have two long dips. One way to clear this would be to emend to *For his head was rent* (xx/x/); this has the advantage of explaining the ambiguity of MS *his* as a scribal misinterpretation, created while trying to be helpful, but has the disadvantage of making the v. *rent* alone signify 'chopped off', an interpretation too far, perhaps. The other way to achieve metrical regularity would be to omit the word *For*, but this effects a somewhat crass closure.

K127 *lyft vp oloft* 'brought up into the open [from the deep, underground cell]', retaining the earlier sense of 'into the air'.

K128 *lake* 'pit, cell'; cf. *a.* 1500 *Mirror Salv.*p. 7: 'And Daniell in þe lake of lyouns'.

þat lurdeyn to lef Either 'to the pleasure of that scoundrel' (*lef* being a n.), as in, e.g., *c.*1175 *PMor.* (Lamb) 250: 'þer inne boð þa þe was to lof [vr. lef] wreche men to swenchen'; or 'to please that scoundrel' (*to lef* being the inf. from OE *lufian*). The latter is more idiomatic of Spalding.

K129–32 This episode of the story is taken from the early part of the legend where, immediately after her conversion of the rhetoricians and before he has her scourged in prison, the emperor likewise tempts Katherine. The *vulgata* text is quite specific on the lack of marital overtures in this matter (see *Passio* 570–85). Voragine, writing at least a century later, puts this episode after the conversion of the queen and Porphiry, and is more arch on the subject (see *Leg.Aurea* 1209.93–4). Some vernacular versions follow the *Passio*, some, with less restraint, *Leg.Aurea*. The decision here hinges on the word *after*, which can mean 'second to [my wife]', signifying that the wife is the *first chosyn*, or 'according as if you were [my consort]', meaning that Katherine would be the *first chosyn*, his concubine. I have interpreted it as the former; the decided *lack* of sexual overtones of the *Passio* appears to be followed by both Spalding and Bokenham.

K130 *And send* 'if you will but proffer'. See also K133.

schame Here '[physical] harm'; cf. *a.* 1400 *Roland & O.* 284: 'Lete Duke Naymes lenge at hame To kepe pareche walles fro schame'. The line might alliterate aa/ax (or aa/xx if alliteration on [s] and [ʃ] was not part of the authorial plan; see p. xxxviii and n. 77). However the original might well have been *grame* 'affliction', giving the more acceptable alliterative pattern aa/bb.

K131 *goddesse* Gen. fem. without -*s* inflexion, as in, e.g., 'Ladi(e) Dai'.

croft 'enclosure', sometimes with a sense of sanctuary; cf. *c.*1350 *NHom.(2)PSanct.*83/38: 'þat o greyne won al vr wele whon greyne on grounde was sowe In Marie lond, þat Mylde croft'.

K133 *faynt* Normally 'flag, weaken', as in *a.* 1400 *Destr.Troy* 6287: 'He [Hector] was . . . Euer frike to þe fyght, fayntid he neuer'; but here more like 'blench, quail, dread, be drained of courage [in the face of the planned torture]'.

K134 *freye* 'terror' [OF *affrai*]; cf. *c.*1410 Lovel.*Merlin* 512: 'It Nis non wondyr thowgh ʒe han Fraye of the torment that is ʒow befalle'. Heuser reads MS *frepe* as *freþe* [OE *freht*]—a Germanic synonym, as in, e.g., 1440 *PParv.* 177: 'Freyhte [vrr. freyt, freyth] or feer: *Timor, pavor, terror*'—but the scribe's East Midland -*th* spelling of the spirant cannot be represented by a thorn, so his case is not convincing.

may feel 'may prevail [upon]'. Holthausen emends to *fail*, but more certainly the v. derives from OE *befēolan* (see ASD Suppl.) Northern and North Midland 'prevail upon, influence, impel'; cf. *Greg.Dial.* 156.1: 'He mid gemalicum benum befealh þam halgan were þer him wære alypfer ut to farenne [*importunis precibus ut relaxaretur imminebat*]'. The semantic relationship between this specific sense in ME and the sense 'bury', found in K111 and K198 (see 'Glossary'), as well as with a further sense 'adhere', is obscure, but can be deduced lexically as all deriving from a fundamental meaning of 'enter into'.

K135 *Qwyles þat þou meue mayst* Word-play on *mef / meue*. In the first instance the word is used transitively 'bring about a change (in you)'; in the second Katherine is the subject, so 'physically move [i.e. be alive]'.

K136 *feel* Here (and in K270) 'feel, be sensate (of)' [OE *gefēlan*]. See preceding Note.

  greue The interpretation 'bodily affliction, pain' [OF *gref*], rhyming on *meue*, *leue* and *preue*, is phonologically sound; cf. *a.* 1200 *Ancr.*(Recl.) 106a: 'Me lauerd þu seist hwerto? ne mahte he wið leasse greue habben arud us?'. The reading *gru* 'iota' [OF *gru* 'a grain'] has been discounted on phonological grounds, despite the fact that in ME it was often written with *eu* as the stressed vowel. The *Katherine* scribe would probably have written the word as *grw* in any case; see, e.g., *rwd* (K15).

K137 *punchyng* Either verbal n. from v. *pouncen* 'stab' (cf. 1440 *PParv.*416: 'Punchyn, or bunchyn; *Trudo, tundo, impello*'; cf. *a.* 1475 *N-Town* 328/30: 'The naylis gun his lemys feyn (= ?make faint), and þe spere gan punche and peyn'); see MED *pouncinge* ger.; or a form of 'punish'; see MED *punishing(e* ger. Neither cites this instance.

  peles 'spikes'; see MED *pel* n. [OF *pel*].

K139 *Prestly þou preue mayst* 'promptly you can prove through experience, experience at first hand'.

K141 *wrenchis and wylys* Concatenation is effected through the sound of two different words: 'wheels' (from previous line) and 'wiles'. Although such esprit is sometimes found in mid-stanza iteration (as in, e.g., K120–1 and K134–5) it is not otherwise found in stanza-linking concatenation.

K142 The b-verse is unmetrical; prep. *to* was almost certainly an original *for to*, as in K145 and 146.

K144 *sley3t . . . gynne* The aa/xx alliterative pattern is not satisfactory, but hardly allows improvement. The collocation is common.

  K145–6 *made he . . . to medyl hire with mischef* 'he caused (that maiden) to involve herself in duress' (see Note to K146 *s.v. mischef*, below). For *made he*, see MED *maken* v. 15. The rest of the phrase is a variation of common *merren with mischef*, but v. *medlen*, in its sense 'embroil [in]', is not otherwise found in a causative function, more often appearing in refl. usage, 'have dealings [with]', as in *a.* 1465 Shirley *Death Jas.*12: 'He was a lusti man, full amorous, and much medeled hym with loves arte'.

K145 *hir* MS *hís*. Emendation has been made on grounds of sense: the tyrant would not be causing Katherine to be involved with violence in order to change *his* intention, but rather *hers*. Spelling is based on fully written adj. poss. *hir* found in 17 instances (e.g., K16). For similar scribal errors with pronouns see K8, K46, K86, K115 and K126.

hir mynde for to make 'in order to coerce her attitude [to create the resolution he wanted from her]'; see MED *maken* v. 14c., with sense of 'force', e.g., 1381 *Pegge Cook.Recipes* p. 94: 'Kest hem al in the broth, and mak it thorw a clothe, and boyle it'.

K146 *mischef* 'adversity'. In a state of war *mischef* was the final agent of the enemy's undoing; cf. to be *at mischef* 'to be in great danger of falling/ succumbing', as in *c.*1410 Lovel.*Grail* 20.267: 'Pompee . . . drof these Felouns Into the Cave . . . And putten hem Alle to Mischef'. The phrase implies 'to place her under an *ultimate* duress'.

mynne On the evidence of the rhyming vowel sound, this can not be an aphetic form of *minen* 'undermine' [OF *miner*], which is used figuratively only of hearts (as in, e.g., *c.*1422 Hoccl. *JWife* 476: 'Shee wolde for no thyng bowe & enclyne; Hire hertes Castel kowde they nat myne'), but more likely 'diminish' [from OF *(di)minüer* or ME adj. *min(n)(e)*/ON *minni*)], which also would be more likely to be used of *miȝt*.

K147 *Passio* 960–5: 'Necdum uerba uirgo finierat, et ecce angelus Domini, de celo descendens, molem illam, uehementi turbinis ictu impactam, tanto impetu concussit ut, ruptis compagibus, partes auulse super infusum populum tanta ui excuterentur ut quattuor milia de ipsa turba gentilium uno turbine necarentur . . .'. But for *turbinis ictu* (where most manuscripts of the 'Shorter' Vulgate have *fulminis ictu*) see *Seinte Katerine*, Note to line 728, s.v. *þunres dune*; see also further below.

so deuly 'so violently, awfully' [from OE *dēofolīce*], but giving the sense of 'with such ferocious downward-driving impetus'. Although the sense, when qualifying the deed of an angel, is odd, its usage had developed to extreme intensifying, as in *c.*1400 *Sultan Bab.*265: 'The Dikes were so develye depe, Thai helde hem selfe Chek-mate'; *a.* 1450 *Siege Jerus.*(Lamb) 454: 'Deflich many [Ld: a ferlich nonbr] Busked to batail'. A reading as adv. *deuly* [from OF *dëu*, adj.], giving 'justly, deservedly', has been rejected on the grounds that it is not implied in the L legends. It is conceivable that MS *so deuly* stands for an original *sodenly* (see also K159 *sodanly*), translating the immediacy of the deliverance after Katherine's prayer (cf. 'et ecce . . .' in *Passio*, above); this would provide the optimum alliterative pattern: aa/aa. However, I adopt the *lectio difficilior* which leaves the scribal word division unaltered and gives the pattern aa/ax, found in twenty other lines.

K148 See Note to K147, but also see *Leg.Aurea*: 'Et ecce, angelus domini molam illam cum tanto impetu diuellendo concussit quod quatuor milia gentilium interemit' (1210.104)—where the force might be translated as 'with such displacing impetus'. It is not easy to work out how Spalding visualised the decimation of the crowd of heathens: whether they were forced down by the chunks of the wheels into a very sparse entity, or whether the force flung them out very widely into the same. The adv. suggests the latter.

thyrst A metathesized form of ON *prȳsta* which can mean 'to compress, force down'; cf. Misyn *FL* I.V.2: 'To god þai ȝelde no deuocion, for þe byrdyn of riches with þe whilk þai ar þirstyn to þe erth'; and Spalding uses the word more or less in this sense in K49; but more often than not he uses a root in different ways, and the plausible image of the heathens being 'forced' or 'flung out very widely' into a wide circle of dead ones is even more attractive, as if a meteorite had hit a sheaf of corn.

thynne 'from there', a Northern and North East Midland form. See MED *thīne* adv. 1 (b); cf. *a.*1400 *Cursor* (Göt) 6676: 'If he to min auter fly, Men sal him þein [Vsp: þeþen] draw to die'.

K149 *thyn* The iterated sound is now in the adj. 'thin on the ground, decimated'; cf. MED *thin(ne* adj. 2 (c), cf. *a.*1400 *Morte Arth. (2)* 280: 'Was none so stiff agayne hym stode; Fulle thynne he made the thikkest prees'.

K152 This episode is not mentioned in the *Leg.Aurea*. The *Passio* gives: 'Que cum ad locum passioni prefixum properaret, respiciens uidit turbam multam uirorum et mulierum sequentium se atque plangentium, inter quas precipue uirgines et matrone nobiles lamentabantur. Conuersa igitur ad illas, dixit: "O generose matrone, o uirgines clarissime, nolite, obsecro, passionem meam lamentabili planctu onerare sed, si nature pietas uos ulla erga me incitat ad miserationem, congaudete, precor, michi potius, quia uideo Christum me uocantem, qui est amor meus, rex et sponsus meus; qui est merces copiosa sanctorum, decus et corona uirginum, Vos uero planctum istum lacrimabilem, quem inanter in me deperditis, in uos ipsas conuertite, ne uos in hoc gentilitatis errore dies suprema deprehendat, pro quo fletus eternos subeatis"' (1095–1106). Such a portrayal could only have been based on that of the daughters of Jerusalem in the life of Christ in Luke 23: 27–8: 'Sequebatur autem illum multa turba populi et mulierum quae plangebent et lamentabant eum. Conuersus autem ad illas Iesus dixit: "Filiae Ierusalem, nolite flere super me, sed super uos ipsas flete et super filios uestros"'. See also Note to K156, below.

more and myn The scribe may have changed the common collocation *more and myn* for the peculiar MS *more and manp* by dittography of *Ma(tro)n(es)*, compounded with *may(dens)* in the next line. The adj. *myn* is required for both rhyme and sense; see *Passio* 1098–9, cited above. The spelling of the emendation is not expanded, as the scribe appears to favour long forms in the octets (e.g., K142–8: *wynne, gynne, mynne* and *thynne*), which, then, in the sestets (K149–53), are followed by the shorter forms (almost as if to

emphasize the short lines): *thyn*, *gyn*, *blyn*, and thus, presumably, *myn* for
MS *manþ*.

K155 *brast on a breyd* 'burst out in an [impassioned] utterance/reproof'.
The forms of *brast* here and of *brest* in K218 are notably closer to OI/ON
bresta (inf.) and *brast* (pa. 3 sg.) than to English *berstan* (inf.) and *bærst* (pa.3
sg.).

breyd Some reproof can be read into Katherine's utterance, as in the tone
of her words to the weeping women in the *Passio* (see Note to K152). MED
distinguishes *breid* n. (2), which carries the sense of reproof [from OE v.
ābregdan], from *breid* n. (1), which came to mean merely an 'utterance' [(see
MED n. (1) (e)) 'deriving from the OE n. *ge)bregd*']. The distinction seems
unnecessary when the latter could obviously carry the sense of reproof
equally well, as in, e.g., *a.* 1325 *Cursor* (Vsp) 15712: 'For mi god ded he
[Judas] sal me giue A waful hard braid [Trin-C: breide]'.

K156 See Note to K152. MS *a booue / a boone*. Three good readings are
possible here: (1) as n. *a boone* [from ON *bōn* 'a prayer'], (2) as adv. *abooue*
[OE *a bufan*], (a) 'above' or (b) 'openly', with word division analogous to
MS l. 2, *be low*, here edited as *below* (K3). Of the two adverbial readings,
'above' (assuming that the noble women were watching the execution from a
high place) is rejected on the grounds that in the sources the women came to
Katherine. For the adopted reading, see MED adv. sense 5 (c), e.g.,
Rich.(Brunner) 1679: 'Kyng Roger spak ffyrst aboue'. Read as adv. of
manner the clause *abooue sche hem bilde* 'openly she entreated', gives one of
Spalding's most common grammetrical frames, adv.+nom.(+acc.)+v., as in
prestly sche preyd in the following line. Although I have read the MS *n/u*
graph as *u*, it is equally likely that a common reflex of OE *abufan*, such as
aboun or *abowen*, was intended; see MED *above(n* adv.

bilde Interpretation of the line depends on definition of this v. (see Note
to K152). It can not derive from v. 'to submit' (from AN n. *bille* (ultimately
L *bulla*)), as the vowel of this was short in ME, rhyming with nouns such as
'skill', as in, e.g., *c.*1350 *Leg.Holy Rood* 138: 'Pardon in book is billed'.
Emendation to *ȝilde* (presupposing that *bilde* arose from the common scribal
habit of alliterating over and above the authorial pattern) gives good sense
(cf. *c.*1400 *WarsAlex.*5318: 'Bot lat þi semblance be sadd quen þou þi saȝe
ȝildis'), but there could be few palaeographical grounds for misreading ȝ as
b. The strongest reading is based on ME v. *belden* (A *bældan*, *beldan*)
'embolden, encourage', which overlaps *bilden* (West Saxon *bieldan*, *byldan*)
'instruct, edify', in both form and meaning, giving a similar usage and form
as in *Maldon* 168–70: 'þa gyyt þæt word gecwæð Har hilderinc, hyssas
bylde, bæd gangan forð gode geferan'.

K158 The previous editors each read this line differently, but rely on the
MS *hir pert pouste* to mean Katherine's power. The emendation to *paynie*

'heathen lands' (see MED *paienie*) has been made in accordance with tentative suggestions made by the late Basil Cottle, and by Thorlac Turville-Petre, to whom I am grateful. It has been elected from four possible readings, and depends upon *hir* in the a-verse being read as 'their' (as in K268). It maintains the alliterative pattern aa/aa on *þ* in two lines, and contrasts neatly with *peyne* in K157. However, it creates a weak caesura; it may be appropriate to take out the following word, *hit*, not only to regularize the rhythm, but to strengthen the caesura. There may have been disorder around an *i* graph in the tradition. Holthausen's reasonable emendation to *in* [*v*]*ayne hit was þilde* should also depend upon *hir* in the a-verse being read as 'their'.

K160 *freschely* 'boldly, openly, freely'; see MED *freshli* adv. 3 (a) . . . '*fresshelyche* [*L liberius*] . . .'.

fylde 'corrupted, defiled'. See *Passio* 1080: 'Quamquam tu omnium horum rea sis quos, arte magica deprauatos, mortis compendium subire fecisti, si tamen ab erroris proposito animum reuocares'.

K161 *leyd* 'destroyed'; see MED *leien* v. (1) 5(a).

K162 'Her neck was very acquiescent in proffering that beautiful member [her head]'; see MED *launchen* v. 1.(a), and its idiomatic slaughtering imagery.

lym MS *lpm̃*. Although some of the nasal contractions over *n* have been expanded (see pp. xv and xcv–xcvi), the spelling *lymm* is not otherwise recorded, and the sign has been read as a flourish.

K163 *feythful to fynde* 'found to be faithful, i.e. proved faithful when put to the test', inf. in the passive sense 'to be found'.

K165–7 This is a technical statement about the properties of this specific saint (see Note to K1–4, above); the spare, almost legalistic tone suggests an association with guild patronage (see K268 and Note), where 'frendchip' of the saint was so important.

K166 *hem bynde* MS *bþnd hem*. The patently necessary emendation restores rhythm and rhyme, and it is probably correct to add the *-e* in conformity with the uniform spelling pattern of the rhymes, as found throughout the text; see MED *binden* v. 7 a.(a) and its senses 'as of being bound to an oath'.

K168 *To fende hem* This is not refl., but the predicate of *prayed* in K165. Katherine was praying *to* God 'to defend' her devotees from hellfire.

K169 *ful hendly* 'very noble, courteous' [from OE *hende*, adj.]; Spalding normally keeps the qualifiers within the same half-line as their n. or v., so despite no parallel late ME evidence, *hendly* is almost certainly adj. qualifying the greeting, and not adv. 'graciously' describing the manner in which Katherine (nom.) received her greeting. Cf. *mytthyly* K47.

K170 *he þat was hyȝest* Periphrasis for God.

K171 *Trewth* 'Righteousness', i.e. God (see also Note to K58).

K172 'because those [who] have learnt about your love will live according to your desire'. The relative is omitted; see also Note to K33.

loue The MS reading is completely clear, but the n. *lore* would have been more epigrammatic; cf. *a.* 1325 *Cursor* (Vsp) 1832: 'þai wald noght lere [Göt: trou; Trin-C: leue; Frf: liue] on noe lare'. The most appropriate significance of *loue* is that it is Katherine's love for God that is exemplary.

K173–4 'I intend to save you without delay / to protect you from [those] devils [who] would make you frightened'; see also Note to K33.

K173 *I am at asent* 'I intend'. The phrase *at asent* is normally used to mean 'in agreement', as in *c.*1330 *Otuel* 515: 'Ich wele ben at acent þat þou sschalt wedde belecent'; but the sense here must be closer to that defined in MED *assent* n. 3(b) 'will, intention' (a sense not otherwise found in the phrase *at a(s)sent*); cf. *a.* 1500 *Degrev.*(Cmb) 863: 'Hyt ys my lordys assent With-ynne for to be'.

K175 *meyne of myrþe* 'company of joy', i.e. the angels of heaven. The collocation here seems to be unique.

hely 'solemnly, strongly, entirely', from *hole* adj. [OE *hǽl*]; see MED *holli* adv.5; *c.*1475 *Cath.Angl.* 59b 'Hally [Monson: Haly]: *firmiter, firme*'. Spalding normally accommodates the qualifiers in the same half-line as the n. or v. that they qualify, so this is almost certainly adv., and not adj. 'holy' qualifying the angels. See also Note to K169.

haue mente Use of the pl. v. with collective n. is idiomatic; see also K213.

K176 *qwen myth hath þe merde* 'when violence has disfigured or destroyed you'. The alliterative collocation is common.

K178 *lyȝth* Almost certainly the common 'ease, comfort' [OE *līhtan*], and not an unparalleled 'make illustrious' [OE *lēohtan*]. Cf. *a.* 1325 *Cursor* 5727: 'He liht [Göt: helpid; Trin-C: halpe; Frf: confort] þam o þair wa'.

K179 *hyȝe* Read as adv. 'highly, eminently'.

K180 *oure* The royal or divine pl. (God still talking); cf. *c.*1400 *Bk.Mother* 39/23: 'Make we a man to oure ymage and to oure liknesse'.

K181 *oriȝth* A rare form of the more usual *ariȝht* 'on right', but cf. *SGGK* 40: 'þis kyng lay at Camylot vpon krystmasse . . . With rych reuel oryȝt and rechles merþes'.

K182 *þour* 'through, by means of', a metathesized form more common in Northern ME. OED does not illustrate this spelling, but cf. the textual variants in Chaucer *CT.Fkl.*865. See also MED *thurgh* prep. 4 (d).

stiffenes of steuen 'firmness of pledge [i.e., My word].' The n. *steven* was used of the command of God particularly in Early ME and Northern religious texts, e.g., *a.* 1450 *Yk.Pl.*9/15: 'Noght by my strenkyth but by my steuyn, a firmament I byd apere'.

K183 *pytte* Superimposed on a previously written *putte*. Glossing is equivocal because the form is so unusual; it could be a derivation of **picchen*, as in K27, but is more likely to be a rare form of ME *putten* [OE *pȳtan*], sounding much the same in the poet's dialect, but employed here for the rhyme (though see also *put* K212, K256). Cf. *a.* 1400 *Firumb.*(2) 596: 'Lo, here ys the spere . . . That longes pyt in hys hert' (though compare *a.* 1475 *N-Town* (see Meredith, *Appendix 4* 19–20): 'For Longeus . . . A ryth sharpe spere to Crystys herte xal pyth'—more likely from *picchen*).

K184 *preuyd hirself purly* 'proved herself to be completely worthy'.

K185 *faunchon MS fauuchon/faunchon.* Elsewhere *fauchon*, a useful alliterative synonym for a sword. It is, more precisely, a scimitar, an apt execution weapon of an eastern potentate. Superfluous *n* occurs also in *mawment* (K11), *reyngnest* (K239) and *dyngnite* (K257).

K186 *throng* The normal sense of 'crushed' or 'pressed' is here stretched to mean 'issued, surged' as in *a.* 1400 *Morte Arth.*3755: 'Thare they thronge in the thikke, and thristis to the erthe Of the thraeste mene thre hundrethe'.

ful thik The opposite of *ful thynne* in K148, and, again, an adverbial construction. As such, it is often employed for intensifying effect.

K187 *þus was þe cors knytt of a kaytyf vnknyit* 'Thus was the [divinely] wrought body undone through the agency of a villain'. The adverbial construction is similar to that in K99 (*þus sterved þe qween strongly of hym þat was sterne*). I am grateful to Myra Stokes for the observation that the doctrinal idea expressed here is that murder undoes what God has made; cf. *c.*1378 *PPl.B.*(Trin-C) 17.281–91: 'And whoso morthereth a good man, . . . He fordooth the levest light that Oure Lord lovyeth . . . Ac this is the worste wise that any wight myghte Synnen ayein the Seint Spirit—assenten to destruye . . . that Crist deere boughte . . . Forgyve be it nevere That shente us and shedde oure blood—forshapte us, as it semed: *Vindica sanguinem iustorum*'. The senses of 'make' and 'unmake', both occurring the same line, are found in, e.g., *c.*1412 *Hoccl.RP* 2564: 'Al-thogh a kyng haue habundance of myght In his land, at his lust knytte & vnknytte'.

vnknyit (*Hs, Hlt*: *unknytt*) 'destroyed'. Although the main vowel here and in the rhyming *flyit*, below, rhymes with *pytte* and *kitte*, no pressing reasons have been found to change the manuscript spelling in either case. In the case of *flyit*, especially, the orthography suggests a different v. from *flien* [OE *flēogan*], namely *flitten* [ON *flytja*]. Such orthography is consistent with the similar doubling of the vowel to *iy* in the invariably monosyllabic *giyld* in K268; below, yet the retained spelling rhymes on the single short vowel in a monosyllabic word, and this pp. must be the same as *knytt* in the same line, so the matter is problematic. Note also the same rhymes in *a.* 1425

*NHom.(3) Leg.Suppl.Hrl.*81/57: 'In his lufe so he hir knyt, þat þarfro wald scho neuer flit'.

K188–90 Lines 188 and 190, which have come to stand adjacent in the witness, have been editorially reversed in order to restore the mid-stanza iteration (bringing it to 16 of the 20 stanzas). This also makes better sense of the story and recovers the consecutive alliteration on the same letter for two lines. It is not clear how the lines came to be juxtaposed; their present MS arrangement suggests that the overall format of one exemplar in the tradition was different, probably in the arrangement of the sestets; the word *qwen* occurring twice at the beginnings of lines would make transposition easy.

K188 *vnworthi* The force is adverbial. There is no recorded parallel use.

K189 Details of Katherine's espousal with Christ (such as with a ring) belong rather to late medieval legends of the saint, but cf. *Passio* 625–6: 'Christus me sibi sponsam adoptauit, ego me Christo sponsam', 760: 'immortali sponso', 1102: '. . . qui est amor meus, rex et sponsus [etc.]'.
fresch All the usual senses of 'young, joyous, lively' prevail, but a gloss of 'bright, vivid' is also apt here, giving the images of the sloughing off of the old body contrasting with the new, brightly coloured *heavenly* body.
fere Noun regularly used of a *bird's* mate, apt with the bird imagery.
flyit Hs, Hlt: flytt; see also Note to *vnknyit*, K187. Here 'flew lightly, softly or rapidly', as appropriate verbs used of a 'bird', but other current significances resonate, e.g., the sense of 'departing', as in *a.* 1475 *N-Town* (Meredith 2) *Appendix 2*, 41: 'Now þese sefne fendys be for me flytt'; the sense of betaking oneself away from something, as in a turning away from sin towards Christ, e.g., *c.*1200 *Orm.*15853: 'Uss birrþ aȝȝ Uss flittenn towarrd Criste'; and the sense of changing or transforming, which, although always otherwise used in a derogatory sense, is fitting here, where the butchered carcass of the following line is seen as being transformed into a *fresch fesaunt*.

K190 *qwen* A received notion that 'at the same moment' as the body fell to the earth, the soul fluttered up to the bridegroom in heaven; see, e.g., the fourteenth-century wall painting in the Holy Sepulchre Chapel, Westminster. The same event, with the same 'chronology' of 'soul first', is expressed with clarity in Bokenham's version: 'And wyth oo stroke went þe same stounde The soule to heuene & the body to ground' (*Lyf*, ll. 7337–8).
fayntly A form with vowel *a*, not recorded in the dictionaries.
foundyed The form must have developed from *founden*, a variation of *foundren* (OF *fondrer*); see MED *founden* v. (5) and *foundren* v. (1). But cf. also OE *fundian*.
flayn Katherine's body was 'flayn' from the scourging by whips

(*scorpionibus*) that she received in prison (see *Passio* 649 and *Leg.Aurea* 81), but Spalding does not otherwise depict this part of her torture.

flik Always otherwise a *side* (not whole carcass) of a slaughtered animal.

K192–6 *Angeles* All medieval versions of the *passio* state that Katherine's body was transported by air to the top of Mount Sinai by angels. In wall paintings in Little Kimble Church, Bucks (and in those cited in Note to K190), two angels lower Katherine's body into a tomb, their wings spread out above her; in Ulm Cathedral one of three white-robed angels points to the top of the mountain as they carry Katherine on a cloth bier. Butler (quoting Archbishop Falconio of Santa Severina) provides an example of how the embellishment of a medieval legend could develop: 'As to what is said, that the body of this saint was conveyed by angels to Mount Sinai, the meaning is that it was carried by the monks of Sinai to their monastery, that they might devoutly enrich their dwelling with such a treasure. It is well known that the name of angelical habit was often used for a monastic habit, and that monks on account of their heavenly purity and functions were anciently called *angels* . . . "Angelical life" and "angelical habit" are still current and usual expressions in Eastern monasticism' (*Butler's Lives of the Saints*, ed. Herbert Thurston S. J. and Donald Attwater, 4 vols (London, 1956), IV. 420–1); cf. *c.*1384 WEV Apoc. 2: 8: 'To the aungel of the chirche of Smyrna, wrijte thou'. Modern exegesis is divided on whether this means guardian angel or human custodian, which is possibly why MED is not clear on this usage, despite the last example in OED *s.v. angel n.*3, 'pastor or minister'.

K196 *Syna* Mount Sinai in the Sinai peninsula of Egypt, a famous pilgrim-shrine in the Middle Ages. The church and monastery were built there long after the third century when Katherine is said to have died, and it is worth noting that the legend was not known to the earliest pilgrims to the mountain—indicating, as might be expected, a later medieval source of the more fabulous elements of the story. In 527 the Emperor Justinian built a fortified monastery for the hermits of this place, dedicated to the Virgin Mary. The supposed body of St Katherine was taken there in the eighth or ninth century since when the monastery has borne her name. The alleged relics are still there in the great monastery, in the custody of monks of the Eastern Orthodox Church. For bibliography and details about the mountain, monastery and relics see Lina Eckstein, *A History of Sinai* (New York, 1921).

K197–9 Sources stress that angels immediately whisked the body to Sinai, four hundred miles away, and that the burial there was done with great honour and glory.

K198 *pat feipful* MS *fepiful*. Once the meaning of *farly to feel* is established (see p. xlii above and further below), it then becomes clear that MS *fepiful* must be a substantive. It could be argued that the *p*-spelling represents *yi* as in *knyit* and *flyit* in K187–9. This would give the form *feyiful*, consistent with a possible *fayful* in K269, but the emendation here (as with that in K269) has been based on the fully written *feythful* in K163. Thus, the graphs have been read as *piþi*, a switching of them at some point has been presumed, and an emendation has been made to *fe[iþ]ful* here and *fa[i]þful* in K269.

   farly to feel 'to bury fairly / honourably'. For Northern simplification of *ai* diphthong, see Jordan §132. The position of the adverbs after the caesura in K197 and 199 might help substantiate a reading of *farly* (K198) as adv. meaning 'at a great distance'. This adv. is not recorded in MED, but is found, in fact, in the *TowneleyPl.* 'Ascension' (ed. Stevens, p. 392, l. 190): 'Farlee may we fownde and fare'. Either reading must depend on the poet's consistent notice of the caesura, as adverbial (rather than as adj. or as adj. used substantively in the sense of 'wondrous' and qualifying *þat feiþful*); see p. xlii.

K199 *curteys comly* See Note to K197–9, above.
   comly adv., [OE *cȳmlice*] 'properly, with good intentions'.

K201 *Myȝtthily o þat mount with melodye* Cf. the Northern Homily *De Sancta Katerina historia*: 'þai toke þat bode clene and faire, /And bare it up into þe ayre, /And so furt with grete melody /Vnto þe mownt of Synay' (ed. Horstmann, *Altenglishe Legenden*, p. 173, ll. 751–4). Although this line has 10 syllables, an average count, the b-verse, *with melodye*, is strikingly brief and unmetrical (x/x/). There is probably an adj. 'much' missing before *melodye*, as in *St.Kath*(2) (*Cai*) 751: 'þe soule com to Jhesu euene / Wiþ moche merthe and melody'; but it is difficult to envisage one determinate word for this slot, and the sense is satisfactory without emendation. MED has *melodi(e* n. qualified 18 times; of these *gret* occurs as adj. 10 times, *sweet* twice and *moche melodi* (the only alliterating phrase) once, though the lines cited last above are not noted.

K202 One might ask why these angels aim to 'mirth us' on every occasion; it is not part of the narrative. It might be imaginative depiction, rare in the poem.

K203 The line has only 8 syllables as compared to an average 11. It is noticeable that in this octet most of the long lines are shorter than usual, and the b-verses of K201 and 203 are unmetrical. Together with the major crux of K204, the pervasive aberrations suggest multiple corruption in this stanza. The first hemistich is peculiarly short, alliterates oddly and lacks a long dip. One suspects the omission of a pron. Pron. *we* with *thanke* works, but would spoil the imp. mood which informs all subsequent stanzas; the manuscript reading seems marginally better.
   herborogh MS *herborgh*. The emendation has been made in the most

restrained way possible to restore metricality to the b-verse. The n. is found in many different forms, as graphically witnessed in the multiple witnesses of, e.g., *PPl.* and *CT*; and the emended trisyllabic *herborogh* is as prevalent as the bisyllabic MS *herborgh*. Holthausen's suggestion of 'improving' the line by emendation *[on] hye* is reasonable, but such means (e.g., inserting *her* before *herborgh*, presupposing homoeoteleuton through the presence of a double *her(-)*, or qualifying the n. with adj.) are yet more excessive, and there are no strong grounds for interfering by means of such addition when the sense is satisfactory.

K204 *qwer, fro hire, realy, oyl-riueres reel* Refers to the rivers of healing oil that flowed from the saint's bones on Mount Sinai (see *Passio* 1141–6 and *Leg.Aurea* 135).

   oyl-riueres reel MS: opl riueres reu'es reel. The penultimate word is read as *reueres* from the clear indication that some kind of dittography has occurred. It could equally well have been read as *ren'es rennes* as Heuser reads it, giving an interesting b-verse. This has, however, been rejected on the grounds that a genitive construction is not idiomatic of the poet, and because the n. *ren* is rare and was not otherwise used of *river* courses until about 1600. Naturally, this is no argument that Spalding was not employing this n., as it can be seen from elsewhere in the text that his vocabulary and usage are innovative and inventive, but the palaeographical argument already presented is stronger; and the metrical argument is stronger again: the inclusion of *rennes* would mean that it, as the main n., would take the first b-verse lift (~*oyl-riueres rennes reel* xx(x)x//), and it would be the only place in the poem where Spalding fits three syllables (at the minimum) into an initial first dip, making a most uncharacteristic rhythm. The present reading scans with the lifts on *riueres* (here trisyllabic) and *reel* (x/xx/).

   reel 3 pl. of *relen*, a v. not uncommon in ME in its sense of 'whirl' (as when giddy or drunk), but not otherwise found in its later sense of 'fall as if unwinding'; but cf. 1593 Drayton *Eclog*.viii.36: 'From whose high top the high soon'st downward reele'.

K207 *Sekenes to socure* See *Passio* 1144–6.

K208 *soft* The *vulgata* texts qualify 'uidetur manare' with 'indeficienter' (*Passio*, 1143) and Voragine qualifies 'manat' with 'indesinenter' (*Leg.Aurea*, 135), both of which adverbs are best translated as 'incessantly'. From rarer usages it can be seen that *soft* here can be translated as 'gradually and easily'; see MED *soft(e* adv.6. A reading as adj. has been rejected, despite the lack of adverbial *-e*; it is too far removed from the n., and not idiomatic of this poet. The omission of adverbial *-e* can be explained by the scribal patterning of the spelling of the rhymes (see p. xliv above).

K209 *croft* 'sanctuary'; see also Note to K131.

K210 *Hir to honoure* 'in order to honour her'. See MED *honouren* v. 2(c)., but could mean 'in her honour', as the phrase *þat lurdeyn to lef* in K128 can be rendered as 'to please that villain'. As with K128, it has been assumed that the verbal phrase is the more idiomatic of Spalding.

K211-14 'This pain that she experienced, I advise that you [should] ponder it, / so that she might deliver you from prison where pain is very quick to appear; / because she guards against disaster all those who honour her, / and [she], who directs them to [eternal] rest, rules them correctly.'

K211 *preuyd* Here 'tested, experienced', as in MED *preven* v. 10. See also the sense in K184.

K212 *prison* Hell, commonly envisaged as a dungeon of torture from which there is no escape.

ful prest The literal sense of 'very ready' can be rendered by 'always imminent'.

K213 *with wondur* 'against disaster/dirty deeds'. Prep. *with* is not normally used in this sense in fifteenth-century texts, and is rare in late fourteenth-century texts.

K215 *tempest of hayl or of thondur* As with *charp schowres* in K253, these elemental images are all used of bombardments of earthly afflictions, but protection from these is part of this saint's special powers; see *Passio* 1109-17.

K217 *surauns* The more concrete 'pledge' rather than the more general 'assurance of security, safety' is Katherine's speciality, especially for guild members.

K219 *þor* A North Eastern, especially Lincs, form of OE *þar* (see LALME, dot map 322).

K220 The mood of this line must be subj., although the rest of the stanza is ind. (the pr. 3 sg. always otherwise indicated by *-s* or *-þ* endings). This is also conspicuous because the subj. is more often written without etymological final *-e*.

Wytty The force could possibly be adverbial, thus 'showing good judgement'; though such usage is not otherwise found in ME. More likely is '[the] sensible people'.

K221 *þat* 'those who'.

K223 *graunt* pa. 3 sg. The author occasionally runs dentals together in words of French derivation. See also *commaund* (K34), *departe* (K86), and Notes.

K224 *Qwere* 'at the moment when'. This is not quite precise, as Christ promised her this at the moment before her execution, but the sense is 'during her passion'.

K227 *hem þat are of Adam heres here, alle* MS: *he þᵗ are of adam her' all'*. The line is short of at least two syllables. Holthausen emends to *hem þat are [ofspring] of Adam here, alle* (suggesting omission of one *of(-)*, and then the rest of the word); this is intelligent and is conceptually pleasing, but creates a genitive syntax that cuts across the caesura in a way not otherwise found in this text (and very rarely in any strong-stress verse). The present emendation, from *here* to *[heres] here*, is founded on suspicion of a different omission: that of one *here*; cf. *c*.1376 *PPl.A(1)* (Vrn) 2.70: 'To habben and to holden and al heore heyres aftur'.

K228 *auert* MS *awtur*. The MS word is the only lexical item in the text that cannot satisfactorily be explained, and, being imp., requires a trisyllabic inf.; for that reason the unique entry: 'aut let him go' (from a possible but otherwise unrecorded v. *auter*?) in only one early Anglo-Norman dictionary must be discounted (see R. Kelham, *A Dictionary of the Norman or Old French Tongue* (London, 1779), *s.v. aut* (in unusual order on p. 26)). For the same reason a French v. *hauncer* (?scribal *haunter*) 'to raise up', a second otherwise attractive proposition, must be rejected. Neither a word like *awtur* nor anything resembling a trisyllabic doublet form appears in any other AN or OF dictionary or in DEAF (see Kurt Baldinger, with Jean Denis, *Dictionnaire étymologique de l'ancien français* (Quebec, 1971–1974)). The phonology of other reflexes of *aw* in the text (as in, e.g., *mawment* and *bawmyng*) gives little help, and it is also hard to account for the *-ur* ending, which elsewhere this scribe employs for derivations of some OF infinitives in *-erer* and OE Class IV weak verbs such as *tempure* (K115), *pondur* (K211), *sondur* (K217). The n. 'altar' is frequently spelt with *w* for *l* in ME, as are many other words, and phonologically this would point to the v. *alteren* [L *alter-are*] 'alter, change'; however this v. is not otherwise used in a trans. manner and does not happily take the prep. *fro*. Corruption of a word from OE *āteran* 'tear away' might be suspected (as in, e.g., Greg.*Past.Care* 359.20: 'Hie mid ðæm anum yfele atera of ðaere menniscan heortan alle ða godan cræftas'); this would fit with the other potent imperative verbs in the prayer, such as *dryue, qwith, schere, schaf, pales, kille*, but is somewhat nullified by its probable alliteration in ME on *t* rather than *a*. The first five letters have been read rather as a scribal corruption of part of *a(d)verten*—a word of L and OF derivation. This v. is often used with prep. meaning 'away from', and note especially the same alliterative collocation in the acrostic poem in *a*. 1475 *N-Town* Mary (ed. Meredith) 49/546–7: 'M. mayde most mercyfull, and mekest in mende; *A*. auerte of þe Anguysch þat Adam began'. From the late fourteenth century the classical L prefix *ad-* is frequently resorted to, as in, e.g., Lydg. *FP* 24043: 'And beestis which be rage off ther nature, He can aduerte & make hem li ful stille'; 1500 *Craft Dying* 408: 'þe deuyll . . . is besy to aduerte fully a man fro þe feiþe'. An original *-du-* or *-dv-* might account palaeographically for a large *Anglicana w*, but one cannot be sure that Spalding would have intended this, as the reversion to the classical L spelling was a pedantic fashion; the emendation has been made in conformity with the spelling in the geographically proximate and stylistically similar *N-Town Play*.

K230 *towchyn* 'affect, afflict'; see MED *tŏuchen* v. 8 (c).

K234 The scribe rubricates the acrostic *k a t e r i n a* with the graph *i* against the initial capital *J* of *Jentyl*. See also Notes to K239 and K259.

K236 *Now swynk þou for vs swith þere* In return for their stalwart devotion, a guild saint up above should work hard for her 'clientele' below; see also Notes to K260 and K263.

K237 *kiþ* MS: *hiþ* Hs: *hiy*. Heuser's bizarre reading destroys the rhyme, but there are some grounds for retaining the MS reading; see MED *hōten* v. 4c 'assure, give assurance of'. Holthausen's emendation, however, is idiomatic, rhymes with 'blyth' and 'swith' in other texts, makes pleasing sense, and promotes the optimum alliterative pattern.

K239 The scribe uses the graph *i* for the second letter of the acrostic *Ri car d us* whereas the graphs of the poem are *Rp*. See also Notes to K234 and K259.

K240 *redyn on* There is no recorded parallel to this phrase. The straightforward meaning 'read about' is somewhat incongruous with the 'rwd', and does not encompass the belief that Katherine could work wonders if 'thought about' at certain crucial moments. The sense may have been 'perceive, grasp the meaning of, interpret' (as in *c.*1350 *Alex.Maced.*856: 'þe swerd sweetlich imade, in sweven too rede, Bitokneth . . . þat hee shall grow full grim'), rendering something more like 'ponder, meditate on, ingest'. However, the poem was composed for the private devotion of, for example, one lady patron, the standard sense, 'read', would work well.

    rent pp. used adjectivally; so also *adent* K244.

K241-2 The mood now changes to that of jussive imp.: '[May] speaking of your graciousness keep us from that knife / that accursedly rends us when we assent to sin'.

K241 *Carpyng of* 'speaking of' continues the petition in the established grammatical mode, and is more straightforward than to read the phrase as Katherine's intercession, i.e. 'speaking [to God] on our behalf'.

    þat cnyf A metaphoric 'devil's knife' which 'carves us' when we relapse into sins such as, say, anger; see Chaucer, *CT* 2091: 'Hoold nat the develes knyf ay at thyn herte—Thyn angre dooth thee alto soore smerte'.

K242 *qwen we to synne sent* The aphetic form of *assenten* is rare but found in *a.* 1382 WEV Judith 12: 10: 'Go and sweteli moue this Ebru, that . . . she sente (WLV 'consent') to dwelle with me'.

K243 *Dyntes of deuelys* 'devils' [?hammer] blows'.

K244 *þat* Must refer back to the *deuelys*.

deply Otherwise, in ME, the meaning is 'grievously, intensively', but here the meaning is both literal and figurative, suggesting the depths of Hell; for the devils were hurled down into and fixed (see next) in darkness soon after the Creation; and MED records the occurrence in *Katherine* as the only literal example of this adv. (though see 1573 Tusser *Husb.*xlviii 104: 'Three poles to a hillock . . . set deeplie and strong').

adent From OF *adenter* 'to mortice, fasten as with teeth' (see also last); see Note to E17 *s.v. endent* and citations there from *Pearl*. See also OED's succinct entry *s.v.* †*Adent, v.*

K245–7 '[At the place] where you are bride, reward us [by means] of the powers of Him / with whom you have departed, who potently created everything; / by the agency of [Him with] whom you are departed now, / procure salvation [for] us now'.

K245–6 For the phonology and grouping of the alliterating letters, especially the alliteration and possible stopping of the OE [hw] reflex in *qwere*, see p. xlvii. See also the concatenation of *qweles* and *wylys* in K140–1. As a Lincs authorial dialect is established, K245 appears to alliterate on unstopped [hw] and initial [w] in *vertues* (aa/aa).

K245 *quith* MS *quich*. Every other *t*-graph in the MS is crossed, but it is likely that they were confused in an exemplar.

K250–3 The syntax is elliptical, but logical: 'Now you make their griefs annulled—/ [i.e. of those who] learn [of] you, ascended [to Heaven], now, / sunbeam so bright'.

Her bales makyst þou blent MED suggests reading *blont*, inexplicably, for this would destroy a good rhyme with no less than seven other words with vowel [e]. The MS reading *mayst* would require *blent* to be read as inf., but this v. inf. never ends in *-t*, and the inf. ending *-t* is not otherwise found in this witness. The pp. is common (cf., e.g., *a.* 1393 Gower *CA* 1.1127: 'So was the pleine trowthe blent Thurgh contrefet Ipocrisie'). The emendation to *makyst* is necessary so that *blent* can be read as pp. of *blenden* [OE *blendan*] 'to dull, mitigate'.

K251 *To lerne þe asent* Spelling of the pp. might suggest a derivation of OE *āsendan* 'send', giving the sense 'sent [to the world for our benefit]'; cf. *c.*1350 *NHom.*(2) *PSanct.*97/55: 'þus was he asent to folfille Al þat crist hedde I-seide him tille'; but there is no recorded instance of the prefixed form after this date. Altogether more characteristic would be an original word from OE *āscendan* 'dishonoured'; cf. *c.*1425 *Glo.Chron.A* (Hrl) 263:

'þo gonne hii to fle; Ac hii adde alle ybe assend [vrr. ssent, yshent] ȝy[f] þe nyȝt nadde y be'; however there is little evidence that our scribe would have spelt the word in this way, even in error (see, e.g., the pp. *schente* K64 and *schenchip* K254). The word has been read as a derivative of the L or OF *ascender(e)* (ME *assenden* rather than *ascenden*), giving the attractive '[now] ascended [up to heaven]'; cf.1420 Lydg. *TB* 1.1384: 'þe kyng . . . Ascendid is in-to his royal se'.

K253 *Schere away* 'excise', a significance that has occasionally been used figuratively. See also Note to K254.

þat schap vs to schrik The pl. v. is trans., giving 'that cause us to shriek' (see also K92). There may have been a ME v. *schricken*, cognate with OHG *schreken* 'to terrorize', but no examples have come to light. The English form could have developed from a factitive umlauted v. (see W. Müller and F. Zarncke, *Mittelhochdeutsches Wörterbuch* (Leipzig, 1866), s.v. *schrëken*). Note also that the sense 'terrify' is close to that found in the prefixed trans. or inchoative forms, ibid., s.v. *erschrecke*; cf. *Parzival*, ed. E. Martin (Halle, 1920), 457.27: 'mich hât der ber und ouch der hirȝ erschrecket dicker denne der man'. Certainly *-vs to schrik* 'prepare to terrify us' would be more idiomatic of Spalding in this poem.

K254 *schrunk be in schenchip* The v. *shrinken* is frequently associated with nouns *shame* and *schenchip*. The notion is that one shrinks away, or slinks away in ignominy, or cowers at the thought of one's shameful sins, and there is, in this usage, an element of flinching with mortification. Associated, then, is the sense 'flinch, cower' as in K92. In this line the intrans. v. seems (as if personified) to be used of the *chames* themselves, rendering 'sunk down', or even 'embedded', 'huddled together', 'furtively retreated'; but it is almost certain that this is an example of Spalding's slack but idiomatic use of the relative, *þat* referring to 'us sinful humans' (see also K98, 230, 244 and 246).

K255 *Pales vs* 'fence us in' [from OF *palisser*] 'enclose around, fence in [as with pales]'; not otherwise recorded in figurative usage.

K256 *þis pouert* Sinfulness of heart or soul.

K257 *Draw* The sense is 'raise' rather than 'attract'.

dyngnite Cf. *a.* 1475 *N-Town* 60/89: 'Whan he [Jesus] is gon to his dygnyte he xal send þe sprytt to his discyplis'. The spelling with intrusive medial *n* is characteristic of the scribe; see also *reyngnest* (K239) and *faunchon* (K185).

þis depe dyk Ditch imagery was often employed for the geography of Hell, but is employed here to illustrate base earthly, as compared to eternal, life;

the idea that earthly life is a prison is expressed in c.1380 *Pearl* 1187: 'So wel is me in þys doel-doungoun'.

K258 *dentiwos dool* 'choice apportionment' [OE *dāl*]. MED cites K258 under *dōl* n. (1) 5, 'Bestowal of grace; charity, grace', though it should rather have been placed under n. (1) 2.(a) '(one's) place (in heaven)', especially as it is preceded by the word *to*, and followed by the word *qwere*. Furthermore, the adj. has once already been employed of a concrete thing (the dove) K59. Katherine's *dentiwos dool* is surely her lovely allotted place in Heaven. Cf. *a.* 1400 *Ancr.Recl.*5/18: 'þise two [Peter and Paul] haue þe heiȝest dale in heuene'.

    demschip 'judgement' (in the adverse sense of 'condemnation), making use of the n. *deme*, from the v. *demen*. MED cites this as the only recorded instance of the word, and it could be that *feynthed* (K270) was created by the poet in the same way. The significance of *qwere deieþ euer demschip* is that such judgement cannot operate to the disadvantage of those who have been received into Heaven; thus *deieþ euer* 'does not exist'.

K259 It can be noted that the scribe uses his *þ/y* graph in the rubricated acrostic *S p a l d y n g* to parallel the initial graph *J* of *Joine*. See also Notes to K234 and K239.

    hym lyk '[those who are] like him'.

K260 *chef of our jornay* 'goal of our journey [through life]', and also 'supreme figurehead [per se] of our journey [through life]'. Together with the sense 'leader', etc., understood here, the n. *chef* could simply mean 'the top, head', as in c.1400 *Mandev.*141/35: 'At the chief of the halle is the Emperoures throne'; or, more subtly, 'objective, goal'; cf. *a.* 1420 Lydg. *TB* 2.3758: 'þe chef of his entent Was to recuren his suster Exyoun'. The association with *jornay* may have been influenced by OF phrases, as in to bring an adventure 'à chef', i.e. 'to achieve'; cf. *SGGK* 1081: 'Now acheued is me chaunce'; but see 1519 Horman *Vulg.*281: 'He wanne the chieffe at euerry game [*victor palmam abstulit*]'. This late sense of 'prize' may also have informed Spalding's thought.

    frenchip Such 'friendship' is often the dispassionate goodwill or favour of a superior, and would be the most advantageous characteristic of a guild patron, in order *to encresse* the *mede* of her devotees (see Note to K263, below). Cf. *a.* 1460 *TowneleyPl.*26/122: 'Noe . . . Thou was alway . . . to me trew as stele . . . frendship shal thou fele To mede'; here is the same association with *mede* as in K263.

K262 *God . . . make our mynde* 'may God fasten our thought', a subj. modification of the common phrase *maken minde* 'call attention to'; see MED *maken* v. 12 b.(f) and K145.

K263 *Oure mede to encresse* 'to augment our (heavenly) reward', achieved through the intercession and special powers of the saint; see also Note to K260, *s.v. frenchip.*

K264 *þo pynchars* 'those persecutors [who]'. This demonstrative is used throughout the poem. The adv. 'though' does not otherwise occur, but its likely spelling would be *þoƷ* (the spirant indicated by *w* as in *sawles*).

pynchars 'who wield pincers' (real or metaphoric). The sense here is probably both literal and figurative, covering demons, detractors and tormentors; cf. *a.*1400 *Cloud* 130/19: 'Fleschely ianglers, glosers, & blamers, roukers & rouners & all maner of pynchers, kept I neuer þat þei sawe þis book, for myn entent was neuer to write soche þing to hem'.

K268 *hir giyld* The n. is not otherwise found in figurative use in ME, and almost certainly refers to a real guild of St Katherine; see pp. lxiv–lxviii above. The spelling of the n. is peculiar, but similar to the doubled vowels of *vnknyit* K187 and *flyit* K189, all three apparently representing short *i*.

K269 'Safeguard us, faithful companion, in order that no sinfulness might befall us'.

Fend MS: *Feed*; 3 sg. [from OE *fēdan*], glosses *educāvit* in OE (see ASD *fēdan* v.); the imp. is found in figurative use in *Cædmon* 67: 'Fed freolice feora wocre', 'feed freely the living progeny'; but thereafter the sense is literal, and nourishing her devotees was not one of Katherine's attributes. Furthermore, feeding in order to prevent the onset of *foly* is an odd concept. An original *Fend* makes good sense and is palaeographically most plausible, not only because of the likely substitution of one letter, but because *ee* could have been picked up through eyeskip to the subsequent *feer.*

feer faiþful MS: *feer fapful.* The *sense*, if not the form, of the earlier editors' MS readings *fayful* is correct, but here the MS *p*-graph is read as *þ*, and the adj. has been emended in conformity with *feiþful* (MS *fepiful*) in K198.

K270 *feynthed* On grounds of alliteration and sense, the long *s* of MS *seynthed* can undoubtedly be read as *f*. See similar confusion with *same* (K74), and a possible confusion of long *s* and *l* in K204. However, *feynthed* is a hapax legomenon, perhaps formulated by Spalding by addition of the suffix abstract n. in the same way as in *demschip* (K258). Though palaeo-graphically questionable, the expected word would be *feyntise*, as in, e.g., *SGGK* 2435: 'þe faut and þe fayntyse of þe flesche'. For a similar abstract n., attractively conceived through n. suffix, see *A Myrour to Lewde Men and Wymmen*, ed. Venetia Nelson (Heidelberg, 1987), 71/20: 'Augustyne in his meditaciouns techeþ vs & seith þus: with awakerhed [glossed '*vigilance*'], takynge busy mynde . . . vs byhoueth lerne'.

K271 *qwen þei apere schal* 'when they must appear in God's presence'; cf. *c.*1380 *Pearl* 405: 'And when in hys place þou schal apere, Be dep deuote in hol mekenesse'. For legal nuance in the diction of appearance before the tribunal of the last judgement, see also Note to K236.

K272 *win* MS *w* can make no sense. Holthausen's *wis* makes sense, but the repetition of *wysse* in K277 jars. An original *wī* may have been read as the present MS *w*, and this more probable reading is proposed. Cf. MED *winnen* v. 7a.; cf. *c*.1475 *Wisd*. 584: 'Thus by colours gyane [vr. and false gynne] Many a soule to helle I wyn'.

woo wyde 'widespread, ubiquitous [earthly] tribulation'.

K273–9 'Katherine, summon us to that King who is most gracious, / who was born our brother, so that we might live in bliss. / Katherine, ⟨us⟩ to that King / who hung for us on the cross / you can lead us all. / [May] he bring us to that paradise / where angels will hymn us'.

K278 *blisse* MS *bilsse* makes no sense; MED cites under *blis(se* n. with the MS spelling, as if a metathesized form, but this has no precedent, and the emendation, though necessary, jars with the ultimate *blysse* (K280). The word is also used at K274, thus making a total of three occurrences (*blis*, *blisse*, *blysse*) in the last 7 lines. No better solution presents itself; the poet may have been winding up fast with a typically unreflective ending.

Notes to *The Alliterative John Evangelist Hymn*

E3 *with* 'by' (see OED *with prep*. III.b); e.g., *c*.1390 *Gawain* 948–9: 'an auncian . . . heʒly honowred with haþelez aboute'.

E5 *louede* 'praised' [OE *lofian*, *lofode*]; voiced fricative consonant *u* is also found in *saluede* (E72) and *lyueande* (E20), but see *lufe* (E224).

lugede 'lodged, dwelling' [OF *logier*]. Verbal forms are more usually used of army camps or with unfavourable connotations; e.g., *a*. 1500 *O fresch floure* 42: 'I wold he were locched with lucifer'. The collocation appears to be original.

E6 *relyde* See MED *relien* v.3 [OF *reliier*] 'rallied, called to his heavenly company', rather than 'rallied, called to his company' at Galilee (see E55 and the probable content of E46, E47). Although the first reading is not supported by other texts, the latter does not appear to inform the opening context where the beatified John is praised.

E10 *His:* Enjambement, particularly after a rhyming adj. poss., is most unusual in alliterative verse, but see also E17–18, E69–70, E145–6 and K71–2. On these grounds the alternative reading of pron. poss., 'his people', has been rejected.

E13 *þou vs wysse* In this text subj. as well as imp. verbs are written with a final *-e* (e.g., *lede* E265, *loke* E237), but in *Katherine* and *Baptist* the tone of the end-of-stanza addresses is imperative, and that is how this second-person verb has been read.

E14 *John* MS; *P*: *Jhon*. Probably a scribal slip on the lines of the abbreviation for *Jhesu*.

E15–17 The jewel imagery is based on the well-known description of the heavenly Jerusalem in Rev 21: 18–21, but probably also on Ezek 28: 13–15: 'in deliciis paradisi Dei fuisti, omnis lapis pretiosus operimentum tuum: . . . topazius et iaspis, . . . sapphirus et carbunculas . . . Cum cherub extento et protegente te posui te, in monte sancto Dei fuisti, in medium lapidum ignitorum ambulasti, in die, qua conditus es, praeparata sunt . . . perfectus in viis tuis a die conditionis tuae, (donec inventa est iniquitas in te)'; these jewel-clad bodies of the virgins in heaven were especially relevant to John's exemplary virginity (see E57–70 and Notes to E58 and E62).

E15 *gete* 'precious stone, either amber, or black jet' [OF *jaiet, gaiet*]. The jewel is often cited in comparisons (e.g., 'as black as ~'), but is not otherwise found in the literary convention of the lapidary eulogy, which is more inclined to include jewels from exotic locations. These stones are chosen for their consonants.

gem dere and MS *germandir* 'germander'—the name of a not-especially esteemed herb [ML *germandr(i)a*], at a pinch cited for its blueness. It is peculiar to find an undistinguished, or any, plant name in a eulogistic list of precious stones, and it is a pity to lose such an attractive concrete image in the editorial process; but an original *gem dere and gente* may easily have led to the problem that MS *germandir* poses. One scribe need only have involuntarily reversed the words *dere and* to *and dere* for the next copyist to have read the minims of *gemme* as *germ*, giving *germander* – in turn being copied with Thornton's *-ir* ending as in, e.g., *philosophir* (E215). A similar collocation is found in *Pearl* 118: 'emerad, saffer, oþer gemme gente', where the specific jewels are followed by the general 'gemme'. The emended phrase with its successor altogether improves the syntax. For a more drastic emendation see Kennedy, 'Alliterative Katherine Hymn', pp. 394–5.

E16 *jasper* an especially precious green or dark stone [OF *jaspe*]; cf. *a.* 1500 *Peterb.Lapid* 93: 'Sent Iohn seyþe in apocolypse þat he say in heuenly kyndome of ierusalem þat þe ferst fundament wase Iaspe'; cf. also 1325 'Ichot a burde in a' 3: 'Ichot a burde . . . ase iaspe þe gentil þat lemeþ wiþ lyht'.

perry 'jewels' [AF *perree, pirie*]; cf. *a.* 1398 Trev. *Barth*.187b/b: 'Sardinium . . . is better þan marbul and most profitable among perreye [L *gemmas*]'.

E17 *drowry* 'precious gift, treasure' [OF *drüerie*]; cf. *a.* 1450 *Yk.Pl*.217/519: 'Hayll, dyamaunde with drewry dight, Hayll, jasper gentill'.

endent 'set, mounted (e.g., in gold), enclosed' [pp. from OF *endenter*]; cf. *c*.1380 *Pearl* 1021: 'þe topasye twynne-hew þe nente endent'. If a reading based on enjambement of E17 is adopted, the figurative meaning of *endent* is: 'As jasper (the jewel of noble jewels), so were you, precious as a love-token treasure, enfolded in the actions of Him who, for sorrow [over mankind], deigned to die'. A rather different figurative usage is found in c.1380 *Pearl* 629: 'Anon þe day, wyth derk endente þe niȝt of deth dotȝ to enclyne'. See also Note to K244, *s.v. adent.*

E18 *endeynede* 'condescended' [OF *deignier*]; cf. *c.*1375 Chaucer *CT.Mk.*B.3324: 'For with no venym deigned [vr. deynede] hym to dye'.

E19 *þou was lufed of þat lorde* See John 8: 23–6, 19: 25–7, 20: 2–10, 21: 7, 20–23, 24.

E20 *He lete mare by* He regarded more highly; see MED *leten* v. 15 (d). See also Note to E194.

E21 'Nor, of those who went with Him, any living person'.

E24 *ay-whare* 'always wherever, everywhere'—a Northern-sounding usage, not recorded in MED or OED, but evidently founded on *ay* 'forever' (see OED *ay* adv. 5) and *ywhere* [OE *gewhǣr*].

E25 *by-dene* an adv. found only in Northern and North Midland texts. For the etymology [?OE *dēn, doen*] see MED *bidene* adv. and the article by Skeat referred to there. More usually the word is employed as an emphatic filler, 'indeed', but here fits with an attested meaning 'completely, entirely, utterly', as in, e.g., *c.*1333–1352 Minot *Poems* 29/74: 'Oure horses . . . Er etin vp ilkone bidene', and *a.* 1450 *Yk.Pl.*502/162: 'Before vs playnly bese fourth brought þe dedid þat vs schall dame be-dene'. See also E50.

E29 See Matt. 4: 21, Mark 1: 19, Luke 5: 10.

   gome was þou get 'you were begotten as a boy-child'; John was born and spent his boyhood in Galilee.

E31 *Zebede* Zebedee, a Galilean fisherman, mentioned in each of the Synoptic Gospels as the father of James and John.

   fude probably 'person' as in E76. A reading based on the meaning 'food' is possible, with an enjambement into 'he fedd the'.

   fet 'shaped, created' from *feten*; cf. *fet* n. and *faiten* v. [OF *fait*, pp. of *fair* 'to make']; cf. the spelling in *c.*1419 York *MGame.*17: 'yfetyd'. Perry glosses as 'brought into being', a strained usage of *fecchen* 'to fetch, bring'. The more precise meaning 'reared', is found in a syncopated derivation from the OF *?afaiter* in *a.* 1387 *PPl.C* (Hnt) 9.30: 'And faite thy faucones to culle wylde foules'.

E34 *Mary* John's mother was Mary Salome, the half-sister of the Virgin Mary. The genealogy derives from various apocryphal sources (see Wolfgang A. Bienert, 'The Relatives of Jesus', in *Hennecke New Testament Apocrypha*, I. 470–2); for a methodical Middle English explanation see Weatherley, *Spec.Sacer.*, pp. 144–6. The *Leg.Aurea* has no mention of John's parents, but Caxton elaborates to: 'Saynt Johan thappostle and euangelist was sone of Zebedee / wyche had maryed the thirde suster of our lady to wyf / and that was brother to saynt James of galice' (*The Golden Legend*, ed. William Caxton, London, 1483, f. xxxvii^r). The Wycliffite Bible calls her by another of her sanctioned names, *Maria Jacobi* 'Mary of James', after her son, the brother of John; WLV Mark 16: 1: 'And whanne the sabat was passid, Marie Maudeleyne, and Marie of James, and Salomee bouȝten swete smellynge oynementis'.

menesyng 'mentioning, mention' [?OE *mynsung*, from *myne* 'mind, memory' or *gemyne* 'mindful']. The only other occurrences in Middle English are in *a.* 1338 Manning *Chron.Pt.1* p. 326: 'Of hym ys mynsyng wiþ-outen ende, ffor he made a cite of ioye'; and ibid., *Pt.2* p. 201: 'þi misdede bi in þi mynsyng [vr. memore], Euer more to drede'.

men mase 'is made'. The pron. impers. takes both sg. and pl. verbs; here the v. is a Northern contracted form, shown by the rhyme to be archetypal, but also found in other texts of the Thornton Lincoln MS, e.g., *c.*1350 *Mirror St.Edm*(*4*).17/10: 'þou aske me: "What mase man haly?"', and *a.* 1375 *Abbey HG*(*Thrn*) 58/25: 'þe whete . . . of þe whilke man mase gud brede'.

E35 See Matt. 20: 20–23: 'Tunc accessit ad eum mater filiorum Zebedaei cum filiis suis, adorans et petens aliquid ab eo. Qui dixit ei: "Quid vis?" Ait illi: "Dic ut sedeant hi duo filii mei unus ad dexteram tuam et unus ad sinistram in regno tuo"'. See also Mark 10: 35–41, where the brothers ask for the seat themselves.

E36 *sere* 'particular, singular' [ON *sér*]. The MS witnesses a b-verse that lacks a long dip, and the final *-e* on *sere* is not etymological. As with so much of this text, the same collocation is found only in *a.* 1450 *Yk.Pl.*394/398: 'To solace sere þai schall be sende'; therefore the words are read as authorial. It is difficult to envisage an alternative, more metrical substitution, and easy to imagine that the poet must have intended an unetymological stress on the final *-e* of *sere*.

E38 *Pereles of Pousté* 'Peerless of Power' [from OF *per* adj. and AF *pousté*]. The collocation is otherwise found only in *a.* 1450 *Yk.Pl.*476/78: 'God . . . pereles is of poste'; and *a.* 1460 *TowneleyPl.*200/172: 'He commys to fulfull the law, A pereles prynce most of pauste'. As in E86, the rhyme is on the accented final *-e*.

E40 *fre* this could be an adverbial usage—'freely, readily'; cf., e.g., *a.* 1300 *Tristrem* 2730: 'Ȝif þine houndes . . . comes oȝain to þe fre'; but is perhaps more likely to be adjectival 'noble, good', as in E149.

E43–50 Because of the regular structure of the stanzas throughout all three hymns, there should be little doubt that the missing lines of this octet are scribal, not authorial. It seems that they are E46 and 47, for the reasons that follow. E49 and 50 make sense together, alliterate on the same letter (*l*), and are joined to the sestet by the iteration of *by-dene*, so they must remain where they are. It is unlikely that a scribe would omit the first line of a stanza, as it would almost invariably have been marked by at least the stanza spacing, if not a large initial or rubrication; thus the stanza probably did open with the words 'Thi modir [etc]', to follow the itemization started in E40 and 41 ('thi fadir . . . Schipe and nett of þe see . . .'); the alliteration on *m* is sustained for two lines, so these should be kept together. The question then remains as to whether the two missing lines come between the edited E44 and E45, or E45 and E47. The problem is unfortunately compounded by the ictus on the initial-*w* words as well as on *kep-* in E45; this means that a line alliterating on either of these letters could have occurred next. The MS does have a line alliterating on *c/k*, but surely a line alliterating on *w/ vowel* and containing a main verb must have followed E45, followed, in turn, by a line alliterating on *c/k*, the sense of which proceeded into 'To cayre with þat cumly'. Line 45 continues on the subject of worldly goods, begun in the two opening lines, and its commencement with *Of* requires a main verb that is not satisfactorily supplied by 'thou keste the' in the next MS line. A reflexive use of *casten* is well-attested (see MED *casten* v. 23 b.), and there is no reflexive usage that includes a prep. *of*, giving 'rid yourself of', as might be envisaged. With this line satisfactorily glossed (see Notes to E48, below), the one unresolved phrase is that beginning with *Of* in E45. Therefore the lacuna has to be between the edited E45 and E48.

The *Leg.Aurea* oddly omits the call by Galilee, and it seems that little more could be added by this poet to the Gospel accounts in the missing lines of the text; but in a curious passage in the third-century Gnostic Books of Jeû the apostles say: 'We have left behind father and mother, we have left behind vineyards and fields, we have left behind goods ($\kappa\tau\eta\sigma\iota\zeta$) and the greatness of rulers and we have followed thee'; see *The Books of Jeu and the Untitled Text in the Bruce Codex*, ed. C. Schmidt, trans. Violet Macdermot (Nag Hammadi Studies 13, Leiden, 1978), p. 40. The Gnostic accounts professed to record the conversations of Christ with his apostles. In the early days of Christianity there were two conflicting schools of thought about the social standing of the apostles: the detractors liked to say that they were as disreputable as Mary Magdalene, but promoters (as all medieval poets were) would argue the opposite, citing, for example, the hired servants left by James and John (see Mark 1: 20).

E44 *aftir myght mene* 'might yearn after'; see MED *menen* v. (2) 3.(d); cf. *a.* 1325 *Cursor* (Vsp) 19360: 'þai went forth ioifuller þan are, Ne noght þam mened o þair sair'; *a.* 1350 *Nicod.(1)*.212: 'If we him reyne, it mun vs rew, euermore þaron to mene'. As far as can be ascertained, the v. is not otherwise found with this prep., which adds an applicable connotation of hankering after worldly goods.

E45 *wanes* 'dwellings, property' [ON *ván*]—a decidedly Northern form.

E50 *lythes* 'people, members of a household' [ON *lyðr*]; see MED *lith* n. (4); cf. *a.* 1400 *Wars Alex*.3750: 'A hundreth thousand, I hope, we be . . . þa leues in oure lede, oure lithis to defend'.

by-dene see Note to E25.

E56 *As witnese the buke* The desertion of their occupation by the fishermen is witnessed in all three Synoptic Gospels, Matt. 4: 18–22, Mark 1: 16–20, Luke 5: 11; but only in the last of these do we find 'relictis omnibus'.

E57 *þi werkes vnwylde* a second predicate of the a-verse verb; this collocation does not appear elsewhere in alliterative verse.

vnwylde 'not wanton, temperate' [from OE *wilde* + un-7; but cf. MDu *onwilt*]. This adj. is not otherwise found in Middle English, and has been employed for alliteration and metre, just as, e.g., the *Wars Alex.* poet uses the adj. *vnrid(e)* in ll. 460, 862 and 994 (1990 edn), or the Northern alliterative poet, Tickhill, *c.*1397 finds a suitable noun (see Kennedy, 'Bird in Bishopswood', ll. 12–13): 'I had lenyd me long . . . In vnlust of my lyf'. See also *vnmyste* in E257.

E58 The line can translate as 'You guarded yourself against activities that were despicable', and, because of the last adj., must refer to John's own actions rather than those of others; the reference is to John's exemplary virginity, which is the subject of the entire stanza; see also Notes to E15–17 and E62. Legends of John's ideal virginity are of Docetic or Gnostic origin, and arose in the second century; see Junod and Kaestli, *Acta Johannis*, *passim*.

werede the fro 'defended/protected yourself from' [OE *werian, werʒan*]; cf. *a.* 1325 *Cursor* (Vsp) 11168: 'Hir sun he sal and fader baþe Be to wer his folk fra waþe'.

E59 *methe* 'modest, unassuming', from the noun *meth(e)* [OE *mæþe*, measure, etc.]; cf. *a.* 1325 *Bonav.Medit.(1)* 156: 'So meke and so myþe a mayster to tray'.

for mylde 'as far as mildness is concerned'. The use of *mylde* as noun is rare, but cf. *a.* 1425 *This is goddis* [Wheatley MS] 113: 'Lete mylde and mekenes mette þin herte'.

E61–70 These lines refer to one of John's four particular features—that of being an exemplary virgin. See Notes to E15–17, E58 and E62.

E61 *fayntles* 'steadfast, tireless', a rare adj., from *feint* 'weak, unreliable'. Here it probably has the sense of 'constant in your virginity'. The only other extant occurrence is in *a.* 1376 *PPl.A(1)* (Trin-C) [2.99]f.5b: 'Fals is a faitour, feyntles of werkis'.

E62 *fere* 'mate, spouse'. The scene of John leaving his bride is apocryphal (see Meyer and Bauer, *Hennecke New Testament Apocrypha*, p. 269). The even more imaginative idea that John was the groom at the wedding at Cana is certainly present in one preface to Augustine; see *Joannis Evangelium, Prefatio Incerti Auctoris ad S. Aurelius Augustinius*, PL 35.1450, and *Der Saelden Hort: Alemannisches Gedicht vom Leben Jesu, Johannes des Täufers und der Magdalena*, ed. H. Adrian (Deutsche Texts des Mittelalters 26, Berlin, 1927), 101, n. to l. 5632; and even Aelfric describes the wedding of 'Iohannes se godspellere, cristes dyrling'; see *Aelfric's Catholic Homilies: The First Series*, ed. Peter Clemoes and M. R. Godden (EETS, ss 17, 18, 1997, 2000) I. 206, and note (II, 29–30). The lore that his betrothed was Mary Magdalene and that Christ prevented John from marrying her was emphatically scotched by Voragine; the *Leg.Aurea* celebrates John as one who kept his virginity even when he 'would marry': 'in ipso enim fuit gratia uirginalis unde et de nuptiis uolens nubere a domino uocatus' (87.8). Caxton's version has 'our lord kepte to hym hys vyrgynyte / lyke as saynt Jerome saith / For he was at hys wedding / and he abod a clene virgyne' (Caxton, *Golden Legend*, f. c^r); and from the life of Mary Magdalene Caxton translates: 'Some say þat mary magdalene was wedded / to Seynt Johan theuangelyst whan crist called / him fro þe weddyng / and when he was called fro her she had therof indignacion / þat her husbond was taken fro her / & went and gaf her self to alle delyte' (ibid., f. ccxix^r). The subject is not present in the *Cursor* or Northern Homily cycles.

E64 *vnchangide of chere*: not entirely a line filler, but refers to John's demeanour reflecting a perpetual inexperience of sexuality.

E71–4 'The son of the sister of her whose lovely body provided the cure for our distress [i.e. son of the sister of the Virgin Mary]'. John was son of Mary Salome, the half-sister of the Virgin, and therefore cousin to Christ; see Note to E34.

E71 *hir syster sone hir* refers to the Virgin Mary (a reference resumed with the relative *whas* in E72); *syster* refers to Mary Salome; and *sone* refers to John. The b-verse verse lacks a long dip, as if an original gen. inflexion has been omitted by a scribe; but see also Duggan, 'Final -e', p. 139, on the relative fixity of the Middle English noun phrase in alliterative verse.

E72 *Whas* 'whose', relates back to *hir* (i.e., referring to the Virgin Mary) in the a-verse of the previous line.

E73 *byrde so bryghte* i.e. Mary, mother of Christ.
  with birdyn 30de bun '(who) with child, went prepared'. The final adjectival pp. is from ON *búin-n*. The noun *birdyn* refers here to something carried within the body. The v. *30de* is pa.3 sg. of *gon* [OE *ēode*].

E74 *alþer beste* 'best of all'; *alþer* is the original gen. pl. of *al*. The compound is more usually found in adverbial use, as in *c.*1387–1395 Chaucer *CT.Prol.*A.710: 'Wel koude he rede a lessoun or a storie, But alderbest he song an offertorie'.

E75 *frayste* 'experience, test, prove' [ON *freista*]. For the collocation see also B73. See also usages in E148, E228 and E239.

bese fun 'proves to be' (see MED *finden* v. 10); cf. *c*.1385 Chaucer *TC* 4.1659: 'I nevere unto Criseyde . . . Was fals . . . it shal be founde at preve'. The 3 sg. *bese* was a Northern dialect form of OE *biþ* perhaps influenced by the 2 sg. *bist*; cf. *a.* 1325 *Cursor* (Frf) 3762: 'My hert bese [Trin. beþ] neuer broȝt in rest'; *fun* is pp. of *finden* [OE *a)ge)findan*; *funden*]; cf., *c*.1375 *NHom.(3)Leg.*9/444: 'A man's face was neuer ȝit fun Like to a-nother in al making'.

E76 *frely fude* i.e. Christ.

E78 *ware* 'were'; see, e.g., E23, E58, etc.

E79 *ware* 'where', otherwise found as *whare* (E12 and E24), and probably miswritten here through contamination from the last.

E82 *helde þe* 'kept yourself'; cf. *c*.1300 *NHom.(1)Gosp.*p.110: 'Thar mai we graithe ensample take . . . And hald us Imang wise men'.

E86 *publischede* 'revealed, divulged'; not commonly found; cf. 1429 *RParl.*4.343a: 'Often tymes . . . matiers . . . spoken and treted in the seide Counseill have be publysshead and discovered'. The collocations are not found elsewhere.

priuaté See also rhyme on final -*é* in E38.

E87–8 These lines refer to the Transfiguration (Matt. 17: 1–9, Mark 9: 2–8, Luke 9: 28–36.7).

E88 *fone* 'few' a Northern blend of *whon* 'a small quantity or number' [from OE *hwōn*] and *feu* 'few' [from OE *fēa*]; cf. *a.* 1425 *MOTeste* 5459: 'And his folke ware bot fone with swylke a streng forto stryfe'.

E89–90 The basis for these lines appears to be the intense utterances at the end of John 12, which are followed in John 13: 2 by 'Et in cena', and resume with yet more similar material, to the end of John 17.

E92 *tuke at* see also E201 where the sense is apparently 'carried out'. The phrase is a sure sign of Northern origin and may have been influenced by the ON phrase *taka at* 'begins', as in *take at ganga* 'begin to go' (see OED *take v.* 62); though here the meaning is different.

þat refers back to Christ.

E96–101 A reference to John 19: 26–27: 'Cum vidisset ergo Iesus matrem et discipulum stantem, quem diligebat, dicit matri: "Mulier, ecce filius tuus". Deinde dicit discipulo: "Ecce mater tua". Et ex illa hora accepit eam discipulus in sua'.

E101–2 It seems likely that John stayed in Jerusalem with Mary until her death in *c*.AD 42—the same year as the general dispersion of the apostles. An enormous body of legend accumulated concerning the death or 'Dormition' of the Virgin Mary; see Note to E146.

E102 *soghte* 'went, departed'; see MED *sechen* v. 11; the sense is well-attested, cf., e.g., *a.* 1450 *Yk.Pl.*9/128: 'þou hast to þe forest soght'; ibid., 41/25: 'Out of our sight nowe is it soghte'; but this intrans. use does not occur without prep. and indirect object. For this reason, and in light of the possible enjambement in other parts of the composition (e.g., E145–6, E199–200 and E225–6), the intended sense was possibly 'went to Asia'. Such a reading, however, would disrupt the caesura in E103, and a simpler reading with end-stopped line is preferable.

E103 *Asye* Paul had already introduced the Christian faith into Asia Minor; John went to consolidate Paul's work. This is the final line of the poem with a biblical source, and is based on Rev. 1: 10–11: 'Fui in spiritu in dominica die et audivi post me vocem magnam tamquam tubae dicentis: "Quod vides, scribe in libro et mitte septem ecclesiis: Ephesum et Smyrnam et Pergamum et Thyatiram et Sardis et Philadelphiam et Laodiciam"'.

E109 *Gret kirkes* See Rev. 1: 4, 11, as in last.

E110 *þe Emperoure* Named in E113 as 'Domycyane'—Titus Flavius Domitianus, 'Domitian', emperor of Rome, AD 81–96. He was of Roman birth, conservative and repressive, and sought to safeguard civil order rather than achieve military conquests. He became mad and inequitable and was finally murdered (see 'Domitian', in *Suetonius*, ed. J. C. Rolfe, 2 vols (Loeb Classical Library, London, 1913, 1914), vol. II, 339–85).

E112 Domitian's persecution of the 'sons of David' (i.e. Jews and Christians) was regarded as being as terrible as Nero's, but though there were executions in AD 95, there were no legendary or especially diverting martyrdoms; see Suetonius, 'Domitian', *passim*.

E113–26 No source can be detected for the alliterative descriptions of the servants of the emperor. The collocations are not all formulaic, and some appear to be fresh.

E113 *dedeyned* 'was offended, angered' [OF *desdeignier*]; cf. *a.* 1382 WEV Job 32: 3: 'But aȝen the thre frendis of hym he dedeynede (WLV hadde indignacioun aȝens, *Vulgate*: *indignatus est*)'.

E116 *toylede* 'entrapped, caught', from the noun *toil* 'trap' [OF *teile* 'web, net']. See OED *toil v.*[2] and *till v.*[1] 'to set a trap' [from OS *tilian* 'obtain']. No source comes to light for this part of the account, which appears to be the poet's alliterative inventiveness.

E118 *Portelatyn* a gateway to the Via Latina at the extreme south-east corner of the outer Aurelian walls of Rome; cf. *c.*1300 *SLeg.John* (Ld) 60: 'þis wes in rome bi-fore a ȝat . . . þat men cleopeden þe porte latin'. In all Latin martyrologies one of John's feast days (6 May) is called 'De Sancto

Johanne ante portam latinam'. The other feast is that of his assumption, 27 December. If Tertullian's legend of John's martyrdom in boiling oil at Rome has any foundation (see Notes to E121–6), its venue must have been a probable site of execution outside the old city, where the Porta Latina was to be built more than two centuries later.

E119 *boustoure* typical ranting description, visualized as in the medieval drama, used to describe the emperor, Domitian.

   barett 'argument, furore' [OF *barat*]. See also Note to E120. The sense of 'derision' may have come from the shaving of John's head in Voragine: 'Iussu igitur Domitiani Romam deducitur et deducto omnes capilli pro derisione a capite preciduntur' (471.3). The word has also a sense of 'sorrow'; see MED *barat* n. 2. Perry glosses 'sorrow, pain', but there is no justification for this in the sources.

E120 *with bale for to bye* 'to suffer, be punished with pain' [from *bien* (OE *bycgan*)]; cf. *a*. 1400 *Destr.Troy* 4865: 'If þai might be . . . of mayne strenght, We mut bye it full bitterly, þe baret we make'.

E121–6 The legend of the boiling oil is not found in Eusebius, who merely records that Domitian sent for John and questioned him himself; see *Historia ecclesiastica* iii, Cap. xix and xx (PG 20.252, 253); nor is it found in the apocryphal *Acta Johannis*, but it is mentioned in Tertullian's third-century *Liber de praescriptionibus adversus haereticos* Cap. xxxvi.6: 'apostolus Joannes, posteaquam, in oleum igneum demersus, nihil passus est, in insulam relegatur' (PL 2.59–60). The matter is dealt with in only two sentences in Voragine's legend of 'Johanne ante portam latinam' (471.3–4; see also Note to E122), as also in *a*. 1325 *Cursor* 21042: 'In a tun was welland hat fild of oyle he did him schott'.

E122 *tonn* 'vat' [OE *tunne*]. *Leg.Aurea*: 'eum in dolium feruentis olei . . . mitti iussit' (88.15), and 'in doleum feruentis olei igne desubter candente mitti iubetur' (471.3). See also Note to E121–6.

E123 *wellande* 'boiling' [from OE *weallan* 'to boil']. See also Notes to E121–6 and E122, above. The same phrase is found in *Cursor Mundi* 21042 (see Note to E121–6) and in line 57 of Bodleian MS Harley 4196, the Northern Homily version: 'þe oyle war wellande warme' (see Horstmann, *Altenglische Legenden*, p. 35).

E124–6 The word *seþen* gives reason to believe that the poet was writing about a subsequent torture, which would give this text at least one unique point of interest, for no other source or record of such a torture seems to exist. Either the poet has been uncharacteristically inventive in order to finish his stanza in style, or he has erroneously introduced the plates of iron of the legends of, e.g., St Margaret or St Vincent; see *Sc.Leg.Saints xxviii* (*Marg.*) 552: 'þane wer of Irne mony plat Layd til hyr sydis, brynnand het';

see also the South English and Northern Homily Legendary versions of these saints' lives. A third, and most likely, interpretation is that the iron plate was some sort of technology (e.g., a grid) involved in the boiling-oil torture.

E128 *dede* Thornton has deleted this word by means of horizontal crossing-out. However, it seems necessary for the sense, and his deletion is understandable in that the word is followed by *dide*. Probably, in the haste of copying, Thornton thought that he had repeated a word.

E131 *Pathmos* the rocky island of Patmos in the Aegean Sea, close to the Turkish coast. Its salt mines, where John probably worked, were used by the Roman emperors as a penal colony. Rev. 1: 9: 'Ego Ioannes, frater vester et particeps in tribulatione et regno et patientia in Iesu, fui in insula quæ appellatur Patmos, propter verbum dei et testimonium Iesu'. The eleventh-century monastery dedicated to John survives on Patmos today. See also Eusebius, *Historia ecclesiastica* iii, Cap. xviii (PG 20.252).

　　apace 'straightaway' [from OF phrase *à pas* 'in steps']; cf. *a.* 1450 *Gener.*(2) 4453: 'On he goth a pase Vnto hir horse, as fast as euer he may'. The syntax of MS *a place* makes the Middle English adv. *aplace* 'in(to) existence' inapplicable, and the poet is not so weak as to have written a noun phrase 'a place', in apposition to *Patmos*. The emendation is warranted on palaeographical grounds in that the error was probably caused by eyeskip to *þat place* in the next line. It also makes sense, for John was banished to Patmos immediately after his ordeal in Rome.

E132 *free* 'noble, illustrious' [OE *freo*]; cf., e.g., *a.* 1450 *St.Editha* 2986: 'þey brouȝton þese relekes fre'; *c.*1380 *Cleanness* 203: 'þer he forȝet all his fre þeweȝ'. The word cannot be an adv. here, or adv. *Wysely* that follows would be syntactically incorrect. Further, the phrase *with a pen* would be tautologous.

E139 *wysses* either 'instructs' [OE *wissian*], or 'directs' [OE *wīsian*]. The former has been read here.

E140 *Goddes grace* See the opening words of *Leg.Aurea*: 'Iohannes interpretatur domini gratia uel in quo est gratia uel cui donatum est uel cui donatio a deo facta est. Per hoc intelliguntur quatuor priuilegia que fuerunt in beato Iohanne' (87.1–2). Cf. B127–8. There could be allusions not only to the Holy Name as found in the Holy Name texts of the *Gracia Dei*, but also to the holy book, *Gracia Dei*, and possibly to Mount Grace itself. See pp. lxix–lxx. If the poem is missing a final stanza (see p. lxxxiv), then this concatenation on the word 'grace' would link two stanzas at exactly the halfway point of the poem and make a literary, devotional, visual, numerological sign. On this see, e.g., Susanna Fein, 'Quatrefoil and Quatrefolia: The Devotional Layout of an Alliterative Poem', *Journal of the Early Book Society for the Study of Manuscripts and Printing History*, 2

(1999), 26–45. On the other hand, perhaps the author merely needed the rhyme.

E142 See Thornton's witness, *On Prayer*, f. 233ᵛ: '. . as all oþer gudnes & gyftes ere gyffene'; see pp. xix and lxix above.

E143 *Domycyane* See Note to E110.

E144 *semle* 'meeting, battle'. Domitian actually met his death by civil murder (in AD 96); and when his successor, the relatively benign Nerva, pardoned those who had been exiled, John returned in triumph to Ephesus.

E145 *gysed* 'prepared', from the substantive *gise* 'manner' [OF *guise*]. The verb has been brought in for the alliteration; more usually it means 'dressed'.

E146 *Ephesym* 'Ephesus', now the Turkish village of Ayassoluk, south of Izmir (Smyrna) near the Aegean coast, about eighty miles by sea and land from Patmos. The Latin acc. ending is found in most Middle English citations. Ephesus was possibly the most important of the Roman empire's Hellenistic cities of Asia Minor in the first century, and noted for its dedication to the goddess Diana (see Acts 19). The church which Paul had established here *c.*AD 50–60 was governed by Timothy and John. Certain of the Marian legends state that Ephesus was also the last home of the Virgin, who was lodged near the city by John and died there; see O. Sinding, *Mariä Tod und Himmelfahrt* (Christiania, 1903), *passim*.

gates þat ware gayne 'paths, routes that were most direct, shortest' [ON *gata* and ON *gegn*]; cf. 1440 *PParv.*189: 'Geyne, redy, or rythge forthe: *Directus*'.

E147 'many people [there], from whence you came [i.e. Rome], were your supporters'—the last being the Christians of Rome. For *þe toþer*, see Note to E148 below.

E148 *frayste of thi fare* 'make enquiries about your progress', 'take an interest in your (apostolic) mission'; cf. the more terse use without prep. in *SGGK* 409: 'þen may þou frayst my fare' (cf. *SGGK* 2494: 'of his fare'). See Note to E75 and the usage in E228 and 239.

þe toþer 'the rest' [formed by false division in spelling of OE *þæt ōþer*]; i.e. the Christians already established in Ephesus by Paul, Barnabas, Timothy and John *c.*AD 50–60, who would have been anxiously awaiting news of John's trial at Rome. John had, in fact, been bishop at Ephesus before his banishment. The pron. is only rarely found denoting a pl. number, but cf. 1494 Fabyn.*Chron.*vii.339: 'xviii were conuycte and hangyd, & the tother remayned longe after in pryson'.

E151–4 At this point (though nowhere else) there is an echo, especially in one rhyme, of ll. 56–8 of the Scottish Legendary version: 'þan a-gane wes sancte Iohn brocht in honore, / quhen ded wes þe emprioure, / to þe citte of effesy, / quare all þe puple in-to hy / sad he was rycht welcum *hame*, / þat þar of god come in þe *name*' (ll. 53–8, emphasis mine); see *Legends of the Saints in the Scottish Dialect of the Fourteenth Century* (*MS. Cambr. Univ. Gg II.6*), ed. W. M. Metcalfe, 3 vols (STS 23, 25, 35, 37, Edinburgh, 1896), p. 110. However, the common source is the phrase from Matthew 21: 8–9, Mark 11: 8–10, Luke 13: 35, 19: 37–38, John 12: 12–13; so *Leg.Aurea*: 'Sicque factum est ut sanctus Iohannes qui cum iniuria in insulam deportatus fuerat cum honore Ephesum remearet, occurrente ei uniuersa turba et dicente: "Benedictus qui uenit in *nomine* domini"' (88.19–20, emphasis mine). I am indebted to Christopher Bright for the train of thought that follows. The Gospel accounts of Christ's entrance into Jerusalem ultimately derive from Psalm 117: 26 (in Vulgate; 118: 26 in Hebrew and modern versions). This psalm (cf. verses 19–20) has the theme 'entrance into the city', as it apparently was sung as the priests entered the Temple in procession. Although the most popular Vulgate version of the Psalms, that based on the Septuagint, has 'venturus sit' for the Hebrew Bible's 'venit', the resonance here seems appropriate to John's return as bishop, and not as arrogant as the Gospel references might at first suggest.

E151 *hailsed* 'greeted, welcomed' [ON *heilsa*]; cf. *a.* 1325 *Cursor* (Vsp) 5156: 'Quen þai come all wit in a rutte, And hailsand forwit him þai lute'. The v. is not found with the adv. 'home', but cf., e.g., *a.* 1325 *Cursor* (Vsp) 15060: 'þin aun folk . . . welcums þe hame'.

E155 *Drucyane* Drusiana. She does not occur in the Bible, but in the late apocryphal Acts of John. She was the hyper-virtuous wife of Andronicus, with whom John stayed in Ephesus. She had parted from her husband in order to remain chaste, was then wooed by another and chose to let herself die rather than commit 'that abominable act' with him; so she took to her bed and expired. The apocryphal tale continues with more deaths and then attempted necrophilia by the second suitor, at which point John intervenes and raises Drusiana from the dead (see McWilson, 'Acts of John', p. 242). The simple retelling here is very close to that of *Leg.Aurea* (88–9.21–37).

E156 *delfynge* 'burying', more often 'digging' [OE *delfung*]; cf. 1440 *PParv.*118: 'Delvynge: *Fossura, fossatura*'.

E158 *Thou* Perry reads, or emends to, *Then*. MS *o* and *u* could be read as Thornton's round *e* and *n*, but the ligature is identical to all the others for *ou*, and, more cogent, in the other eight instances of OE *þænne/þanne* the vowel is *a* (as in, e.g., *thane* E155).

bare the body was naked because the second suitor, 'inflamed by the fiercest lust', had unwound the grave clothes and was about to enjoy with it 'what its owner wouldn't assent to while alive' (McWilson, 'Acts of John', p. 265; see Note to E155).

pare 'where'; see also E8 and E147.

E159–60 See *Leg.Aurea*: 'Tunc iussit feretrum deponi et corpus resolui dicens: "Dominus meus Ihesus Christus suscitet te, Drusiana. Surge et uade in domum tuam et para mihi refectionem!". Statim illa surrexit et cepit ire sollicita de iussione apostoli, ita ut sibi uideretur quod non de morte, sed de sompno excitasset eam' (88–9.27–30).

E166 *no thynge* i.e. material things, as in E40–56.

E168 *By fondyng* 'through temptation' (cf. *fanding* E62); i.e. the Devil caused some of them to go back to their heathen ways. The sense would have been clearer if *And* in E167 had been *But*.

E168–9 If a stanza is missing from the poem (see also p. lxxxiv above), it would almost certainly be after the twelfth stanza. The present thirteenth stanza opens with a pronoun, *þay*, and *þe caytefs* it refers to in the next line are the young men of the tale (told quite expansively by Voragine) of two rich young men who sold all to comply with the behests for asceticism of a non-Christian philosopher, usually named Aristodemus in the sources; see *Leg.Aurea* 92.75. Our poet employs the name of Crato for the sources' bishop who, later in the story, put John through trial by poison (see Note to E212).

E169–82 This is an extremely brief retelling of the legend of the rich young men (see last). Here, the poet seems to think that they had given up all they had to follow the Christian teachings of John. The wealthy youths soon regretted their decision when they saw their servants dressed better than themselves (here E169–70). John sent them to pick up sticks, which he turned for them into golden rods, and stones which he turned into gems, so that they were then as rich as before, though they had thus lost the kingdom of heaven. This legend is linked with that of the resurrection of the dead youth (Isidore, *De ortu et obitu patriarcharum*, Cap. lxxii, 183–4 (PL 83)—see E185–91 and Note to E192–6).

E173–4 At this late point in the composition this is the first of the three imperfect couplets of the hymn where the alliteration on the same main letter for two lines is not totally regular (see also E203–4 and E257–8); however the iteration of alliterating *w* does fall on the rhyming words, to give the couplet the alliterative pattern aa/aa, bb/ba.

E173 *þaire will* the young men had wanted to have their wealth back again.

wandes 'sticks' [ON **vandu-r*]—a word found more often in Northern dialects; cf. 1300 Hampole *Pr.Consc.*5878: 'þe wande sal chace foly out of þe childes hert'; *a.* 1450 *Yk.Pl.*11/146: 'Before the kyng cast downe thy wande And it sall seme as a serpent'.

E175 *saynede* 'signed with the sign of the Cross, blessed'; a Northern form of OE *segnian* and OF *seignier*, *sain(n)er*; see also E229 and E230. Cf. *a.* 1460 *TowneleyPl.*239/340: 'Primus tortor . . . "Sayn vs, lord, with thy ryng"'; *a.*

1450 *Yk.Pl.*28/287: 'I schalle þe sayne . . . In þe name of my fadir . . . in heuene [etc]'. See also Note to E229.

E176 *saphirs* 'sapphires'—only here for the alliteration. *Leg.Aurea* has 'pretiosas gemmas', *Cursor Mundi* (*Göt*) 'stanis precius' and Caxton's *Golden Legend* 'precyous stones and jewellis' (f. cjʳ).

E179–80 In the three hymns, the sestets divide naturally into two groups of three lines each (*Katherine* and *Evangelist*: ccd ccd; *Baptist*: bbc ddc); for this reason the third line (metrically a shorter b-verse type) is naturally end-stopped, and sentences that run on between these two groups are barely found except in this one odd instance—an example of the *Evangelist*-poet's distinctive style; this is found also in some of the long lines. In *Baptist* something similar occurs between B67–8, in *Katherine* not at all. Even in the sestets of the two 14-line stanza York Plays (see p. xxx and n. 49), which have a distinctive rhyme scheme, and one more conducive to enjambement, cd cccd, there is no enjambement between the c-rhyming lines, that is lines 3 and 4 of the sestets.

E181 Of several possible readings, the most viable might be to interpret *wone* (*wane* in E183) as a noun in the genitive case, giving 'in greater abundance'; see MED *wone* n. (3) 3. (d).

E183 *more wane* See above; the complete interchange of vowels in the concatenation of stanzas 13 and 14 can be noted.

bewane 'had possession of, possessed' [OE *ge)winnan*]. MED, under *bewinnen* v., specifies only singular -*an* endings; cf. *a.* 1338 Manning *Chron.Pt.2* p. 323: 'Of all þat grete tresoure þat euer he biwan'; but pl. forms in -*an* from the pa. pl. OE *ge)wunnen* are certainly found without the prefix, as in, e.g., *a.* 1400 *Morte Arth.*22: 'How they whanne . . . wyrchippis many'.

E187 *many mane* because of the source material, this has to mean 'many (a) man', i.e. 'a great number of persons, company', rather than 'great lamentation' as it does in the next line; see *Leg.Aurea*: 'Veniens igitur mater, uidua et ceteri qui eum flebant, ad pedes apostoli prociderunt rogantes' (91.51). See also *men*, E217.

E188 *mane* 'lamentation' [from OE **mænan* v.]; cf. *c.*1440 *Ihesu cryste saynte* 29: 'Ihesu, to þe I make my mane; Ihesu to þe I calle and crye'.

mele myghte thay noghte 'they could not speak' (for grief) [OE *mælan*, ON *mæla*].

E189 *Leg.Aurea*: 'Flente igitur apostolo diutius et orante' (91.60).

E192–6 The resurrected youth told the two rich young men that while he was dead he had seen heaven prepared and the angels weeping, and hell prepared and devils rejoicing, because the rich young men had regretted their decision. For sources see Note to E169–82.

E194 *þat* 'those who', an indefinite relative. The sense of the verb *leten* with prep. *by* is similar to the usage in E20; see MED *leten* v. 15 (d).

E197 *thay* the two wealthy young men.

weryede 'regretted, cursed' [OE *wærgan*]; cf., e.g., *c.*1390 Chaucer *CT.ML* 372: 'This Sowdanesse, whom I thus blame and warye, Leet prively hire conseil goon hire way'; 1440 *PParv.*516/2: 'Weryyn or cursyn, *imprecor, maledico, execror*'.

E200 *Ʒoo* an anomalous Southern form of the affirmative adv. [OE *gēa* Late West Saxon *iā*]. The form is not found in Yorkshire texts, but is, however, employed for the rhyme in the North West Midland *c.*1420 *Avow.Arth.*xxiv: 'Gauan asshes, "Is hit soe?" To tother knyƷt grauntus, Ʒoe'. All four rhymes here may be scribal.

E201 *tuke at* see Note to E92.

E202 *þat þay it fledde froo* 'that they [had] fled from it/ [had] abandoned it' (i.e. John's teaching).

E203–4 The alliteration on the same letter is not carried through the couplet—an isolated, apparently authorial blemish that appears to have been unavoidable, given the precise source material of this narration. See also Notes to E173–4 and E257–8.

E205 *in degre* 'in constitution' (explained by 'in thaire kynde' in the previous line); cf. *a.* 1395 Gower *CA.*1.2243: 'Riht such am I in my degree, Of fleissh and blod, and so schal deie'; 1445 ?Lydg. *Cal.*117: 'Myne yƷe is blynd in his degree'.

E206–7 Horstmann (ll. 204–5) punctuates against the line-ending: *in degre As þaire kind was, to bee Stones as þay ware*. Although the *Evangelist*-poet employs a greater degree of enjambement than most alliterative verse writers, such counterpoint is extremely bold, and does not seem idiomatic (see also Note to E102).

E208 *free* adv. 'readily'.

E209 *þan þat syghte fra thay see* 'from [the time] when they saw that sight'.

E210 *Myse* 'misdeeds'. See also E217.

E212 *Craton þe Cunande* 'Crato', confused by this poet with *Leg.Aurea*'s bishop Aristodemus (92.75); see also Notes to E221–32 and E169–82. In *Leg.Aurea* 'Craton philosophus' influences the two youths to give up their worldly goods for his pagan philosophy (89.31) The name is probably borrowed from that of Crates, the Theban philosopher, said to have shown his contempt for riches by throwing his own away.

E213 *þat he gun in lende* 'that he lived among'.

E217 'In this way he prevented the people from amending their misdeeds'.

E218 *mony a* Perry reads, or emends to, *mon a*. As this makes little sense, I assume it to be a slip. The MS is altogether clear.

E219 *Thurgh thaym* either 'on account of them (the idols)' or, more likely, 'in the name of them'; see MED *thurgh* prep. 4.

E221–32 See *Leg.Aurea*: 'Aristodemus autem pontifex ydolorum in populo seditionem maximam concitauit ita ut una pars contra aliam ad prelium pararetur. Cui apostolus: "Quid tibi uis? Faciam ut placeris". Cui ille: "Si uis ut credam in deum tuum, dabo tibi uenenum bibere et si nullam in te lesionem intulerit, uerus deus dominus tuus apparebit". Cui apostolus: "Fac ut locutus es". Et ille: "Volo ut alios inde morientes uideas ut sic amplius pertimescas". Pergens igitur Aristodemus ad proconsulem duos uiros decapitandos petiit et coram omnibus eis uenenum dedit; qui mox ut uenenum biberunt spiritum exhalarunt. Tunc apostolus calicem accipiens et signo crucis se muniens totum uenenum bibit et nullam lesionem incurrit. Quapropter deum omnes laudare ceperunt' (92.75–83). This legend, first related in Isidore (see Note to E169–82), may have had an origin in Christ's words to John and James, and in their reply: '"Nescitis quid petatis; potestis bibere calicem, quem ego bibiturus sum?" Dicunt ei: "Possumus"' (Matt. 20: 22 and Mark 16: 15–18).

E223 *noyede* 'harmed' [OF *anoier*]; cf. *c.*1280 *SLeg.Pass.(Pep)* 2338: 'ʒif hi drinkeþ dedlich þing, hit ne shal ham nouʒt anuye' (see Mark 16: 18).

E224 *lufe* from the sense of the source (see Note to E221–32, above) one would expect 'honour' [OE *lofian*], but in later ME such derivations are invariably spelt with vowel *-o-* (as in *louede*, E5). The derivations of *lufian* (of which this must be one) are spelt with *-uf-* throughout (see E19, E50, E237 and E246).

E226 *was puneschede in pyne* '(who) were enduring legal retribution in prison'. *Leg.Aurea*: 'duos uiros decapitandos petiit' (92.80). See MED *punishen* v. 3a.: *ben punished*; cf. *c.*1350 *Alex.&D.*395: 'We miht aftur Ben ypunched in paine'.

pyne '(condition or place of) imprisonment' [OE *pīnian*, *pīnung*]. Cf. *c.*1380 Chaucer *HF* 3.1511: 'Proserpyne, That quene ys of the derke pyne'.

E227 *felyd* 'tasted' [OE *ge)fēlan*]; see MED *felen*. v. (1) 2.

E228 *fylthe* 'evil' [OE *fylþ*], here 'poisonous constituent'. See also E69.

E229 *sauede* the graphs *n* and *u* are indistinguishable in the MS. Perry reads *sanede* (see Note to E175). This is unlikely because the word is found in the next line. Emendation to *saluede* (also found in E72) would be most apt, but the MS reading of *sauede* is satisfactory enough, because in the sources the philosopher asks the saint to raise the dead men to life (albeit after John's own survival of the cup of poison). Such adjustments of the ingredients of the legends are common in all three hymns.

seande a pr. p. construction, 'in the sight of'.

E230 *saynede* see Note to E175.

swetely Perry reads Thornton's sigma *s* as an *o*, giving *owtely* – a reading which does not make sense and does not alliterate. Furthermore, Early Middle English *outliche* 'utterly' appears to have died out by *c*.1300.

off 'of'; the phrase translates as 'sipped out of it then'.

E231 'the most majestic in hall [i.e. Crato] beheld that you took no harm.'

E232 *hally* 'entirely, unanimously' [from OE *hāl*, adj.] (see also *holly* E233); cf. *c*.1440 *Alex*.48/24: 'þay . . . said vn-till hym, hallely wit a voyce, "þou . . . es a godd."'

heledide see MED *helden* 2 b.(b).

E233 *holly* see Note to E232; cf. *c*.1439 Lydg. *FP* 3.1443: 'Hir fadir Iacob & hooli hir kynreede Ageyn this Sichem gan inwardli disdeyne'.

E237–8 That John repeated Christ's Commandment to Love (Matt. 22: 39, Mark 12: 13, Luke 10: 27–37, John 13: 34) is thought to have come from Jerome; see *Epistle ad galatas* vi. x (PL 26.462); but the idea is also found in the Johannine writings, e.g., 1 John 4: 7–11.

E239–40 'You bade them be noble in their behaviour when it came to be tested.'

E239 *frayste* See Notes to E75, E148 and E239–40.

E241 *Mone* 'tell, elucidate' [ON *muna* 'remember']; cf. *a*. 1338 Manning *HS* 11888: 'þe poyntes twelue . . . Prestes oghte hem all to kunne, lewed men to teche and monne'. Horstmann interprets as *moue*, presumably from *meven*, giving an unidiomatic reading.

E242 *mencyon* 'reference (to), account (of)' [OF *mencion*]; cf. *a*. 1398 Trev. *Barth*.128a/a: 'In þe gospel . . . is mensioun and mynde of [L *agitur de*] þe victorie of crist'.

mynde 'record' [OE *gemynd*]; cf. *a*. 1450 *Yk.Pl*.471/188: 'A prophette . . . Johell . . . spekis þus in his speciall spell, And of þis matere makis he mynde'.

E243 'It is the commandment of Christ that I am declaring to you'; see Note to E237–8 and next.

E245 *releue* 'help, succour' [OF *relever*]; see MED *releven* v. 2 (a).

þat lykes ȝoure lare 'that behaviour is favoured by your (own) teaching/ faith'.

E246 *as ȝour-selfe* See Gospels cited in Note to E237–8.

E254 *Weled the for worthi* MS *wothi* can be read as a misspelt adj. 'worthy', used substantively, as in E77. This is the only logical reading, adopted by both Perry and Horstmann. See MED *welen* v. 'choose' [ON *velja*].

thi wirchip to welde 'to hold your position of honour' (i.e. the bishopric that John had governed before his torture and exile).

E255 *blethely* 'readily, gladly' [OE *blīðelīce*].

E256 *belde* 'supporter, protector' [A *bældo, beldo*]; cf. *c.*1400 *Perceval* 1412: 'þay solde gare hym byde þat was hir beste belde'; *a.* 1450 *Yk.Pl.*114/76: 'Now, gud God, þu be my bilde [rhyme: unwelde]'.

E257–8 These two long lines constitute one of the three couplets (out of 75 extant in the text) that do not alliterate on the same letter. It seems impossible to restore to the established pattern; I assume an authorial inability to resolve the alliteration. See also Notes to E173–4 and E203–4.

manhede 'homage' [from OE *man* n.]; cf. *c.*1300 *Glo.Chron.A* 5197: 'Hii dude him anon hor manhede [vrr. honoure, homage]'.

mytir vnmyste 'not lacking the [bishop's] mitre'. A tag. Cf. Note to E57.

E258 *frythe* Horstmann misreads as *firthe*, a common variant.

E261 *thi mede* John's reward was specific: a seat at Christ's right hand in heaven (see Note to E35).

E263 *heþen paste* 'went from here (this earthly life)' [ON **heðan*]; cf. *c.*1300 *LFMass Bk.*295: 'And for þo soules þat hethen are past, þat þai haue rest þat ay shal last'.

Notes to *The Alliterative John Baptist Hymn*

B3 *to thi fader soght* The v. *sechen* takes a direct object. A more typical authorial line with an aa/bb alliterative pattern, as compared with this rather defective one, might run: 'Gabriel ful godely ‖ thi sire he soght'; however, cf. MED *sechen* 10, ~ *unto*, 'approach'.

B8 *with myrthe schul mete* Luke 1: 14: 'Et multi in nativitate ejus gaudebunt'.

B10 *To the soule sete* 'wholesome for the soul'. The adj., found in Northern texts such as *SGGK*, is from ON *soetr* 'sweet' (cf. also OE *-saete*); see MED *sete* adj. (b).

B11 *Nedeful to neuen* 'needful to be named', probably referring to the mirth of B8, or possibly referring to John's name, efficacious when uttered at the hour of death.

B13 *þer we schal long lende* 'to the place where we will dwell for a long time'—reference to the afterlife, for which John's powers of intercession are needed. MS *þat* makes no sense.

B14 *He bring vs* 'may he bring us'. See also B14.

B17 John was regarded as the last and greatest prophet after Christ. See Luke 7: 28: 'Dico enim vobis: Maior inter natos mulierum propheta Ioanne Baptista nemo est'.

B19 *myght gone* 'might go/walk'. Omission of the auxiliary gives an unmetrical b-verse, and is almost certainly corrupt; *on ground [þat] myght gone* improves the metre.

B20 *markyd on molde* 'fashioned (in human form) on earth/in the world'; see MED *marken* v. 13; cf. E1–2.

myghty in mede Literally 'great in reward', meaning there is no saint so rewarding to be connected with as John.

B23 *3e* The saint is always otherwise addressed as *þou / þow* and Day emends to *þow*. However, although one would expect the form *3i(e)* in a Northern composition, *3e* is here read as an authorial affirmative 'yea, yes' [ON *jā*, OE *gēa*], but perceived by a scribe as pron. sing., addressing John; cf. 1440 *PParv.*(W) 549: '3etyng, with worshyp, seying 3e not þu: *Vosacio*'.

B24–5 This must surely be read with enjambement: *At spede of God to gete grace* 'successful in procuring grace from God'.

B26 *He bring vs* as in B14.

B28 *His* i.e. God's.

B29 *good* 'good words, praise'; see MED *god* n. (2) 3.(b); cf. *a.* 1400 *Orolog.Sap.*373/13: 'I schulde come to þat holy sacramente, wher-of I haue herde so many goodes spoken'.

B30 *Al-holy* 'wholly, entirely'; cf. 1440 *PParv.* 9: 'Alle hooly [vr.al-holy]: *Integre, integraliter, totaliter*'. See also B133.

holde 'possession, control'. MS *honde*. The emendation restores the rhyme, and makes better idiom; cf. *c.*1395 Chaucer *CT.WB.D.*599: 'al myn herte I yaf vnto his hoold'.

B31 *forgoher* Probably copied in error; the MS is clear but no similar form occurs elsewhere, and no other superfluous *h* occurs in the witness. An unfamiliar *foreganger, forgraiþer* (see MED *for(e-greithen* v.), or similar, from the poem's Northern origins may have distracted a scribe. The epithet refers to one of John's typological functions as herald and messenger of Christ; see Luke 7: 27, where this is explicit. Cf. *a.* 1325 *Cursor* (Trin.) 13206–9: 'To helle bifore crist he ferd / As he dud in to þis werd / þerfore is he called forgoer / And cristis owne messanger'.

B35–84 See Luke 1: 5–25, 57–79. When the angel Gabriel told Zacharias that his aged wife, Elizabeth, would bear a child, Zacharias' disbelief caused him to be struck dumb until the angel's words should be fulfilled; when the child was born, neighbours and cousins proceeded to name him after his father, but Zacharias wrote, 'His name is John' on a writing tablet, and, as was prophesied, his speech was restored.

B35 *þis* MS *þí*. Day emends to *þat*, but my emendation to a similar demonstrative includes the MS *i* graph.

þer þei bothe stode The clumsy MS reading is retained because the words could refer to Zacharias and the angel, and may have been influenced by the widespread iconography of the scene. The phrase 'þer þi sire stode' would alliterate and make better sense (see also B3). If the reference is to Zacharias and his wife (the obvious reading), there is some discrepancy with the New Testament story and all medieval derivations—which have the angel appear to Zacharias, who then goes home to tell the tidings to Elizabeth. Day suggests that *þat bright* (B36) is Christ, and that B35 refers to the annunciation to Mary and Joseph, but such a reading is not consonant with the episode of Zacharias and the angel that follows in B37–42.

B38 *many-folde* See MED *mani-folde* adv. intensive; it could be translated here as 'clearly'. Myra Stokes has suggested the apt proposition of an archetypal *on folde* 'on earth', which contrasts the divinity of the angel with the human on the human plane. The line, in either case, is not metrical (see pp. xxxiii–xxxv) and would be improved by the omission of a syllable. In the MS, with its inverted verses, there is a word 'many' at the beginning of the next verse only three lines on, and eyeskip may have caused this rather useless phrase. Nevertheless, there is probably insufficient evidence for emendation.

B39 *neuend on-one* 'pronounced a name at once'. Day's alliterating emendation ('And neuend [a] no[m]e') provides a reading that does not rhyme with *stone*. She was perhaps influenced by the word division of the MS (*o none*) (l. 67 in MS and Day), which also led her to the emendation of B67 (l. 39 in MS and Day); but the orthography of the rounded vowels is not unusual (see MED *an-on*). See also Note to B67. This repetition of tags in each of the eleventh lines could easily have led to the juxtaposition of the stanzas in this tradition.

B40 The line, though possibly authorial, has two long dips. 'For he nolde þe aungel leue' improves the metre.

B43 *roser* 'rosebush' [OF *rosier*]; cf. *c.*1425 *St.Mary Oign*.179/25: 'She songe of seint Stephen, whom she clepyd Rosyer of paradys'.

B44 *mekeful* Although *menskful* 'honourable, exalted' makes the best sense in the context, there can be no sound justification for Day's addition of two letters, as *mekeful* is well-enough attested, e.g., in *c.*1390 *Maidstone PPs.*(V) 87: 'Mekeful (vr. merciful) lord, þou make hit sene Wiþ-inne my herte'. Alternatively, the MS *mekeful* was possibly an authorial (and more prevalent) *milceful* ('merciful', used commonly of Mary), the original *i* graph transmuting to *e*, and *l* + *c* to *k*; cf. another variant in the above psalm: (Vrn: 'þou art, fader, so milsfull kyng').

B45 *maste is of myght* MS *þat is ful of myght*. Following Day, I read the poet's intention to alliterate on this easy b-verse tag; cf. *Evangelist*: *þat maste es of myghte* (E1). The alteration to straightforward syntax with the inclusion of *ful* exemplifies characteristic scribal corruption in strong-stress verse. The vowel in *maste* follows relics in rhymes in B109 and B112. See also 'Prayer to the Blessed Virgin', Day, *Wheatley MS*, p. 11, l. 172: 'of myghtes maste'.

B46 *þat swete* Understood to be Mary because of the pronouns that follow in B47.
   sawes The Magnificat, Luke 1: 41–55.

B47 *pertly a-plight* 'straightaway, assuredly'—shortened from *I þe aplight* 'I assure you', or *on plight* 'on my word' [from OF *apert* and OE *plihtan*].

B48–9 In Gospel versions Mary departed after three months and before Christ was born (Luke 1: 56–7), but, apocryphally, she was the first woman to touch John, and, in this midwife role, presumably to clothe him (as at B49); see Petrus Comestor, *Historia scholastica*: 'et legitur in libro Justorum quod beata virgo eum primo levavit a terra' (PL 198.1538) and *Leg.Aurea*: 'Mansit ergo uirgo beata cum cognata sua tribus mensibus ministrans ei natumque puerum suis sanctis manibus de terra leuauit, ut habetur in hystoria scholastica, et quasi morem gerule officiosissime peregit' (542–3.4–5); cf. *a.* 1325 *Cursor* (Vsp) 11062–4: 'Maria . . . was hir-self þe first womman þat lifted fra þe erth iohan'.

B49 *cawte in clothes* Mary dressed the newborn John. This is not found in Middle English versions of the John legend or lives of Christ, but appears to be a natural development from the Latin source (see Peltier, *S. Bonaventurae*, p. 518). Nicholas Love translates 'oure lady lift vp first from þe gronde, & after bisily diȝt & treted as it longet to him' (Sargent, *Love's Mirror*), p. 32; see also Voragine and *Cursor* in preceding Note. However, a later translation (*c.* 1609) gives: 'our Ladie receiued firste into hir handes, and after pretilie dressed him' (*The Miroure of the Blessed Life of Christ*, ed. D. M. Rogers (English Recusant Literature 392), p. 67). Rogers does not state from which of the longer Latin lives of Christ or Mary this may have come, or whether it is a reworking of Love. For Latin texts see Peltier, *S. Bonaventurae*, and Sarah M. Horrall, *The Lyf of Oure Lady* (Middle English Texts 17, Heidelberg, 1985); no manuscripts in British libraries mention clothes or dressing. For an illuminating discussion of the importance in such narratives of cloth, cloths and clothing in the 'feminization' of devotion, through service, see Gail McMurray Gibson, *The Theater of Devotion: East Anglian Drama and Society in the Late Middle Ages* (Chicago, 1989), especially pp. 51–65.

B50 *loutid to Jhesu* Refers to John quickening in Elizabeth's womb when the pregnant Mary greeted her, and is, characteristically in this composition, not sequential with its biblical source.

B51 *lett* MS *leet*. Many vowels in this witness are doubled to indicate a degree of length (see 'Language', above). This instance appears to be a mere error. The rhymes are on short *e* and are straightforward.

B53 *Oure fadres be-forne* MS *oure fadres be borne* makes no sense. Day's emendation to '[þo] f[o]des [vn]borne' nicely expresses the idea that the unborn John recognized the unborn Christ, but is too strained, when the emendation of one letter gives the unexceptional tag which could be read as an adverbial phrase expressing the later meeting of the adult John and Christ: '(even) before they met in front of our ancestors'. Alternatively *be-forne* could be read as an adj., rendering *fadres be-forne* as 'forefathers'. The first interpretation has been favoured, and the text is punctuated according-ingly; cf. *a.* 1475 *N-Town* 7/195: 'The shepherds xal come hym be-fforn / With reuerens'.

B58 *within bredde* The verb is intrans., 'grew, were nurtured'; cf. MED *breden* v. 2 (b); *a.* 1450 *Yk.Pl.*311/130: 'Woo worthe þe wombe þat I bredde ynne'.

B60 *in stede* 'beset with'; the phrase can be rendered literally as: 'the sorrows in which they were placed'.

B61–6 Certain MS lines have been editorially juxtaposed here. First, B65 and B66 (MS ll. 37 and 38) have been reversed to sustain the iteration between octet and sestet which is otherwise observed throughout the other nine stanzas. This reversal also improves the sense of the story, because the relatives went to see what Zacharias had written (Luke 1: 62–3). Second, B61 and B63 (MS ll. 33 and 35) have been reversed to effect some rationality in the narrative where, at this point, the MS makes no sense. Relatives who knew of the baby's imminent arrival (MS l. 35) were all around the place of his birth (MS l. 34), for they had zealously gathered themselves together (MS l. 33) because, according to the law, they were to be there for the circumcision and naming on the eighth day (MS l. 36).

B61 *kyde* 'familiar', but perhaps best read as 'recognized, rightful', to give a sense of John's endorsement by the extended Holy Family.
   wist The word creates the poor alliterative pattern aa/xx and may be scribal. A more Northern form *ken(ne)d* or *kent* (see *kist* B47) would restore the fundamental aa/ax pattern.

B62 *þanne* MS *þam* gives a non-idiomatic phrase that is dialectally out of place (see *þem*, B69), and was possibly occasioned by a nasal bar in the tradition. Spelling is in line with *þanne*, B35, B36 and B106. The emendation is still imperfect in that it retains the ungrammatical *was*, but this may have been authorial.

B63 *for gadrid togedir* MS *for togedir* is unmetrical. As the kinsmen gathered together for the circumcision and naming of the child (Luke 1: 58–9), it can be surmised that, rather than Day's conjectural *gamen*, a past or present participle of the verb *gaderen* occurred here. The form with vowel *a* has been selected as being the most common. Although a form with vowel *e* might have caused scribal homoeoteleuton, similar collocations of *gaderen* and *togedir* demonstrate that disparate vowels are more often found than assonating ones. The pp. ending conforms with *callid* and *combrid* in the same stanza. Cf. *c.*1384 WEV Matt. 2: 4: 'He, gedrynge to gidre alle the princis of prestis'; *c.*1450 *Alph.Tales* 214/30: 'He garte gadur to-gedur yong men'.

B64 *were þei lede* This passive construction works in an idiomatic reflexive way. The sense is that they betook themselves to the birthplace. See next.

B65 *hem lede* A reflexive usage that is not otherwise encountered after the early fourteenth century. See MED *leden* v. 10 (refl. 'betake oneself'); cf. *a.* 1325 *Cursor* (Vsp) 24620: 'Vnto þe tun þan i me ledd'.

B67 *frayned* See Luke 1: 62–3: 'Innuebant autem patri eius quem vellet vocari eum. Et postulans pugillarem scripsit dicens: "Ioannes est nomen eius"'.

on-one MS *o none*. As in B39, Day emends to *[a] no[m]e* and spoils the rhyme (MS and Day l. 39). The naming is mentioned in the next line. The tag 'at once', as in B39, is appropriate here, and makes sense of the clear MS reading. The emendation conforms with the spelling in B39; hyphenation is editorial. See also Note to B39.

B71–81 The editorial punctuation reflects one of several possible readings of the syntax.

B73 *frestyng* 'proving', from *fraisten*, to put to the test [ON *freista*]. The only other occurrence of the verbal noun is in *a.* 1450 *Yk.Pl* 428/48–9: 'So frendfull we fonde hym in fraistyng . . . In frasting we fonde hym full faithfull and free'.

B74 *sekir* 'sure, secure' [OE *sicor*]. MS *sokir* was probably caused by eyeskip to *socour* in the line below.

B76–8 MS *blowe* and *knowe* rhyme with *lawe* and *sawe*, suggesting scribal alteration from original Northern vowels. See also B109 and B112.

B76 *whennes* A form of the rare *whenso* [representing OE **swā hwanne swā*]; cf. 1423 Jas.I *Kingis Q.*cxviii: 'Quhenso my teris dropen on the ground'. Here the monosyllabic form appears to have been chosen for its metrical applicability; cf. *c.*1175 *Lamb.Hom.* 85: 'In þe deie of liureisun hwense god almihtin wule windwin þet er wes i þorschen'.

B77 *hende* MS *honde* does not rhyme, and a pl. form would make better sense; cf. the Northern pl. *hend(e)* [from OI *hönd*, ON *hendr*]; see *a.* 1325 *Cursor* (Vsp) 17142: 'Tak ute mi hert bituix þine hend', and *c.*1400 *Maundev.*(Roxb.) ii.5: 'þe pece . . . to þe whik his hend ware nailed'.

B80 *in a throwe* 'in a short while' [OE *þrāg/þrāh*]; surely originally Northern *thrawe*, rhyming on *lawe* (B72), *sawe* (B74) and original Northern *blawe* and *knawe* (B76, B78).

B81 *A poyntil hade he hent* MS *hade he hent*; cf. *c.*1384 WEV Luke 1: 63: 'He, axinge a poyntel, wroot seyinge, "John is his name"'; *a.* 1325 *Cursor* (Vsp) 11087: 'Asked þan sir zachari Tables and a pontel [Ld: poyntele] tite'. The conjectural *i*-ending is adopted in conformity with, e.g., *wildirnesse* (B86), *purpil* (B87) and *watir* (B94).

B89–90 For the interpretation of the biblical *locustae* (Matt. 3: 4) subsequent to Pliny, see Day's useful Note to B89–90 (Day, *Wheatley MS*, p. 103). The English commonly understood it to be a form of grass such as oats (see also next); see also *a.* 1425 *Wycl.Serm.*2.5: 'Sum men seien þat locusta is a litel beest good to ete. Sum men seien it is an herbe þat gederitþ honey upon him; but it is licli þat it is an herbe þat mai nurishe men, þat þei clepen hony soukil; but þis þing varieþ in many contrees'.

B89 *Hawes* 'hawthorn berries' of temperate climates [OE *haga*]. The pl. in -*s* makes hawthorn berries [OE *haga*], seen as subsistence food, the most likely reading. See also the poetic usages: *a.* 1500 *Orfeo* (Hrl) 22/241: 'In somer he lyueþ by hawys'; *c.*1380 Chaucer *Form.A.* 7: 'They eten mast, hawes, and swich pounage, And dronken water of the colde welle'; but see MED *haver* n. (2) 1.(a) for ON *hafur*, L *avena* 'cereal, oats'. As the *Legenda Aurea* has *locustas* here (see preceding Note), there may have been a general confusion about what the saint did eat. There is some conflation of meaning with the sense of brushwood, or whatever is growing in the desert, exemplified in 1440 *PParv.* 230: 'Hawe, frute; *Cinum, cornum, ramnum*'. *Cinum* is dogwood, etc. Note *ryse* 'brushwood', also in B89.

hent MS *toke* does not alliterate, and was almost certainly picked up by the scribe from the preceding line. Day's emendation is very sound (see also use of *hent*, B81) and changes a bad xx/aa alliterative pattern to a regular aa/bb.

B90 *borionand bere* 'sprouting barley' [OF *borjoner, burjuner,* etc. 'to burgeon'; OE *bere* 'barley']. MS *borion and bere* suggests that a non-Northern scribe in the MS tradition did not understand the pr. p. -*and* ending. Day, inexplicably, hyphenates to produce *borion-and*.

blomyng 'spring (i.e. time of blooming)'; not otherwise found, but obviously from the verb *blomen*. The ME v. appears to derive from an OI verbal n.: *blīōmandi* 'blooming, flourishing', and this hapax legomenon may have come directly from language current in the Danelaw.

B91 Day's helpful way of making sense of this line was to emend MS *and* to *for*, also adopted here. The saint was lacking rich food in the desert; *þis* relates to *ryche mete*.

B92–9 Editorial punctuation is drastic in order to make some sense of the wording.

B92 *þow* This is perfectly distinct in the MS and the only significant variation from Day's reading.

B96 *sydir* 'spiritous drink'. It would be nice to visualize English apple cider going down with the hawthorn berries, roots and barley in the Middle Eastern desert, but see MED *sider* n. (b) 'strong drink'. The phrase *sydir ne wyne* comes not from any of the Gospel descriptions of John in the desert but from the words of the angel to Zacharias (Luke 1: 15): 'et vinum et siceram non bibet'. The letter *c* of L *sicera* (Gk σικερα, Hebrew *sēkhār* 'strong drink') became *d* (probably via *z* and *th*) in romance languages to give OF *cidre* (see OED *cider* n.). However, cf. *a.* 1325 *Cursor* 10977: 'And [noþer win] ne ciser drinc'.

B101 *withouten any were* 'without any doubt', a b-verse tag. The Anglian, Northern and Scots *were*, sometimes *war* [OHG *werra*], translates as 'confusion, perplexity'; cf. *c.*1485 *Digby Myst.*III. 1027: 'With-owtyn ony wyre, þer xall ye se hym'.

B103–4 The MS makes no sense. Christ's baptism was in his thirtieth year; hence the complex emendations that render 'the thirtieth year from the nativity'. Apocryphal knowledge had it that, just as Christ first appeared to the pagan (three kings) on the twelfth day after his birth, so he appeared to be baptized at the onset of his ministry on the twelfth day after his thirtieth year (6 January). Cf. *c.*1425 *Spec.Sacer.*(Add) 18/ 34(Epiphany): 'In that day ye schall haue þe feste of the apperynge of oure lorde, borne . . . and beynge þer in the cribbe, schewyde his godhede . . . And in the same day a xxx.ti yere that he was so worschipped of the kynges it is red that he was baptysed of John Baptist in the Flom Jordan'; *c.*1200 *Orm.*11047: 'Jesu Crist wass fullhtnedd Rihht o þatt daȝȝ . . . þatt twellfte daȝȝ iss nemmnedd'.

B104–5 The MS reads: *As fel on þe twelft day he peryd. / Vn to þe holy gost of heuene he come to þere.* Day's cogent emendation demonstrates the confusion of metre and sense that arose when a scribe changed an original Northern *til* to *to* in an exemplar that was possibly not set out in verse lines. Day drops the MS *vn*, presumably reading *peryd* as bisyllabic; however the alliterative metre throughout scans mostly with *unstressed* uninflected pa. t. syllables (e.g., *busked* B63); and monosyllabic *peryd* would retain MS *vn* and ensure asymmetry in the b-verse.

B105–12 There was a widespread misconception that the Holy Ghost descended onto John and not Christ at Christ's baptism; cf. 1460 *TowneleyPl.* 25/69–72 [John]: 'The holy gost from heuen discende As a white dowfe downe on me than; The fader voyce, oure myrthes to amende, Was made to me lyke as a man'. This may have arisen from a misunderstanding of Mark 1: 9–10: 'venit Iesus a Nazareth . . . et baptizatus est in Iordane ab Ioanne. Et statim . . . vidit . . . columbam descendentem . . . in ipsum'.

B112 *moost* The rhyme points to an original Northern *maast*; see also B72–8.

B114 *profet* Read as past tense (see MED *profiten* v.), and this verse as qualifying the previous one. The innovatory and Christ-like 'points of peace' that John uttered to the people in, e.g., Luke 3: 10–14 were quite unlike the 'Resones and right' (see Note to B116) that John enunciated to Herod and his wife (Mark 6: 17–18); see especially the *Cursor* poet's interpretation of this: 'To kyng heroude seide seynt Ion Do wey fro þis wicked wommon þou louest hir muche aȝeynes þi lif And ȝitt is she þi broþer wif Whom þou shuldes not haue with lawe If þou dredded goddes awe, etc.' (Vsp 13048–56).

   poyntes 'distinguishing qualities'; cf., e.g., Luke 3: 10–14.

B115 *Herode* Herod the tetrarch, one of the three sons of the Herod the king; cf. *a.* 1325 *Cursor* (Vsp) 13004–13: 'not þat heroude wile ȝe wele þat slowȝe þe childer of israele, But anoþer þat so hat Of þre sones þat he gat', etc.

   Herodias Herod the tetrarch's wife; she had been the wife of his deceased brother, Philip. See Mark 6: 17: 'Ipse enim Herodes misit ac tenuit Ioannem et vinxit eum in carcere propter Herodiadem uxorem Philippi fratris sui, quia duxerat eam'.

B116 *rekynde on ryse* Perry glosses as 'enumerated in order' [Late OE *recenian*; *ge)reconod*, OE *ræw* 'row'], probably because of the prep.; cf. *a.* 1450 *Yk.Pl.* 20/50: 'Rede youre resouns right on rawes'. More probably the original phrase was *in rees*, i.e. 'in outrage' [OE *ræs*, ON *rás*]; whatever the case, the form *ryse* is an odd mutation. See Mark 6: 18: 'Dicebat enim Ioannes Herodi: "Non licet tibi habere uxorem fratris tui"'. See also Note to B114.

B119 *led . . . likyng* '[Herod] did not conduct himself lawfully in his pleasure'; see MED *leden* v. 4. (e) refl. See also Notes to B64 and 65.

B120 *For* 'because of'. See also Note to B115.

B123 *hyr* MS *hym.* I assume that Herodias is the subject of the two sentences of the sestet, and the verb is reflexive. See Mark 6: 19. In medieval legend Herodias was worried about separation from Herod if John prevailed, so *Cursor*, II, 13040–1: 'Sco cried and mad ful mikel dole, Als sco þat was a neber fole'; *La Légende doréé par Jacques de Voragine*, trans. M. G. B[runet] (Paris, 1843), II, 414–9: 'La dame auoit moult grant frisson / Que herodes aler ne laissast'.

B124–6 See Matt. 14: 8: 'At illa, praemonita a matre sua: "Da mihi, inquit, hic in disco caput Ioannis Baptistae"'.

B128 *betokenith Goddes grace* 'John' derives, through Latin and Greek, from Hebrew *Johanan* 'God is gracious'. The phrase here shows that the meaning was understood in the medieval period. In this instance the impetus is from the discourse on the name that opens each of Voragine's legends, though, in the case of this saint the etymology is not spelt out (see *Leg.Aurea* 540. 1–2: 'Johannes baptista multipliciter nominature [etc.]'). However, cf. E140, 'Thi name is Goddes grace' and accompanying Note. See also *Leg.Aurea* 541–8.12–129 for a long passage on the threefold grace which John received in his mother's womb.

    clere MS *lere*. See 1440 *PParv.*81: '"Cleryn", or make clere a thynge þat ys vnknowe: *Clarifico, manifesto*'. There is one other aa/ax line in the poem, B72, but MS *lere* gives a self-rhyme. I have followed Day in emending to *clere*, but doubtfully, for this produces a different self-rhyme with the adj. *clere* in B134, and also because, surprisingly, the collocation of *clerk* and *cleren* is not otherwise found in alliterative verse. However the emendation restores the prevalent alliterative pattern of the composition, aa/aa.

B129 *on* MS *of.* Day emends to *[in]*, **involving an unnecessary change of two letters; for** *on . . . maners*, see MED *manere* n. 3b.

B130 *lere* MS *bere* does not make good sense. See also Note to B128.

B133 *holy* 'wholly', as also in B30.

B134 *lantern of light* The phrase was used of any notably holy person (cf. K3), but most particularly of John the Baptist, seen as the lantern heralding Christ's ministry (John 5: 35: 'Ille erat lucerna ardens et lucens'). Cf., e.g., *a.* 1325 *Cursor* (Trin-C) 12910: 'He þe chees for þi lantern Bifore his face þe liȝt to bern To go bifore his comyng'; *c.*1450 *Interpol.Rolle Ps.*(Bod 288) 57: 'Joon Baptist was lantirne bifore þe sunne'.

    The b-verse is in 'forbidden' anapaest metre; . . *scynyng ful clere* is a metrical possibility, or the disyllabic *scyneth* may have been substituted for an original, more Northern *scynst* (cf., e.g., *hast*, B30, and cf. *schinest* in the iteration of B135).

GLOSSARY

The glossary records the sense and forms of all words in the texts. Except when confusion might arise, only the first five occurrences of a word are recorded. Proper names are found at the end of the glossary. The letter ȝ has a separate alphabetical entry after g; vocalic y is treated as i; consonantal i is treated as j; the letters th and and þ have been treated as identical. Emended words are distinguished by an asterisk. Words in the critical apparatus are not included. The abbreviations for grammatical forms are those recommended by EETS and listed in, for example, *The Ayenbite of Inwyt*, ed. Pamela Gradon (EETS, 278, 1979), p. 235.

a *art.* a *B81; *see also* **ane**

abyde *v. intrans.* live, remain K274; **byde** E8, E9; **habyde** halt, wait E157; *we to ~ our souls to remain* (there) K274; *pa. 3 sg.* **abode** inhered K18

abooue *adv.* openly K156

aboute, abowt *prep.* about, around B62, K77

adent *pp.* fastened down (in), gripped (in) K244

aferde *pp.* frightened K174

affy *v. trans.* trust, believe E216

after, aftir *prep.*; *of congruence*: after K132; *of pursuit*: after, for E44, E102

agayne *adv.* back, to their former state E204, E205

aȝens *prep.* against K118

ay *adv.* always E6, E153, K228, K237, K261, K262, K264, &c.; constantly E82

ay-whare *adv.* everywhere E24

al(l), alle *n., pron.* all (people, things), everything E162, K1, K213, K246; *gen.* **alþer** ~ **beste** best of all E74

al(l) *adj.* all, entire, the whole of E1, E43, E45, E127, K32, K88, K143, K158, &c.; *pl.* **al** K229, K267; **all** E142; **alle** B69, E229, K31, K36, K120; *with pl. v.*: **alle** K175

al *adv.* entirely, totally K38; *as intensive* K77; **~-holy** entirely B30

almost *adv.* very nearly, well-nigh K90

alone *adv.* solely, entirely; *was of on here ~ was entirely due to her* K42

alow *v.* permit K55

als *see* **as**

also *adv.* besides, also E141

alsone *adv.* immediately, at once E229

alþer *see* **al(l), alle** (*n.*)

am *1 sg.* am K173; *see also* **are, art, be, is, was**

and *conj.* and B1, E10, *E15, K12, &c.; if K130

ane *art.* an E126

angeles *see* **aungel**

angwysch *n.* torment K228

apace *adv.* at once, immediately *E131

apere *v. intrans.* appear (in God's presence) K271

ap(p)ertely *adv.* clearly, openly B114, E105

a-plight *adv.* assuredly B47

appon *prep.* in E203; *see also* **vp**

are (*v.*) *see* **art**

are *adv.* before E171, E172

art *2 sg.* are, art B21, K3, K245; *as auxil.*: ~ **went** have gone K246, K247; *3 pl.* **are** are K227; *see also* **am, be, is, was**

as, als *conj. & rel. adv.* when B66, B104; as, like B21, B64, B78, B79, B128, B137, E17, E56, E59, E63, E111, E206, E222; as (if) E160, K113, K189, K190; in (such) a manner (as) B32, B32, B108, E171, E172, K13, K101; when, in (such) a manner E30; in the form of B106; being one who was K163; as if she were one who was K188; being (one who is, those which are) B42, E15, E16, E207, K180; as if (you were, he were) E115, E246; in this way, thus, ?besides K107, K108, K110, K111; als . . . als as . . . as E227; ~ **þat** because K116

aschamyd *pp.* ashamed, reluctant K66; *see also* **schamed**

asent *n.* agreement; *am at ~ have decided* K173; *see also* **sent**

asent *v.¹, pp.* having ascended K251

assentand *v.²*, *pr. p.* assenting E67; *see also* **sent**

aste *pa. 3 sg.* asked E35

astonyd *pp.* stunned, dazed K89

at *prep.* at E89, E113, E144, K44, K202; at a time of, when in B22, B23, B76; according to E84, K172; *tuke* ~ took to, ?assimilated E92, E201; ~ *spede* in a state of prosperity B24; *am* ~ *asent* have decided K173

auert *v. imp. sg.* avert, deflect *K228

aungel *n.* angelic messenger B35, B40; heavenly messenger B133; *pl.* **a(u)ngeles** angels K192, K279; ~ *of angwysch* angels of torment, devils K228

away, awey *adv.* hence B12; away K105, K229, K253, K254

bachilere *n.* young knight K105

bad(d)e *pa. 2 sg.* commanded E157, E179, E239; *pa. 3 sg.* bad K50; **bedde** E119; *pa. 3 pl.* **bedde** asked, begged E255

bayne *adj.* desirous E99

balde *see* **bolde**

bale *n.* torment E120; grief E186; trouble, misfortune E256; *pl.* **bales, balys** (everlasting) torments, pains, evils B2, K4, K218, K219, K250

baptim *n.* baptism B131

baptist *v. pa. 2 sg.* baptized B101

baran *adj.* infertile B2

bare *v.¹* uncover, make naked E120; *pp.* E121, E158; *with adj., adv. force*: unrelieved, unremitted; *bales ful* ~ extreme tortures K4; ?manifestly B57

bare (*v.²*) *see* **berene**

barett *n.* derision, furore E119

barne *n.* child E8, E74, E185

bathe *see* **bothe**

bawmyng *vbl. n.* balm, application or effusion (of balm) K78

be *v.* be E239, E255; **bee** E206; *3 pl.* are K240; **beene** K77; *subj. 2, 3 sg.* B140, E256; *1 pl.* B56; *imp. sg.* B1, B15, B113, B127, E3, E5, K66; *pl.* E237, E244; *as auxil. (with pp.) forming passive: 3 sg.* be B7, B34, B133, E153, K64, K65, K68, K119, K161; **bese** E75; *3 pl.* K254; **ben** K244; *pa. 2 sg.* E134, E135; *pa. 3 sg.* E156; *pp.* **bene** E172; *see also* **am, are, art, is, was**

be (*prep.*) *see* **by**

become *pa. 3 pl.* became E235

bedde *see* **bad(d)e**

beene *see* **be**

beerd(e), byrde *n.* maiden E7, E73, K17, K26, K155; woman B2; *pl.* **beerdes** ladies K156

before *prep.* in front of B28, K32, K35; **be-forne** *B53

behelde *pa. 3 sg.* saw, beheld E231

bekende *pa. 3 sg.* committed, entrusted E98

belamy *n.* fair friend (ironical), rascal, knave K17

belde *n.* encourager, defender E256

beleue *n.* belief, faith K81

below *adv.* (on earth) below K3

bemes *n.¹ pl.* trumpets B76

bemus *n.² pl.* beams, rays K77

ben(e) *see* **be**

bent *pa. 3 sg.* overcame K17

bere *n.¹* barley B90

bere *n.²* bier E157

berene *v.* bear, carry K105; *pa. 3 sg.* **bare** bore, gave birth to E74, E186; *pp.* **born(e)** born B1, B57, B78, E7, K274; **bourn** B34

beryen *v.* bury K106

beschope *n.* bishop E255

bese *see* **be**

besyde *prep.* near, beside K270

besoghte *pa. 2 sg.* beseeched E190, E191

beste *adj.superl.* best E8, E74; *as adv.* E256

bete *v.* conquer, vanquish B2

betokenith *3 sg.* signifies B128

better *adj.comp.* better B17

bewane *pa. 3 pl.* (had) possessed E183; *see also* **wynne**

bewte *n.* courtesy K18

by, be *prep.* by the agency of E22, E168, K48; according to E162, E163, E194, E214, K214; by B72, E184; ~ *name* by title K80; *adv.* with respect to E20

by (*v.*) *see* **by(e)**

biddyng, byddyng *vbl. n.* command, authority E100, K32

byde *see* **abyde**

by-dene *adv.* completely, entirely, utterly E25, E50, E51

by(e) *v.* pay, make amends E120, E121

bygane *pa. 2 sg.* began E189

bilde *pa. 3 sg.* appealed, entreated K156

bynde *v.* bind, pledge K166; *pa. 3 pl.* **bonde** K32

byrde *see* **beerd(e)**

birdyn *n.* burden (of child in womb) E73

bythe *n.* environment, abode; *in his* ~ in its place (in him) K18

bytwene *prep.* between E116

blamyd *pp.* accused, censured K65

blede *v.* shed blood B18

blely *adv.* willingly, gladly, cheerfully K31

blent *pp.* mitigated, annulled; *makyst þou* ~ render null and void K250

blethely *adv.* readily, gladly E255

blyn *v.* desist, cease K153

blis(se), blys(s), blysse *n.* state of eternal happiness, joy B26, E8, E9, E100, E107, K219, K233, K274, *K278, K280; happiness, joy K78

blyssede *pa. 2 sg.* blessed E158; *pp.* blissed(e) made blessed B1, B15, &c., E153; **blyste** sanctified E255

blyth(e) *adj.* happy, joyful E159, K233

blod(e), blood *n.* blood B18, K92, K93; flesh B17, K106, *K107

blomyng *vbl. n.* springtime B90

blowe *v.* sound B76

body *n.* body B58, E74, E120, E158; corpse K193; human being, person B17, B34, E99, E186

bokes *see* **buke**

bold(e), balde *adj.* healthful B34; rude, presumptuous E119, K105

bonchef, bonchif *n.* cheerful behaviour K18; a good outcome K218

bonde *see* **bynde**

bone *n.* bone B17; *pl.* bones K106, K107

borionand *pr. p. as adj.* sprouting B90

born(e) *see* **berene**

bostful *adj.* bragging, arrogant, menacing, threatening K17

bot, but *conj.* but, however E157, E225, E229, K38, K58, K88; but rather K6; except for B18; unless (with *subj.*) K133

bot, but *conj., adv.* but, only B88, E54

bothe *adv.* both B32, B35, B99, B111, K80; **bathe** E75, E81, E232

bourn *see* **berene**

boustoure *n.* braggart E119

bouxsom *see* **buxum**

bowand *adj.* compliant, agreeable E100

bowed *pa. 3 pl.* bowed (down to), deferred (to) K31

brast *see* **brest**

bredde *v. intrans. pa. 2 sg.* grew, were nurtured B58

breyd *n.* commotion, outburst K155

brest *v. trans.* burst asunder, dissolve K218; *pa. 3 sg.* **brast**; ~ *on a breyd* burst out in an utterance K155

briddes, briddus *n. pl.* birds (*fig.*) K78, K79

bright, bryghte, bryth *adj.* beautiful, radiant, good E7, E73, K26; bright, glittering E195; *as subst.* paragon B36; *superl.* **briȝthest** K155

briȝtnes *n.* brightness, light K77

brynge *v.* bring E93; *3 sg.* **brynges** K218; *subj. 3 sg.* **bryng** K278; *imp. sg.* **bring(e)** B14, B26, E8; *pa. 2, 3 sg.* **broght(e)** brought B36, E100; delivered E106, E107; **brogth** rendered K78, K79; *pp.* **broght** delivered (into the world) B1; **broghte** brought, reduced E186

bryth *see* **bright**

broghte, brogth *see* **brynge**

brothir, broþur *n.* brother K274; *gen.* B120; *pl.* **brothire** E235

buke *n.* book, Bible E56; *pl.* **bokes** books, authorities B137

bun *adj.* prepared E73

buntiful *adj.* beneficent, charitable K156

burghe *n.* town E185

busked *pa. 3 pl.* prepared B63

but *see* **bot**

buxum *adj.* obedient, pliant B58; **bouxsom** obedient and willing E99

cayre *v.* go, travel E48

caytyf *n.* villain K117; **caytef** *K33; **kaytyf** K187; *pl.* **caytefs, kaytefs** young men E169; wretches K2

calle *v.* name B68; *3 pl.* **calle** cry unto, beseech K225; *imp. sg.* **cal** call, summon K273; *pa. 3 sg.* **called** summoned E39; *pa. 3 pl.* **callede** knew him by the name of E212; *pp.* **calde, callid, callyd** named B7, B70, B133

calle *n.* summons, bidding E55

camel *n. gen.* camel's B88

cantly *adv.* keenly, ferociously K34

care, kare *n.* misery, ill, suffering B59, K6; envy, ill will E169; *pl.* **kares, karis** K200, K216, K226; (eternal) woe, Hell K2

carpyng *vbl. n.* talking K241

cast *n.* stratagem, contrivance K142

cawte *pa. 3 sg.* wrapped B49

certayne *n.* certainty; *in* ~ truly E144

chames *see* schame

charp *adj.* sharp K253

chaste *adj.* chaste E63, E65

chees *see* chese

chef *n.* head, leader K132; aspiration, goal K260

cheftane *n.* leader E64

chere *n.* demeanour E64, E65, E159

chese *1 sg.* chose, select K132; *3 sg.* chesus K259; *1 pl.* chees K260; *pa. 3 sg.* chose chose E64; chese selected to espouse B120, B121; *pa. 3 pl.* to-ches came by K40; *ppl. adj.* icore, chosen chosen, appointed E63, K33; *ppl. adj. as subst.* chosyn; *after my first* ~ as the one selected by me K132

child(e) *n.* child B5, B68, E63, E192; son B110

chose(n) *see* chese

clargy *see* clergi

cledde *pp.* clothed, dressed E170

cleen, clene *adj.* chaste, pure, free from sin K249; new, pristine E170

clene *adv.* purely, virtuously E48; *comly and* ~ in a fitting and virtuous manner K75

clere *v. 3 pl.* make apparent, instruct *B128

clere *adv.* clearly, brightly B134, B135; absolutely E244

clergi, clergy *n.* learning, knowledge, doctrine E212, K25; clargy K22

clerke *n.* learned person E211; *pl.* clerkes B78, B79, B128

clethyng, clothyng *n.* clothing B88, E170

cnyf *n.* knife (*fig.*) K241

comandement *n.* decree E243

combrid, cumbyrde *pp.* burdened B59; ensnared E169

comes *v. 3 sg.* comes E154; commeth issues K209; *3 pl.* (*pr. historic*) com come K75; *pa. 2, 3 sg.* com(e) came B105, E55, E187; *pa. 3 pl.* come came E150; *pp.* comen arrived, born B59

comly *adj.* beautiful; *as subst.* gracious one K164; fair one K185; cumly E48; *superl.* cumlyest K2

comly *adv.* fittingly, in a manner glorious to hear K199; purely, virtuously, with good intentions K75

commaund *pa. 3 sg.* commanded K34

commen *v.* communicate, converse K76

commeth *see* comes

commyneres *n. pl.* citizens K34

conceyue *v.* conceive B5; *pp.* conceyued B45

connande, cunande *adj.* clever, adept E212, E244

coppe *n.* cup E230

cors *n.* body K187

cosyn *n.* cousin B47; *pl.* cosyns B61

couetede *pa. 3 pl.* coveted, craved E195

couetyse *n.* avarice E169

court *n.* court, courtyard K131

couthe *pa. 3 pl.* could E127

craue *v.* long, yearn for B124

crye *3 pl.* pray K199

cristen *adj.* Christian K81

croft *n.* enclosure, sanctuary K131, K209

cumbyrde *see* combrid

cumly(est) *see* comly

cunande *see* connande

cuntre *n.* country E130, E211

cursed, cursud *ppl. adj.* accursed, wicked, evil, execrable K33, K113

cursurdly *adv.* damnably, abominably K242

curtays, curteys *adj. (as subst.)* gracious lady K76, K199; *superl.* most gracious K1

curtesy *n.* graciousness K241

day(e) *n.* day B104, E156, K232; day (of judgement) B76; *pl.* dayes K53; *gen. pl.* E200

daynte *adj.* precious E17

darlyng, derlyng(e) *n.* darling one B115, B136, E96, K171; beloved friend E155

declare *1 sg.* announce, pronounce E243

dede *n.* deed, action K110; *in* ~ in fact, actually K90; *pl.* dede(s), dedis E18, E25, E113, E127, E128, E262

dede *adj.* dead E155, E185, E227

dedeyned *pa. 3 sg.* was offended, angered E113

dedis *see* dede

dedly *adv. (as intens.)* intensely, vehemently K104

deel *v.* give (vent to), act out K104

defaste *pp.* defiled, spoilt E69

defende *pa. 3 sg.* forbade, proscribed E215

defoulede *pp.* contaminated, polluted E62

degre *n.* constitution E205

deieþ *see* dye

deyse *n.* dais, throne B122

delfynge *vbl. n.* interment, burial E156

demyd *pa. 3 sg.* judged E114

demschip *n.* judgement K258

dentiwos, dentywos *adj.* beautiful K59, K258

departe *3 pl.* separate, part K86

depe *adj.* deep K257

deply *adv.* deeply, grievously K244

derckenesse *see* derknes

dere *n.* harm, injury E128

dere *adj.* dear B115, B136, *E15, E155, K171; *as subst.* noble one K86

dere *adv.* with love K243

derely *adv.* exquisitely E17

derfe, derue *adj.* dreadful E127; dreaded, painful K85

derknes, derckenesse *n.* darkness K60, K244

derlyng(e) *see* darlyng

derne *adj.* deceptive, cunning K103

derue *see* derfe

deserte *n.* desert B100

deth(e) *n.* death K67, K84, K85, K123

deueles *n. gen.* devil's K103; deuyls E113; *pl.* deuelys K243

deuly *adv.* intensely; *so~* with such awesome impetus K147

dewre *v.* endure K59

did(d), dide, dyd *see* doo

dye *v.* die E18, E114, K85 ; *3 sg.* deieþ K258; *pa. 2 sg.* dyede E128

dyk *n.* dungeon, slough K257

dill *adj.* obtuse, foolish E127

dyngnite *n.* position of honour K257

dyntes *n. pl.* blows, strokes K243

dysciples *n. pl.* disciples E11

discry *v.* perceive, discern B129

disjoyned *pp.* thrown apart, shattered K150

dispised *pa. 3 sg.* reviled K104

dyth *pa. 3 sg.* put, delivered K60

doghter *n.* daughter B124

doynge *vbl. n.* behaviour, deeds E114

doluyn *pp.* buried K244

doo *v.* do, carry out E127; *3 sg.* doth does K13; *pa. 1 sg.* dyd did K110; *pa. 3 sg.* didd, dide E128, E210; *auxil. forming pa. 3 sg.* did, dyd K38, K93, K184; *pp.* done put E122; *be ~* be consigned E156

dool *n.* lot, apportionment K258

doth *see* doo

doumbe *adj.* dumb B42

doute *see* dowte

dowf(e) *n.* dove B106, K59

down(e) *adv.* down E157, E227

dowte *3 pl.* dread, fear K85; *imp. sg.* doute doubt B5

draw *v. imp. sg.* draw, raise K257

drede *n.* fear, terror K86

dredeful *adj.* fearful, awesome B76

dredles *adv.* assuredly, certainly E156, K103

drynkyng *pr. p.* drinking B94

dryue *v. imp. sg.* drive K243; *pa. 3 sg.* drof K86

drowry *n.* precious gift, treasure E17

dule *n.* grief, compassion E18; suffering, torment E114

dwellyng *pr. p.* living B100

eyþer *conj.* either; ~ . . . *or* either . . or K106

encresse *v.* increase K263

endeynede *pa. 3 sg.* humbled, submitted E18

endent *pp.* set, mounted, enclosed E17

enmyes *n. pl.* enemies, foes K231

entende *v.* heed, consider K116

entent *n.* frame of mind, purpose, resolve K62; *take* ~ heed, pay attention to K171

entyr *v. trans. imp. sg.* register, submit K232

entrik *v. imp. sg.* entrap, ensnare K231

es *see* is

euen *adv.* directly, exactly E193

euer *adv.* ever, yet E33, E182, E183; always K124, K231, K260; eternally E266, K258

euerei, euerilka, euerilk(e) *adj.* every K232; *euer ilka* each and every K202; *euer-ilk(e)-a* each, every E3, E85, E137, E139, E240

face *n.* face E32, E87; face, person B28, E252; *his* ~ *þere before* immediately in front of him K35

fader, fadir *n.* father B3, B38, B80, E31, E40; *pl.* fadres forefathers B53

fayn *adj.* glad, rejoiced K192; eager E148, E149

faynt *v.* faint, ?flinch K133

fayntles *adj.* steadfast, tireless E61

fayntly *adv.* feebly, wearily K190

faire *adj.* comely, attractive E32, E61

fayre *adv.* well K69

faith, faythe *n.* faith, doctrine B102, E75, E216

faiþful, fayth(e)ful(l) *adj.* faithful, constant, trustworthy B73, E92, E240, *K269; **feythful** steadfast K163; *as subst.* **feiþful** faithful, true one *K198

falle *v.* fall E227, K231; *subj. 3 sg.* **fal** might befall K269; *pa. 3 sg.* **fel** happened, befell B104

famen *n. pl.* foemen, adversaries E130

famyd *pp.* renowned K68

fanding, fondyng *vbl. n.* tempting, temptation, testing E62, E168

fare *n.* coming, arrival B61; doings, concerns E76, E148, E239, E258

fare *v.* go, deal E26

farly *adv.* fairly, honourably K198

fast *adv.* vigorously E215, K114; firmly, absolutely K133; instantly, soon E227

faunchon *n.* scimitar K185

fecchen *v.* bring (round), save, gain K120; *pa. 3 sg.* **fet** brought up, nurtured E31; *pa. 3 pl.* **fett** fetched K193; *pp.* **fet** fetched K198

fedd *pa. 3 sg.* nurtured E32

feel *v.¹* veil, conceal, bury K111, K198

feel *v.²* experience, perceive K136; attempt, prevail upon; *may ~ þe to meſ* may move you K134; *1 pl.* be aware of K270; *pa. 2 sg.* **felid** E129; *pa. 3 pl.* **felyd** tasted E227

feele *adj.* many E147

feer, fere *n.* companion, mate K189; mate, spouse E62; companion E240; friend K269; *pl.* **feres, ferys** associates K120, K160

fees *v.* punish K36, K37

feynthed *n.* faintness, (human) weakness *K270

feythful, feiþful *see* **faiþful**

fel *see* **falle**

felawys *n. pl.* colleagues, associates *K36

felde *n.* field E258

felid, felyd *see* **feel** (*v.²*)

fell *n.* strong, harmful, deadly E228

fende *n.* fiend, devil E168; *pl.* **fendys, fyendys** K168, K174

fend(e) *v.* defend K120, K168, K174; fend off K235; *imp. sg.* **fend(e)** B73, *K269; *pa. 3 sg.* **fende** defended K121

fere *adv.* far B99

ferde *pa. 2, 3 sg.* went E83, E147

fere(s), ferys *see* **feer**

ferly *n.* marvel, wonder E88

ferly *adv.* quickly K35

fersly *adv.* violently K185

fesaunt *n.* pheasant K189

fet, fett *see* **fecchen**

fyendys *see* **fende**

fyfti, fyfty *num.* fifty K21, K30, K48; *as subst.* K36

filede, fylde *pp.* defiled E61; defiled, corrupted K160

filthe, fylthe *n.* sexual activity E61, E69; toxic element E228

fynde *v.* find K261; *with passive force:* prove, be found K163; *pp.* **fun** found; *bese ~* proves to be E75

fyne *adj.* excellent B97, K21; exquisite E178; subtle E228

fyre *n.* fire K13, K35, K36, K37

flayn *ppl. adj.* flayed, lacerated K190, K191

fledde *pp.* fled; *it ~ froo* abandoned it E202

flemede *pa. 3 pl.* banished, exiled E130

flesche *n.* body E62, E129

flye *v.¹, 3 pl.* fly K197

flyit *v.², pa. 3 sg.* flew lightly, softly or rapidly K189

flik *n.* flitch, slaughtered creature K190, K191

flynt *n.* flint K13

fode, fude *n.* living thing, creature E31, E76; body K111

foly *n.* (moral) folly, sinfulness K120, K121, K269

folk(e) *n.* people B71, B92, E147, E149, E215; chosen companions E88

folowe *v.* follow E76; *subj. sg.* **folow** follow, observe K133; *pa. 2 sg.* **folowede** E91; *pa. 3 pl.* **folowed** E258

fondyng *see* **fanding**

fone *n.* few E88

foo *n.* enemy, adversary E143; *pl.* **foos** B73, K235

for *conj.* because, since B40, B63, E91, E128, E170, K12, K39, K40, K91, K126, K144a, K160, K172, K175, K200, K213, K223; so that E256, K68, K111 (*see note*)

for *prep.* (*of cause*) for, because of B60a, B60b, B113, B120, E114a, E134, E189, E262, K5, K119, K270; concerning E59; (*of benefit*) for the sake of B18, B131, E50, E198, E220, K64, K65, K70, K71a, K199, K236; *~ hyng vs* hung for us K276; (*with neg. as intensive of refusal*)

K144b, K144c; *(of ind. obj.)* B139, E18,
E24, E35, E254, K154, K165, K199; *(of
equivalence)* E178; instead of B91; as
K143; *(with inf.)* B125, E49, E114b,
E120, E148, E160, E165, E228, E252,
E261, K67, K114, K202; in order to
B68, E217, K71b, K95, K115, K129,
K145, K146, K217, K235, K238, K268

forgoher *n.* foregoer, precursor B31

forme *v.* make, construct K35

forsothe *interj.* indeed E36, E176, E220

forsuke *pa. 2 sg.* left E40, E53

forth(e) *adv.* forward K183; forth B1,
E83; *~-broght* nurtured, brought up B1

forthi *adv.* for this reason, on that
account E63, E173; accordingly E77;
consequently E130

forthynkyng *vbl. n.* remorse, contrition
E202

forthir *adv.* more, farther E26

fosterde *pa. 3 sg.* raised, nurtured E32

foulely *adv.* heinously E129

foullede *pa. 3 pl.* injured E129

foundyed *pa. 3 sg.* sank, stumbled K190

four *adj.* four K148

fra *see* **fro**

fraynd *pa. 3 pl.* asked B67

frayste *v.* test, prove E75; experience
E148; taste E228; *be free to ~* be noble
at the proof, test E239; *see also* **frestyng**

framyd *pp.* shaped, devised K69

frede *v.* suffer, experience *K97

fre(e) *adj.* free, noble E40, E92, E132,
good E149; independent E93, E239

free *adv.* readily E208

freely *adv.* readily E258

freelte *n.* frailty, moral weakness K270

freye *n.* fear, terror K134

frely *adj. as subst.* free, noble one E76, E87

frenchip(e) *n.* goodwill K261; interest on
our behalf E75, K260

frende *n.* friend, helper B71; friend and
leader E83; *pl.* **frendes, frendys** E147,
K165

frendely *adj.* sympathetic, benevolent
E240

fresch *adj.* fresh, new K134; bright,
young, lively K189

freschely *adv.* readily K160

frestyng *vbl. n.* testing, putting to the
proof B73; *see also* **frayste**

frythe *n.* wood, forest E258

fro *prep.* from B55, B73, E58, E60, E66,

E93, K2, K4, K60, K86, K120, &c.; **fra**
E106; away from E147, E202, K50;
from the time of *B103; from the time
that E209

fude *see* **fode**

fulfille *v.* fulfil B102

ful(l) *adv.* very B3, B4, E39, E48, K4,
&c.; most B63; exceedingly (far) K148

fun *see* **fynde**

gadrid *pp.* gathered *B63

gafe *see* **gyfes**

gayne *adj.* shortest, most direct E146

game *n.* way of life, pursuit K76, K82

gan(e) *v. auxil. equivalent of* did: *pa. 2 sg.*
did B6; **gun** E260; *pa. 3 sg.* did, began
B41, B123, K101; **gun** E213; *pa. 3 pl.*
B65; **gun** E204, E227

gaste *n.* spirit E68, E260

gates *n. pl.* paths, routes E146

geder *3 pl.* gather, draw; *~ to* draw to; *~
þe to hir giyld* adopt you as patron saint
of their guild K268

gem *n.* a precious stone *E15

gente *adj.* noble E15

gentill *adj.* noble E16

gerne *adv.* readily E145

get *pp.* engendered E29

gete *n.* jet E15

gete *v.* obtain B25

gyde *v.* guide K268

gyfes *pa. 3 sg.* gives E142; *pa. 2 sg.* **gafe**
bestowed (to) E174, E181; *~ the to*
applied yourself to E145; *pp.* **gyffen**
bestowed upon E141

gyftes *n. pl.* gifts E142

giyld *n.* fraternity K268

gyn, gynne *n.* (evil) strategy K144;
instrument, device K150

gysed *pa. 2 sg.* prepared E145

go *see* **goo**

god *n.* (pagan) god, deity K138

goddesse *n. gen.* goddess's K131

gode *adj.* good B100; *see also* **gude**

godely *adv.* graciously B3, B48

golde *n.* gold E174, E195; golden objects
E204, E208

golde *adj.* golden E180

gome *n.* man, a boy child E29

gone *see* **goo**

goo *v.* go E145; change, revert E204; *3 pl.*
(pr. historic) go turn, transmute E205;
pp. **gone** B19

good *n.* open-heartedness B29; *see also* **gude**

good(e) *adv.* properly, well K102, K110

governe *v.* govern, guide, direct K267

grace *n.* grace, favour B6, B25, B48, B128, E30, E89, E140, E141, E249, K82

gracyous *adj.* generous, full of God's grace; *most* ~ most empowered by grace, having the most power of holy grace K267

grame *v.* harm, afflict K83

granted *see* **graunt(e)**

graythely *adv.* readily E29, E146

graue *n.* grave K112

graunt(e) *v. imp. sg.* give E249; *pa. 3 sg.* granted *B126, K223; *pp.* **gra(u)n-ted(e)** E30, E141

gref *v.* injure, oppress K130

gret(e) *adj.* great B6a, E109, E141, E248, K88; *comp.* **gretter** B19

grete *v.¹* greet, salute B6b; *1 sg.* B29, K267; *pa. 3 sg.* **grett** B48

grete *v.²* weep, lament E189; *pa. 3 sg.* **grett** E189

gretly *adv.* very much, exceedingly B123

gretter *see* **gret(e)** *(adj.)*

greue *n.* grief, pain K136

greue *v.* trouble, worry B123; disturb, incommode B41

grymme *n.* fury, wrath K83

grysely *adj.* dreadfully E189

grof *pa. 3 sg.* buried K102

ground *n.* earth; *on* ~ in the world B19

gude *adj.* good, pure E68, E174, E262; *see also* **gode**

gudnes *n.* goodness E30, E142, E190

gun *see* **gan(e)**

ȝare *adv.* readily B63

ȝe *interj.* yes B23; **ȝoo** E200

ȝe *pron. 2 pl.* you E199, E237, E245, E246; *dat. pl.* **ȝow** (to) you E243, E249; *adj. poss. 2 pl.* **ȝoure** your E245

ȝelde *v.* surrender E260; give, render E261

ȝere *n.* year B103

ȝit *adv.* yet E129

ȝode *pa. 3 sg.* went E73

ȝonge *adj.* young E185

ȝoo *see* **ȝe** *(interj.)*

ȝoure, ȝow *see* **ȝe** *(pron)*

ȝoure-selfe *pron. 2 sg.* yourself E246

ha(a)st *n.* haste B109; *in* ~ in a hurry K21

habyde *see* **abyde**

had, hadd, hade, haf, hafe *see* **haue**

hayl *n.* hail K215

hailsed *pa. 3 pl.* greeted, welcomed E151

halden *see* **helde**

hall *n.* hall E231

hally, holly *adv.* wholly, only E232, E 233; **hely** solemnly, strongly, fully K175

hame, home *n.* home E151, E184

hande *n.* hand; *hade no thynge in* ~ owned nothing E171; **hende** *B77

harme *n.* harm, injury E231

hast *(n.)* *see* **haast**

hast *(v.)* *see* **haue**

hate *adj.* hot E123

hath, haþ *see* **haue**

hatrede *n.* hatred, hostility E112

haue *v.* possess B125; maintain K157; hold, bear K167; *2 sg.* **hast** B30; *3 sg.* **hath** B132; *1, 3 pl.* **hafe** E242; **haue** hold, keep K221; *subj. 3 sg.* **hafe** E36; *pa. 2, 3 sg.* **hade** experienced, felt E45, E112, E231; *pa. 3 pl.* **had(e)** had, possessed E169, E171a, E183, E202, K44; took K39; felt, experienced E161; **hadde** E182; *pp.* **hadde** owned, possessed E171c; *as auxil. forming perf. t.: 1 sg.* **haue** K69; *3 sg.* **hath, haþ** K48, K117, K176, K177; *3 pl.* **haf** K172, K264; **haue** K46, K175; *as auxil. forming pluperfect t.: 3 sg.* **had(e)** B45, B81, E69, E160, K160; *3 pl.* **had** E171b; **hadd** E196, K198; **hade** E172

hawes *n. pl.* hawthorn berries B89

he *(pron. 3 sg. fem. nom.)* *see* **sche**

he *pron. 3 sg. masc. nom.* he B6, B14, B26, B32, B37, E1, E4, E10, E20, E32, K8, K9, K10, K19, K37, &c.; *acc.:* **hym** B6, B41, B119, E186, E212, E260a, K14, K57, K88, K101, K125; *dat.:* **him**, **hym** B120, E21, E42, E78, E80, E260b, K54, K99, *K115; to him B84, K74, K259; from him *K126; *refl.:* **hym** E18, K121, K122, K124; **Hymselfen** E102; **hymselue** K90; *adj. poss.* **his**, **hys** B7, B8, B18, B28, B70, B84, E9, E10, E18, E30, E44, K10, K11, K16, K104, &c.; *see also* **hit**

hede, heed *n.* head, life K126; *hir* ~ her person, her existence K98; **heued** B125

heel *n.* health, salvation; ~ *þou vs hent* obtain salvation for us K248 heghe, heyest *see* hye, hyȝe

heylyng *vbl. n.* act of salutation, greeting K169

helde *intrans. pa. 2 sg.* kept; ~ *þe* accompanied E82; *trans. pa. 3 sg.* held B77; *pp.* halden held, considered E172

heledide *pa. 3 pl.* bowed E232

hely *see* hally

helpe *subj.3 sg.* help, guide E251

hem *see* thay

hende *(n.) see* hande

hende *adj. as subst.* worthy (one) E82; *superl.* hendeste E231

hendly *adj.* gracious, courteous K169

hent(e) *v. imp. sg.* obtain; *heel þou vs* ~ obtain salvation for us K248; *pa. 2 sg.* obtained, found, took *B89; *pa. 3 sg.* received K169; *3 pl.* took; *þei hem* ~ got hold of for themselves K21; *pp.* hent obtained, brought B81

her(e), hir(e), hyre *(adj. poss.) see* sche and thay

herandys *n. pl.* missions, business, petitions K232

herborogh *n.* shelter, dwelling *K203

herde *pa. 3 sg.* heard K170

here *adv.* here, on this earth K85, K163, K164, K166, K167, K200, K225, K227

heres *n. pl.* heirs *K227

hert *n.* heart B30, K113

heþen *adv.* hence, from this earthly life E263

heued *see* hede

heuen *n.* heaven B14, B140, E196, E262, K179; *gen.* heuene B105

hye, hyȝe *adj.* lofty, high K203; *superl.* hyest *þe* ~ *were hythe* were called the highest, were of greatest renown, were the most reputable K22; heyest K23; hyȝest greatest, most exalted K170

highte *pp.* called, known as, acknowledged E34; hythe K22, K23

hyȝe *adv.* in a high position, eminently K179; heghe E94

him, hym, hymselue *see* he *(masc.)*

hyne *n.* attendants, household E232, E233

hynge *v.* hang, be crucified E94; *pa. 3 sg.* hyng hung, was crucified; *on crosse for* ~ *vs* hung for us on the cross K276

hir, hyr, hyre, hirself *see* sche *and* thay

his, hys *see* he *(masc.) and* it

hit *see* it

hythe *see* highte

holde *n.* keeping, protection *B30

holy *adj.* holy B133

holly *see* hally

home *see* hame

hony-comes *n. pl.* honeycombs B91

honoure *v.* honour, dignify, make renowned K210

how *adv.* how E196

hurt *n.* harm, injury K39

I *pron. 1 sg.* I B29, E22, E28, E111, E174, E243, K1, K7, K69, K110, K111, &c.; *acc. (of impers. v.)* me; ~ *liketh* it is pleasing to me B112; *dat.* me K64, K65, K118; *adj. poss.* my B30, B110, K132, K138, K171

ibore *pp.* born; *blessed hire* ~ blessed the day she was born, blessed her existence K31

icore *see* chese

if *conj.* if E223

ilk(e) *adj., adv.* each E246; *(as intens.)* same, truly B49, E186; *euer(e) ilk(e) a* each and every E3, E246, K202; every specific E60

ilkone, ylkone *pron.* each one E11, E180, E238

ille *n.* harm, impairment E129

in *prep.* in B15, B16a, B16b, B20, B21, E4, E5, E6, E7, E9, K18, K20, K21, K30, K34, &c.; among E213; to, unto K90, K151; into B7, B95, E122, K113; on account of B8; on K196; throughout K22

incarnacion *n.* incarnation B103

into *prep.* into E103

in-with *prep.* within E52

yren *adj.* iron E126

is *3 sg.* is B45, B70, B110, B127, K85, K212, K239, K273; es E1, E8, E10, E92, E140, E243; *see also* am, are, art, be, was

it *pron. 3 sg. neut. nom.* it B41, B97, B108, B128, E37, E75, E158, E160, E223, E228, E243; hit K38, K158; *acc.* it B7, B95, B98, B129, E51, E133, E202, E226, E227, E230, E241, E244, K211; *adj. poss.* his its K18

jasper *n.* jasper E16

jentyl *adj.* gracious, generous K234

jewel, jowell *n.* jewel B72, E16

joy(e) *n.* joy B72, K280

joyne *v. imp. sg.* join; ~ *vs to* unite us with K259

jornay *n.* journey or pilgrimage (through life) K260

jowell *see* jewel

jugged *pp.* judged, evaluated B72

kache *v. imp. sg.* snatch; ~ . . . *fro* preserve . . from K226

kayesere *n.* emperor, ruler K113

kaytyf, kaytefs *see* caytyf

kare, kares, karis *see* care

karueth *see* kerf

keel *v.* cool, assuage, relieve, comfort K200

kende *pp.* known, recognized E211

kepe *v.* defend, protect E244, K25; *subj.3 sg.* **kep(e)** B54, K241; *imp. sg.* **kepe** K225; *vbl. n.* **kepyng(e)** defence K2; possession E45; protection E97

kerf *v.* cut (off) K95; *3 sg.* **karueth** bites, cuts, rends K242

kest *v.* cast, set free K216; *pa. 2 sg.* **keste**; *thou* ~ *the* you devoted yourself E48

kyde *see* kiþ

kille *v. imp. sg.* destroy K265

kyn *n.* kinfolk, relations B61

kynd *adj.* kind, gracious K164, K265; *superl.* **kyndest** K273

kynde *n.* nature, constitution E204, E206

kyndly *adv.* naturally, readily, lovingly K216

kyndnes *n.* benevolence, goodwill K237

kyngdames *n. pl.* kingdoms, realms K22

kirkes *n. pl.* churches E109

kist *pa. 3 sg.* kissed B47

kiþ *v.* make known, manifest, demonstrate *K237; ppl. adj.* **kyde** recognised, rightful B61

kitte *pp.* cut, smitten K185

klay *n.* clay; *krepen in* ~ lie buried K226

knaues *n. pl.* evildoers E170

knytt *ppl. adj.* joined, whole K187

knowen *v.* learn, find out, discover K76; *1 sg.* **know** am familiar with, am aware of K1; *3 pl.* **knowe** B78, B79; *pa. 3 pl.* **knewe** knew K200; *pp.* **knawen** noted E211

koueres *3 sg.* rescues K216

krepen *3 pl.* creep, lie motionless, lie still; ~ *in klay* lie buried K226

labowrid *pa. 3 sg.* belaboured, upbraided *K88

laddes *n. pl.* louts E118

laghte, laȝgth *see* lawth

laye *v.¹ intrans. pa. 3 sg.* lay E158

layede *v.² trans. pa. 1 sg.* laid, buried K112; *pp.* **leyd** laid down, destroyed, taken K161

laythely *adv.* harshly, with dishonour E118

laytheste *adj. superl.* most loathsome E117

lake *n.* lake, pit, cell K128

land(e) *n.* land E213, E259; country, nation B64; *pl.* **landis** E164

lantern(e) *n.* lantern, guiding light B134, K3

lare, lore *n.* teaching, faith taught, religious persuasion E194, E214, E245, K28, K29

laste *v.* endure E266

lawe *n.* law B64, B72; *pl.* **lawes** E214

lawe *adv.* low E95

lawfully *adj.* licitly B119

lawnch *v.* put forth, proffer; *to* ~ in the proffering of K162

lawth *pa. 3 sg.* caught; ~ *to here lore* brought to her persuasion K29; **laghte** took, caught up (to himself) E260; *pp.* **laȝgth** taken K128

leche *v.* heal, save, redeem K3

lede *n.* person E20, E245; *pl.* people, subjects, following E213, K88; *in* ~ among humankind E117

le(e)de *v.* guide, conduct K4; lead, take in tow K30; *subj.3 sg.* **lede** E265; *refl.* **lede betake** oneself B65; *pa. 3 sg.* **led** conducted B119; *pa. 3 pl.* **ledden** E118; *pp.* **ledd** guided E214; **lede** gathered at B64

lees *n.* leash *(fig.)* K30

lef *v.* please K128

lefte *pa. 2 sg.* forsook E50, E51; *pa. 3 pl.* E164

leyd *see* layede

lende *v.¹* abide B13, E80; remain E49; *gun in* ~ lived among E213

lende *v.²* bow E95

lenger *adv. comp.* longer, more K87

lente *pa. 3 sg.* bestowed E19

lepe *pa. 3 pl.* leapt, hastened, came over to the side of K28

lere *v.* learn *B130, E247; imp. pl.* E246; *pp.* **lerede** learnt K172

lerne *v.* teach K101; learn of, meditate on; *to* ~ at the learning of K251; *pa. 2 sg.* **lerned** instructed B92

lesson *n.* instruction E246

lett *n.* obstacle, reluctance B50, *B51

lete *pa. 3 sg.* regarded; *He ~ mare by* (whom) he regarded more highly E20; *pa. 3 pl.* **lett** took heed of; *þat ~ by þi lare lyghte* who regarded your teachings with indifference E194

leue *n.* leave, permission B126

leue *v.* believe in B40, K138

leue *adj.* dear, prized K84

licherouse *adj.* licentious, corrupt E117

lyf(e) *n.* life E19, K161

lif(e) *v.* live E6, K172; *pa. 2 sg.* **lyffede** dwelt E259; *pr. p.* **lyueande** E20

lyft *pp.* raised K127

light, lyghte *n.* light B134; enlightenment E138; **lyth** K3; eternal light, glory E5, E251, E265

lyghte *adv.* lightly, indifferently E194

ly3th *v.* ease, gladden K178

li3thly, lythly, litthly *adv.* lightly, easily K30; readily, willingly K101; immediately, promptly K161

lyk *adj.* like; *hym ~* (those who are) like him K259

lykes *3 sg.* likes, honours E245; *impers.* liketh; *me ~* it pleases me B112; *pa. 3 sg.* **lyked(e)**; *hym ~* it pleased him, he chose E80, E260

likyng, lykyng(e) *vbl. n.* desire, wish B92, B93, E49; gratification B119; *in ~* according to his will E6

lym(e) *n.* limb, part K162; *deueles ~, deuyls ~* limb of Satan E113, K103

lyste *pa. 3 sg.* desired, chose E259

listen *v.* hear, take heed B130

lyth *see* **light**

liþ *adj.* gentle, kindly K234

lythes *n. pl.* people, members of a household E50

li(t)thly *see* **li3thly**

lyueande *see* **lif(e)** (*v.*)

long *adv.* for a long time B13

longly *adv.* for a long time K88

lorde *n.* master, husband *K87; *þat ~, oure ~* Christ E6, E19, E49, E259

lore *see* **lare**

lorne *pp.* forsaken B56

lost(e) *pp.* forfeited E196; lost K87

loue, lufe *n.* love E50, K101, K234; love (of God) K172

loue, lufe *v.¹* love E246; *3 pl.* love K4; *pr.*

p. **lufande** loving E237; *pp.* **lufed** beloved E19. *See also* **lufe** (*v.²*)

louede *see* **lufe** (*v.²*)

louely *adj.* ordinary, humble B92

loutid *see* **lowte**

low *v.* humble K54

low *adj.* base, deep K128

lowte *v.* bow, make obeisance K87; *pa. 3 sg.* **loutid** B50

lufe (*n.*) *see* **loue** (*n.*)

lufe *v.²* honour E224; *pp.* **louede** praised, venerated E5; *see also* **loue, lufe** (*v.¹*)

lufly *adj.* lovely, beautiful K127

luf(e)ly *adv.* gladly, properly B130, E5, K29

lugede *pp.* lodged, living E5

luke *v. imp. pl.* look, see to it E237, E245

lurdeyn *n.* scoundrel, evil-doer K128; *pl.* **lurdans** E117

lust *n.* pleasure, desire K172

lusty *adj.* beautiful K162

made *see* **make**

may *3 sg.* may, can B133, E12, E241, K100, K134, K222; *impers.* B129; *2 sg.* **mayst** K135, K136, K138, K139, K250; *auxil.2, 3 sg.* **mote** may, must E153; **mut** K277; *pa. 2, 3 sg.* **myth, myght(e)** could B19, E35, E44, E256, K83, K97; *pa. 3 pl.* **myghte** E188

mayden *n.* maiden, girl, virgin E59, K145, K186; *pl.* **maydens** unmarried girls K153

mayn(e) *n.* strength, power E142, K194

maystry *n.* miracle, wonder E218

make *v.* make K174; make, turn (to his will) K145; *3 pl.* **mase**; *men ~* is made E34 ; *subj. 3 sg.* **make** put, set, centre K262; *imp. sg.* **make**; *vs at spede* ensure we are successful B24; **makyst**; *~ þou blent* render null and void *K250; *pa. 2, 3 sg.* **made** B124, E174, E218, K52, K59, K145; created E1; caused to be built E109; *pa. 3 pl.* **made** E188; *pp.* **made** made, constituted K24; *~ bare* stripped E121

man(e) *n.¹* man, (a) person B20, E44, E246; **mane** K47; *pl.* **men** men, people, humans B60, E241, E253; populace E217; **mane** attendants E187; *pron. impers.* one, it E33; **men** B52, B129, E34

mane *n.²* lamentation E188

maner(e) *n.* kind, sort E43; case, situation E60; *pl.* **maners** ways B129

manhede *n.* homage E257

many *adj.* many B8, B71, B129, E187; **mony** E218; many (a) E90; *as subst.* many people B62

many-folde *adv.* clearly B38

mankynde *n.* mankind E1, E244, K47

mare *see* more

markyd, merkede *pp.* appointed, destined B20, E2

mase *see* make

maste *see* more

matere *n.* matter, subject E242

matrones *n. pl.* respectable married women K152

mawment *n.* idol, false god K11; *pl.* mawmetis E218

me *see* I

mede *n.* reward B20, B140, E261, K96, K263

medyl *v. refl.* meddle herself with, have dealings with K146

meel *n.* occasion K202

mef, meue *v.* move, alter your attitude K134; move, live K135; *pa. 2 sg.* moued turned, safeguarded E60

meyne *n.* household; ~ *of myrþe* company of joy, heavenly host K175

meke *adj.* gentle B111, E59

mekeful *adj.* merciful B44

mekenes *n.* meekness, long-suffering, obedience E27, K122

mele *v.* speak E188

melody(e) *n.* music K176, K201

men *see* man(e) (*n.¹*)

mencyon *n.* description; ~ *of* knowledge of, example of E242

mende *v.* amend E217, K122; restore, rectify K125; improve upon, restore K238

mendynge *vbl. n.* amending, repentance E108

mene *v.¹* describe E28; mean, signify E241; *imp. sg.* mone explain E241

mene *v.²* complain, yearn; *aftir myght* ~ hanker after E44

menesyng *vbl. n.* mentioning, mention E34

menȝe *n.* company E236

menskede *pa. 3 pl.* honoured E257

mente *see* mynt

merci *n.* mercy K125

merde *pp.* destroyed K176, K177

merkede *see* markyd

merrede *pa. 3 sg.* prevented E217

messager *n.* messenger B33

mesured *pp.* appraised E2

mete *n.* food B91, K55

mete *v.* meet, experience B8, B9; *pa. 3 sg.*, *pl.* mett B44, B52, E33

methe *adj.* modest, unassuming E59

mett *see* mete (*v.*)

meue *see* mef

my *see* I

myght(e), myȝth, myht, myth *n.* power, strength B45, E1, E191, E248, K10, K24, K96, K146, K194, &c.; ardour E135; force, violence K176, K177

myght(e) (*v.*) *see* may

myghty *adj.* great, abundant B20; *so* ~ in such esteem E172

myȝtthily *adv.* greatly K201; *see also* mytthyly (*adj.*)

mylde *n.* mildness; *for* ~ as far as mildness is concerned E59

milde, mylde *adj.* gentle, meek, acquiescent K162; courteous B33, B77; gentle B111; *superl.* myldeste E33

myldely *adv.* gently E81

milk *n.* milk K186

myn *adj.* lesser (in rank); *more and* ~ high and low (in rank), all *K152

mynd(e) *n.* intention K145; thought, mind E44, E60, *K96, K167, K221, K262; recollection E242

mynne *v.* diminish, reduce K146

mynt *pa. 3 sg.* aimed K10; *pa. 3 pl.* aimed, intended K202; *pp.* mente intended, decided K175

myracle *n.* miracle B82

myrth(e), myrþe *n.* joy, exultation B8, B9, B83, E12; *meyne of* ~ company of joy, heavenly host K175; *pl.* myrthes, myrthys joys B27, K238

myrthe *v.* gladden, console K176, K202

mischef *n.* evil, harm K146

mys(s)e *n. sg.*, *pl.* misdeed(s), transgression(s) E60, E108, E210, E217

misse, mysse *v.* be without, lack E12, K222; *3 pl.* mys B27

myth (*n.*) *see* mygth(e)

myth (*v.*) *see* may

mytir *n.* (bishop's) mitre E257

mytthyly *adj.* extensive K47; *see also* myȝtthily (*adv.*)

mytthynes *n.* strength, greatness; ~ *of mode als* so fearlessly, too K108

mobles *n. pl.* property, goods E43

mode *n.* state of mind B33, E33; anger K104; courage, daring K108

moder, modir *n.* mother B44, E34, E43, E97, E187

molde *n.* (the) earth B20, E2

momyl *v.* babble; *to ~ on his mawment* to (make you) babble prayers to his idol K11

mone *see* mene (*v.²*)

mony *see* many

moo *see next*

more, mare *adj., adv. comp.* more B16, B20, E27, E181, E183, E210, E241, E266; **moo** B129; greater (in rank); *~ and myn* high and low (in rank) K152; *subst.* more E20; *superl.* **maste** *B45, E1; **most** B15, K267; **moost** most of all B112; in the highest degree, to the greatest extent K24

mote *see* may

moued *see* mef

mount *n.* mountain K201

mouthe *n.* mouth, speech E28

murnande *pr. p.* mourning E187

mut *see* may

na *see* no *(adj.)*

name *n.* name B7, B70, B127, E140, E154; *be ~* by title K80

nane *see* none

ne *conj.* nor B19, B87a, B96, E21, E62, K144; *neþer . . . ~* neither . . . nor K18; *no . . . ~* neither . . nor E242; nor (either) B17b, B20; *~ neuer* nor ever B17a; nor (did not) *B95; or B87b

nede *n.* need; *at ~* in exigency, distress B22, B23

nedeful *adj.* necessary B11

neghe *v. imp. sg.* draw near, approach B22, B23; *pa. 2 sg.* **neghed** approached, touched B98

neythir, neþer *conj.* neither; *~ . . . ne* neither . . nor K18; *~ . . . ne . . . ne* neither . . nor . . or B87

nek *n.* neck K162, K183

nere *adv.* near B99

neþer *see* neythir

nett *n.* net E41

neuen *v.* name, invoke B11; *pa. 3 sg.* **neuend** named, called B39

neuer *adj.* not ever (a) B16, B17, K47; *adv.* not ever B19, B97, K118

newe *adv.* newly K191, K192, K195; immediately K194

no, na *adj.* no B20, B132, E20, E21, E61, E62a, E62b, E166, K5a, K5b, K41, K55, K83, &c.

no *adv.* not, no K87

noght(e) *see* not

noyede *pa. 3 sg.* harmed E223

non *adv.* not at all B27

none, nane *adj.* no, not any E129, E176, K39; *as pron.* **non** no one B19, E177

not, noght(e) *adv.* not B40, B56, B98, B118, B119, E12, E67, E124, E128, E172, K5, K16, K66, K91, K97, &c.; not at all, by no means K8, K85; *with subst. force* **nought** nothing at all B5

now(e) *adv.* now, at the present E26, E247, K46, K100, K247, K248, K250, K251, K261; *as emph.* K236

o *see* on

of *prep.* of, belonging to B6, B31, B48, B61a, B82, E2, E16, E45, E74, E88, K3, K5, K24, K72, &c.; pertaining to B25, B114, E41, E86, E104; with respect to B43, B45, B72, E1, E32, E33, E36, E38, E43, E64, E138, E142, K22; from E130, E173, K61, K227; **off** E230; about B36, B61b, B132, E27, E110, E148, E161, E242, E253, K16, K76, K241; by means of E30, E190, E248, K8, K137, K245; at the hands of K99; out of E1a, E127, E167, K1, K13; by B2, B34, B58, E19, E7, K187; *~ . . . ~* (either) of . . . (or) of B17; *thank ~ vs* (for) thought about us, graciousness towards us, for our sakes K6; *was ~ on here alone* was entirely because of her K42

oft *adv.* often, frequently K133, K205

oyl(e) *n.* oil E123; (healing) oil K205

oyl-riueres *n. pl.* rivers, streams of (healing) oil K204

oloft *adv.* on high K206; *lyft vp ~* brought up from below K127

on *prep.* on, upon B19, B31, B104, B106, B107, B122, K96, K157, K262, K276; o K201; one E94, E126; to K11; because of; *was of ~ here alone* was entirely because of her K42; in B20, *B129, K155; one E60; *~ ryse* in rows

B116; in (the ways of) K172; of, about K240

on-one *adv.* at once B39, *B67

one *see* **on**

or *conj.* or E15, E80, K215; *eyþer . . . ~ either . . or* K106

or *adv.* before B52

oriȝth *adv.* rightly, indeed K181

orison *n.* prayer K170

oþer *n.* (the) other one E238

ouerthrow *v.* be cast down, stumble K5

our(e) *see* **we**

owen *adj.* own B28

owte *prep.* out E130

paynes *see* **peyne**

paynie *n.* heathendom *K158

pales *v. imp. sg.* fence (*fig.*), enclose, shelter K255

palle, pelle *n.* raiment B87, E225

pappes *n. pl.* breasts K95

paryng *vbl. n.* impairment, injury K41

passede, paste *pa. 3 sg.* went E131, E263

pees, pesse *n.* peace B114, K266

peyne *n.* pain, suffering, torment K157, K184, K211, K212; **paynes** eternal torment E106

peles *n. pl.* stakes, spikes K137

pelle *see* **palle**

pen *n.* pen; *with a ~ free* in noble written expression E132

penance *n.* the pains of purgatory E106; penalty, penitential sentence E200

pepul *n.* people, populace K114; **puple** E105

pere *n.* equal B132

pereles *n.* unequalled; *~ of Pousté* Matchless One of Might (God) E38

peryd *pa. 3 sg.* appeared B104

perry *n.* jewels E16

pert *adj.* manifest, acknowledged K158

pertly *adv.* openly, unhesitatingly B47, K73

pesse *see* **pees**

philosophir *n.* intellectual authority E215

pik *v. imp. sg.* strip, extract, pluck K255

pilde *pp.* stripped K158

pynchars *n. pl.* persecutors, attackers K264

pynd(e) *pp.* tortured K224, K264

pyne *n.* torture, legal retribution E226

pyte *n.* pity, compassion K255; *~ on* distress for K157

pyth *pa. 3 sg.* pitched, threw (at), put (to) K27

pytte *see* **put**

place *n.* place E85, E132, E137

plate *n.* grid E126

ples(e) *v.* delight K38; allay, cajole, induce K74

poyntes *n. pl.* explanations, arguments B114, K27; **poyntis** constituent details E86

poyntil *n.* writing implement *B81

pondur *v.* consider, think about K211

porter *n.* gatekeeper, guard K74

pouert *n.* (spiritual) penury K256

pouste, *n.* power, authority K158; **pousté;** *Pereles of ~* Matchless One of Might (God) E38

prayed *see* **prey**

prechide *pa. 3 sg.* preached E105

prechyng *vbl. n.* preaching B113

precyouse *adj.* precious E178, E203

prees *n.* press, throng, crowd K32

prey *v. imp. sg.* pray B139; *pa. 3 sg.* prayed, **preyd** requested, begged, pleaded K74, K157; made petition K165

pres *v.* affect, afflict *K41; *pa. 3 sg.* **presed** pressed forward, hurried K73

presoners *see* **prisonere**

prest *adj.* ready, quick to appear K212

prestly *adv.* promptly K139; at once K157; readily K183

preuaté *n.* privacy, exclusivity E86

preué *pp.* intimate E85

preue *v.* experience K139; *pa. 3 sg.* **preuyd** proved (her worth) K184; experienced K211

price *n.* value, cost B87

pride *n.* (the sin of) pride K255

prik *v.* stab, assail, torment K184

prikkynge *vbl. n.* urging goading E106

prynce *n.* prince (Christ) E85

prison *n.* prison, bondage, servitude (of Hell) K212

prisonere *n.* captive K183; *pl.* **presoners** prisoners E226

profe *v.* test E221, E225

profet *pa. 2. sg.* prophesied, taught B114

profor *v. imp. sg.* offer, grant K266; *pa. 3 sg.* **profirde** gave to E226

prophet *n.* prophet B133

prouddeste *adj. superl. as subst.* most arrogant E225

publischede *pa. 3 sg.* revealed E86

puyson *n.* poison E221, E225
punchyng *vbl. n.* stabbing K137
puneschede *pp.* was ~ were suffering punishment E226
puple *see* pepul
purly *adv.* wholly, fully K184
purpil *n.* (aristocratic clothing of) purple B87
put *v. subj. 3 sg.* may remove K212; *imp. sg.* remove K256a; lead, raise K256b; *pa. 3 sg.* pytte put K183

queen, qween, qwene *n.* queen K73, K80, K91, K99
quod *pa. 3 pl.* said E241
qwan, qwen *see* when
qwat *see* what
qweles *n. pl.* wheels K140
qwene *see* queen
qwer(e) *see* whare
qwerefore *adv.* therefore, on account of which K49
qwith *v. imp. sg.* reward; *us* ~ *of* reward us with *K245
qwyles *see* whils
qwo *pron. interrog.* who, which (of them) K20; *dat.* whom B112; qwom K246, K247; *gen.* whas whose E72
qwoso *pron. indef.* whoever K166; whoso B130

ranne *pa. 3 pl.* ran, were consistent with K45; *pr. p.* rynnande running, hastening E150; *pp.* ronne run, undergone (the course of martyrdom) K46
rase *pa. 3 sg.* rose, raised himself E192
realy *adv.* splendidly K204
reche *v.¹ imp. sg.* obtain (for), bestow (on) K233
recheþ *v.² 3 sg.* prepares, directs K214
rede *n.* advice ; *to* ~ as advice B66
rede *v.¹ 1 sg.* advise, urge K211
rede *v.² read* B137; learn E264; *3 pl.* redyn read K240
redy *adj.* ready E264
reel *see* releþ
rees *n.* (a) rush, haste K34
reygn *3 pl.* reign K46; *2 sg.* reyngnest K239
rekynde *pa. 2 sg.* enumerated B116
releþ *3 sg.* flows K205; *3 pl.* reel K204
releue *v.* assuage, alleviate the suffering of E245

relyde *pa. 3 sg.* rallied, called (to his company), assigned (to eternal life) E6
rent *n.* payment K126; income E164
rent *pa. 3 sg., pl.* lacerated K14, K15; *pp.* rent lacerated K240
repent *v.* repent E105; *pa. 3 pl.* regretted (it) E167
resoun *n.* reason; *be* ~ correctly K214; *pl.* reson(e)s arguments, argumentation B116, K14, K15, K45
rest *n.* (heavenly) peace K214
rest *v.* abide K181; *pa. 3 sg.* restid endured B31
retorikes *n. pl.* rhetoricians, scholars K21, K30
reuleþ *see* rewlyst
rewle *n.* rule, religious precept, religious belief K16
rewly *adv.* wretchedly, piteously K46
rewlyst *2 sg.* govern, control K240; *3 sg.* reuleþ governs K214
rial, ryal *adj.* royal, magnificent K45, K239
rially *adv.* majestically K46
rialte, ryalte *n.* royal status, regal power K16, K239
ryche *adj.* rich B91
ryf *adj.* great, abounding K239
right, ryght(e) *n.* righteousness B43, B116; ryth K45
ryghte *adv.* truly E136; just, exactly E185; properly, correctly E247
rynnande *see* ranne
ryse *n.¹* brushwood B89
ryse *n.²* rows, sequence B116
ryth *see* right
rithe *adj.* right, correct K16
riueres *see* oyl-riueres
ronne *see* ranne
rood *n.* cross B31; rude E94
roser *n.* rose bush B43
rotes *n. pl.* roots B89
rowth *pa. 3 sg.*; ~ *not of* cared nothing for K16
rude *see* rood
rwd *adj.* lowly, ignorant K240; *as subst.* violent person K15

sacrifice *n.* sacrificial offering K130
saye, sene *v.* say E160, say, tell K71; *3 sg.* saith B131; *pa. 2 sg.* said(e), sayd said E199, E236; spoke B117; *pa. 3 sg.* sayd(e), seid, seyd(e), seyed said B4,

B109, K64, K109, K117, K129, K159, &c.; spoke K115; *impers.* said B52; *pa. 3 pl.* said(e) said E152, E200

saiyng *vbl. n.* utterance, words B117

saynede *pa. 2 sg.* made the sign of the cross over E175, E230

sake *n.* sake; *for þi* ~ for you K70, K71

salf *n.* salve (*fig.*) K63, K208

sall *see* schal

saluede *pa. 3 sg.* healed E72

same *adv.* together, with each other K74

saphirs *n. pl.* sapphires E176

sare *n.* wound (of original sin) E72

sare *adv.* in an excruciating manner E125; sore grievously B41

sat(t) *see* sitte

saue(de) *see* save

sauyour, saueoure, savyour *n.* Saviour E71, K61, K72

save *v.* save, preserve K62; rescue K173; *imp., subj. sg.* saue B55, K271; *pa. 2 sg.* sauede E229

savyour *see* sauyour

sawe *n.* doctrine, faith B74; *pl.* sawes words, announcement B4; words, declaration B46; discourses, doctrines K20

sawe (*v.*) *see* se(e)

sawles *n. pl.* souls K271

schaf *v. imp. sg.* strip away K254

schake *pp.* shaken K147

schal, schalt *v. auxil. 1, 3 sg.* shall, will B5, B7, K130, K131, K178; sall E266; *2 sg.* schalt K64, K65, K68, K119, K133, &c.; *1, 3 pl.* schal, schul B8, B13, B76, K172, K279; must K271; *forming subj.: pa. 1 sg.* schuld would K111; *pa. 3 sg.* schuld, sulde might K20; was going to K92, E156, K98, K161, K200; *pa. 3 pl.* suld(e) were going to E120, E198; must E216

schame *n.* disgrace, a shameful fate K72; disgrace, harm K130; *pl.* chames disgraces, harms K254

schamed *pa. 3 sg.* dreaded; ~ *not his showte* was not abashed by his shouting K91; *see also* aschamyd

schap *3 pl.* prepare; ~ *vs to schrik* make us shriek K253; *pa. 3 sg.* schap determined, appointed K72; schope ~ *hir to schrynk* prepared or planned to make her shrink or desist (for horror) K92

scharply, scherply *adv.* immediately, keenly, efficiently B117, K197

sche *pron. 3 sg. fem.* she B45, B46, B47, B49, B124, K15, K16, K29, K78, K79, &c.; he K26; scho E35, E74, E159, E160, E186; *acc.:* hir(e), hyre K31b, K92, K102a, K102b, K105, K112, K203, &c.; *dat.:* hir(e) E102, K31a, K204, K206, K208, K223; hyr(e) *B126, K77; here B48b, K42; *refl.:* hir(e), hyr *B123, E35b, E159, K146a; hirself K184; *adj. poss.* her K28, K93, K129; here B46, B47, B48a, K29, K96, K143; hir B77, B124, E35a, E71, E99, E101, E187, K16, K82, K94, K95, *K145, &c.; hire K32, K78, K87, K161, K189; hyr K30, K106, K170; hyre K15, K20, K76

schede *v.* shed K92, K93

scheen *adj.* bright, shining K252

schenchip *n.* shame, disgrace K254

schente *pp.* destroyed, brought to nothing K64

schere *v. imp. sg.* cut, shear away, excise K253

scherply *see* scharply

schewd *v. trans. pa. 3 sg.* showed, made known to K63; schewede E90; *intrans. pa. 3 sg.* schewed appeared B35

schinest *2 sg.* shine B135; *3 sg.* scyneth shines B134

schipe *n.* boat E41

scho *see* sche

schofferes *n. pl.* detractors K19

schope *see* schap

schortly *adv.* quickly K91

schowres *n. pl.* assaults, pains K253

schowte *n.* uproar, shouting K91

schrik *v.* shriek K253

schrynk *v.* cow, make cower; *schope hir to* ~ prepared or planned to make her shrink or desist (for horror) K92; *pp. (intrans.)* schrunk sunk deep K254

schul, schul(d) *see* schal(t)

scort *v.* curtail, cut short K20

see *n.* sea E41, E175

se(e), sene *v.* see E88, E203; see, visit K74; find out K20; behold E252, K71; *pr. p.* seande in the sight of E229; *pa. 3 sg.* sawe perceived (you to be) K62; *pa. 3 pl.* see witnessed E209; *pp.* sene seen (before) E176, E177

seemly *adv.* becomingly, graciously K64

seet *n.* seat, place (in heaven) E35

segge *n.* man E144

seid, seyd(e), seyed *see* saye, sene

seke *v.* look for, search for K19; *pa. 3 sg.*
sothe sought, found K61, K71;
soght(e) B3, E102, E219

sekenes *n.* sickness, infirmity K207

sekir *adj.* sure, secure *B74

selcouyth, selcouthe *adj.* wondrous,
strange, marvellous E90, K151

semede *pa. 3 sg.* seemed, appeared E160

sem(e)ly *adj.* fair E72; resplendent E203;
becoming, comely K180; *as subst.* prin-
cely one E101; fair one, beautiful lady
K129; good man B4

semely *adv.* in a beautiful and fitting
manner B46

semle *n.* meeting, battle E144

senatour *n.* governor K159

send *v. subj. sg.* offer; *and* ~ if you were to
offer K130; *imp.* sende render B75; *3
sg.* sendys sends K217; *pa. 3 sg.* sent
E101; sent forth K19; sente brought,
sent K60; *pp.* sent restored B84

sene (*v.*) *see* se(e), sene *and* saye, sene

sent *1 pl.* assent, agree K242; *see also*
asent, assentant *and* send

sere *adj.* particular, singular E36

sergauntes *n. pl.* officers K19

serteyn *adj.* unfailing, trustworthy B75

seruede *pa. 2 sg.* cared for E101

sese *v.* cease, desist B118

sete *adj.* sweet B10

seþen *conj.* then E89, E124, E190; sythen
E102

sett *v.* set E157; *pa. 2 sg.* set; ~ . . . *bot
smalle* considered that insignificant E54;
pa. 3 sg., pl. set, placed E125, K196; ~
hir vp raised herself up E159; related
B46; *pp.* sett placed, situated E35

seuen *adj.* seven E200

sybbe *n.* cousin (to) E71

sydir *n.* cider B96

sydis *n. pl.* body, womb E72

syghte, siȝth, syȝth, sythe *n.* sight, view
E90, E209, K180; *in his* ~ before his
face, before him, in his presence K20;
selcouyth in ~ wondrous to behold K151

syll *n.* hall E203

syn *see* synne

syne *conj.* then E230

synful *adj.* K271; *(as n).* (the) sinful B75

syng *v.* rejoice, hymn, sing to K279

synne *n.* sin, transgression B55, B60,
K242; syn E67

syre *n.* lord, god K130

syster *n.gen.* sister's E71

siþ *causal conj.* because, since K138

sythe *see* syghte

sythen *see* seþen

sitte *v.* sit, remain K53; *pr. p.* sittyng
B122; *vbl. n.* syttynge E36; *pa. 3 sg.*
sat(t) alighted, sat B106, B107

skyn *n.* skin B88

slayn(e) *pp.* slain, struck down K195;
killed E144

sleyȝt *n.* cunning, contrivance, trickery
K144; contraption K147

slely *adv.* cunningly, treacherously, ?skil-
fully K147

slepede *pp.* slept E160

slounge *pp.* cast, thrown K119

smal(l)e *adj.* little E175; insignificant E54

so *adv. demons.* in such a way, to such a
degree B85a, B85b, B97, B135, B136,
E4, E73, E95, E155, E172, E189,
E228a, E228b, E255, K16, K45, K47,
K48, K79, &c.; *adv.* in this way B131,
E17; *adv. rel., conj.* because of this
K17a; ~ . . . *that* to such a degree . .
that K17b-18, K147-8; *see also* qwoso

soche *adj.* such K27; swylk(e) E34, E176,
E177

socour, sokour *n.* aid, help B75, K63

socure *v.* relieve, succour K207

sodanly *adv.* immediately K159

soft *v.* allay, abate, ameliorate, assuage
K129

soft *adv.* gently, softly K208

softely *adv.* gently E159

soght(e) *see* seke

solace, solas *n.* consolation, comfort B74,
E36, E37, K60, K61, K72

sonbeem *n.* sunbeam K252

sondur *v.* separate, put away, abolish
K217

sone *n.* son B34, B48, E71, E101; *pl.*
sones E35

sone *adv.* soon, directly E167, E200; *ful* ~
at once, without delay K173

sonne *n.* sun K50

sore *see* sare

sory *adj.* wretched, vile K159; *as subst.* the
afflicted B74

sorow *n.* sorrow, affliction B60; *pl.* sorowes K62, K129, K217

sothe *n.* truth E160

sothe (*v.*) *see* **seke**

soth(e)ly, soþly *adv.* absolutely, unconditionally E199; in truth, assuredly K61, K197

souerayne *adj.* utmost E89

soule *n.* soul B10

spare *v.* show mercy E124, K8, K9; *pa. 3 sg.* **spared** omitted, refrained K114

speche *n.* speech, ability to talk B84; words K114

spede *n.* help; *at* ~ successful B24

spende *v.* discharge, vent K114

spere *n.* spear K113

sprede *pp.* spread, gathered B62

sprong *pa. 3 sg.* rose up, reacted, jumped up K113; *subj. pa. 3 sg.* **sprunge** were embedded (in); *as spere in hert* ~ as if a spear had struck, were quivering in his heart K113

stalworth *adj.* stalwart, unshakeable B21

stande *v. imp. sg.* stand, be B22; *pa. 2 sg.* **stode** stood firm, confronted B118; *pa. 3 sg., pl.* **stode** stood B35, B42, K89; stood firm, withstood K100

stanes *see* **stone**

stede *n.* place, abode B35

stede *pp.* established in; *in* ~ beset with B60

stedefastly *adv.* firmly, uncompromisingly B118

stedfast *adj.* strong, staunch, dependable B21

sterf *v. trans.* cause to die, destroy K98; *intrans. pa. 3 sg.* **sterved** died, perished K99

sterne *adj.* fierce, harsh, cruel K99

steuen *n.* utterance, promise, agreement K182

stiffenes *n.* firmness K182

stifly, styfly *adv.* stoutly, unyieldingly B22, K12

still(e), styll *adv.* quiescently, motionlessly B106, B107; quietly, privately E39; steadily E81; submissively E199

stynte *pa. 2 sg.* stood firm K12

stirt *v.* start, flinch *K100

stytly *adv.* valiantly, stoutly, undismayed K100

stode *see* **stande**

stone *n.* stone B21, B42, E178; *pl.* **stones** E203, E207; **stanes** E175

story *n.* story, legend B131

stowre *n.* time of affliction or adversity B21

stowte *adj.* strong, menacing, arrogant K89

stranglyd *pa. 3 sg.* choked K90

strof *pa. 3 sg.* struggled, rampaged K90

strongly *adv.* violently K99

sturdy *adj.* violent, fierce K89

suffire *v.* suffer, undergo E199

suggeourned *pa. 2 sg.* lived, stayed E143

suyle *n.* soil, country E143

suld(e) *see* **schal**

sum *pron. indef.* some E167

supere *n.* (the last) supper E89

suppede *pa. 2 sg.* drank E230

surauns *n.* assurance, pledge K217

swerd(e) *n.* sword K97, K161

swete *adj.* sweet, gracious B4; lovely B49; *as subst.* lovely one, gracious one B46

swetely *adv.* devoutly E230

swylk(e) *see* **soche**

swynk *v. imp. sg.* labour, exert influence K236

swith *adv.* very much K236

take *v.* take, receive K67; *imp. sg.* receive B7; take, pay K171; *pa. 2 sg.* **toke, tuke** B88, B95; ~ *at* took to, ?assimilated E92; *pa. 3 sg.* **tuk** seized E115; *pa. 3 pl.* **toke, tuke** took B66, E166; ~ *at* took to, ?assimilated E201; *pp.* **take** taken, understood K143

talle *adj.* noble, mighty K229

tame *adj.* submissive K78, K79

tarying *pr. p.* provoking K57

techyng(e) *vbl. n.* teaching, instruction E92, E201

tellen *v.* tell, utter K115; *pa. 3 sg.* **tolde** told E193; apprised, notified B33, B36, B37

tempest *n.* storm K215

tempure *v.* temper, assuage K115

tene *n.* wrath, rage K115; suffering, harm, grief K230

tent *n.* attention E166

tent *v.* take care of E99; *pa. 3 sg.* **tente** took care of K58

thay, þai, þay, thei, þei *pron. 3 pl. nom.* they B35, B52, B63, B64, B65, E116, E120, E188a, E188b, E189, K21, K23, K28, K31, *K46, &c.; *acc., dat.*: **þam, thaym(e), þem** B69, E106, E107, E116, E157, E167, E174, E219; **hem** K3, K4,

K37, K38, K83, *K86, &c.; *refl.*: hem
themselves B63, B65, K32, K41, K166;
for themselves K21, K40; *adj. poss.*
thaire, þaire, thayre their E36,
E128, E188, E204, E256, &c.; her(e),
hir K44, K158, K250, K268
than(e), þan(e), þanne *conj., adv.* then
B35, B36, *B62, B106, E119, E131,
E145, E155, E185, K19, K23, K24,
K26, K27, &c.; when; ~ . . . *fra* from
the time when E209
þan *conj., prep.* than E182, E183
thank *n.* thought, consideration, goodwill;
~ *of vs* in consideration of us, for our
sakes K6
thanke *v. imp. sg.* thank K203
thankles *adj.* ungracious, unmoved K49
thare, þare *see* þer(e)
thareby *adv., conj.* on those aforesaid
things E54; *see* þer(e)
þartyll *adv.* to that; *traysted* ~ put their
trust in it E201
thase *see* this
þat *pron., nom.* that E73; *acc.*: that fact
E245
þat *rel. pron.* that, which, who(m) B18,
B31, B33b, B45, B50, B60, E1a, E1b,
E4, E7, E100, E243, K1, K4, K46,
K72b, K85b, &c.; (you) who E231a; of
him who E142; (those) who E194,
K221; (of those) who E162, K254; *as*
~ in a manner in which K116
that, þat *adj. demons. retaining sense of def.
art.* that, the B4, B26, B33a, B34b, B35,
E2, E6, E8, E13, E19, K15, K17a,
K17b, K33, K49, &c.
þat *conj.* that B34a, E22, E120, E198,
K166, K200; so that K148a, K186a; in
order that B56, B140, E216, K212,
K269; to such a degree that K18; *luke*
~ see to it that E237; *qwyles* ~ as long as
K135; in that E202
þe, the *def. art.* the B6, B10, B40, B48,
B64, *B68, E2, E15, E41, E45a, E45b,
K1, K7a, K26, K32, K50, &c.; *see also*
þat (*adj. demons.*)
þe (*pron.*) *see* þou
thede *n.* nation E115
thef *n.* evil man, villain K49; theefe E115
thei, þei *see* thay
þer(e), þare, thare *adv.* there E20,
E104, E122, E175, E177, E234,
E235; *adv. demons.* there, at that junc-

ture, at that place B49, B62, B105,
E161, K9, K10, K12, K13, K33, &c.;
conj., rel. where B27, B35, E8, E10,
E147, E158; to where *B13; *adv., conj.*
thereat, thereupon K103; þor K219,
K220, K222, K223; *indef. before v.*
there K77
þer(e)fore *adv.* therefore, for that reason
K66, K203
these *see* this
thi, þi, þin *see* thou
þider *adv.* to that place B64
thik, thyk *adv.* thickly, at a great depth
K50, K51; abundantly K186
thykly *adv.* deeply, intensely K6
thyn *adj.* thin, thinned-out, sparsely
peopled K149
þin, thyne (*pron.*) *see* thou
thyng(e) *n.* thing E43, E166, E171
thynk *v.* think, consider E35; *pa. 2 sg.*
thoght deigned B118; *pa. 3 sg.* thoghte
calculated E222
thynne *adv.* from that place K148
thyrst *pp.* thrown, dispersed K148
thyrsted *pa. 3 sg.* tormented, oppressed
K49
þis, þisse *pron.* this person B110; this
thing B91, E110, E241, E247, K133,
K223
this, þis *adj. demons. sg.* this B16, *B35,
B59, E4, E21, E242, E246, K211, K256,
K257, K272; *pl.* thase, these these
E117, E118, E241
þo *adj. demons. pl.* those K36, K44, K78,
K79, K156, K160; *incl. towards def. art.*
the K156, K264
þo *adv.* then K45, K93, K94, K96, K97
thoght (*v.*) *see* thynk
thoght(e) *n.* mind, consideration E202;
take it in ~ bear this in mind B7; *ne
toke it in* ~ did not consider it B95
tholyd *pa. 2 sg.* suffered, endured K6
thondur *n.* thunder K215
þor *see* þer
thorgh(e), thurgh(e) *prep.* through B82;
by means of, by the agency of B6,
B48, E89, E106, E142, E218, E219;
thorowe E108; þour through, by
K182
thou, þou, thow, þow *pron. 2 sg. nom.*
you, thou B1, B15, B21, B29, B30, E3,
E5, E13, E17, E19, K3, K5, K12, K43,
K58, &c.; *acc., dat.*: þe, the thee B29,

B62, B104b, E30, E37, E86a, E98, K4, K7b, *K8, K9, K49, K71, &c.; *refl.* the yourself B5, B91, E58, E82; *adj. poss.* thi, thy, þi your, thy B3, B5, B30, B38, B74, E22, E24, E27, E31, E34, K14, K44, K45, K56, K57, &c. (*before vowel*) þin K62; thyne E52

þour *see* thorgh(e)

thowsand *n.* thousand K148

thraly *adv.* violently E116

thralle *n.* enslavement E93

thref *n.* company, multitude, throng K148

threte *n.* threat, torment K5

threted *pa. 3 pl.* menaced, treated ill E116

threteth *num.* thirtieth *B103

throghe *adv. intens.* thoroughly, firmly; *throw* ~ imprisoned fast K58

throng *n.* pressure K5; crowd K149

throng *pa. 3 sg.* issued, flowed out K186

throw *v.* throw, cast K50; *pp.* throw constrained, imprisoned K58

throwe *n.¹* short while B80

throwe *n.²* (spell of) torment K50, K51

thurgh(e) *see* thorgh(e)

thurgheowte *prep.* throughout (the sphere of) E212

thus, þus *adv.* thus, so, in this way B6, E152, E217, E259, K15, K29, K43, K51, &c.

tyde *n.* time; *that* ~ in those days E2

till *see* to

tyme *n.* time, moment B83

tynt *pa. 3 sg.* failed, neglected, omitted K8, K9

tyraunt *n.* tyrant, villain K7; *pl.* tyrauntez E115

to *prep.* to, towards B3, B4, B14, B26, B38, E8a, E100b, E107, E118, E131, K28, K29, K32, K45, K54a, &c.; into B59, E208, K81, K119, K219, K256, K268, &c.; unto B10, B71, B74, B75, E37, E67, E86, E88a, E90, K114, K156, K171, K199, K232, &c.; in response to E55; to a state of E186; *with inf.* to B2, B9, B11, B25, B66, *B68, E8b, E9, E18, E26, E75, K3, K4, K8, K9, K35, &c.; *we* ~ *abyde* our being to remain (there) K274; in order to B102, E6, E48, E88b, E121, E221, K11, K19, K20, K25, K30, &c.; *that you should* E244, E246, *for* ~ in order to B125, E49, E120, E252; E247; ~ *hym chese* selected for himself

B120; ~ *tent* in the tending of E99; till, tyll E101, E146, E240

to-ches *see* ches

togedir *adv.* together B63

toylede *pa. 3 pl.* entrapped, caught E116

toke *see* take

tolde *see* tellen

tonn *n.* vat E122

toþer *n.* that other (company), the rest E148

towchyn *3 pl.* smite, afflict K230

towchyng *vbl. n.* touching, affliction K8

trace *n.* track, footsteps, way of conduct E91

tray *n.* pain, affliction K230

trayfoly *adv.* grievously K7

trayste *adj.* secure, trusty E91

traysted *pa. 3 pl.* trusted E201

traytour *n.* false one, betrayer K57; *pl.* traytures deceivers K229

traytury *n.* treachery K119

transfegurede *pa. 3 sg.* transfigured E87

tredyd *pa. 3 sg.* oppressed, crushed, trampled down K57

tretest *2 sg.* deal with K215

trewe *adj.* righteous E91; trw assured; *trw tutor* assiduous adviser, mentor K116

trew(e)ly *adv.* truthfully B36, B37; assuredly, absolutely E234

Trewth, Trewþe *n.* Truth, Righteousness (i.e. God) K58, K171

trow *1 sg.* believe, think, am sure K7; *pa. 3 pl.* trowede believed; ~ . . . *to þe* put their faith in you E234

trw *see* trewe

tuk(e) *see* take

tunge *n.* speech, words K115

turment *n.* torment, torture K119; *pl.* turmentys afflictions K230; *see also* turnement

turne *v.* turn, convert from the faith K7; overthrow, convert, subvert K56, K57; *imp. sg.* turn K229; *pa. 3 sg.* turnede transformed (back) E208

turnement *n.* turning, torture, racking K8

turnyng *vbl. n.* rotation K140

turtyl *n.* turtle dove (*fig.*) K229

tutor *n.* mentor K116

twelft *num.* twelfth B104

twelue *num.* twelve *K53

two *num.* two E226

uirgyn *see* virgyn
us *see* we

verray *adj.* true E70
vertues *n. pl.* qualities, potencies, powers K245
vertuus *adj.* powerful, miraculous K143
virgyn, uirgyn *n.* virgin E70, K249
vnchangide *pp.* consistent E64
vnknyit *pa. 3 sg.* unknitted, disjointed, destroyed K187; *see also* knytt
vnmyste *ppl. adj.* not lacking E257
vntill(e), vntyll *prep.* to, before B104; towards, to E42, E131
vnto *prep.* to E128, E152; into (a state of) E198; in accordance with B92, B93
vnwylde *adj.* not wanton, not intemperate E57
vnwysely *adv.* foolishly E184
vnworthi *adj. with adv. force* as if unworthy, wrongly, undeservingly K188
vnwrapped *pa. 3 pl.* unloosed, took off K94
voyce *n.* voice B109
vp *adv.* up E158, K127, K179, K20
vpe-ryghte *adv.* upright E192
vs *see* we

way(e) *n.* way, path E13, E78, E103, E163, E184
wald(e) *see* wil (*v.*)
walke *v.* walk, go E78
walle *n.* dwelling; *in-with* ~ in your habitation E52
wandes, wandis *n. pl.* sticks E173, E179, E208
wane(s) *see* wone (*n.²*)
wanne *see* wynne
wanted *pa. 3 sg.* lacked B91
wardeþ *3 sg.* guards, protects K213
war(r)e (*v. and conj.*) *see* was and whare
ware *adj.* sentient B85
warely *adv.* prudently E103
warre *adj.* aware E111
was *pa. 2, 3 sg.* was B16, B64, B86, B108, E17, E20, E22, E32, E33, K16, K42, K47, K82, K84, &c.; *auxil. forming pass.* B84, E7, E19, E29, E63, E121, E141, K33, K87, K127, K143, K147, &c.; *subj. 3 sg.* ware, were B97, E78; *pa. 2, 3 sg.* ware, were B59, E23, E134, E136, K58, &c.; *pa. 3 pl.* ware, were

E58, E127, E146, E147, E148, E149, K22, K23, K148; warre E176; was B62, E176, E177; *auxil. forming pass.* ware, were B57, B60, B64, B78, E169, E170, E172; warre E214, was E226; *see also* am, are, art, be, is
waste *adj.* profitless, vain E66
wate *1 sg.* know E22; wysse know, ?make known E111; *pa. 3 pl.* wist B61; wyste E253
watir *n.* water B94
wax *pa. 3 sg.* grew, turned, became K103
we *pron. 1 pl. nom.* we B12, B13, B56, B137, E242, E264, K242, K260, K270, K274; *acc.:* vs us B14, B22a, B22b, B23, B24, B26, B54, B55, E8, E13, E19, E93, E100, E142, E251, E265, K202, K230, K241, K242, K245, K253, K255a, K256a, K256b, K257, K259, K264, K269a, K272, K273, K275, K277, K278; us K245; *dat.:* vs us B18, B73, B128, B139, E241, K6, K236, K243, K253, K255b, K270, K276, K279; for us K233, K248; to us K266, K269b; *adj. poss. sg.:* our(e) B72, B140, E64, E71, E72, E259, K61, K130, K131, K180, K260, K263, K274 ; *pl.:* our(e) B53, B73, K200, K231, K232, K235, K238, K271
wed(e) *n.* clothing K94; shroud K102; *worthi in* ~ meritorious (a) human B16
welde *v.* hold E254
wele *n.* prosperity B32
wele *adv.* well B78, B79, E23, E35, K200
weled *pa. 3 pl.* decreed, ordained E254
wellande *ppl. adj.* boiling E123
welthe *n.* wealth E45, E198; abundance E181, E183
wende *v.* go, travel E79, E165; turn E198; *1 pl.* go, proceed B12; *pa. 2, 3 sg.* went(e) went, departed E21, E42, E103, E163, K123; *pa. 2, 3 pl.* E162, E184; *pp.* went gone, departed K246, K247; *see also* wene
wene *1 sg.* believe, assert E174; *pa. 1 sg.* wende believed, expected *K118; *pa. 3 sg.* wende; ~ *him* expected, trusted K124
went(e) *see* wende (*v.*)
wepe *v.* weep K154; *pa. 3 pl.* wepede E197
were *n.* confusion, doubt B101
were (*v.*) *see* was

werede *pa. 2 sg.* guarded E58
weryede *pa. 3 pl.* regretted, cursed E197
werk(e) *n.* work, deeds, actions E134, E162, E197, K143; *pl.* **werkes** E22, E24, E57, E66, E104, E253
werlde, world(e) *n.* world B16, B59, E4, E21, E53, E198
whan *see* **when**
whare, qwer(e) *conj.* to where E12; **ware** where, wherever E79; whence, from where K204; in which K212, K258; (at) the place where K224, K239, K245, K279
whas *see* **qwo**
what(e), qwat *adj.* whichever E78; *interrog.* what E241, K105, K117
when, whan, qwan, qwen *conj.* when B12, B57, B44, B59, B65, E55, E87, E179, E183, E260, K7, K10, K44, K58, K59, &c.
whennes *conj.* when, where B76
whils, qwyles *conj.* as long as, while E143, E259, K134; ~ *þat* during the time that, as long as, while K135
whom, whoso *see* **qwo** *and* **qwoso**
wychcraft *n.* sorcery, witchcraft K143
wyde *adj.* wide, great, large; *þis woo* ~ the woe of this world or life K272
wyde *adv.* wide rangingly E4
wyes *n. pl.* people E161
wyf(fe) *n.* wife B5, B120, B121, K245
wight, wiȝth, wyȝhte, wyȝth *n.* being, person B16, B49, B132, E3, E21, E139, E161, E250, K142, K154; *pl.* **wyȝthes** K44, K48
wyȝthly *adv.* powerfully K246
wik *adj.* wicked K188
wil, wyl(l), will(e) *n.* will, purpose B100, B108, E78, E79, E133, K44, K144; desire, intent E84, E173, E197
wil *v. auxil. 1 sg.* will E28; *2, 3 sg.* **wil(l)** B130, K55; *2 pl.* E199; *pa. 2 sg.* **wald** E77; **woldest** K5; *pa. 3 sg., pl.* **wald(e), wold(e)** wanted to, intended to B32, B34, E94, E95, E124, K7, K37, K87; would B40, K116, K153, K166; *subj.* **wolde** B18; *pa. 3 pl. forming cond. & ind. future:* **wald(e)** E224, K174
wildirnesse *n.* wilderness B86
wylys *n. pl.* wiles, ruses, stratagems K141
wyn *n.* joy B54
win (*v.*) *see* **wynne**
wyne *n.* wine B96

wynne *v.* win, overpower K142; *imp. sg.* **win** bring *K272; *pa. 2 sg.* **wanne** prevailed over K43; *pp.* **wonne** expended K44; overcome, outdone K48; see also **bewane**
wirchip(e) *n.* honour, E254, K256; distinction, renown E104
wirchiped(e) *see* **worchipes**
wirkyn *v.* work, act K118
wyrkynges *vbl. n. pl.* actions, deeds E58
wys(e) *adj.* wise B85, E57, E253
wysely *adv.* intelligently E133
wysse *v.¹* guide K277; *2 sg.* **wysses** E139; *3 subj.* may she guide K220; *imp. sg.* lead E13
wysse, wist, wyste (*v.²*) *see* **wate**
wit, witt(e) *n.* intellect E133; wisdom K43; mind, wits, reason K56, K57
with, wyth *prep.* with B8, B9, B29, B33, B44, B59, B100, E21, E48, E49, E73, E85, E119, E133, E257a, E257b; K76, K88, K108, *K115a, &c.; by E3; with, by means of E28, E115, E123, E132, E214, K8, K78, K122, K137, K141, K161; against K213; by the agency of E61, E62a, E62b; by the agency of, from K247; by, alongside B22, E77, E78, E82, E83, E165; supplied with, in a state of B54, E120; together with B90, E114, E133, E135, E159, E187
within *prep.* within B58
withouten *prep.* without B50, B51, B101
witnes *n.* witness E138
witnese *3 sg.* witnesses, as is witnessed by E56
witt *see* **wit**
witty, wytty *adj.* intelligent, wise B15, E57, E253; *as n.* sensible people K220
wittily, wyttily *adv.* wisely, cleverly K43, K48
woo *n.* adversity B32; dreadful thing, evil dispensation K117; eternal torment E198; *þis* ~ *wyde* the troubles and afflictions of this world or life K272
wode *n.* wood B86
woful *adj.* miserable, wretched K188
wold(e), woldest *see* **wil**
wonde *pa. 3 sg.* wound, wrapped K102
wondir, wondur *n.* amazement, marvel E161; disaster K213
wondur *adv.* exceedingly K103
wondurful *adj.* prodigious, awesome K142

wone *n.*¹ habitation B15; *pl.* **wanes** dwellings, property E45

wone *n.*² *gen.* of possessions; *mare* ~ in greater measure or abundance E181; **wane** E183

wonyng, wonnyng *n.* dwelling B86, K272

wonn *v.* go, travel E77; *pr. p.* **wonnande** faring E4

wonne (*v.*) *see* **wynne**

worchipes *3 pl.* honour K213; *pp.* **wirchiped(e)** honoured, revered E3, E134, E135; *pa. 3 pl.* **wirchipede** E162

worde *n.* tidings B36; speech, teaching, discourse, utterance K48; *pl.* **wordes** K44

world(e) *see* **werlde**

worthi, worthy *adj.* admirable, praiseworthy B127, B132, E22, E23, E134, E136, E250; *as substant.* **worthi** B16, E77, *E254

worthyly *adv.* commendably E104

woundid, wowndyd *pp.* wounded K102, K188

wow *n.* vow K52

wrake *n.* vengeance, persecution K141

wrate *pa. 2 sg.* wrote E133; *pa. 3 sg.* **wrote** B69

wrechid *adj.* wretched E58

wrenchis *n. pl.* tricks K141

wroght(e), wro3gth, wrogth *pa. 2, 3 sg.* worked, effected B32, E104, E173, K141; performed, carried out K144; wrought, created E4, K246; behaved E184; ~ *at* behaved according to E84; concocted E220

wrote *see* **wrate**

wrunge *pp.* twisted, affected, coerced K117

INDEX OF PROPER NAMES

Adam Adam, the first man K227

Apocalips The Book of Revelation or *The Apocalypse* E132

Asye Asia E103

Baptist John the Baptist B1, B15, B29, B43, B57, &c.

Bedleme Bethlehem E7

Craton Crato or Crates E212

Crist, Criste Christ B18, B139, E243, K199, K223, &c.

Domycyane Domitian (Titus Flavius Domitianus, Emperor of Rome) E113, E143

Drucyane Drusiana E155

Ephesym Ephesus (*acc.*) E146

Euaungelist John the Evangelist E3, E14

Flume Iordan River Jordan B102

Gabriel The Angel Gabriel B3

Galylee Galilee E29

God(d) The God of the Christians B6, B25, B54, E30, E190, E191, E248, K262; *gen.* **Goddes** B34, B128, B136, E140, E154; **Goddys** K125

Herod, Herode Herod the Tetrarch, son of King Herod B115, B126

Herodias Herodias, wife of Herod, above B115

Holy Gost Holy Spirit B105

Ihesu, J(h)esu Jesus B50, B101, E250, K259

John Saint John the Evangelist *E14, E15, E77, E216, E220

Jon, Joon Saint John the Baptist B7, B70, B138; **Seint Jon þe Baptist** B138

Katereyn Saint Katherine of Alexandria K1, K29, K43, K71, K74, &c.; **Katereyne** K273, K275; **Kateryn** K265

Mary The Virgin Mary, Mother of Christ B33, B44, B77; Mary, wife of Zebedee and mother of John the Evangelist E34

Pathmos The Aegean island of Patmos E131

Pereles of Pousté Matchless One of Might, i.e., God E38

Philip Philip, deceased brother of Herod the Tetrarch B120

Porfiri Porphirius (or Porphiry), the

legendary adviser to the tyrant, and captain of his guard K73; **Porphiri** K109, K124; **Porphyri** K101

Portelatyn The Latin Gate: gateway to the Via Latina in ancient Rome E118

Syna Mount Sinai in modern-day Egypt K196, K197

Zebede Zebedee, father of John the Evangelist E31